◆ 世界史专业英语教材 ◆

世界史文献解读

张乃和 主 编
袁跃华 副主编

Commentaries on World Historical Documents

U0790884

人民东方出版传媒
People's Oriental Publishing & Media
東方出版社
The Oriental Press

图书在版编目（CIP）数据

世界史文献解读 / 张乃和主编 ； 袁跃华副主编 . 北京 ： 东方出版社， 2024.12. -- ISBN 978-7-5207-4101-9

Ⅰ. K107

中国国家版本馆CIP数据核字第2024TN6270号

世界史文献解读

SHIJIESHI WENXIAN JIEDU

主　　编：张乃和
副 主 编：袁跃华
责任编辑：李小娜
出　　版：东方出版社
发　　行：人民东方出版传媒有限公司
地　　址：北京市东城区朝阳门内大街166号
邮　　编：100010
印　　刷：定州启航印刷有限公司
版　　次：2024年12月第1版
印　　次：2024年12月第1次印刷
开　　本：710mm×1000mm　1/16
印　　张：29.25
字　　数：595千字
书　　号：ISBN 978-7-5207-4101-9
定　　价：95.00元
发行电话：（010）85924640

版权所有，违者必究

如有印装质量问题，我社负责调换，请拨打电话：（010）85924640

本书为2023年天津市普通高等学校本科教学改革与质量发展建设研究计划项目“历史学专业课程体系优化与教学内容改革研究与实践”（项目编号：B231006514）阶段性成果

本书受天津市高等学校创新团队培养计划项目“欧洲文明与现代化”（项目编号：013-ZXCX14005）资助

目　录

Contents

Preface
序 言

当前，我国世界史专业建设面临着前所未有的挑战和机遇，在当前和今后一个时期的首要任务是，聚焦世界史一流专业建设中心工作，锚定培养具有全球胜任力的世界史专业人才目标，优化课程体系，改革教学内容，加强双语和外语授课，推动专业升级优化，实现高质量发展。

本书是在新文科建设背景下，对大学世界史文献解读进行的新思考和新探索，旨在围绕立德树人根本任务，以本科教育教学审核评估为契机，以一流本科专业建设为牵引，以一流师范生培养为重点，以教育教学信息化、智能化为重要驱动，全面提升本科教育教学质量。本书最终是为了探索有独特优势的世界史专业英语教育教学体系，以教育自信推动树立历史自信、文化自信，为党育人、为国育才，培养合格的社会主义建设者和接班人。

在教学目标方面，为进一步深化教育综合改革，推进历史学专业体系优化升级，坚持课程思政常态化、规范化、制度化，我们需要从根本上提高历史学专业学生的“五基”——基本价值立场、基本理论方法、基本文献史料、基本专业知识、基本学术前沿——的素养和水平；全面培养学生听、说、读、写、译、用等各方面的专业英语能力，重点培养学生运用英文文献读写专业学术论文的科研创新能力，为深入开展国际学术交流、构建自主的历史学知识体系打下坚实基础。

因此，本书的定位是，放眼世界百年未有之大变局和中华民族伟大复兴的战略全局，落实立德树人根本任务，聚力数字赋能，高起点、高质量编写世界史专业英语教材，在教学内容、教学方法、教学资源、教学团队等方面，全面提升数字化、智能化水平，提高学生的世界史文献解读和利用能力。

本书坚持以下原则：

1. 突出思政元素。以权威的英文版本为参考，收录马克思、恩格斯、列宁等马克思主义者的经典文献与关于中华优秀传统文化的基础文献，这些共同构成本书的第一编。

2. 突出世界历史主线。以文明交流互鉴为主线，收录世界上古、中古、近代、现当代四个时段的典型文献。每个时段为一编。

3. 突出学科和专业特色。以我国历史研究的新方向——经济社会史、欧洲文明史为特色和优势，兼顾世界历史的主线与全局。

4. 突出原始文献的选用。以整理出版的原始文献为主，兼顾未经整理出版的历史档案，特别是手稿和近代早期印刷出版文献的选取具有典型性。

本书按照世界史的概念与理论、世界上古史、世界中古史、世界近代史、世界现当代史五编的顺序，每编则以时间为序编排所收录的文献。每篇文献由导读，正文，常用术语、单词与短语，思考与练习，延伸阅读等部分组成。在导读中，主要是对所选取文献的历史背景、文献责任者和文献本身的情况进行介绍和评价。重视对文献进行史源学说明，尤其是文献本身的“书谱”与文献责任者的“学谱”。为了便于理解正文，本书重点解释了正文中有一定难度的字词和短语。在思考与练习中，本书重点放在培养原始文献意识，锻炼文献史料的理解力和解释力上。在延伸阅读部分，本书不仅重视传统文献，更重视网络数据库资源以及影视资料等现代影音文献，增加了原始文献汇编参考书目或数据库、网站等教育教学资源。

迄今为止，就编者所见，国内编写的世界史文献解读类图书主要有10余部。①

---

① 参见尤天然、王寅编著：《世界历史文选》，华东师范大学出版社1986年版；尤天然、王寅编著：《世界历史文选》，华东师范大学出版社2002年版；王寅、尤天然编著：《历史英语文选》，上海辞书出版社2009年版；陈文海主编：《历史学专业英语》，长春出版社1999年版；陈文海主编：《历史学专业英语新编》，长春出版社2013年版；刘德斌主编：《世界历史与国际关系专业英语选读》，吉林大学出版社2003年版；张德明：《历史专业英语》，武汉大学出版社2007年版；高芳英、范菊华主编：《史学专业英语》，群言出版社2008年版；王绍梅编著：《历史学英语》，复旦大学出版社2013年版；王宪明选编：《西方历史学经典选读》，中国人民大学出版社2008年版；亓佩成：《大学历史专业英语教程》，山东大学出版社2019年版；周丽新主编：《历史与文化专业英语教程》，上海交通大学出版社2011年版；冯佳：《历史学英文文献阅读与论文写作》，山东大学出版社2022年版；[美]沙露茵、马紫梅编著：《历史学专业英语教程》，北京大学出版社2005年版；孟广林主编：《西方历史文献选读》五卷本，社会科学文献出版社2015—2016年版；等等。

编者通过学习，初步体会到其突出优点有以下几个方面：第一，在体例上，以历史时代变迁为主线，兼顾地区、国别或专题，选取了每一个历史时代主要地区或国家的代表性文献。第二，在内容上，这些代表性文献以历史作品为主，兼顾一定的原始文献，重点选取了历史上著名史学家、政治家等人物的作品。第三，在课程目标及课程理念上，以掌握英文文献的阅读理解与中英文翻译为主，重点是对专业英语语言的学习和使用。

但是，现有这类图书留给我们努力的空间也许值得关注：第一，课程思政元素可以更加鲜明。迄今为止，我们尚未见到在世界史文献解读中收录马克思主义经典文献和中华优秀传统文化基础文献者。第二，以往所收录的文献侧重于传统的政治史、军事史，图书有必要反映当今中国史学重视经济社会史、文化和文明史的新趋势。第三，课程目标及课程理念不仅要强调语言技能学习，还要重视专业素养和技能的培养。因此，本书将在吸收以往相关图书编写经验和优长的基础上进行探索性尝试。本书可作为普通高等学校世界史专业教材。

Part I

Introduction to the Concepts and Theories of World History

世界史的概念与理论

本编以马克思主义为指导，将明确界定世界史的概念，引导学生阅读和理解马克思主义有关世界历史理论的经典著作。

国内外学术界对世界史概念的界定至今仍见仁见智。在努力摆脱欧洲中心论和苏联史学模式固化的过程中，中国学者逐渐形成了独具特色的世界历史概念。这就是以吴于廑先生为代表的中国世界史学界对世界历史的界定。这是吴于廑先生整体世界史观的逻辑起点。早在 1982 年 10 月，在云南昆明举行的中国世界中世纪史研究会第三次年会上，吴于廑先生就作了题为《世界历史上的游牧世界与农耕世界》的大会报告，首次集中阐发了整体世界史观。随后，吴于廑先生先后发表"4 篇宏文，加上他为《中国大百科全书 · 外国历史卷》（1990 年出版）撰写的总条'世界历史'，构架了大致完整的世界史体系，从学理上阐释和勾勒了历史发展为整体世界史的脉络"[①]。以整体世界史观为基础编写的 6 卷本大学世界史教材，从 20 世纪 90 年代至今一直是高校基本教学用书。这套教材就是以吴于廑先生为《中国大百科全书 · 外国历史卷》撰写的"世界历史"条目为总序言。本编的世界史概念正是以此为基础，首次尝试把该总序言主要内容翻译为英文。

为了加深对世界史概念的理解和把握，我们还把中国学者编纂的《马克思主义大辞典》《世界历史名词》中对世界历史的界定翻译成了英文，同时把密歇根大学诺斯罗普对世界历史概念的思考作为对照，从而进一步印证中国学者的世界史概念不仅符合马克思主义，而且从某种程度上已经超越了欧洲中心论和西方学者的认知。在此基础上，从我国的外语教学与研究出版社、苏联的莫斯科进步出版社等权威出版社出版的马克思主义经典著作英文版中，我们选取了 5

---

① 刘景华：《"整体世界史观"从这里启航——忆四十二年前的一场学术盛会》，《历史评论》2024 年第 1 期。

篇有关历史和世界史重要论述的文献，以便让学生进行重点阅读和理解。为了更好地传承发展中华优秀传统文化，把马克思主义基本原理与中华优秀传统文化有机结合起来，本编还选取了《大学》《中庸》的部分章节，以期厚植中国人的文化根基，加快构建中国特色的世界史学科体系、学术体系、话语体系，最终建构中国自主的世界史知识体系。

Unit 1

Concepts of World History

世界史的概念

历史就是过程（process），包括自然史和人类史。[①] 其中，自然史（nature history）就是自然界演化的过程，人类史（human history）就是人类社会变迁的过程。那么，何谓世界史呢？这里的世界史是指人类史，不是指自然史。人类创造的历史展现在作为矢量（vector）的历史时间和历史空间中。历史学就是时空整合学（temporal and spatial integration science）。然而，国内外学界对历史和历史学的理解和认识见仁见智，迄今难以达成共识，对世界史和世界史学科的概念界定也不例外，“全球史”概念也经常与世界史互用。自 20 世纪末至今，吴于廑先生对世界史的界定已被中国学术界接受。因此，本编首先译介了吴于廑先生对世界史的概念界定，同时译介了《马克思主义大辞典》和《世界历史名词（2013）》中对世界史的理论概括和推荐标准，并与国外学者有关世界史的论述进行对照，以期中国人能够树立正确的世界历史观，更期待向国际学术界展示这一世界历史观，从而推动中外交流互鉴。

吴于廑（1913—1993），祖籍安徽休宁，成长于江苏宝应。中国世界史学科创建者，历史学家、历史教育家。1935 年毕业于东吴大学。毕业后曾在南开大学经济研究所学习经济史，1941 年赴美留学。1944 年和 1946 年先后获得哈佛大学文学硕士和哲学博士学位。1947 年回国任武汉大学历史系教授，先后任历史系主任、副校长，以及中国世界中世纪史研究会会长、中国世界上古史研究

① 参见《马克思恩格斯文集》第 1 卷，人民出版社 2009 年版，第 517—519 页。

会会长。曾与周一良共同主编了新中国第一部世界历史教材《世界通史》(4卷本)。改革开放后与齐世荣共同主编了教育部委托的高校世界历史教材《世界史》(6卷本)。

I. Different Definitions of World History

1. Wu Yujin's definition of world history①

World history is an important subdiscipline of history, and its content is to explore and expound systematically the process of the historical development from the primitive, isolated and scattered groups into the closely interacted world of integration. In terms of the whole situation point of view, the main mission of world history is to make comprehensive investigations into histories of all regions, countries and nations, and to research and explain the evolution of human history with academic achievements of cultural anthropology and archaeology so as to reveal the laws and trends of historical development.

2. World history in *A Dictionary of Marxism*②

A period in the development of human history. There're two periods in human history, i. e., the periods of national history and world history. It's in the period of world history that all nations break through the closed status to make human history in larger scale and on deeper level. Emerging from the age of capitalism, world history resulted from the development of the productive forces. It includes diverse aspects of economics, politics, and culture etc., and embodies the forces of production becoming global, the scope of communication international, the interdependence among all nations enhanced, the form of social governance unified. World history itself is also on the

① 吴于廑.《总序》,吴于廑、齐世荣主编:《世界历史·古代编》上卷,高等教育出版社2011年版,第1页。

② 徐光春主编:《马克思主义大辞典》,崇文书局2017年版,第2—3页。

process of continuous development. It's the proletariat who make the world history, and communism is the inevitable outcome of the world history. The discipline of world history is an important subdiscipline of history, which with overall views on the world makes comprehensive investigations into histories of all regions, countries and nations, and to research and explain the process, trends and laws of the emergence, development and evolution of world history.

3.World history in *Chinese Terms in World History*①

An important historical discipline. Its content is to explore and expound systematically the process of the historical development from the primitive, isolated and scattered groups into the closely interacted world of integration, and to research and explain the evolution of human history so as to reveal the laws and trends of the historical evolution.

4. Global history

(1) Global history in *Chinese Terms in World History*②

A kind of method and theory for reconstructing world history arising in the late twentieth century West, which has close connection with the emergence and development of globalization, and now has been regarded as a new school of history.

(2) Global history in the West③

What is global history, in a sense beyond merely a collection of histories of all parts of the globe? What might truly cosmopolitan global history look like? It was in the late eighteenth century that European historians began, arguably for the first time, to think of history in global or planetary terms and to pose these questions. The idea that there was a universal community of all mankind itself had, to be sure, a long history running through medieval Christian understandings of a humanitas universalis back to Roman accounts

---

① 世界历史名词审定委员会：《世界历史名词》，商务印书馆 2013 年版，第 1 页。

② 世界历史名词审定委员会：《世界历史名词》，商务印书馆 2013 年版，第 1 页。

③ Prasenjit Duara, Viren Murthy, and Andrew Sartori eds., *A Companion to Global Thought*, Chichester: Blackwell Publishing Ltd., 2014, p. 184.

of the orbis terrarum, the inhabitable world of the contiguous continents of Europe, Asia, and Africa, and Greek ideas of the oikoumene, also a notion of a connected human community.

5. Douglas Northrop's review on world history[①]

But what happens if these institutional and intellectual pathways are disrupte—if historical questions are asked in new ways, stretching across the boundaries of the existing fields? Can time and space be stretched, and historians take a new, broader, perspective? This is precisely what practitioners of world and global history aim to do. They represent a young "field," at least by the standards of professional history, one that by most measures has only come into its own over the past quarter-century. World history is still in some ways embattled, harshly criticized by self-styled disciplinary gatekeepers, including some specialists in nationally defined fields—Japanese history, Russian history, American history, etc.. World history may represent a practical threat (as a new claimant to limited institutional resources) but is more likely to be attacked in intellectual terms, as a marginal, even doomed approach, too general, impossibly broad, obviously too superficial to permit serious scholarship. Yet world history—as a professional arena—is populated by a diverse and rapidly growing group of scholars and teachers who have worked hard to show the contrary.

II. Common Terms, Words and Phrases for the Text

world history 世界史

Marxism 马克思主义

Marxist 马克思主义者

Marxist history 马克思主义史学

dialectical materialism 辩证唯物主义

① Douglas Northrop, "The Challenges of World History", in Douglas Northrop ed., *A Companion to World History*, Chichester: Blackwell Publishing Ltd., 2012, p. 1.

historical materialism 历史唯物主义

basic contradictions of society 社会基本矛盾

forces of production（productive forces）生产力

relations of production（productive relations）生产关系

mode of production 生产方式

economic base 经济基础

superstructure 上层建筑

formation of society（social formation）社会形态

dynamic of social development 社会发展动力

law of social development 社会发展规律

idealism 唯心主义

positivism 实证主义

eurocentricism 欧洲中心论

Asian mode of production（Asiatic mode of production）亚细亚生产方式

genetic method 发生学方法

economic and social history 经济社会史

comparative history 比较史学

oral history 口述史

public history 公共史学

quantitative history 计量史学

psychohistory 心理史学

division of labour 劳动分工

property 所有制

property right 产权

ownership 所有权

primitive society 原始社会

slavery society 奴隶制社会

feudal society 封建社会

capitalist society 资本主义社会

socialist society 社会主义社会

communist society 共产主义社会

historicism 历史主义

historiography 历史编纂学

historiographer（historian）史官、史学家

Annals 法国年鉴学派

universal history 普遍史

total history 整体史

big history 大历史

global history 全球史

ethnic group 族群

race 种族

nation 民族

values（view of value）价值观

circa 大约（简写为 c., ca. or cir.）

III. Exercises and Thinking

1. According to Wu Yujin's theory on the integrated world history, do you agree with such an opinion that China history is also a field of world history?

2. Please summarize different concepts of world history, and make some comparisons among them, then share your reflections with your classmates.

3. Please comment on Douglas Northrop's review on world history.

IV. Further Readings and Internet Links

1. Further Readings

吴于廑:《吴于廑文选》，武汉大学出版社 2007 年版。

徐光春主编:《马克思主义大辞典》，崇文书局 2017 年版。

世界历史名词审定委员会:《世界历史名词》，商务印书馆 2013 年版。

大辞海编辑委员会:《大辞海·世界历史卷》，上海辞书出版社 2011 年版。

朱孝远:《如何学习研究世界史》，北京大学出版社 2011 年版。

Douglas Northrop ed., *A Companion to World History*, Chichester: Blackwell Publishing Ltd, 2012.

David Walker, Daniel Gray, *Historical Dictionary of Marxism*, Lanham and Toronto: The Scarecrow Press, Inc., 2007.

2. Internet Links

中国世界史研究网（中国社会科学院世界历史研究所主办）：http://iwh.cssn.cn/

Journal of World History（美国夏威夷大学《世界史》期刊）：https://www.jstor.org/journal/jworldhistory

Journal of Global History（英国剑桥大学出版社《全球史》期刊）：https://www.cambridge.org/core/journals/journal-of-global-history#

Unit 2

The German Ideology

《德意志意识形态》

随着英国工业革命的完成和资本主义社会的确立，思想敏锐、深邃的马克思和恩格斯分别从理论思考和现实观察两个角度，对资本主义社会开展了深入的研究和批判，并得出了相同的结论。正如马克思所说的那样："自从弗里德里希·恩格斯批判经济学范畴的天才大纲（在《德法年鉴》上）发表以后，我同他不断通信交换意见，他从另一条道路（参看他的《英国工人阶级状况》)，得出同我一样的结果。"[①] 正是在此基础上，1845—1846 年，这两位巨人在布鲁塞尔共同撰写了马克思主义经典巨著《德意志意识形态——对费尔巴哈、布·鲍威尔和施蒂纳所代表的现代德国哲学以及各式各样先知所代表的德国社会主义的批判》。这部巨著首次对历史和历史唯物主义进行了系统、明确的阐述，对历史转变为世界史的逻辑与实践进行了科学、准确的把握；同时对以前的德国哲学信仰进行了全面清算，对黑格尔哲学进行了深刻批判。尽管这部巨著在马克思和恩格斯生前并未全部出版，只有第 2 卷的第 4 章得以发表，但其中阐发的历史唯物主义基本原理至今仍然闪耀着真理的光辉。因此，这部巨著是我们学习、研究世界历史的基本遵循和指南。

卡尔·海因里希·马克思（Karl Heinrich Marx, 1818—1883），马克思主义的创立者，世界无产阶级和国际共产主义运动的伟大领袖和导师，人类历史上最有影响力的思想家之一。弗里德里希·冯·恩格斯（Friedrich Von Engels，1820—

① 《马克思恩格斯文集》第 2 卷，人民出版社 2009 年版，第 592—593 页。

1895），马克思的亲密战友，马克思主义的创立者之一，世界无产阶级和国际共产主义运动的伟大领袖和导师。这里选取的内容出自莫斯科进步出版社 1976 年出版的《德意志形态》英译本。

I. Conclusions from the Materialist Conception of History: History as a Continuous Process, History as Becoming World History, the necessity of Communist Revolution①

History is nothing but the succession of the separate generations, each of which uses the materials, the capital funds, the productive forces handed down to it by all preceding generations, and thus, on the one hand, continues the traditional activity in completely changed circumstances and, on the other, modifies the old circumstances with a completely changed activity. This can be speculatively distorted so that later history is made the goal of earlier history, e. g., the goal ascribed to the discovery of America is to further the eruption of the French Revolution. Thereby history receives its own special goals and becomes "a person ranking with other persons" (to wit: "self-consciousness, criticism, the unique", etc.), while what is designated with the words "destiny", "goal", "germ", or "idea" of earlier history is nothing more than an abstraction from later history, from the active influence which earlier history exercises on later history.

The further the separate spheres, which act on one another, extend in the course of this development and the more the original isolation of the separate nationalities is destroyed by the advanced mode of production, by intercourse and by the natural division of labour between various nations arising as a result, the more history becomes world history. Thus, for instance, if in England a machine is invented which deprives countless workers of bread in India and China, and overturns the whole form of existence of these empires, this invention becomes a world-historical fact. Or again, take the

① Marx and Engels, *The German Ideology*, Moscow: Progress Publishers, 1976, pp. 58–62.

case of sugar and coffee, which have proved their world-historical importance in the nineteenth century by the fact that the lack of these products, occasioned by the Napoleonic Continental System, caused the Germans to rise against Napoleon, and thus became the real basis of the glorious Wars of Liberation of 1813. From this it follows that this transformation of history into world history is by no means a mere abstract act on the part of "self-consciousness", the world spirit, or of any other metaphysical spectre, but a quite material, empirically verifiable act, an act the proof of which every individual furnishes as he comes and goes, eats, drinks and clothes himself.

In history up to the present it is certainly likewise an empirical fact that separate individuals have, with the broadening of their activity into world-historical activity, become more and more enslaved under a power alien to them (a pressure which they have conceived of as a dirty trick on the part of the so-called world spirit, etc.), a power which has become more and more enormous and, in the last instance, turns out to be the *world market.* But it is just as empirically established that, by the overthrow of the existing state of society by the communist revolution (of which more below) and the abolition of private property, which is identical with it, this power, which so baffles the German theoreticians, will be dissolved; and that then the liberation of each single individual will be accomplished in the measure in which history becomes wholly transformed into world history. From the above it is clear that the real intellectual wealth of the individual depends entirely on the wealth of his real connections. Only this will liberate the separate individuals from the various national and local barriers, bring them into practical connection with the production (including intellectual production) of the whole world and make it possible for them to acquire the capacity to enjoy this all-sided production of the whole earth (the creations of man). *All-round* dependence, this primary natural form of the *world-historical* co-operation of individuals, will be transformed by this communist revolution into the control and conscious mastery of these powers, which, born of the action of men on one another, have till now overawed and ruled men as powers completely alien to them. Now this view can be expressed again in a speculative–idealistic, i.e., fantastic, way as "self–generation of the species" ("society as the subject"), and thereby the consecutive series of interrelated individuals can be regarded as a single individual, which accomplishes the mystery of generating itself. In this context it is evident that individuals undoubtedly make *one another,* physically and mentally, but do not make themselves, either in the nonsense of Saint Bruno, or in the sense of the "unique" , of the "made" man.

Finally, from the conception of history set forth by us we obtain these further conclusions: (1) In the development of productive forces there comes a stage when productive forces and means of intercourse are brought into being which, under the existing relations, only cause mischief, and are no longer productive but destructive forces (machinery and money); and connected with this a class is called forth which has to bear all the burdens of society without enjoying its advantages, which is ousted from society and forced into the sharpest contradiction to all other classes; a class which forms the majority of all members of society, and from which emanates the consciousness of the necessity of a fundamental revolution, the communist consciousness, which may, of course, arise among the other classes too through the contemplation of the situation of this class. (2) The conditions under which definite productive forces can be applied are the conditions of the rule of a definite class of society, whose social power, deriving from its property, has its *practical*–idealistic expression in each case in the form of the state and, therefore, every revolutionary struggle is directed against a class which till then has been in power. (3) In all previous revolutions the mode of activity always remained unchanged and it was only a question of a different distribution of this activity, a new distribution of labour to other persons, whilst the communist revolution is directed against the hitherto existing *mode* of activity, does away with *labour,* and abolishes the rule of all classes with the classes themselves, because it is carried through by the class which no longer counts as a class in society, which is not recognized as a class, and is in itself the expression of the dissolution of all classes, nationalities, etc., within present society; and (4) Both for the production on a mass scale of this communist consciousness, and for the success of the cause itself, the alteration of men on a mass scale is necessary, an alteration which can only take place in a practical movement, a *revolution*; the revolution is necessary, therefore, not only because the *ruling* class cannot be overthrown in any other way, but also because the class *overthrowing* it can only in a revolution succeed in ridding itself of all the muck of ages and become fitted to found society anew.

Summary of the Materialist Conception of History

This conception of history thus relies on expounding the real process of production —starting from the material production of life itself—and comprehending the form of intercourse connected with and created by this mode of production, i.e., civil society in its various stages, as the basis of all history; describing it in its action as the state, and also explaining how all the different theoretical products and forms of consciousness, religion, philosophy, morality, etc., etc., arise from it, and tracing the process of their formation from that basis; thus the whole thing can, of course, be depicted in its totality (and therefore, too, the reciprocal action of these various sides on one another). It has not, like the idealist view of history, to look for a category in every period, but remains constantly on the real *ground* of history; it does not explain practice from the idea but explains the formation of ideas from material practice, and accordingly it comes to the conclusion that all forms and products of consciousness cannot be dissolved by mental criticism, by resolution into "self-consciousness" or transformation into "apparitions", "spectres", "whimsies", etc., but only by the practical overthrow of the actual social relations which gave rise to this idealistic humbug; that not criticism but revolution is the driving force of history, also of religion, of philosophy and all other kinds of theory. It shows that history does not end by being resolved into "self-consciousness" as "spirit of the spirit", a but that each stage contains a material result, a sum of productive forces, a historically created relation to nature and of individuals to one another, which is handed down to each generation from its predecessor; a mass of productive forces, capital funds and circumstances, which on the one hand is indeed modified by the new generation, but on the other also prescribes for it its conditions of life and gives it a definite development, a special character. It shows that circumstances make men just as much as men make circumstances.

This sum of productive forces, capital funds and social forms of intercourse, which every individual and every generation finds in existence as something given, is the real basis of what the philosophers have conceived as "substance" and "essence of man" , and what they have deified and attacked: a real basis which is not in the least disturbed, in its effect and influence on the development of men, by the fact that these philosophers revolt against it as "self-consciousness" and the "unique" . These conditions of life, which different generations find in existence, determine also whether or not the revolutionary convulsion periodically recurring in history will be strong enough to overthrow the basis of everything that exists. And if these material elements of a complete revolution are not present—namely, on the one hand the existing productive forces, on the other the formation of a revolutionary mass, which revolts not only against separate conditions of the existing society, but against the existing "production of life" itself, the "total activity" on which it was based—then it is absolutely immaterial for practical development whether the *idea* of this revolution has been expressed a hundred times already, as the history of communism proves.

II. Common Terms, Words and Phrases for the Text

history 历史

material 材料，物质的

materialist 唯物主义者，唯物主义（者）的

conception 概念

circumstances 环境，经济状况

French Revolution 法国大革命

goal of history 历史的目的

self-consciousness 自我意识

abstraction 抽象

intercourse 交往

Napoleonic Continental System 拿破仑的大陆体系

world-historical fact 世界历史性的事实

transformation 转变，转型

world spirit 世界精神

metaphysical 形而上学的，高度抽象的

empirical fact 经验事实

alien 异己的

world market 世界市场

communist revolution 共产主义革命

baffle 难住，阻隔

theoretician 理论家

intellectual production 精神的生产

cooperation 协作，合作社

speculative 思辨的，投机性的

idealistic 理想主义（者）的，唯心主义（者）的

subject 主体，主观

means of intercourse 交往手段

oust 剥夺，驱逐

social power 社会权力

communist consciousness 共产主义意识

process of production 生产过程

form of intercourse 交往形式

civil society 市民社会

depict 描述，描绘

in totality 总体上，总共

reciprocal 相互的，互惠的

idealist view of history 唯心主义历史观

formation of ideas 观念形态

material practice 物质实践

apparition 幽灵，异象

whimsy 怪念头，离奇的东西

humbug 骗子，鬼话

social relations 社会关系

driving force of history 历史的动力

substance 实体

essence of man 人的本质

deify 神化，崇拜

convulsion 震动，动乱

recur 反复出现，再现

immaterial 非物质的，无关紧要的

III. Exercises and Thinking

1. According to the document, please define the conception of history.

2. Is there any goal for the process of history?

3. How can you understand the transformation of history into world history?

4. Please sum up the main body of the materialist view of history.

IV. Further Readings and Internet Links

1. Further Readings

马克思、恩格斯:《德意志意识形态》，人民出版社 2018 年版。

《马克思恩格斯文集》第 1 卷，人民出版社 2009 年版。

恩格斯:《英国工人阶级状况》,《马克思恩格斯全集》第 3 卷，人民出版社 2002 年版。

2. Internet Links

中共中央党史和文献研究院：https://www.dswxyjy.org.cn/

国家哲学社会科学文献中心：https://www.ncpssd.cn/

中国社会科学院历史理论研究所：http://lls.cssn.cn/

《过去与现在》英文期刊：https://academic.oup.com/past

Unit 3

Manifesto of the Communist Party

《共产党宣言》

“一个民族要想站在科学的最高峰，就一刻也不能没有理论思维。”[①]1848年发表的《共产党宣言》，又称《共产主义宣言》，是马克思、恩格斯为世界上第一个共产党组织——共产主义者同盟起草的纲领，是国际共产主义运动的第一份纲领性文献。这部文献首次系统阐述了科学社会主义理论，是马克思主义诞生的标志。

共产主义者同盟（Communist League）是首个以科学社会主义为指导的无产阶级政党。其前身是1836年成立的正义者同盟，一个流亡到法国的德国工人秘密组织。在马克思、恩格斯的帮助下，正义者同盟接受了马克思、恩格斯创立的科学社会主义理论。1847年6月，正义者同盟在伦敦召开大会，在马克思、恩格斯的直接领导下正式改组，更名为共产主义者同盟。[②]早在1848年欧洲革命之前，马克思、恩格斯就完成了《共产党宣言》的写作，对欧洲革命运动起到了重要的推动作用。1850年11月9日，英国宪章派机关刊物《红色共和党人》首次开始刊载《共产党宣言》的英文版。

第一位英文版《共产党宣言》的英译者的信息至今仍不够清晰完整。当时该译者化名霍华德·默顿（Howard Morton），曾在多个杂志上发表文章，号召工人参加革命运动。恩格斯曾指出，这位译者是海伦·麦克法林女士：“第一个英译本是由海伦·麦克法林女士翻译的，于1850年刊载在乔治·朱利安·哈尼

---

① 《马克思恩格斯文集》第9卷，人民出版社2009年版，第437页。

② 徐光春主编：《马克思主义大辞典》，崇文书局2017年版，第369页。

的伦敦《红色共和党人》杂志上。”[1] 但是，有关她的情况，至今人们只知道她住在兰卡斯特的伯恩利（Burnley），是一位英国宪章派成员，也是马克思、恩格斯的友人，没有其他更多的信息。[2]《红色共和党人》的编辑哈尼在首次刊发的英文版《共产党宣言》的序言中明确指出，《共产党宣言》这一文献的作者是马克思、恩格斯，并且该文献“已被德国共产主义者各派别所接受”，“英国读者通过该文献的杰出译本将能够评判德国最先进的革命党人的计划和原则”。[3] 从马克思主义文献学和史源学角度而言，第一个英译本的相关问题仍然值得深入研究。

本书选取的内容则出自 1888 年恩格斯亲自编校的英文版《共产党宣言》。该英文版是最为权威的英译本。恩格斯还专门为该英文版撰写了序言，在谈到这一版本的编校和翻译时他明确说：“本版译文是由译过马克思《资本论》一书大部分的赛米尔·穆尔先生翻译的。我们共同把译文校阅过一遍，并且我还加了一些有关历史情况的注释。”[4] 因此，恩格斯亲自编辑、校阅的英文版是经典版本。在中国，恩格斯编校的版本于 1965 年由当时的外文出版社出版发行，1968 年重印。这里选取的内容是其绪言和第一部分。

I. Excerpt from *Manifesto of the Communist Party*[5]

A spectre is haunting Europe—the spectre of Communism. All the Powers of old Europe have entered into a holy alliance to exorcise this spectre: Pope and Czar, Metternich and Guizot, French Radicals and German police-spies.

Where is the party in opposition that has not been decried as Communistic by

---

① 《马克思恩格斯文集》第 2 卷，人民出版社 2009 年版，第 11 页。

② John Saville introduction, *The Red Republican and The Friend of the People,* Vol. 1, London: Merlin Press, 1966, pp. xi–xii.

③ 参见 John Saville introduction, *The Red Republican and The Friend of the People,* Vol. 1, London: Merlin Press, 1966, pp. xi–xii. p. 161; ODNB, Vol. 25, p. 355。

④ 《马克思恩格斯文集》第 2 卷，人民出版社 2009 年版，第 15 页。

⑤ Karl Marx and Frederick Engels, *Manifesto of the Communist Party*, Peking: Foreign Languages Press, 1968, pp. 29–39.

its opponents in power? Where the Opposition that has not hurled back the branding reproach of Communism, against the more advanced opposition parties, as well as against its reactionary adversaries?

Two things result from this fact.

I. Communism is already acknowledged by all European Powers to be itself a Power.

II. It is high time that Communists should openly, in the face of the whole world, publish their views, their aims, their tendencies, and meet this nursery tale of the Spectre of Communism with a Manifesto of the party itself.

To this end, Communists of various nationalities have assembled in London, and sketched the following Manifesto, to be published in the English, French, German, Italian, Flemish and Danish languages.

BOURGEOIS AND PROLETARIANS

The history of all hitherto existing society is the history of class struggles.

Freeman and slave, patrician and plebeian, lord and serf, guild-master and journeyman, in a word, oppressor and oppressed, stood in constant opposition to one another, carried on an uninterrupted, now hidden, now open fight, a fight that each time ended, either in a revolutionary re-constitution of society at large, or in the common ruin of the contending classes.

In the earlier epochs of history, we find almost everywhere a complicated arrangement of society into various orders, a manifold gradation of social rank. In ancient Rome we have patricians, knights, plebeians, slaves; in the Middle Ages, feudal lords, vassals, guild-masters, journeymen, apprentices, serfs; in almost all of these classes, again, subordinate gradations.

The modern bourgeois society that has sprouted from the ruins of feudal society has not done away with class antagonisms. It has but established new classes, new conditions of oppression, new forms of struggle in place of the old ones.

Our epoch, the epoch of the bourgeoisie, possesses, however, this distinctive feature: it has simplified the class antagonisms. Society as a whole is more and mote splitting up into two great hostile camps, into two great classes directly facing each other: Bourgeoisie and Proletariat.

From the serfs of the Middle Ages sprang the chartered burghers of the earliest towns. From these burgesses the first elements of the bourgeoisie were developed.

The discovery of America, the rounding of the Cape, opened up fresh ground for the rising bourgeoisie. The East-Indian and Chinese markets, the colonisation of America, trade with the colonies, the increase in the means of exchange and in commodities generally, gave to commerce, to navigation, to industry, an impulse never before known, and thereby, to the revolutionary element in the tottering feudal society, a rapid development.

The feudal system of industry, under which industrial production was monopolised by closed guilds, now no longer sufficed for the growing wants of the new markets. The manufacturing system took its place. The guild-masters were pushed on one side by the manufacturing middle class; division of labour between the different corporate guilds vanished in the face of division of labour in each single workshop.

Meantime the markets kept ever growing, the demand ever rising. Even manufacture no longer sufficed. Thereupon, steam and machinery revolutionized industrial production. The place of manufacture was taken by the giant, Modern Industry, the place of the industrial middle class, by industrial millionaires, the leaders of whole industrial armies, the modern bourgeois.

Modern industry has established the world market, for which the discovery of America paved the way. This market has given an immense development to commerce, to navigation, to communication by land. This development has, in its turn, reacted on the extension of industry; and in proportion as industry, commerce, navigation, railways extended, in the same proportion the bourgeoisie developed, increased its capital, and pushed into the background every class handed down from the Middle Ages.

We see, therefore, how the modern bourgeoisie is itself the product of a long course of development, of a series of revolutions in the modes of production and of exchange.

Each step in the development of the bourgeoisie was accompanied by a corresponding political advance of that class. An oppressed class under the sway of the feudal nobility, an armed and self-governing association in the mediaeval commune; here independent urban republic (as in Italy and Germany), there taxable "third estate" of the monarchy (as in France), afterwards, in the period of manufacture proper, serving either the semi-feudal or the absolute monarchy as a counterpoise against the nobility, and, in fact, corner stone of the great monarchies in general, the bourgeoisie has at last, since the establishment of Modern Industry and of the world market, conquered for itself, in the modern representative State, exclusive political sway. The executive of the modern State is but a committee for managing the common affairs of the whole bourgeoisie.

The bourgeoisie, historically, has played a most revolutionary part.

The bourgeoisie, wherever it has got the upper hand, has put an end to all feudal, patriarchal, idyllic relations. It has pitilessly torn asunder the motley feudal ties that bound man to his "natural superiors," and has left remaining no other nexus between man and man than naked self-interest, than callous "cash payment." It has drowned the most heavenly ecstasies of religious fervour, of chivalrous enthusiasm, of philistine sentimentalism, in the icy water of egotistical calculation. It has resolved personal worth into exchange value, and in place of the numberless indefeasible chartered freedoms, has set up that single, unconscionable freedom—Free Trade. In one word, for exploitation, veiled by religious and political illusions, it has substituted naked, shameless, direct, brutal exploitation.

The bourgeoisie has stripped of its halo every occupation hitherto honoured and looked up to with reverent awe. It has converted the physician, the lawyer, the priest, the poet, the man of science, into its paid wage-labourers.

The bourgeoisie has torn away from the family its sentimental veil, and has reduced the family relation to a mere money relation.

The bourgeoisie has disclosed how it came to pass that the brutal display of vigour in the Middle Ages, which Reactionists so much admire, found its fitting complement in the most slothful indolence. It has been the first to show what man's activity can bring about. It has accomplished wonders far surpassing Egyptian pyramids, Roman aqueducts, and Gothic cathedrals; it has conducted expeditions that put in the shade all former Exoduses of nations and crusades.

The bourgeoisie cannot exist without constantly revolutionising the instruments of production, and thereby the relations of production, and with them the whole relations of society. Conservation of the old modes of production in unaltered form, was, on the contrary, the first condition of existence for all earlier industrial classes. Constant revolutionising of production, uninterrupted disturbance of all social conditions, everlasting uncertainty and agitation distinguish the bourgeois epoch from all earlier ones. All fixed, fast-frozen relations, with their train of ancient and venerable prejudices and opinions, are swept away, all new-formed ones become antiquated before they can ossify. All that is solid melts into air, all that is holy is profaned, and man is at last compelled to face with sober senses, his real conditions of life, and his relations with his kind.

The need of a constantly expanding market for its products chases the bourgeoisie over the whole surface of the globe. It must nestle everywhere, settle everywhere, establish connexions everywhere.

The bourgeoisie has through its exploitation of the world market given a cosmopolitan character to production and consumption in every country. To the great chagrin of Reactionists, it has drawn from under the feet of industry the national ground on which it stood. All old-established national industries have been destroyed or are daily being destroyed. They are dislodged by new industries, whose introduction becomes a life and death question for all civilised nations, by industries that no longer work up indigenous raw material, but raw material drawn from the remotest zones; industries whose products are consumed, not only at home, but in every quarter of the globe. In place of the old wants, satisfied by the productions of the country, we find new wants, requiring for their satisfaction the products of distant lands and climes. In place of the old local and national seclusion and self–sufficiency, we have intercourse in every direction, universal inter–dependence of nations. And as in material, so also in intellectual production. The intellectual creations of individual nations become common property. National one–sidedness and narrow–mindedness become more and more impossible, and from the numerous national and local literatures there arises a world–literature.

The bourgeoisie, by the rapid improvement of all instruments of production, by the immensely facilitated means of communication, draws all, even the most barbarian, nations into civilisation. The cheap prices of its commodities are the heavy artillery with which it batters down all Chinese walls, with which it forces the barbarians' intensely obstinate hatred of foreigners to capitulate. It compels all nations, on pain of extinction, to adopt the bourgeois mode of production; it compels them to introduce what it calls civilisation into their midst, *i.e.*, to become bourgeois themselves. In one word, it creates a world after its own image.

The bourgeoisie has subjected the country to the rule of the towns. It has created enormous cities, has greatly increased the urban population as compared with the rural, and has thus rescued a considerable part of the population from the idiocy of rural life. Just as it has made the country dependent on the towns, so it has made barbarian and semi–barbarian countries dependent on the civilised ones, nations of peasants on nations of bourgeois, the East on the West.

The bourgeoisie keeps more and more doing away with the scattered state of the population, of the means of production, and of property. It has agglomerated population, centralised means of production, and has concentrated property in a few hands. The necessary consequence of this was political centralisation. Independent, or but loosely connected provinces, with separate interests, laws, governments and systems of taxation, became lumped together into one nation, with one government, one code of laws, one national class–interest, one frontier and one customs–tariff.

The bourgeoisie, during its rule of scarce one hundred years, has created more massive and more colossal productive forces than have all preceding generations together. Subjection of Nature's forces to man, machinery, application of chemistry to industry and agriculture, steam–navigation, railways, electric telegraphs, clearing of whole continents for cultivation, canalisation of rivers, whole populations conjured out of the ground—what earlier century had even a presentiment that such productive forces slumbered in the lap of social labour?

We see then: the means of production and of exchange, on whose foundation the bourgeoisie built itself up, were generated in feudal society. At a certain stage in the development of these means of production and of exchange, the conditions under which feudal society produced and exchanged, the feudal organisation of agriculture and manufacturing industry, in one word, the feudal relations of property became no longer compatible with the already developed productive forces; they became so many fetters. They had to be burst asunder; they were burst asunder.

Into their place stepped free competition, accompanied by a social and political constitution adapted to it, and by the economical and political sway of the bourgeois class.

A similar movement is going on before our own eyes. Modern bourgeois society with its relations of production, of exchange and of property, a society that has conjured up such gigantic means of production and of exchange, is like the sorcerer, who is no longer able to control the powers of the nether world whom he has called up by his spells. For many a decade past the history of industry and commerce is but the history of the revolt of modern productive forces against modern conditions of production, against the property relations that are the conditions for the existence of the bourgeoisie and of its rule. It is enough to mention the commercial crises that by their periodical return put on its trial, each time more threateningly, the existence of the entire bourgeois society. In these crises a great part not only of the existing products, but also of the previously created productive forces, are periodically destroyed. In these crises there breaks out an epidemic that, in all earlier epochs, would have seemed an absurdity—the epidemic of over–production. Society suddenly finds itself put back into a state of momentary barbarism; it appears as if a famine, a universal war of devastation had cut off the supply of every means of subsistence; industry and commerce seem to be destroyed; and why? Because there is too much civilisation, too much means of subsistence, too much industry, too much commerce. The productive forces at the disposal of society no longer tend to further the development of the conditions of bourgeois property; on the contrary, they have become too powerful for these conditions, by which they are fettered, and so soon as they overcome these fetters, they bring disorder into the whole of bourgeois society, endanger the existence of bourgeois property. The conditions of bourgeois society are too narrow to comprise the wealth created by them. And how does the bourgeoisie get over these crises? On the one hand by enforced destruction of a mass of productive forces; on the other, by the conquest of new markets, and by the more thorough exploitation of the old ones. That is to say, by paving the way for more extensive and more destructive crises, and by diminishing the means whereby crises are prevented.

The weapons with which the bourgeoisie felled feudalism to the ground are now turned against the bourgeoisie itself.

But not only has the bourgeoisie forged the weapons that bring death to itself; it has also called into existence the men who are to wield those weapons — the modern working class—the proletarians.

In proportion as the bourgeoisie, *i.e.*, capital, is developed, in the same proportion is the proletariat, the modern working class, developed — a class of labourers, who live only so long as they find work, and who find work only so long as their labour increases capital. These labourers, who must sell themselves piecemeal, are a commodity, like every other article of commerce, and are consequently exposed to all the vicissitudes of competition, to all the fluctuations of the market.

II. Common Terms, Words and Phrases for the Text

manifesto 宣言

communist party 共产党

holy alliance 神圣同盟

spectre 幽灵，幻象，幻觉

exorcise 驱除，消除

decry 反对，谴责

opponent 对手，敌手

hurl 投掷，压倒

reproach 责备，指责

reactionary 反动的

adversary 敌手，对手

nationality 国籍

bourgeois 资产者

bourgeoisie 资产阶级

proletarian 无产者

proletariat 无产阶级

class struggle 阶级斗争

patrician 贵族（古罗马与中世纪意大利和德意志的）

plebeian 平民（古罗马与中世纪意大利和德意志的）

lord and serf 领主与农奴

guild-master 行会师傅

journeyman 雇工

oppressor 压迫者

oppressed 被压迫者

reconstitute 改组，复原

epoch 时代，时期

orders 社会等级

gradation 层次，阶段

vassal 封臣，附庸

apprentice 学徒

sprout 生长出，萌芽

antagonism 对抗，对立

class antagonisms 阶级对立

burgher 自治市市民

burgess 自治市居民

impulse 推动

totter 动摇，蹒跚

world market 世界市场

commune 公社

counterpoise 抗衡力，砝码

patriarchal 家长的，族长的

idyllic 田园诗般的，田园风光的

motley 混杂的，形形色色的

ecstasy 狂热，入迷

philistine 平庸的，庸人

sentimentalism 感情主义，多愁善感

exploitation 剥削

halo 光轮，荣光

reverent 恭敬的，虔敬的

awe 敬畏，恐惧

paid wage-labourer 雇佣劳动者

disclose 揭露，使显露

reactionist 反动派

pyramid 金字塔

aqueduct 渡槽，高架水渠

cathedral 主教座堂，教区总教堂

exodus 离开，迁徙

disturbance 干扰，动荡

agitation 焦虑不安，骚动

ossify 僵化，骨化

profane 亵渎

sober 冷静的，素淡的

cosmopolitan 世界性的，见多识广的

chagrin 失望，懊恼

dislodge 强行去除，逐出

indigenous 本地的，本土的

clime 地区，气候带

seclusion 与世隔绝，清净

self-sufficiency 自给自足

inter-dependence 相互依赖

one-sided 片面的，一边倒的

narrow-minded 气量小的，狭隘的

instruments of production 生产工具

obstinate 固执的，棘手的

capitulate 屈服，投降

idiocy 愚昧

agglomerate 成团，汇聚

lump 归并

conjure 变魔术，变戏法

slumber 沉睡，睡眠

fetter 束缚，桎梏

asunder 碎，散

gigantic 巨大的，庞大的

sorcerer 术士，巫师

nether 下方的，较低的

the nether world 阴间，地狱

over-production 生产过剩

disposal 除掉，处理

forge 锻造，伪造

wield 运用，支配

piecemeal 零敲碎打的，零星的

vicissitude 沉浮，荣枯

III. Exercises and Thinking

1. Please discuss the thesis " The history of all hitherto existing society is the history of class struggles".

2. Describe the development of the bourgeoisie, and define concepts of bourgeois and proletarian.

3. Evaluate the historical role of the bourgeoisie, and tell us the future of it.

IV. Further Readings and Internet Links

1. Further Readings

马克思、恩格斯：《共产党宣言》，人民出版社 2014 年版。

《马克思恩格斯文集》第 2 卷，人民出版社 2009 年版。

Karl Marx and Frederick Engels, *Manifesto of the Communist Party*, Peking: Foreign Languages Press, 1968.

2. Internet Links

中共中央党史和文献研究院：https://www.dswxyjy.org.cn/

国家哲学社会科学文献中心：https://www.ncpssd.cn/

中国社会科学院历史理论研究所：http://lls.cssn.cn/

Unit 4

The Capital

《资本论》

列宁指出："自从《资本论》问世以来，唯物主义历史观已经不是假设，而是科学地证明了的原理"，唯物史观成为"唯一科学的历史观"。[①] 19 世纪 40 年代，马克思、恩格斯共同撰写了《德意志意识形态》，创立了唯物史观。为了进一步检验唯物史观的科学性，马克思经过长期研究，于 1867 年出版了《资本论》第一卷。马克思在该卷的第一版序言中明确提出，他是以英国为典型实例，以英国的社会统计资料为主要历史文献依据，以科学的客观态度，"把经济的社会形态的发展理解为一种自然史的过程"，"最终目的就是揭示现代社会的经济运动规律"。[②] 恩格斯在《资本论》第一卷甫一出版就撰写书评提出，该经典著作"对于论题的切实的正面的叙述"，"直接丰富了科学。作者在那里用完全新的唯物主义的自然历史的方法考察了经济关系"。[③] 不仅如此，恩格斯还说："这本书，不管它的倾向如何，包含着值得所有的人注意的科学研究和实际材料"；这是因为马克思不仅坚持和运用唯物史观进行研究，而且通过科学研究和历史文献来检验和发展唯物史观，"他没有一个地方以事实去迁就自己的理论，相反地，他力图把自己的理论表现为事实的结果。这些事实他总是取自最好的来源，而涉及现代的情况时，则取自真实的可是德国还不知道的来源，即英国议会的报告"。[④] 马克思正是以科学的态度，以令人信服的历史文献为基础，来检验和发

---

① 《列宁选集》第 1 卷，人民出版社 2012 年版，第 10 页。

② 《资本论》第 1 卷，人民出版社 2018 年版，第 8—10 页。

③ 《马克思恩格斯全集》第 16 卷，人民出版社 1964 年版，第 254 页。

④ 《马克思恩格斯全集》第 16 卷，人民出版社 1964 年版，第 257—258 页。

展理论，这就使理论具有了令人信服的科学性和说服力。因此，恩格斯在1886年为《资本论》英译版所作的序言中说，“毫无疑问，在这样的时刻，应当倾听这样一个人的声音，这个人的全部理论是他毕生研究英国的经济史和经济状况的结果”①。马克思正是通过研究英国的经济史和经济状况，验证了唯物史观的科学性。

值得注意的是，《资本论》还是在唯物史观指导下解读和运用历史文献的典范。恩格斯在为《资本论》第一卷所作的书评中说：“我们不能不注意，他同时向我们提供了大量极有价值的历史材料和统计材料，这些材料几乎毫无例外地全部是从各种调查委员会向英国议会所做的正式报告中拿来的。”②在英国，议会的委员会制度始于14世纪，到16世纪中叶就已基本成形，为调查经济社会状况以及进行法律改革提供了重要依据。③1836年，英国议会对特别委员会进行了改革，委员会成员数额稳定在15名，成员名单向社会公布，委员会成员向证人或专家所提出的问题应以速记的方式确定下来，从而大大提高了委员会调查报告的准确性和可信度。④因此，即使在西方，人们也认为英国议会委员会的调查报告文献价值很高。⑤马克思、恩格斯不仅从形式上而且从内容上高度重视英国议会委员会的调查报告，并且指出，英国“定期指派委员会去调查经济状况”，这些委员会“有全权去揭发真相”，他们调查的对象有“工厂视察员”“医生”，与“调查女工童工受剥削的情况以及居住和营养条件等等的”“内行、公正、坚决的人们”。⑥恩格斯也提出，“这样的委员会，——当然，如果有合适的人在里面，——对于人民来说，是认识自己的最好的手段”⑦。恩格斯还以英国的调查委

① 《资本论》第1卷，人民出版社2018年版，第35页。

② 《马克思恩格斯全集》第16卷，人民出版社1964年版，第260页。

③ Joseph Redlich, tr. by A. Ernest Steinthal, *The Procedure of the House of Commons: A Study of Its History and Present Form*, Vol. II, Archibald Constable & Co. Ltd., 1908, p. 203.

④ Joseph Redlich, tr. by A. Ernest Steinthal, *The Procedure of the House of Commons: A Study of Its History and Present Form*, Vol. II, Archibald Constable & Co. Ltd., 1908, p. 213.

⑤ P. Ford and G. Ford, *A Guide to Parliamentary Papers*, Oxford: Basil Blackwell, 1956, p. 35.

⑥ 《资本论》第1卷，人民出版社2018年版，第9页。

⑦ 《马克思恩格斯全集》第16卷，人民出版社1964年版，第260页。

员会对工业部门劳动条件的调查为例，具体说明了这一点。[①]可见，马克思、恩格斯重视这些调查报告，主要是因为这些材料来自人民大众，贴近社会生活实际，具有广泛的代表性，因而具有高度的准确性和可信度。这就是说，马克思、恩格斯更加重视历史文献的社会主体性，而不是其外在形式和类型。这对我们重新认识中国学者提出的史源学理论无疑具有重要启示。

本书所采用的马克思所著《资本论》英文版有关内容，主要依据恩格斯生前亲自编校的《资本论》英文版第一卷。令人遗憾的是，恩格斯生前未能实现编校出版《资本论》英文版第二卷和第三卷的愿望。[②]因此，该版第一卷也是恩格斯生前编校出版的最后一部马克思的经典著作的英文版，具有很高的可信度和权威性。英文版第一卷最初由英国法学家、国际会员赛米尔·穆尔（Samuel Moore）和英国马克思主义活动家爱德华·艾威林（Edward Aveling）翻译成英文出版。[③]此前马克思曾对该卷的德文版和法文版进行了修订，一度计划亲自编校该卷的英文版，但因身体健康情况而中断，改由恩格斯编校。恩格斯带领穆尔和艾威林于1886年翻译出版了英文版第一卷之后，又亲自为德文版第四版提供更多材料，并反复对照法文版及马克思手稿的注释，对该卷进行了补充。美国人欧内斯特·昂特曼（Ernest Untermann）依据恩格斯的补充，在第一版英文译本的基础上，最后形成了《资本论》第一卷最为完整的英文版。这就是1906年在纽约出版的《资本论》第一卷英文版，[④]也是本书采用的版本。

---

① 《马克思恩格斯全集》第16卷，人民出版社1964年版，第261页。
② 《资本论》第1卷，人民出版社2018年版，第900页。
③ 《资本论》第1卷，人民出版社2018年版，第31—32页。参见ODNB, Vol. 2, pp. 1017–1019。
④ 参见Karl Marx, *Capital: A Critique of Political Economy*, Vol. 1, New York: The Modern Library, 1906, pp. 8–9。

I. Excerpt from *Capital: A Critique of Political Economy*[①]

Chapter XXVI THE SECRET OF PRIMITIVE ACCUMUEATION

We have seen how money is changed into capital; how through capital surplus-value is made, and from surplus-value more capital. But the accumulation of capital presupposes surplus-value; surplus-value presupposes capitalistic production; capitalistic production presupposes the preexistence of considerable masses of capital and of labour-power in the hands of producers of commodities. The whole movement, therefore, seems to turn in a vicious circle, out of which we can only get by supposing a primitive accumulation (previous accumulation of Adam Smith) preceding capitalistic accumulation; an accumulation not the result of the capitalist mode of production, but its starting point.

This primitive accumulation plays in Political Economy about the same part as original sin in theology. Adam bit the apple, and thereupon sin fell on the human race. Its origin is supposed to be explained when it is told as an anecdote of the past. In times long gone by there were two sorts of people; one, the diligent, intelligent, and, above all, frugal elite; the other, lazy rascals, spending their substance, and more, in riotous living. The legend of theological original sin tells us certainly how man came to be condemned to eat his bread in the sweat of his brow; but the history of economic original sin reveals to us that there are people to whom this is by no means essential. Never mind! Thus it came to pass that the former sort accumulated wealth, and the latter sort had at last nothing to sell except their own skins. And from this original sin dates the poverty of the great majority that, despite all its labour, has up to now nothing to sell but itself, and the wealth of the few that increases constantly although they have long ceased to work. Such insipid childishness is every day

① Karl Marx, *Capital: A Critique of Political Economy*, Vol. 1, New York: The Modern Library, 1906, pp. 784–787.

preached to us in the defence of property. M. Thiers, e.g., had the assurance to repeat it with all the solemnity of a statesman, to the French people, once so *spirituel*. But as soon as the question of property crops up, it becomes a sacred duty to proclaim the intellectual food of the infant as the one thing fit for all ages and for all stages of development. In actual history it is notorious that conquest, enslavement, robbery, murder, briefly force, play the great part. In the tender annals of Political Economy, the idyllic reigns from time immemorial. Right and "labour" were from all time the sole means of enrichment, the present year of course always excepted. As a matter of fact, the methods of primitive accumulation are anything but idyllic.

In themselves, money and commodities are no more capital than are the means of production and of subsistence. They want transforming into capital. But this transformation itself can only take place under certain circumstances that centre in this, *viz.*, that two very different kinds of commodity possessors must come face to face and into contact; on the one hand, the owners of money, means of production, means of subsistence, who are eager to increase the sum of values they possess, by buying other people's labour-power; on the other hand, free labourers, the sellers of their own labour-power, and therefore the sellers of labour. Free labourers, in the double sense that neither they themselves form part and parcel of the means of production, as in the case of slaves, bondsmen, &c, nor do the means of production belong to them, as in the case of peasant-proprietors ; they are, therefore, free from, unencumbered by, any means of production of their own. With this polarisation of the market for commodities, the fundamental conditions of capitalist production are given. The capitalist system presupposes the complete separation of the labourers from all property in the means by which they can realise their labour. As soon as capitalist production is once on its own legs, it not only maintains this separation, but reproduces it on a continually extending scale. The process, therefore, that clears the way for the capitalist system, can be none other than the process which takes away from the labourer the possession of his means of production; a process that transforms, on the one hand, the social means of subsistence and of production into capital, on the other, the immediate producers into wage–labourers. The so–called primitive accumulation, therefore, is nothing else than the historical process of divorcing the producer from the means of production. It appears as primitive, because it forms the pre–historic stage of capital and of the mode of production corresponding with it.

The economic structure of capitalistic society has grown out of the economic structure of feudal society. The dissolution of the latter set free the elements of the former.

The immediate producer, the labourer, could only dispose of his own person after he had ceased to be attached to the soil and ceased to be the slave, serf, or bondman of another. To become a free seller of labour–power, who carries his commodity wherever he finds a market, he must further have escaped from the regime of the guilds, their rules for apprentices and journeymen, and the impediments of their labour regulations. Hence, the historical movement which changes the producers into wage–workers, appears, on the one hand, as their emancipation from serfdom and from the fetters of the guilds, and this side alone exists for our bourgeois historians. But, on the other hand, these new freedmen became sellers of themselves only after they had been robbed of all their own means of production, and of all the guarantees of existence afforded by the old feudal arrangements. And the history of this, their expropriation, is written in the annals of mankind in letters of blood and fire.

The industrial capitalists, these new potentates, had on their part not only to displace the guild masters of handicrafts, but also the feudal lords, the possessors of the sources of wealth. In this respect their conquest of social power appears as the fruit of a victorious struggle both against feudal lordship and its revolting prerogatives, and against the guilds and the fetters they laid on the free development of production and the free exploitation of man by man. The chevaliers d'industrie, however, only succeed in supplanting the chevaliers of the sword by making use of events of which they themselves were wholly innocent. They have risen by means as vile as those by which the Roman freed–man once on a time made himself the master of his *patronus*.

The starting–point of the development that gave rise to the wage–labourer as well as to the capitalist, was the servitude of the labourer. The advance consisted in a change of form of this servitude, in the transformation of feudal exploitation into capitalist exploitation. To understand its march, we need not go back very far. Although we come across the first beginnings of capitalist production as early as the 14th or 15th century, sporadically, in certain towns of the Mediterranean, the capitalistic era dates from the 16th century. Wherever it appears, the abolition of serfdom has been long effected, and the highest development of the middle ages, the existence of sovereign towns, has been long on the wane.

In the history of primitive accumulation, all revolutions are epoch–making that act as levers for the capitalist class in course of formation; but, above all, those moments when great masses of men are suddenly and forcibly torn from their means of subsistence, and hurled as free and “unattached” proletarians on the labour market. The expropriation of the agricultural producer, of the peasant, from the soil, is the basis of the whole process. The history of this expropriation, in different countries, assumes different aspects, and runs through its various phases in different orders of succession, and at different periods. In England alone, which we take as our example, has it the classic form.

II. Common Terms, Words and Phrases for the Text

capital 资本

primitive accumulation 原始积累

surplus–value 剩余价值

presuppose 以……为先决条件，预先假定

labour–power 劳动力

vicious circle 恶性循环，循环论证

original sin 原罪

anecdote 逸闻趣事

diligent 勤勉的，煞费苦心的

intelligent 明智的，有才智的

frugal 节俭的，廉价的

rascal 流氓，无赖

riotous 暴乱的，放纵的

condemn 谴责，宣告有罪

brow 面颊，额头

come to pass 发生

insipid 乏味的，无特色的

solemnity 庄重，严肃

spirituel（法语）优雅的，风趣的

crop up 发生，被提到

notorious 众所周知的，声名狼藉的

enrichment 致富，浓缩

means of production 生产资料

means of subsistence 生活资料

bondsman (bondman)（中世纪的）农奴

peasant-proprietor 自耕农

peasant economy 小农经济

unencumbered 不受妨碍的，没有负担的

polarisation (polarization) 极化，两极分化

dissolution 瓦解，融化

regime 政体，管理制度

impediment 妨碍，阻碍

serfdom 农奴制

bourgeois historian 资产阶级历史学家

expropriation 剥夺，侵占

industrial capitalist 工业资本家

potentate 统治者，有权势的人

prerogative 特权

exploitation 剥削

supplant 取代，排挤掉

chevalier d'industrie（法）冒险家，骗子（字面意思是“工业骑士”）

chevalier of the sword 佩剑骑士

vile 卑鄙的，可耻的

patronous（拉丁语）庇护人，赞助人

servitude 奴役，苦役

sporadic 零散的，个别的

epoch–making 划时代的

lever 杠杆，方法

labour market 劳动力市场

III. Exercises and Thinking

1. Please say why the primitive accumulation is necessary, and try to define it.

2. How can you understand the development of the bourgeois and proletarian?

3. Please evaluate the role of the bourgeoisie and the mission of the proletariat.

IV. Further Readings and Internet Links

1. Further Readings

马克思：《资本论》，人民出版社 2018 年版。

Karl Marx, *Capital: A Critique of Political Economy*, Vol. 1, New York: The Modern

Library, 1906.

2. Internet Links

中共中央党史和文献研究院：https://www.dswxyjy.org.cn/

国家哲学社会科学文献研究中心：https://www.ncpssd.cn/

中国社会科学院历史理论研究所：http://lls.cssn.cn/

Unit 5 The Origin of the Family, Private Property and the State
《家庭、私有制和国家的起源》

《家庭、私有制和国家的起源》是恩格斯于1884年撰写的关于古代社会发展与国家起源的历史唯物主义经典著作。恩格斯撰写这部经典著作的缘起是，1883年3月马克思逝世以后，恩格斯在整理其遗稿时发现了马克思对摩尔根《古代社会》一书的摘要和批语。① 以此为基础，恩格斯运用历史唯物主义对古代社会发展和国家起源问题进行了专题研究。列宁在《论国家》中曾推荐阅读恩格斯的这部著作："这是现代社会主义的基本著作之一，其中每一句话都是可以相信的，每一句话都不是凭空说的，而是根据大量的史料和政治材料写成的。"② 列宁指出，这部著作为研究国家问题"提供了正确观察问题的方法。它从叙述历史开始，讲国家是怎样产生的"③。

这部经典著作共分九章。第一章为史前文化各阶段，主要讲述了史前人类社会历史的各个阶段。这里的"史前"是指国家出现以前，也就是"成文史"以前。史前主要包括蒙昧时代与野蛮时代，这两个时代各自经历了低、中、高级阶段。同时，恩格斯还把史前文化各阶段放在人类历史全程中来考察，指出人类迄今经历了三个历史时代：蒙昧时代、野蛮时代、文明时代，而摩尔根的《古代社会》只是关注了前两个时代以及向第三个时代的过渡问题。第二章为家庭，主要讲述了人类社会的细胞即家庭形式的演变。这主要体现为蒙昧时代的

① 《马克思恩格斯文集》第4卷，人民出版社2009年版，第15页。
② 《列宁全集》第37卷，人民出版社2017年版，第64页。
③ 《列宁全集》第37卷，人民出版社2017年版，第64页。

群婚制与野蛮时代的对偶婚制，文明时代则是专偶制。第三章至第八章主要讲述国家产生的过程。这六章分别以易洛魁人的氏族、希腊人的氏族、雅典国家的产生、罗马的氏族和国家、凯尔特人和德意志人的氏族、德意志人国家的形成等为题，分析了他们从氏族、胞族、部落、部落联盟到国家产生的全过程。第九章主要讲述了国家产生的经济条件。从社会分工到生产劳动分工，从生产力结构和水平到生产关系的性质和特征，这一章系统地讲述了生产力发展和生产关系变革为国家产生提供的经济条件。"在经济发展到一定阶段而必然使社会分裂为阶级时，国家就由于这种分裂而成为必要了"①，"国家是文明社会的概括"②。随着国家的产生，人类就进入了文明时代。

这里采用的英文版本是我国外文出版社 1978 年版的单行本。

I. Excerpt from *The Origin of the Family, Private Property and the State: In Connection with the Researches of Lewis H. Morgan*③

Chapter 1 Stages of Prehistoric Culture

Morgan was the first person with expert knowledge to attempt to introduce a definite order into the prehistory of humanity; so long as no important additional material makes changes necessary, his classification will undoubtedly remain in force.

Of the three main epochs—savagery, barbarism and civilization, he is concerned, of course, only with the first two and the transition to the third. He divides both savagery and barbarism into lower, middle and upper stages according to the progress made in the production of food; for, he says:

Upon their skill in this direction, the whole question of human supremacy on

① 《马克思恩格斯文集》第 4 卷，人民出版社 2009 年版，第 193 页。
② 《马克思恩格斯文集》第 4 卷，人民出版社 2009 年版，第 195 页。
③ Frederick Engels, *The Origin of the Family, Private Property and the State: In Connection with the Researches of Lewis H. Morgan*, Peking: Foreign Languages Press, 1978, pp. 23–30.

the earth depended. Mankind are the only beings who may be said to have gained an [almost] absolute control over the production of food... It is accordingly probable that the great epochs of human progress have been identified, more or less directly, with the enlargement of the sources of subsistence.

The development of the family takes a parallel course, but here the periods are not divided by such striking marks.

1. SAVAGERY

(a) *Lower stage*. Childhood of the human race. People still lived in their original habitat, in tropical or subtropical forests, and were partially at least tree-dwellers, for otherwise survival among large beasts of prey cannot be explained. Fruit, nuts and roots served for food. The development of articulate speech is the main result of this period. None of the peoples that became known during the historical period were any longer in this primitive state. Though this stage may have lasted thousands of years, we have no direct evidence to prove its existence; but once the evolution of man from the animal kingdom is admitted, such a transitional stage must necessarily be assumed.

(b) *Middle stage*. Begins with the utilization of fish for food (including crabs, mussels and other aquatic animals) and with the use of fire. The two are complementary, since food fish becomes fully utilizable only by the use of fire. With this new source of nourishment, men became independent of climate and locality; even as savages, they could, by following the rivers and coasts, spread over most of the earth. Proof of these migrations is the distribution over every continent of the crudely worked, unpolished flint tools of the earlier Stone Age, the so-called "paleoliths," all or most of which date from this period. Settlement in new areas, the constantly active urge for discovery, and the ability to produce fire by friction made available new kinds of food: farinaceous roots and tubers, for instance, were baked in hot ashes or in baking pits (ground ovens). With the invention of the first weapons, club and spear, game could sometimes be added to the fare. But the tribes which figure in books as living entirely, that is, exclusively, by hunting never existed in reality; the yield of the hunt was far too precarious. At this stage, owing to the continual uncertainty of food supplies, cannibalism seems to have arisen and was practised from then onwards for a long time. The Australian aborigines and many of Polynesians are still in this middle stage of savagery today.

(c) *Upper stage*. Begins with the invention of the bow and arrow, whereby game became a regular source of food, and hunting one of the normal branches of work. Bow, string and arrow already constitute a very complex instrument, whose invention presupposes long, accumulated experience and sharpened intelligence and therefore knowledge of many other inventions as well. Comparing the peoples acquainted with the bow and arrow but not yet with pottery (from which Morgan dates the transition to barbarism), we in fact find already some beginnings of settlement in villages and some control over the production of means of subsistence; we find wooden vessels and utensils, finger–weaving (without looms) with filaments of bark, plaited baskets of bast or reeds, and polished (neolithic) stone tools. For the most part also, the use of fire and the stone axe have already provided the dug–out canoe and sometimes beams and planks for house–building. We find all these advances, for instance, among the Indians of northwest America, who are acquainted with the bow and arrow but not with pottery. The bow and arrow was for savagery what the iron sword was for barbarism and fire–arms for civilization — the decisive weapon.

2. BARBARISM

(a) *Lower stage*. Dates from the introduction of pottery. In many cases it can be proved, and in all it is probable, that the first pots originated from the habit of covering baskets or wooden vessels with clay to make them fireproof; in this way it was soon discovered that moulded clay answered the purpose without any inner vessel.

Thus far we can regard the course of development as being generally valid for all peoples at a given period without distinction of place. With the beginning of barbarism, however, we reach a stage when the difference in the natural endowments of the two hemispheres of the earth comes into play. The characteristic feature of the period of barbarism is the domestication and breeding of animals and the cultivation of plants. Now, the Eastern Hemisphere, the so-called Old World, possessed nearly all the animals adaptable to domestication, and all the varieties of cultivable cereals except one; the Western Hemisphere, America, had no mammals that could be domesticated except the llama, which, moreover, was only found in one part of South America, and of all the cultivable cereals only one, though that was the best, namely, maize. Owing to these differences in natural conditions, the population of each hemisphere went its own way, and different landmarks divide the particular stages in each of the two cases.

(b) *Middle stage*. Begins in the Eastern Hemisphere with the domestication of animals; in the Western, with the cultivation, by means of irrigation, of plants for food, and with the use of adobe (sun-dried) bricks and stone for building.

We shall begin with the Western Hemisphere, as here this stage was never superseded until the European conquest.

At the time when they were discovered, the Indians at the lower stage of barbarism (comprising all those living east of the Mississippi) were already practising some horticulture of maize and possibly also of squash, melons and other garden plants, from which they obtained a very substantial part of their food. They lived in wooden houses in villages protected by palisades. The tribes in the northwest, particularly those in the region of the Columbia River, were still at the upper stage of savagery and acquainted neither with pottery nor with any form of plant cultivation. The so-called Pueblo Indians of New Mexico, however, and the Mexicans, Central Americans and Peruvians at the time of the Conquest were at the middle stage of barbarism. They lived in houses like fortresses, made of adobe brick or of stone, and cultivated maize and other edible plants, varying according to locality and climate, in artificially irrigated plots of ground, which supplied their main source of food; and they had even domesticated some animals — the turkey and other birds by the Mexicans, the llama by the Peruvians. They could also work metals, with the exception of iron for which reason they were still unable to dispense with stone weapons and tools. The Spanish Conquest then cut short any further independent development.

In the Eastern Hemisphere the middle stage of barbarism began with the domestication of animals providing milk and meat, but plant cultivation seems to have remained unknown far into this period. It was, apparently, the domestication and breeding of animals and the formation of herds of considerable size that led to the differentiation of the Aryans and Semites from the mass of barbarians. The European and Asiatic Aryans still have the same names for cattle, but this is hardly ever the case with the names for the cultivated plants.

In suitable localities, the formation of herds led to a pastoral life: the Semites lived upon the grassy plains of the Euphrates and the Tigris, and the Aryans upon those of India, of the Oxus and the Jaxartes, and of the Don and the Dnieper. It must have been on the borders of such pasture lands that animals were first domesticated. To later generations, consequently, the pastoral tribes appear to have come from regions which, so far from being the cradle of mankind, were almost uninhabitable for their savage ancestors and even for people at the lower stage of barbarism. But having once accustomed themselves to pastoral life in the grassy plains of the rivers, these barbarians of the middle stage would never have dreamed of returning willingly to the native forests of their ancestors. Even when they were forced further to the north and west, the Semites and Aryans could not move into the forest regions of western Asia and of Europe until they became able, by cultivation of grain, to feed and especially to winter their herds on this less favourable land. It is more than probable that here the cultivation of grain originated from the need for cattle fodder and only later became important as a human food supply.

The plentiful supply of milk and meat and especially the beneficial effect of these foods on the growth of the children account perhaps for the better development of the

Aryan and Semitic races. It is a fact that the Pueblo Indians of New Mexico, who are reduced to an almost entirely vegetarian diet, have a smaller brain than the Indians at the lower stage of barbarism, who eat more meat and fish. In any case, cannibalism now gradually dies out, surviving only as a religious act or, what is here almost the same thing, as a means of working magic.

(c) *Upper stage*. Begins with the smelting of iron ore and passes into civilization with the invention of alphabetic writing and its use for literary records. This stage (as we have seen, only the Eastern Hemisphere passed through it independently) is richer in advances in production than all the preceding stages together. To it belong the Greeks of the heroic age, the tribes of Italy shortly before the foundation of Rome, the Germans of Tacitus and the Norsemen of the Viking age.

Above all, we now first meet the iron ploughshare drawn by cattle, which made large-scale agriculture, the *cultivation of fields*, possible and hence a practically unrestricted food supply under the then prevailing conditions. Then came the clearance of forest land for tillage and pasture, which in turn was impossible on a large scale without the iron axe and the iron spade. Population rapidly increased in number, and in small areas became dense. Prior to field agriculture, only very exceptional conditions would have allowed half a million people to be united under a single central direction; probably this never occurred.

We find the upper stage of barbarism at its zenith in the Homeric poems, particularly in the *Iliad*. Developed iron tools, the bellows, the hand-mill, the potter's wheel, the making of oil and wine, well-developed metal-working which had become an artistic craft, the wagon and the war-chariot, shipbuilding with beams and planks, the beginnings of architecture as an art, walled cities with towers and battlements, the Homeric epic and a complete mythology—these are the chief legacy brought by the Greeks from barbarism into civilization. When we compare the descriptions which Caesar and even Tacitus give of the Germans, who stood at the beginning of the cultural stage from which the Homeric Greeks were just preparing to make the next advance, we realize how rich was the development of production within the upper stage of barbarism.

The sketch which I have given here, following Morgan, of the development of mankind through savagery and barbarism to the beginnings of civilization, is already rich enough in new features; what is more, they cannot be disputed since they are drawn directly from production. Yet my sketch will seem flat and feeble compared with the picture to be unrolled at the end of our travels; only then will it be possible to give a full view of the transition from barbarism to civilization and the striking contrasts between the two. For the time being, Morgan's division may be summarized thus: Savagery—the period in which man's appropriation of products in their natural state predominates; the products of human art are chiefly auxiliary instruments in this appropriation. Barbarism—the period during which man learns to breed domestic animals and to practise agriculture, and acquires methods of increasing the supply of natural products by human activity. Civilization—the period in which man learns the further reworking of the products of nature, the period of industry proper and of art.

II. Common Terms, Words and Phrases for the Text

prehistoric culture 史前文化

savagery 未开化状态，蒙昧

barbarism 野蛮状态，粗野

civilization 文明，开化

transition 过渡，转变

supremacy 至上，优势

subsistence 生存，生计

habitat 栖息地，产地

articulate 发音清晰的，善于表达的

utilize 利用

mussel 河蚌，贻贝

aquatic 水生的，水生动植物

complementary 互补的，相配的

nourishment 食物，养料

locality 地区，方位

flint 燧石，硬物

Stone Age 石器时代

paleolith (palaeolith) 旧石器

farinaceous 粉状的，含淀粉的

club 棍棒，球杆，俱乐部

fare 伙食，饮食

tribe 部落

figure 形象，轮廓

precarious 不牢靠的，不稳定的

cannibalism 食人，同类相食

aborigine 土著居民，土生动物

intelligence 智力，智能

pottery 陶器，制陶术

vessel 容器，器皿

utensil 器皿，用具

filament 细丝

bark 树皮

plait 辫子，编织

bast（树木的）韧皮纤维

neolithic 新石器时代的

beam 横梁

plank 木板

firearm 火器

fireproof 耐火，防火

clay 黏土

mould 模子，使成形

endowment 天赋，资助

hemisphere 半球，领域

domesticate 驯化，驯养

llama 羊驼

cultivation 种植

maize 玉蜀黍，玉米

adobe 土坯

supersede 超越，取代

horticulture 园艺，园艺学

palisade 栅栏

edible 可食用的

pastoral 游牧的，畜牧的

fodder 饲料

smelt 冶炼

iron ore 铁矿石

ploughshare 犁铧

zenith 顶点，全盛

wagon 四轮马车，篷车

war-chariot 战车

battlement 城垛

feeble 虚弱的，无力的

appropriation 占用，获取

rework 再加工

III. Exercises and Thinking

1. Please tell the difference between culture and civilization from the perspective of etymology.

2. To what periods do the paleoliths and neoliths refer? Do you consider it a truthful classification between the two hemispheres in the development of barbarism?

3. When does the difference in the natural endowments of the two hemispheres of the earth come into play?

4. How to evaluate the role of geographical factors in the progress of prehistoric culture? Discuss it relating to the geographical determinism.

IV. Further Readings and Internet Links

1. Further Readings

恩格斯：《家庭、私有制和国家的起源》，人民出版社 2018 年版。

《马克思恩格斯文集》第 4 卷，人民出版社 2009 年版。

Frederick Engels, *The Origin of the Family, Private Property and the State: In Connection with the Researches of Lewis H. Morgan*, Peking: Foreign Languages Press, 1978.

2. Internet Links

中共中央党史和文献研究院：https://www.dswxyjy.org.cn/

中国共产党思想理论资源库：http://data.lilun.cn/

Unit 6 Imperialism, The Highest Stage of Capitalism

《帝国主义是资本主义的最高阶段》

《帝国主义是资本主义的最高阶段》是列宁所著的马克思主义经典文献。在19世纪末20世纪初资本主义进入帝国主义阶段的新的历史条件下，第一次世界大战成为帝国主义国家争相瓜分世界的争夺战，国际共产主义运动面临着新的机遇和挑战。针对世界社会主义革命的新形势，1916年列宁在苏黎世撰写了这部马克思主义经典文献。列宁把马克思主义原理与当时的国内外历史实际相结合，丰富和发展了马克思主义的资本主义理论，阐述了科学的帝国主义理论。这部经典文献就是列宁科学的帝国主义理论的集中体现。列宁的科学的帝国主义理论不仅是俄国十月革命和社会主义建设的指南，也是我们理解和把握世界近现代史主线和全局的基本遵循。

这部文献共有十章。第一章到第六章，主要讲述19世纪末20世纪初帝国主义的基本经济状况及其特征。这六章包括生产集中和垄断、银行和银行的新作用、金融资本和金融寡头、资本输出、资本家同盟瓜分世界、大国瓜分世界六个专题，逐一分析了这些经济现象及其背后的实质。第七章至第十章，主要讲述了帝国主义的性质及其历史趋势。这四章分为帝国主义是资本主义的特殊阶段、资本主义的寄生性和腐朽、对帝国主义的批评、帝国主义的历史地位四个专题，科学地界定了帝国主义："帝国主义是发展到垄断组织和金融资本的统治已经确立、资本输出具有突出意义、国际托拉斯开始瓜分世界、一些最大的资本主义国家已把世界全部领土瓜分完毕这一阶段的资本主义。"同时，列宁还指出了帝国主义的经济实质是垄断资本主义，具有内在的寄生性；指明了帝国主义是过渡的、垂死的资本主义，是无产阶级社会革命的前夜。

列宁的《帝国主义是资本主义的最高阶段》，又被称为《帝国主义论》，从资本主义发展的新情况、新形势出发，以马克思主义为指导，守正创新，揭示了资本主义在新的历史阶段所体现出来的特征和性质，提出了帝国主义的历史地位和发展趋势，续写了马克思的《资本论》的新篇章，是科学的帝国主义理论确立的标志。

这里采用的英文版，是我国外文出版社 1965 年出版，1975 年第五次重印的英文版单行本。

I. Excerpt from *Imperialism, The Highest Stage of Capitalism: A Popular Outline*[①]

IMPERIALISM, AS A SPECIAL STAGE OF CAPITALISM

We must now try to sum up, put together, what has been said above on the subject of imperialism. Imperialism emerged as the development and direct continuation of the fundamental characteristics of capitalism in general. But capitalism only became capitalist imperialism at a definite and very high stage of its development, when certain of its fundamental characteristics began to change into their opposites, when the features of the epoch of transition from capitalism to a higher social and economic system had taken shape and revealed themselves all along the line. Economically, the main thing in this process is the displacement of capitalist free competition by capitalist monopoly. Free competition is the fundamental characteristic of capitalism, and of commodity production generally; monopoly is the exact opposite of free competition, but we have seen the latter being transformed into monopoly before our eyes, creating large-scale industry and forcing out small industry, replacing large-scale by still larger-scale

① V. I. Lenin, *Imperialism, The Highest Stage of Capitalism: A Popular Outline*, Peking: Foreign Languages Press, 1975, pp. 104-113.

industry, and carrying concentration of production and capital to the point where out of it has grown and is growing monopoly: cartels, syndicates and trusts, and merging with them, the capital of a dozen or so banks, which manipulate thousands of millions. At the same time the monopolies, which have grown out of free competition, do not eliminate the latter, but exist over it and alongside of it, and thereby give rise to a number of very acute, intense antagonisms, frictions and conflicts. Monopoly is the transition from capitalism to a higher system.

If it were necessary to give the briefest possible definition of imperialism we should have to say that imperialism is the monopoly stage of capitalism. Such a definition would include what is most important, for, on the one hand, finance capital is the bank capital of a few very big monopolist banks, merged with the capital of the monopolist combines of industrialists; and, on the other hand, the division of the world is the transition from a colonial policy which has extended without hindrance to territories unseized by any capitalist power, to a colonial policy of monopolistic possession of the territory of the world which has been completely divided up.

But very brief definitions, although convenient, for they sum up the main points, are nevertheless inadequate, since very important features of the phenomenon that has to be defined have to be especially deduced. And so, without forgetting the conditional and relative value of all definitions in general, which can never embrace all the concatenations of a phenomenon in its complete development, we must give a definition of imperialism that will include the following five of its basic features: (1) the concentration of production and capital has developed to such a high stage that it has created monopolies which play a decisive role in economic life; (2)the merging of bank capital with industrial capital, and the creation, on the basis of this "finance capital," of a financial oligarchy; (3)the export of capital as distinguished from the export of commodities acquires exceptional importance; (4)the formation of international monopolist capitalist combines which share the world among themselves, and (5)the territorial division of the whole world among the biggest capitalist powers is completed. Imperialism is capitalism in that stage of development in which the dominance of monopolies and finance capital has established itself; in which the export of capital has acquired pronounced importance; in which the division of the world among the international trusts has begun; in which the division of all territories of the globe among the biggest capitalist powers has been completed.

We shall see later that imperialism can and must be defined differently if we bear in mind, not only the basic, purely economic concepts—to which the above definition is limited—but also the historical place of this stage of capitalism in relation to capitalism in general, or the relation between imperialism and the two main trends in the working-class movement. The point to be noted just now is that imperialism, as interpreted above, undoubtedly represents a special stage in the development of capitalism. To enable the reader to obtain the most well-grounded idea of imperialism possible, we deliberately tried to quote as largely as possible *bourgeois* economists who are obliged to admit the particularly incontrovertible facts concerning the latest stage of capitalist economy. With the same object in view, we have quoted detailed statistics which enable one to see to what degree bank capital, etc., has grown, in what precisely the transformation of quantity into quality, of developed capitalism into imperialism, was expressed. Needless to say, of course, all boundaries in nature and in society are conditional and changeable, that it would be absurd to argue, for example, about the particular year or decade in which imperialism "definitely" became established.

In the matter of defining imperialism, however, we have to enter into controversy, primarily, with K. Kautsky, the principal Marxian theoretician of the epoch of the so-called Second International—that is, of the twenty-five years between 1889 and 1914. The fundamental ideas expressed in our definition of imperialism were very resolutely attacked by Kautsky in 1915, and even in November 1914, when he said that imperialism must not be regarded as a "phase" or stage of economy, but as a policy, a definite policy "preferred" by finance capital; that imperialism must not be "identified" with "present-day capitalism" ; that if imperialism is to be understood to mean "all the phenomena of present-day capitalism" — cartels, protection, the domination of the financiers, and colonial policy—then the question as to whether imperialism is necessary to capitalism becomes reduced to the "flattest tautology," because, in that case, "imperialism is naturally a vital necessity for capitalism," and so on. The best way to present Kautsky's idea is to quote his own definition of imperialism, which is diametrically opposed to the substance of the ideas which we have set forth (for the objections coming from the camp of the German Marxists, who have been advocating similar ideas for many years already, have been long known to Kautsky as the objections of a definite trend in Marxism).

Kautsky's definition is as follows:

"Imperialism is a product of highly developed industrial capitalism. It consists in the striving of every industrial capitalist nation to bring under its control or to annex larger and larger areas of *agrarian*" (Kautsky's italics) "territory, irrespective of what nations inhabit those regions."

This definition is utterly worthless because it one-sidedly, i.e., arbitrarily, singles out only the national question (although the latter is extremely important in itself as well as in its relation to imperialism), it arbitrarily and inaccurately connects this question *only* with industrial capital in the countries which annex other nations, and in an equally arbitrary and inaccurate manner pushes into the forefront the annexation of agrarian regions.

Imperialism is a striving for annexations—this is what the political part of Kautsky's definition amounts to. It is correct, but very incomplete, for politically, imperialism is, in general, a striving towards violence and reaction. For the moment, however, we are interested in the economic aspect of the question, which Kautsky himself introduced into *his* definition. The inaccuracies in Kautsky's definition are glaring. The characteristic feature of imperialism is *not* industrial *but* finance capital. It is not an accident that in France it was precisely the extraordinarily rapid development of *finance* capital, and the weakening of industrial capital, that, from the'eighties onwards, gave rise to the extreme intensification of annexationist (colonial) policy. The characteristic feature of imperialism is precisely that it strives to annex *not only* agrarian territories, but even most highly industrialized regions (German appetite for Belgium; French appetite for Lorraine), because (1) the fact that the world is already divided up obliges those contemplating a redivision to teach out for *every kind* of territory, and (2) an essential feature of imperialism is the rivalry between several Great Powers in the striving for hegemony, i.e., for the conquest of territory, not so much directly for themselves as to weaken the adversary and undermine *bis* hegemony. (Belgium is particularly important for Germany as a base for operations against England; England needs Bagdad as a base for operations against Germany, etc.)

Kautsky refers especially—and repeatedly—to Englishmen who, he alleges, have given a purely political meaning to the word "imperialism" in the sense that he, Kautsky, understands it. We take up the work by the Englishman Hobson, *Imperialism*, which appeared in 1902, and there we read:

"The new imperialism differs from the older, first, in substituting for the ambition of a single growing empire the theory and the practice of competing empires, each motivated by similar lusts of political aggrandizement and commercial gain; secondly, in the dominance of financial or investing over mercantile interests."

We see that Kautsky is absolutely wrong in referring to Englishmen generally (unless he meant the vulgar English imperialists, or the avowed apologists for imperialism). We see that Kautsky, while claiming that he continues to advocate Marxism, as a matter of fact takes a step back-ward compared with the *social-liberal* Hobson, who *more correctly* takes into account two "historically concrete" (Kautsky's definition is a mockery of historical concreteness!) features of modern imperialism: (1) the competition between *several* imperialisms, and (2) the predominance of the financier over the merchant. If it is chiefly a question of the annexation of agrarian countries by industrial countries, then the role of the merchant is put in the forefront.

Kautsky's definition is not only wrong and un-Marxian. It serves as a basis for a whole system of views which signify a rupture with Marxian theory and Marxian practice all along the line. We shall refer to this later. The argument about words which Kautsky raises as to whether the latest stage of capitalism should be called "imperialism" or "the stage of finance capital" is absolutely frivolous. Call it what you will, it makes no difference. The essence of the matter is that Kautsky detaches the politics of imperialism from its economics, speaks of annexations as being a policy "preferred" by finance capital, and opposes to it another bourgeois policy which, he alleges, is possible on this very same basis of finance capital. It follows, then, that monopolies in economics are compatible with non-monopolistic, non-violent, non-annexationist methods in politics. It follows, then, that the territorial division of the world, which was completed precisely during the epoch of finance capital, and which constitutes the basis of the present peculiar forms of rivalry between the biggest capitalist states, is compatible with a non-imperialist policy. The result is a slurring-over and a blunting of the most profound contradictions of the latest stage of capitalism, instead of an exposure of their depth; the result is bourgeois reformism instead of Marxism.

Kautsky enters into controversy with the German apologist of imperialism and annexations, Cunow, who clumsily and cynically argues that imperialism is present-day capitalism; the development of capitalism is inevitable and progressive; therefore imperialism is progressive; therefore, we should grovel before it and glorify it! This is something like the caricature of the Russian Marxists which the Narodniks drew in 1894-95. They argued: if the Marxists believe that capitalism is inevitable in Russia, that it is progressive, then they ought to open a tavern and begin to implant capitalism! Kautsky's reply to Cunow is as follows: imperialism is not present-day capitalism; it is only one of the forms of the policy of present-day capitalism. This policy we can and should fight, fight imperialism, annexations, etc.

The reply seems quite plausible, but in effect it is a more subtle and more disguised (and therefore more dangerous) advocacy of conciliation with imperialism, because a "fight" against the policy of the trusts and banks that does not affect the basis of the economics of the trusts and banks is nothing more than bourgeois reformism and pacifism, the benevolent and innocent expression of pious wishes. Evasion of existing contradictions, forgetting the most important of them, instead of revealing their full depth—such is Kautsky's theory, which has nothing in common with Marxism. Naturally, such a "theory" can only serve the purpose of advocating unity with the Cunows!

"From the purely economic point of view," writes Kautsky, "it is not impossible that capitalism will yet go through a new phase, that of the extension of the policy of the cartels to foreign policy, the phase of ultraimperialism," i.e., of a superimperialism, of a union of the imperialisms of the whole world and not struggles among them, a phase when wars shall cease under capitalism, a phase of "the joint exploitation of the world by internationally united finance capital."

We shall have to deal with this "theory of ultraimperialism" later on in order to show in detail how definitely and utterly it breaks with Marxism. At present, in keeping with the general plan of the present work, we must examine the exact economic data on this question. "From the purely economic point of view," is "ultraimperialism" possible, or is it ultra-nonsense?

If by purely economic point of view a "pure" abstraction is meant, then all that can be said reduces itself to the following proposition: development is proceeding towards monopolies, hence, towards a single world monopoly, towards a single world trust. This is indisputable, but it is also as completely meaningless as is the statement that "development is proceeding" towards the manufacture of foodstuffs in laboratories. In this sense the "theory" of ultraimperialism is no less absurd than a "theory of ultra-agriculture" would be.

If, however, we are discussing the "purely economic" conditions of the epoch of finance capital as a historically concrete epoch which opened at the beginning of the twentieth century, then the best reply that one can make to the lifeless abstractions of "ultraimperialism' (which serve exclusively a most reactionary aim: that of diverting attention from the depth of *existing* antagonisms) is to contrast them with the concrete economic realities of present-day world economy. Kautsky's utterly meaningless talk about ultraimperialism encourages, among other things, that profoundly mistaken idea which only brings grist to the mill of the apologists of imperialism, viz., that the rule of finance capital *lessens* the unevenness and contradictions inherent in world economy, whereas in reality it *increases* them.

II. Common Terms, Words and Phrases for the Text

imperialism 帝国主义

capitalism 资本主义

capitalist monopoly 资本主义的垄断

free competition 自由竞争

transform 转型，改变性质

merge 合并，融合

manipulate 操作，使用

eliminate 消除，淘汰

friction 摩擦，抵触

hindrance 妨碍，障碍

deduce 演绎，推导

concatenate 连接，串联

bank capital 银行资本

industry capital 工业资本

finance capital 金融资本

oligarchy 寡头

controversy 争论，辩论

resolutely 坚决地，坚定地

financier 金融家，理财家

flat 扁平的，没有趣味的

tautology 同义反复，冗赘

objection 反对，异议

annex 附加，吞并，强占

arbitrary 武断的，任意的

inaccuracy 不准确，差错

glaring 引人注目的，显眼的

intensification 强化，加剧

appetite 胃口，欲望

contemplate 盘算，算计

great power（西方的）大国，列强

hegemony 霸权

undermine 侵蚀，暗中破坏

allege 断言，声称

aggrandizement 扩张，夸大

avow 公开表示，断言

apologist 辩护士，辩解者

mockery 嘲弄，歪曲

un-Marxian 非马克思主义的

rupture 决裂，破裂

frivolous 无意义的，轻浮的

detach 分开，分离

compatible 兼容的，适合的

slur 忽略，马虎

blunt 减弱，变钝

reformism 改良主义

clumsy 笨拙的，粗糙的

cynical 愤世嫉俗的，无所顾忌的

grovel 匍匐，爬行

glorify 颂扬，美化

tavern 小酒馆，小旅馆

implant 培植，移植

conciliation 调和，和好

pacifism 和平主义，不抵抗主义

ultraimperialism 超帝国主义

superimperialism 超帝国主义

nonsense 废话，胡话

proposition 论点，提议

divert 转移，避开

grist 面粉，有利的事

III. Exercises and Thinking

1. Please summarize the fundamental characteristics and nature of imperialism with understanding the definition of it.

2. How did K. Kautsky define the imperialism? Point out where he went wrong.

3. What is the reformism? Say the difference between it and Marxism on the theory of imperialism.

IV. Further Readings and Internet Links

1. Further Readings

列宁:《帝国主义是资本主义的最高阶段》，人民出版社 2014 年版。

《列宁选集》第 2 卷，人民出版社 2012 年版。

V. I. Lenin, *Imperialism, The Highest Stage of Capitalism: A Popular Outline*, Peking: Foreign Languages Press, 1975.

2. Internet Links

中共中央党史和文献研究院：https://www.dswxyjy.org.cn/

中国共产党思想理论资源库：http://data.lilun.cn/

Unit 7

Daxue and *Zhongyong*

《大学》与《中庸》

《大学》《中庸》《论语》《孟子》共同构成中国古代经典“四书”。据考证，《大学》《中庸》这两部经典均出自《礼记》，“四书”之名始于宋代朱熹的《四书章句集注》。[①]

《大学》的主要内容是三纲领和八条目。其中，三纲领是指明明德，亲民，止于至善；八条目是指格物，致知，诚意，正心，修身，齐家，治国，平天下。核心思想是强调为政以德、民为邦本，反映了当时新兴地主阶级巩固阶级统治的要求。《中庸》的主要内容则是宣扬“允执其中”的中庸之道，被称为“孔门传授心法”。核心思想是强调天人合一、厚德载物，反映了当时中国古代哲学的本体论思考已经达到相当高的水准。[②]

尽管《大学》《中庸》有不同的版本，但从国际影响来看，苏格兰汉学家理雅各（James Legge）依据朱熹《四书章句集注》的英译本，占有重要历史地位，至今仍不可忽视。19 世纪中叶，理雅各来到中国，与洪仁玕、王韬等人过从甚密，随后便着手翻译“四书”等中国古代经典著作。他的英译本成为当时的标准，并由此推动了西方汉学成为职业化的学术领域，开创了汉学的“理雅各时代”（Leggian epoch）。[③] 选取这两部中华优秀传统文化经典，不仅有助于提高我国历史学习者和研究者的传统文化基础素养，而且有助于我们理解世界文化文

① （清）永瑢等撰：《四库全书总目》上册，中华书局 1965 年版，第 289 页。

② 参见赵国璋、潘树广主编：《文献学大辞典》，广陵书社 2005 年版，第 49、208 页。

③ ODNB, Vol. 33, pp. 190–191.

明之间的交流互鉴。

这里依据的中文版本是中华书局的朱熹《四书章句集注》，英译本则是依据1914年上海中华图书馆印行的由理雅各翻译的《中西四书》。理雅各把“大学”翻译为“The Great Learning”，把《中庸》翻译为“The Doctrine of the Mean”。在这里除了标题使用汉语拼音之外，正文内容均从其译文。

I. Excerpt from *Daxue* and *Zhongyong*①

1. *Daxue*

The Great Learning

My master, the philosopher Ch'ing, says—"The Great Learning is a book left by Confucius, and forms the gate by which first learners enter into virtue. That we can now perceive the order in which the ancients pursued their learning, is solely owing to the preservation of this work, the Analects and Mencius coming after it. Learners must commence their course with this and then it may be hoped they will be kept from error."

What the Great learning teaches, is—to illustrate illustrious virtue; to renovate the people; and to rest in the highest excellence.

The point where to rest being known, the object of pursuit is then determined; and, that being determined, a calm unperturbedness may be attained. To that calmness there will succeed a tranquil repose. In that repose there may be careful deliberation, and that deliberation will be followed by the attainment *of the desired end*.

Things have their root and their completion. Affairs have their end and their beginning. To know what is first and what is last will lead near to what is taught *in the Great Learning*.

The ancients who wished to illustrate illustrious virtue throughout the empire, first

① L. Y. T., *The Four Books, or The Chinese Classics in English from the Best Previous Books*, Shanghai: The China Book Company, 1914, pp. 1-3, pp. 24-27.

ordered well their own States. Wishing to order well their States, they first regulated their families. Wishing to regulate their families, they first cultivated their persons. Wishing to cultivate their persons, they first rectified their hearts. Wishing to rectify their hearts, they first sought to be sincere in their thoughts. Wishing to be sincere in their thoughts, they first extended to the utmost their knowledge. Such extension of knowledge lay in the investigation of things.

Things being investigated, knowledge became complete. Their knowledge being complete, their thoughts were sincere. Their thoughts being sincere, their hearts were then rectified. Their hearts being rectified, their persons were cultivated. Their persons being cultivated, their families were regulated. Their families being regulated, their States were rightly governed. Their States being rightly governed, the whole empire was made tranquil and happy.

From the emperor down to the mass of the people, all must consider the cultivation of the person the root of *everything besides*.

It cannot be, when the root is neglected, that what should spring from it will be well ordered. It never has been the case that what was of great importance has been slightly cared for, and, at the same time, that what was of slight importance has been greatly cared for.

2. *Zhongyong*

The Doctrine of the Mean

My master, philosopher Ch'ing, says, "Being without inclination to either side is called CHUNG; admitting of no change is called YUNG. By CHUNG is denoted the correct course to be pursued by all under heaven; by YUNG is denoted the fixed principle regulating all under heaven. This work contains the law of mind, which was handed down from one to another, in the Confucian school, till Tsze-sze, fearing lest in the course of time errors should arise about it, committed it to writing, and delivered it to Mencius. The book first speaks of one principle; it next spreads this out and embraces all things; finally it returns and gathers them all up under the one principle. Unroll it, and it fills the universe; roll it up, and it retires and lies kid in mysteriousness. The relish of it is inexhaustible. The whole of it is solid learning. When the skilful reader has explored it with delight till he has apprehended it, he may carry it into practice all his life, and will find that it cannot be exhausted."

What Heaven has conferred is called The Nature; an accordance with this nature is called The Path of duty; the regulation of this path is called Instruction.

The path may not be left for an instant. If it could be left, it would not be the path. On this account, the superior man does not wait till he sees things, to be cautious, nor till he hears things, to be apprehensive.

There is nothing more visible than what is secret, and nothing more manifest than what is minute. Therefore the superior man is watchful over himself, when he is alone.

While there are no stirrings of pleasure, anger, sorrow, or joy, the mind may be said to be in the state of Equilibrium. When those feelings have been stirred, and they act in their due degree, there ensues what may be called the state of Harmony.

This Equilibrium is the great root from which grow all the human actings in the world, and this Harmony is the universal path which they all should pursue.

Let the states of equilibrium and harmony exist in perfection, and a happy order will prevail throughout heaven and earth, and all things will be nourished and flourish.

In the first chapter which is given above, Tsze-sze states the views which had been handed down to him, as the basis of his discourse. First, it shows clearly how the path of duty is to be traced to its origin in Heaven, and is unchangeable, while the substance of it is provided in ourselves, and may not be departed from. Next, it speaks of the importance of preserving and nourishing this, and of exercising a watchful self-scrutiny with reference to it. Finally, it speaks of the meritorious achievements and transforming influence of sage and spiritual men in their highest extent. The wish of Tsze-sze was that hereby the learner should direct his thoughts inwards, and by searching in himself, there find these truths, so that he might put aside all outward temptations appealing to his selfishness, and fill up the measue of the goodness which is natural to him. This chapter is what the writer Yang called it—"The sum of the whole work." In the ten chapters which follow, Tsze–sze quotes the words of the Master to complete the meaning of this.

Chung–ne said, " The superior man embodies the course of the Mean; the mean man acts contrary to the course of the Mean. The superior man's embodying the course of the Mean is because he is a superior man, and so always maintains the Mean. The mean man's acting contrary to the course of the Mean is because he is a mean man, and has no caution."

II. Common Terms, Words and Phrases for the Text

master 专家，学者

learning 学问，学识

virtue 美德，德行

perceive 认识到，理解

commence 开始

renovate 革新，更新

perturb 搅乱，扰乱

tranquil 平静的，静止不动的

repose 安静，静止

deliberation 考虑，研究

complete 完成的，圆满的

completion 结束，实现

regulate 管理，调节

cultivate 培养，陶冶

person 人品

rectify 调正，校正

utmost 极度的

besides 其他的

mean 中庸（的），适度（的）；卑鄙的，微不足道的

inclination 倾向，倾斜

denote 表示，代表

lest 唯恐，免得

commit 付诸，托付

relish 滋味，美味

solid learning 实学，扎实的知识

superior man（gentleman, a man of noble character）君子

mean man（a base person, vile character）小人

manifest 明了的

minute 微小的，极小的

stir 拨动，搅动

equilibrium 平衡，均势，平静

harmony 和谐，协调

perfection 完美，完善

prevail 盛行，占优势

self-scrutiny 自省，自察

meritorious 值得称赞的，有功的，有价值的

sage 圣贤，哲人；贤明的，睿智的

appealing 吸引人的，有感染力的

embody 体现，包含

III. Exercises and Thinking

1. When were the Great Learning and the Doctrine of the Mean compiled and in what places for first learners? Give your answers with historical materials.

2. What's the purpose of the Great Learning? What should we pursue in modern university?

3. How to understand " This work contains the law of mind" in the Doctrine of the Mean?

IV. Further Readings and Internet Links

1. Further Readings

（宋）朱熹:《四书章句集注》，中华书局 2011 年版。

L. Y. T. tr., *The Four Books, or The Chinese Classics in English from the Best Previous Books*, Shanghai: The China Book Company, 1914.

James Legges tr., *The Great Learning and the Doctrine of the Mean*, Shenyang: Liaoning People's Publishing House, 2017.

Andrew Plaks tr. , *Ta Hsueh and Chung Yung (The Highest order of Cultivation and On the Practice of the Mean)* , London: Penguin Books, 2003.

2. Internet Links

爱如生中国基本古籍库：http://dh.ersjk.com/

中华古籍资源库：http://read.nlc.cn/thematDataSearch/toGujiIndex

Part II

Ancient History of the World

世界上古史

本编在马克思主义的理论指导下，选取世界上古史的原始史料，培养学生阅读不同文明、不同风格原始史料的能力。为了确保内容的全面性和深度，本编精心选取了这些文明、国家中具有典型意义的原始史料。在选取史料的过程中，我们既注重各个文明之间的均衡性，力求让每个文明都能得到公正的对待，同时也注重原始史料类型的多样化，力求从不同角度、不同层面展现古代文明的丰富面貌。

然而，由于篇幅的限制，我们并未能将所有文明的原始史料都收入本编。这是出于两方面的考虑：一方面，篇幅的限制使得我们无法对所有文明都进行详尽的探讨，必须有所取舍；另一方面，我们希望通过选取具有代表性和典型性的史料，来达到以点带面的效果，使读者能够通过这些史料了解到各个文明的主要特点和发展趋势。

在本编中，我们选取了《汉谟拉比法典》的法条、《埃伯那之子阿赫摩斯自传》、《荷马史诗》中有关独眼巨人的故事、《贝希斯敦铭文》、《穆尔什里二世年代记》、波利比乌斯《通史》中关于罗马宪政的论述以及司马迁《史记》中的《淮阴侯列传》等史料。这些史料中既有法律文本，也有个人传记，还有史诗传说和历史记载，类型多样，内容丰富。通过对这些史料的深入研究，本编揭示出古代文明的原始史料的多面性和复杂性，为学生提供一个更加全面、立体的古代世界图景。

总的来说，本编在马克思主义的指导下，通过对世界古代史上各个主要文明的典型原始史料的研究，既保证了研究的广度和深度，又兼顾了史料的多样性和均衡性。虽然篇幅有限，但我们仍努力做到了精选史料、深入剖析、以点带面。相信通过这样的研究方式，能够更好地揭示古代文明的真实面貌，为学生提供更加丰富的历史认知和文化体验。

Unit 8

The Code of Hammurabi

《汉谟拉比法典》

古代两河流域文明历来重视法制，早在公元前24、23世纪，拉伽什的国王恩美台那和乌鲁卡基那的铭文中，就提到他们的立法活动，恩美台那宣称“建立了拉伽什的自由”。除了立法活动外，古代两河流域很早就开始进行司法活动，在早王朝时代，私法文书主要涉及土地转让的纠纷事宜。到了乌尔第三王朝时期，古代两河流域的人们编撰了《乌尔纳姆法典》，从此编撰法典成为两河流域乃至整个西亚的法律传统。此后，古代两河流域的人们先后编撰出了《李皮特伊斯塔尔法典》《埃什嫩那法典》《汉谟拉比法典》《中亚述法典》《新巴比伦法典》以及其他一些法典，其中《汉谟拉比法典》是目前保存下来篇幅最长、条理最清晰、保存最完整的法典。

《汉谟拉比法典》刻写在2.25米高的玄武岩石柱上，该石柱是1901年法国考古队发现于古埃兰城市苏萨城，现藏于法国卢浮宫。与古代两河流域其他法典一样，《汉谟拉比法典》由前言、正文与结语构成，其中前言部分主要论述了汉谟拉比的统治权来自神明的赐予，与此同时宣扬了汉谟拉比的功绩，以及汉谟拉比的弱势群体保护人的角色，明确提出了立法的目的是“建立真理与正义”。结语部分主要多次叙述立法的目的是发扬正义、打击奸邪，以及法典对于百姓的重要性，以及对于抹掉石碑铭文的诅咒。正文部分共282条法律条款，涉及司法审判、财产、土地房屋、商业、婚姻、家庭、刑事伤害、行业（医生、理发师等）、农业、租佃和奴隶等方面的内容。该法典内容杂陈，非常复杂，具有诸法合体、刑名不分的特点。

对于以《汉谟拉比法典》为代表的古代两河流域法典的性质，目前学界还没有取得一致认识，有的学者认为这些法典是国王颁布的全国通用的法典，还有学者认为这些法典与泥板上的法庭判例存在矛盾之处，因此，它们可能是过去的判例集或某种意义上的法理学性质的著作，实际的审判中并未完全遵照这些法典。

I. Text①

Laws on Stealing and Receiving Stolen Property

(6) If a man has stolen property from a god or from a temple, that man shall be killed.

Furthermore, anyone who has acquired stolen goods from him shall be killed.

(7) If a man has bought silver, gold, a slave, a slave-girl, an ox, a sheep, a donkey or anything else from a man's son or a man's slave without properly witnessed receipts, even if he has accepted them just to look after them, that man is a thief, and shall be killed.

(8) If a man has stolen an ox, or a sheep, or a donkey, or a pig, or a boat, he shall pay thirty times its value if it belongs to a god or a temple and repay ten times its value if it belongs to a workman. If that thief does not have enough to pay, he shall be killed.

Laws on Soldier's Land and Houses

(26) If a soldier or a trapper has not gone on a royal expedition after being commanded to do so but has hired a labourer and sent him as his substitute, that soldier or trapper shall be killed.

The one who was hired by him shall take over his house.

(27) If they have assigned the field and orchard of a soldier or trapper who ought to have returned with the royal fighting troops to someone else and that person takes over

---

① 本文献选自 M. E. J. Richardson, *Hammurabi's Laws: Text, Translation and Glossary*, London and New York: T&T Clark International, 2004, pp. 44－119。

his duties, but then he does manage to return and reach his city, they shall give him back his field and his orchard, and he shall assume his own duties.

(28) If the son of a soldier or trapper who ought to have returned with the royal fighting troops is able to assume his duties, the field and the orchard shall be given to him and he shall assume his father's duties.

(29) If his son is too small and unable to assume his father's duties, one third part of the field or the orchard shall be given to his mother while she is rearing him.

(30) If the soldier or the trapper has been lazy with regard to his duties concerning his field, his orchard or his house, and has been away and someone else has then decided to take possession of his field, his orchard or his house and has assumed his duties for three years, but then he returns and requires them back, neither his field, nor his orchard nor his house shall be given to him.

The one who has taken them over and assumed the duties shall continue to do so himself.

(31) If he has been away for one year only and has returned, his field, his orchard and his house shall be given to him.

He shall perform his own duties again.

(32) If a merchant has paid a ransom for one particular soldier or trapper who ought to have returned from a royal expedition and enabled him to get back to his city, he shall pay back the ransom himself provided there is silver for ransom in his house; if there is no silver for ransom in his house he shall be ransomed by the temple in his city; if the temple in his city has no silver for ransom the palace shall pay the ransom.

But neither his field, his orchard or his house should be given for his ransom price.

Laws on Duties of Farmers

(42) If a man has rented a field to be cultivated but does not produce grain from the field, they shall charge him with not having worked the field, and he shall pay the same amount of grain to the owner of the field as his neighbour does.

(43) If he has abandoned the field without having cultivated it at all, he shall pay the same amount of grain to the owner of the field as his neighbour; moreover he shall break up the field that he has abandoned with mattocks and harrow it and return it to the owner of the field.

(44) If a man has rented an abandoned field to be developed over a period of three years but he drags his feet① and does not develop the field, he shall break up the field in the fourth year with mattocks, scuffle and harrow it and return it to the owner of the field; furthermore he shall make an assessment of 3000 silas grain per 18 ikurs (of field)②.

(45) If a man has let his field to be cultivated for a rent, and he has received the rental payment for the field, but some time later The Storm③ has eroded away the land or a flood has overwhelmed it, it is the cultivator who has to bear the loss.

(46) If he has not received any rent for his field, or has rented only a half or a third of the field, the cultivator and the owner of the field shall share by agreement whatever grain is produced from the field.

(47) If the cultivator has asked to work the field again because he has not regained his investment for the first year, the owner of the field shall not object.

That same cultivator of his shall work the field and at the harvest he shall collect whatever was agreed.

Laws on Commence

(100) If a merchant has sent an agent on a journey to give or to receive silver, but on the journey the agent...④ if where he went he should have made a profit, he shall work out the interest for the amount of silver he took and count the number of days, and shall recompense the merchant.

---

① 原文直译为“他放下他的手臂”。

② 此处根据原文做了修改。伊库（iku）是古代两河流域的面积单位，1 伊库合 0.36 公顷；西拉（sila）是古代两河流域的容积单位，1 西拉合 1 升。

③ 原文是“阿达德（Adad）”。阿达德是古代两河流域的风暴之神，此处用神来指代风暴。

④ 此处文字破损。

(101) If he has not seen any profit where he went, the agent shall give the merchant twice the amount of silver he took.

(102) If a merchant has given silver to a salesman as a gratuity and where he went he saw a loss, he shall repay the initial amount of silver to the merchant.

(103) If an enemy has made him drop all he was carrying as he travelled on the road, the salesman shall swear by the god and go free.

(104) If a merchant has given an agent grain or wool or oil or any other material to trade, the agent shall set out in order the silver and repay the merchant.

The agent shall receive a sealed document for the silver he has given to the merchant.

(105) If an agent has neglected to obtain a sealed document for the silver he has given to the merchant, any silver without a sealed document may not be counted in the reckoning.

(106) If the agent has taken silver from a merchant and disagrees with him, and that merchant can prove in the presence of god with witnesses that the agent took the silver, the agent shall give the merchant three times the value of whatever silver he took.

(107) If a merchant has entrusted silver to an agent and the agent has repaid him all that he gave him, but the merchant disagrees with him about what the agent had given him, yet that salesman can prove in the presence of god with witnesses that the merchant is wrong, the merchant shall give the agent six times the value of whatever he had taken because he has disagreed with the agent.

Laws on Debt

(113) If a man has lent another man some grain or silver and he takes some grain from a storehouse or from a heap without the owner's permission, they shall prove that that man has taken some grain from a storehouse or from a heap without the owner's permission and he shall bring back whatever grain he has taken.

Moreover he shall forfeit his right to anything at all that he has given.

(114) If a man has not lent another man grain or silver but has seized someone as security, he shall pay a third of a mana① of silver for each secured person.

(115) If a man has lent another man grain or silver and has seized someone as security but the secured person has died inexplicably while on the creditor's property, there is no basis for complaint in such a case.

(116) If the secured person has died on the property of the creditor after a beating or cruelty, the owner of the secured person shall prove the merchant involved guilty. If it was the man's son, they shall kill his son. If it was the man's slave, he shall pay a third of a mana of silver. Moreover he shall forfeit his right to anything at all that he has given.

(117) If a man is gripped in poverty, and he has sold his wife, or his son, or his daughter for silver, or has put them into bound-service, they shall work in the house of their purchaser or of their bond-master for three years but in the fourth year their liberation shall be agreed.

(118) If he has given a slave or a slave-girl into bound-service, the merchant may pass them on and sell them for silver.

The person cannot be reclaimed.

(119) If a man is gripped in poverty and has sold his slave-girl for silver after she has borne him sons, the slave-girl's owner may pay back the silver the merchant had loaned and redeem his slave-girl.

Laws on Marriages

(128) If a man has taken a wife but has not drawn up contracts with her, that woman is not married.

(129) If a man's wife has been caught copulating with another male, they shall tie them up and throw them into water.

If the woman's husband allows his wife to live, so similarly the king may allow his

① 马那（mana）是古代两河流域重量单位，1 马那合 500 克左右。

slave to live.

(130) If a man has restrained another man's wife, who has known no other male, and has actually copulated with her and they have caught him, that man shall be killed, but that woman shall be innocent.

(131) If the wife of a husband has been accused by her husband but she has not been caught copulating with another male, she shall swear a solemn oath and return to her house.

(132) If a finger has been pointed at a man's wife because of some male but she has not been caught copulating with another male, she shall leap into the River① for the sake of her husband.

(133a) If a man has been taken away captive but there is a supply of food in his house, his wife [shall support herself while her husband is away; she shall not enter anyone else's house.]

(133b) If that woman has not kept herself to herself② but has entered someone else's house, they shall prove that woman guilty and throw her into the water.

(134) If a man has been taken captive but there is no supply of food in his house, his wife may enter someone else's house.

That woman has no guilt.

(135) If a man has been taken captive but there is no supply of food in his house, and his wife has entered someone else's house until his return and has given birth to sons, but then later her husband comes back and rejoins his community, that woman shall go back to her first husband.

The sons shall go after their father.

---

① 原文中在“河水”（River）一词前有表示神祇的限定符，有学者认为，这可以理解为跳入河水中接受河神的审判，但也有学者认为，河水前面加上神祇限定符，可能表示的是河水具有神圣性。因此，此处可以翻译为“圣河”。

② 原文直译为“没有守卫好她的身体”。

(136) If a man has abandoned his city and fled, and afterwards his wife has entered someone else's house, but then that man returns and would take his wife back, the wife of a fugitive shall not return to her husband because he has despised his city and fled.

(137) If a man who has fixed his ideas on leaving a priestess who has born him sons, or a temple-woman who provided him with sons, they shall give back her dowry to that woman. They shall give her half the field, the orchard or the goods and she shall bring up her sons.

After she has brought up her sons they shall give her the same share as one son from whatever was given to her for her sons.

She will choose a husband as she likes.

(138) If a man has left his first wife who has born him no children, he will give her as much silver as her bride-price.

He shall pay back the gift she brought from her father's house and leave her.

(139) If there is no bride-price, he shall give one mana of silver as a divorce claim.

(140) If he is a workman, he shall give a third of a mana of silver.

(141) If the wife of a man who has been living in the man's house has made a plan to go away, and has dealt deviously, dissipated her household and belittled her husband, they shall prove her guilty.

If her husband has said he will leave her, he shall leave her. Nothing at all shall be given her for her journey or her divorce claim. If her husband has said he will not leave her, her husband shall marry a different wife.

The other wife shall live in her husband's house like a slave-girl.

(142) If a wife has despised her husband and has said, "You shall not take me" , her situation shall be assessed by her community. If she has been looked after and there is no blame, but her husband has erred and greatly disparaged her, that woman has no guilt. She shall take away her marriage gift and go to her father's house.

(143) If she has not been careful but has erred and dissipated her household and

disparaged her husband, they shall throw that woman into the water.

Laws on inheritance

(165) If a man has granted a field, an orchard or a house to his heir who is the apple of his eye[①] and has written an official document for him and afterwards the father passes to his destiny, he shall keep the gift his father gave him when the brothers share the estate. Apart from that they shall make equal shares of the property in their father's house.

(166) If a man has chosen wives for all the sons he has raised but has not taken a wife for his small son before the father passes to his destiny, when the brothers make the allocation they shall reserve from the property in the father's house something in addition to the normal share to pay for the bride-price for their little brother who has not taken a wife, so allowing him to take a wife.

(167) If a man has taken a wife and she has borne him sons and that woman has passed to her fate, and after her death he has taken a second wife, and she has borne sons, and finally the father has passed to his fate, the sons shall not divide the property according to their mothers.

They shall take the dowries of their respective mothers, but the property of their father's house they shall divide equally.

(168) If a man has come to the decision to dispossess his son and he has stated before the judges, "I will dispossess my son," the judges shall make the decisions about his affairs and the father shall not dispossess his son from his inheritance unless the son has committed an offence serious enough to be disinherited.

(169) If he has committed an offence against his father serious enough to be disinherited, on the first occasion they will turn a blind eye. If he has committed an offence for a second time the father shall disinherit his son.

---

① 原文直译为"在他眼中被接纳的人"。

Laws on Adoption

(185) If a man has taken in a tiny child at birth as a son and has brought him up, that ward shall not be reclaimed.

(186) If a man has taken in a tiny child as a son, and then soon after he has taken him in his father and mother search him out, that adopted child shall return to his father's house.

(187) The son of an official with a position in the palace and the son of a priestess shall not be reclaimed.

(188) If a professional craftsman has taken in a child as a ward and instructed him in manual skills, he shall not be reclaimed.

(189) If he has not instructed him in manual skills, that ward shall return to his father's house.

(190) If a man has not counted together with his own sons, the child whom he has taken in as a son and whom he has brought up, that ward shall return to his father's house.

Laws on Assault

(196) If a man has destroyed the sight of another similar person, they shall destroy his sight.

(197) If he has broken another man's bone, they shall break one of his bones.

(198) If he has destroyed the sight of a working man① or broken a bone of a working man, he shall pay one mana of silver.

(199) If he has destroyed the sight of another man's slave or broken a bone of another man's slave, he shall pay half his value in silver.

(200) If a man has knocked out the tooth of a man who is his colleague, they shall knock out his tooth.

(201) If he has knocked out the tooth of a working man, he shall pay a third of a

① 原文是穆什钦奴（muškēnu），指的是依附于国家的依附民。

mana of silver.

(202) If a man has struck the cheek of a man who is more important than he, he shall be struck in the council 60 times with an ox-tail.

(203) If one man has struck the cheek of another such man of similar status, he shall pay one mana of silver.

(204) If a working man has struck the cheek of another working man, he shall pay ten shekels① of silver.

(205) If a man's slave has struck the cheek of another man, they shall cut off his ear.

(206) If a man has struck another man in a brawl and has injured him, that man shall solemnly declare, "I did not wound him intentionally." It is he who shall be responsible for the physician.

(207) If someone has died in that brawl, he shall similarly make a solemn declaration; and if it was a man's son, he shall pay half a mana of silver.

(208) If he was a working man's son, he shall pay a third of a mana of silver.

(209) If a man has struck the daughter of a man and has made her lose her unborn child, he shall pay ten shekels of silver for the foetus.

(210) If that woman has died, they shall kill his daughter.

(211) If he has made a commoner②'s daughter lose her unborn child by the violence, he shall pay five shekels of silver.

(212) If that woman has died, he shall pay half a mana of silver.

(213) If he has struck a man's slave-girl and made her lose her unborn child, he shall pay two shekels of silver.

(214) If that slave-girl has died, he shall pay a third of a mana of silver.

Laws on Slavers

(278) If a man has bought a slave or a slave-girl and, before they have finished the

① 谢克尔（shekel）是古代两河流域的重量单位，1 谢克尔约合 11 克。

② 法典原文中是穆什钦奴（muškēnu），指的是依附于国家的依附民，但是译者此处却用了 commoner 一词。

first month, sickness has struck them down, he shall return them to the seller and the purchaser shall take back any silver he has paid.

(279) If a man has bought a slave or a slave-girl and then claims are found to exist, the one who sold to him shall be responsible for the claims.

(280) If a man in a foreign country has bought a slave or a slave–girl from someone, and when he is travelling in the land the owner of the slave or the slave–girl has told him that it is his slave or his slave-girl, he shall arrange the emancipation of such slaves and slave-girls without payment provided they are citizens of the land.

(281) If they are citizens of a different land the purchaser shall state the amount of silver he paid in the presence of the god and the owner of the slave or the maid shall pay the silver and redeem his slave or his slave-girl.

(282) If the slave has stated to his master, "You are not my master," his master shall prove that it is his slave and cut off his ear.

II. Common Terms, Words and Phrases for the Text

the apple of his eye 掌上明珠

turn a blind eye 视而不见，听之任之

III. Exercises and Thinking

1. What were the consequences if an individual abandons the rented field without any cultivation?

2. What happened to a woman who was accused by her husband of copulating with another male, but was not caught in the act?

3. Please list the articles about an eye for an eye and a tooth for a tooth in *The Code of Hammurabi*.

IV. Further Readings and Internet Links

1. Further Readings

Martha T. Roth, *Law Collections from Mesopotamia and Asia Minor,* 2nd Ed., Atlanta: Society of Biblical Literature, 1997.

Raymond Westbrook, ed., *A History of Ancient Near Eastern Law*, Leiden and Boston: Brill, 2003.

吴宇虹等:《古代两河流域楔形文字经典举要》, 黑龙江人民出版社 2006 年版。

2. Internet Links

The Code of Hammurabi: https://avalon.law.yale.edu/ancient/hamframe.asp

Code of Hammurabi: https://www.worldhistory.org/Code_of_Hammurabi/

Unit 9 *The Autobiography of Ahmose Son of Abana*

《埃伯那之子阿赫莫斯自传》

从古王国时代起，埃及的贵族与朝臣们便有在墓穴墙壁上镌刻自身荣耀之举，从而铸就了古埃及别具一格的传记文学。古埃及的自传铭文，常刻写在陵寝的墙壁之上，其意在令后世子孙铭记逝者生前的伟业，以及他们所扮演的社会角色和所作出的贡献，更为重要的是，他们希望通过此种方式来获得美好的来世。这些传记铭文不仅勾勒出了死者的生活轨迹及其丰功伟绩，也映射出了当时的社会价值观和历史发展的状况。

新王国时期，埃及的自传文学蔚然成风，其中不乏描绘军旅生涯的功勋记事，《埃伯那之子阿赫莫斯自传》便是其中的瑰宝。这部传记详述了阿赫莫斯的生平功业，尤其聚焦于他的军事经历和所获得的荣誉。这部自传从阿赫莫斯成家立业之前的岁月开始写起，一直叙述至他的暮年。阿赫莫斯出生于埃尔卡伯的一个家庭，母亲名为埃伯那，父亲是巴巴，而祖父则名叫拉因特。在未成家之际，阿赫莫斯承袭父业，投身行伍，成为一名士兵。成家之后，他跟随法老阿赫摩斯一世征讨喜克索斯人，并参与了对努比亚的战争。在阿蒙霍特普一世统治的时代，阿赫莫斯因在对努比亚的战争中表现出色，被赐予"国王勇士"的荣誉称号。在图特摩斯一世统治时期，他晋升为军队指挥官，参与了对努比亚的征战，随后又投身于图特摩斯一世对叙利亚的战役。

这部自传不仅是对阿赫莫斯一生的赞歌，更是对那个英雄时代的生动见证，它以贵族的视角，展现了埃及历史的一段辉煌篇章。这里选取的内容出自立希海姆（Lichtheim）编纂的《古埃及文学读物》英译本。

I. Text[①]

The Crew Commander[②] Ahmose son of Abana[③], the justified; he says. I speak to you, all people. I let you know what favors came to me. I have been rewarded with gold[④] seven times in the sight of the whole land, with male and female slaves as well. I have been endowed with very many fields. The name of the brave man is in that which he has done; it will not perish in the land forever.

He speaks as follows. I grew up in the town of Nekheb[⑤], my father being a soldier of the King of Upper and Lower Egypt[⑥], Seqenenre[⑦], the justified. Baba son of Reonet was his name. I became a soldier in his stead on the ship "The Wild Bull" in the time of the Lord of the Two Lands. Nebpehtire[⑧], the justified. I was a youth who had not married; I slept in...[⑨]

Now when I had established a household,[⑩] I was taken to the ship "Northern," because I was brave. I followed the sovereign on foot when he rode about on his chariot. When the town of Avaris[⑪] was besieged, I fought bravely on foot in his majesty's

---

① 本文选自 Miriam Lichtheim, *Ancient Egyptian Literature*, Vol. 2, Berkeley and Los Angeles: University of California Press, 1978, pp. 12–14。

② 这个官职在古埃及文中写作。

③ 埃伯那是墓主人的母亲。

④ 古埃及新王国时期，通常赏赐给士兵黄金，以表彰其作战勇敢，这种奖励通常被称为"勇气之黄金（ nbw n qnt）"。

⑤ 涅亨布是上埃及第三诺姆的首府，古埃及文写作，读作 nḫb，古希腊语称之为 Ειλείθυιας πόλις，阿拉伯语称之为 Elkab。现在该遗址位于卢克索以南 80 千米处。

⑥ 上下埃及之王是古埃及法老的王衔之一，该王衔产生于第 1 王朝国王登（Den）统治时期，表达了国王对上埃及与下埃及的统治权。

⑦ 古埃及第 17 王朝法老塞肯那拉－塔奥二世（Seqenenre Tao II）。

⑧ 古埃及第 18 王朝法老阿赫摩斯二世的王位名。

⑨ 此处文字破损。

⑩ 建立家室指的是结婚。

⑪ 古埃及第 15 王朝（喜克索斯王朝）的首都，该城市用古埃及文写作，读作 ḥwt-wꜥrt，意思是"地区之家"。该名称用古希腊文写作 Αὔαρις，现在埃及达巴丘（Tell el-Dab'a）遗址。

presence. Thereupon I was appointed to the ship "Rising in Memphis[①]." Then there was fighting on the water in "Pjedku[②]" of Avaris. I made a seizure and carried off a hand[③]. When it was reported to the royal herald the gold of valor was given to me.

Then they fought again in this place; I again made a seizure there and carried off a hand. Then I was given the gold of valor once again.

Then there was fighting in Egypt to the south of this town, and I carried off a man as a living captive. I went down into the water—for he was captured on the city side—and crossed the water carrying him. When it was reported to the royal herald I was rewarded with gold once more. Then Avaris was despoiled, and I brought spoil from there: one man, three women; total, four persons. His majesty gave them to me as slaves.

Then Sharuhen[④] was besieged for three years, His majesty despoiled it and I brought spoil from it: two women and a hand. Then the gold of valor was given me, and my captives were given to me as slaves.

Now when his majesty had slain the nomads of Asia, he sailed south to Khent-hen-nefer[⑤], to destroy the Nubian Bowmen[⑥]. His majesty made a great slaughter among them, and I brought spoil from there: two living men and three hands. Then I was rewarded with gold once again, and two female slaves were given to me. His majesty journeyed north, his heat rejoicing in valor and victory. He had conquered southerners, northerners.

---

① 孟菲斯是埃及古都的希腊语名称。孟菲斯在古埃及文中有不同的名称，常见的是"白城（inb ḥḏ）""永恒之所（ḏd-st）""持久并美丽（mn-nfr）""两土地的生命（ʿnḫ t□wy）"。本传记中用的是mn-nfr，该词后来演变为科普文中的ⲙⲉⲙϥⲓ和希腊文中的Μέμφις。

② 帕杰德库（pꜣ-ḏdkw）是阿发里斯附近的一条尼罗河支流。

③ 古埃及人在战场上计算斩首数量时采用了计算手的方式。

④ 沙鲁亨是巴勒斯坦西南部的城市，古埃及文写作，读作šrḥn，大概在今天加沙地带，学界尚未确定其具体位置，许多学者认为是现在的Tell el-Farah，皮特里认为是Tell el-Ajjul，而雷尼认为是Tel Heror。

⑤ 尼罗河第二瀑布附近的地区。

⑥ 在古代，努比亚人善射箭，因此，古埃及人称之为"弓箭手"。

Then Aata① came to the South. His fate brought on his doom. The gods of Upper Egypt grasped him. He was found by his majesty at Tent-taa②. His majesty carried him off as a living captive, and all his people as booty. I brought two young warriors as captives from the ship of Aata. Then I was given five persons and portions of land amounting to five arurae③ in my town. The same was done for the whole crew.

Then came that foe named Tetian④. He had gathered the malcontents to himself. His majesty slew him; his troop was wiped out. Then I was given three persons and five arurae of land in my town.

Then I conveyed King Djeserkare⑤, the justified, when he sailed south to Kush⑥, to enlarge the borders of Egypt. His majesty smote that Nubian Bowman in the midst of his army. They were carried off in fetters, none missing, the fleeing destroyed as if they have never been. Now I was in the van of our troops and I fought really well. His majesty saw my valor. I carried off two hands and presented them to his majesty. Then his people and his cattle were pursued. and I carried off a living captive and presented him to his majesty.

I brought his majesty back to Egypt in two days from "Upper Well⑦," and was rewarded with gold. I brought back two female slaves as booty, apart from those that I had presented to his majesty. Then they made me a "Warrior of the Ruler."

Then I conveyed King Aakheperkare⑧, the justified, when he sailed south to Khent-hen-nefer, to crush rebellion throughout the lands, to repel the intruders from the desert

① 阿阿塔（ꜣꜣtꜣ）可能是一位努比亚人，但是，有学者认为该词是一个头衔而非人名。

② 坦特塔阿（tnt–tꜣ-ꜥ），位置不能确定，但是，从该词的限定符来看，指的是一个有河流的地方。

③ 阿鲁拉是古埃及面积单位斯塔特（stꜣ-ꜥt）的希腊语称呼。

④ 坦提安（ttjꜥn），从名字看这是一个埃及人。

⑤ 古埃及法老阿蒙霍特普一世的王位名。

⑥ 库什（kꜣš）是古埃及对尼罗河第一瀑布以南的努比亚地区的称呼。

⑦ 未知的地方。

⑧ 古埃及法老图特摩斯一世的王位名。

region. I was brave in his presence in the bad water, in the towing of the ship over the cataract. Thereupon I was made crew commander.

Then his majesty [was informed that the Nubian]...①. At this his majesty became enraged like a leopard. His majesty shot, and his first arrow pierced the chest of that foe. Then those [enemies turned to flee], helpless before his Uraeus②. A slaughter was made among them; their dependents were carried off as living captives. His majesty journeyed north, all foreign lands in his grasp, and that wretched Nubian Bowman head downward at the bow of his majesty's ship "Falcon." They landed at Ipet-sut③.

After this (his majesty) proceeded to Retjenu④, to vent his wrath throughout the lands. When his majesty reached Nahrin⑤, his majesty found that foe marshalling troops. Then his majesty made a great slaughter of them. Countless were the living captives which his majesty brought back from his victories. Now I was in the van of our troops, and his majesty saw my valor. I brought a chariot, its horse, and him who was on it as a living captive. When they were presented to his majesty, I was rewarded with gold once again.

I have grown old; I have reached old age. Favored as before, and loved [by my lord], I [rest] in the tomb that I myself made.

---

① 此处文字破损。

② 蛇标（nsrt）为古埃及法老王冠上的眼镜蛇装饰物，据说它可以帮助法老击杀敌人。

③ 伊潘特苏特（ipt–swt）是卡纳卡神庙的名字。

④ 列藤努（rṯnw）是古埃及人对西奈以北、陶鲁斯以南地区的叙利亚－巴勒斯坦地区的称呼。

⑤ 那哈林（nhrn）是古埃及人对两河流域北部、叙利亚地区的米坦尼王国的称呼。

II. Common Terms, Words and Phrases for the Text

Nekheb 涅亨布

the King of Upper and Lower Egypt 上下埃及之王

the Lord of the Two Lands 两土地之主

sovereign 君主

Avaris 阿发里斯

Memphis 孟菲斯

royal herald 王家传令官

Sharuhen 沙鲁亨

Nubian 努比亚人，努比亚的

Upper Egypt 上埃及

Kush 库什

falcon 鹰隼

Retjenu 列藤努

Nahrin 那哈林

III. Exercises and Thinking

1. What titles or positions did Ahmose achieve throughout his military career?

2. How many times was Ahmose rewarded with gold, and for what reasons?

3. How did Ahmose contribute to Egypt's victories through the roles he undertook during his military service?

IV. Further Readings and Internet Links

1. Further Readings

James Henry Breasted, *Ancient Records of Egypt*, Vol. 2, Chicago: the University of Chicago, 1906.

郭丹彤译注：《古代埃及象形文字译注》（中卷），东北师范大学出版社 2015 年版。

李晓东译注：《埃及历史铭文举要》，商务印书馆 2007 年版。

2. Internet Links

Osirisnet: Tombs of Ancient Egypt: https://www.osirisnet.net/tombes/el_kab/ahmes/e_ahmes_01.htm

Unit 10

The Homer Epic

《荷马史诗》

《荷马史诗》是古希腊最著名的文学作品，反映了当时希腊社会的状况。该史诗描述了公元前 12 世纪古希腊联军对小亚细亚的特洛伊的远征以及战后奥德修斯返回故乡的古史。虽然该作品是文学作品，但是史诗中包含着真实的历史内核。德国考古学家施里曼依靠该史诗的记载，成功挖掘出特洛伊、迈锡尼等遗址。

《荷马史诗》由《伊利亚特》和《奥德赛》构成，这两部分既独立又有联系。《伊利亚特》全诗共 15693 行，分为 24 卷，主要内容是叙述特洛伊战争。虽然叙述特洛亚战争，但诗人并没有像历史叙述那样叙述它的全过程及其多方面，而是撷取其中的一段进行叙述，集中叙述了发生在战争进行到第十年时约 50 天里发生的事件。而《奥德赛》共 12000 多行，分为 24 卷，主要讲述的是英雄奥德修斯的故事。以奥德修斯幸运归返家乡为转折点，全诗内容可以分为两个部分：前半部分主要讲述了特洛伊战争胜利后，奥德修斯被迫漂泊数十年，遭遇种种挫折的艰苦经历；后半部分则讲述了奥德修斯返回家乡后，在神明的指引下，依靠自己的智慧和他人的协助，最终完成复仇的故事。两部史诗的风格也有所不同，前者较多地出现一些雄伟悲壮的场面，后者虽也描写了动人心弦的斗争，但场景瑰丽多姿，格调比较平静。《荷马史诗》是早期希腊重要的精神成果，在世界文学史上有着举足轻重的地位。这里选取的内容出自布彻（Butcher）和朗（Lang）的《奥德赛》英译本。

《奥德赛》中有很多脍炙人口的故事，其中之一就是第九卷中奥德修斯及其同伴与独眼巨人斗争的故事。本卷倒叙了奥德修斯离开特洛伊城后的历险，包括劫杀基科涅斯人、因伙伴酩酊大醉而被迫逃亡、遭遇库克洛普斯（巨人）的袭击并被囚禁在石室中。本文选取了奥德修斯与库克洛普斯斗争的故事的部分内容。故事梗概为：奥德修斯及其同伴来到库克洛普斯的邦界，奥德修斯带着伙伴和醇酒去拜访库克洛普斯，却被库克洛普斯关在石室内当作食物。奥德修斯设计弄瞎了他，第二天又躲在羊群中逃离。

I. Text①

But I commanded the rest of my well-loved company to make speed and go on board the swift ships, lest haply any should eat of the lotus and be forgetful of returning.② Right soon they embarked, and sat upon the benches, and sitting orderly they smote the grey sea water with their oars.

Thence we sailed onward stricken at heart. And we came to the land of the Cyclôpes③, a froward and a lawless folk, who trusting to the deathless gods plant not aught with their hands, neither plough: but, behold, all these things spring for them in plenty, unsown and untilled, wheat, and barley, and vines, which bear great clusters of the juice of the grape, and the rain of Zeus gives them increase. These have neither gatherings for council nor oracles of law, but they dwell in hollow caves on the crests of the high hills, and each one utters the law to his children and his wives, and they reck not one of another.

Now there is a waste isle stretching without the harbour of the land of the Cyclôpes, neither nigh at hand nor yet afar off, a woodland isle, wherein are wild goats unnumbered, for no path of men scares them, nor do hunters resort thither who suffer hardships in the wood, as they range the mountain crests. Moreover it is possessed neither by flocks nor

① 本文选自 S. H. Butcher and A. Lang, trans., *The Odyssey of Homer*, New York: P. F. Collier & Son Corporation, 1909, pp. 137－149。

② 《奥德赛》中，描述了一个国度，那里居住着洛托法戈伊人，他们以花为食。奥德修斯派人去打探情况。被派去的人吃了洛托斯花，就完全忘却了回家乡，只希望留在那里同洛托法戈伊人一起生活。

③ 在古希腊神话中，Cyclops（复数形式为 Cyclôpes）通常被描述为前额中间长有一只眼睛的巨人。他们是乌拉诺斯和盖亚的儿子，是泰坦神族的成员。

by ploughed lands, but the soil lies unsown evermore and untilled, desolate of men, and feeds the bleating goats. For the Cyclôpes have by them no ships with vermilion cheek, not yet are there shipwrights in the island, who might fashion decked barques, which should accomplish all their desire, voyaging to the towns of men (as ofttimes men cross the sea to one another in ships), who might likewise have made of their isle a goodly settlement. Yea, it is in no wise a sorry land, but would bear all things in their season; for therein are soft water–meadows by the shores of the grey salt sea, and there the vines know no decay, and the land is level to plough; thence might they reap a crop exceeding deep in due season, for verily there is fatness beneath the soil. Also there is a fair haven, where is no need of moorings, either to cast anchor or to fasten hawsers, but men may run the ship on the beach, and tarry until such time as the sailors are minded to be gone, and favourable breezes blow. Now at the head of the harbour is a well of bright water issuing from a cave, and round it are poplars growing. Thither we sailed, and some god guided us through the night, for it was dark and there was no light to see, a mist lying deep about the ships, nor did the moon show her light from heaven, but was shut in with clouds. No man then beheld that island, neither saw we the long waves rolling to the beach, till we had run our decked ships ashore. And when our ships were beached, we took down all their sails, and ourselves too stept forth upon the strand of the sea, and there we fell into sound sleep and waited for the bright Dawn.

So soon as early Dawn shone forth, the rosy–fingered, in wonder at the island we roamed over the length thereof: and the Nymphs①, the daughters of Zeus, lord of the aegis, started the wild goats of the hills, that my company might have wherewith to sup. Anon we took to us our curved bows from out the ships and long spears, and arrayed in three bands we began shooting at the goats; and the god soon gave us game in plenty.

① 宁芙诸女神（Nymphs）是古希腊神话中的女神，她们与自然界的各个方面紧密相连，尤其是与森林、山岳、水体等自然环境相关。这些女神被认为是自然的守护者，她们以美丽的少女形态出现，通常与歌舞、生命和繁殖的力量联系在一起。

Now twelve ships bare me company, and to each ship fell nine goats for a portion, but for me alone they set ten apart.

Thus we sat there the livelong day until the going down of the sun, feasting on abundant flesh and on sweet wine. For the red wine was not yet spent from out the ships, but somewhat was yet therein, for we had each one drawn off large store thereof in jars, when we took the sacred citadel of the Cicones①. And we looked across to the land of the Cyclôpes who dwell nigh, and to the smoke, and to the voice of the men, and of the sheep and of the goats. And when the sun had sunk and darkness had come on, then we laid us to rest upon the sea–beach. So soon as early Dawn shone forth, the rosy–fingered, then I called a gathering of my men, and spake among them all:

"Abide here all the rest of you, my dear companions; but I will go with mine own ship and my ship's company, and make proof of these men, what manner of folk they are, whether froward, and wild, and unjust, or hospitable and of god–fearing mind."

So I spake, and I climbed the ship's side, and bade my company themselves to mount, and to loose the hawsers. So they soon embarked and sat upon the benches, and sitting orderly smote the grey sea water with their oars. Now when we had come to the land that lies hard by, we saw a cave on the border near to the sea, lofty and roofed over with laurels, and there many flocks of sheep and goats were used to rest. And about it a high outer court was built with stones, deep bedded, and with tall pines and oaks with their high crown of leaves. And a man was wont to sleep therein, of monstrous size, who shepherded his flocks alone and afar, and was not conversant with others, but dwelt apart in lawlessness of mind. Yea, for he was a monstrous thing and fashioned marvellously, nor was he like to any man that lives by bread, but like a wooded peak of the towering hills, which stands out apart and alone from others.

---

① 在《奥德赛》中，基科涅斯人（Cicones）是色雷斯地区伊斯马洛斯城（Ismarus）的居民。奥德修斯率领的军队攻击了基科涅斯人居住的城堡，杀死了许多民众，并掠夺了妇女和财富。然而，由于麻痹和轻敌，奥德修斯的部队在海滩上庆祝时被基科涅斯人的援军突袭，导致大量士兵死亡。

Then I commanded the rest of my well-loved company to tarry there by the ship, and to guard the ship, but I chose out twelve men, the best of my company, and sallied forth. Now I had with me a goat-skin of the dark wine and sweet, which Maron①, son of Euanthes, had given me, the priest of Apollo, the god that watched over Ismarus. And he gave it, for that we had protected him with his wife and child reverently; for he dwelt in a thick grove of Phoebus Apollo②. And he made me splendid gifts; he gave me seven talents of gold well wrought, and he gave me a mixing bowl of pure silver, and furthermore wine which he drew off in twelve jars in all, sweet wine unmingled, a draught divine; nor did any of his servants or of his handmaids in the house know thereof, but himself and his dear wife and one housedame only. And as often as they drank that red wine honey sweet, he would fill one cup and pour it into twenty measures of water, and a marvellous sweet smell went up from the mixing bowl: then truly it was no pleasure to refrain.

With this wine I filled a great skin, and bare it with me, and corn too I put in a wallet, for my lordly spirit straightway had a boding that a man would come to me, a strange man, clothed in mighty strength, one that knew not judgment and justice.

Soon we came to the cave, but we found him not within; he was shepherding his fat flocks in the pastures. So we went into the cave, and gazed on all that was therein. The baskets were well laden with cheeses, and the folds were thronged with lambs and kids; each kind was penned by itself, the firstlings apart, and the summer lambs apart, apart too the younglings of the flock. Now all the vessels swam with whey, the milk-pails and the bowls, the well-wrought vessels whereinto he milked. My company then spake and besought me first of all to take of the cheeses and to return, and afterwards to make haste and drive off the kids and lambs to the swift ships from out the pens, and to sail over the

① 在《奥德赛》中，马戎（Maron）是色雷斯地区伊斯马洛斯城（Ismarus）的阿波罗的祭司。当奥德修斯和他的手下洗劫伊斯马洛斯城时，他们饶恕了马戎及其妻小的生命。出于感激之情，马戎给了奥德修斯七塔兰特上好的金子、一碗银子和十二罐美味的葡萄酒。

② 阿波罗是古希腊神话中的太阳神、音乐神、医药神、预言神，是奥林匹斯十二大神之一。在古代文献中提及阿波罗的时候，常常加上修饰语“明亮、光明、灿烂（Phoebus）”。

salt sea water. Howbeit I hearkened not (and far better would it have been), but waited to see the giant himself, and whether he would give me gifts as a stranger's due. Yet was not his coming to be with joy to my company.

Then we kindled a fire, and made burnt-offering, and ourselves likewise took of the cheeses, and did eat, and sat waiting for him within till he came back, shepherding his flocks. And he bore a grievous weight of dry wood, against supper time. This log he cast down with a din inside the cave, and in fear we fled to the secret place of the rock. As for him, he drave his fat flocks into the wide cavern, even all that he was wont to milk; but the males both of the sheep and of the goats he left without in the deep yard. Thereafter he lifted a huge doorstone and weighty, and set it in the mouth of the cave, such an one as two and twenty good four-wheeled wains could not raise from the ground, so mighty a sheer rock did he set against the doorway. Then he sat down and milked the ewes and bleating goats all orderly, and beneath each ewe he placed her young. And anon he curdled one half of the white milk, and massed it together, and stored it in wicker-baskets, and the other half he let stand in pails, that he might have it to take and drink against supper time. Now when he had done all his work busily, then he kindled the fire anew, and espied us, and made question:

"Strangers, who are ye? Whence sail ye over the wet ways? On some trading enterprise or at adventure do ye rove, even as sea-robbers over the brine, for at hazard of their own lives they wander, bringing bale to alien men."

So spake he, but as for us our heart within us was broken for terror of the deep voice and his own monstrous shape; yet despite all I answered and spake unto him, saying:

"Lo, we are Achaeans[①], driven wandering from Troy, by all manner of winds over the great gulf of the sea; seeking our homes we fare, but another path have we come, by

---

① 根据《荷马史诗》，阿凯亚人（Achaean）与达那奥伊人（Danaoi）、阿盖奥伊人（Argeioi）一起围攻特洛伊。《荷马史诗》中描述的他们的活动区域，大致在希腊大陆和及其西部岛屿、克里特岛、罗得岛和邻近岛屿（基克拉迪群岛除外），与公元前 14—前 13 世纪迈锡尼人的活动区域重合。

other ways: even such, methinks, was the will and the counsel of Zeus. And we avow us to be the men of Agamemnon①, son of Atreus, whose fame is even now the mightiest under heaven, so great a city did he sack, and destroyed many people;② but as for us we have lighted here, and come to these thy knees, if perchance thou wilt give us a stranger's gift, or make any present, as is the due of strangers. Nay, lord, have regard to the gods, for we are thy suppliants; and Zeus is the avenger of suppliants and sojourners, Zeus, the god of the stranger, who fareth in the company of reverend strangers."

So I spake, and anon he answered out of his pitiless heart: "Thou art witless, my stranger, or thou hast come from afar, who biddest me either to fear or shun the gods. For the Cyclôpes pay no heed to Zeus, lord of the aegis③, nor to the blessed gods, for verily we are better men than they. Nor would I, to shun the enmity of Zeus, spare either thee or thy company, unless my spirit bade me. But tell me where thou didst stay thy well–wrought ship on thy coming? Was it perchance at the far end of the island, or hard by, that I may know?"

So he spake tempting me, but he cheated me not, who knew full much, and I answered him again with words of guile:

"As for my ship, Poseidon, the shaker of the earth, brake it to pieces, for he cast it upon the rocks at the border of your country, and brought it nigh the headland, and a wind bare it thither from the sea. But I with these my men escaped from utter doom."

So I spake, and out of his pitiless heart he answered me not a word, but sprang up, and laid his hands upon my fellows, and clutching two together dashed them, as they had been whelps, to the earth, and the brain flowed forth upon the ground, and the earth

---

① 根据《荷马史诗》，阿伽门农（Agamemnon）是古希腊迈锡尼的国王，阿特柔斯（Atreus）的儿子，是特洛伊战争中希腊联军的统帅。

② 指的是阿伽门农率领希腊联军攻克特洛伊城的行为。

③ 在《荷马史诗》中，aegis是宙斯神奇的胸甲（或盾牌），宙斯将其借给女儿雅典娜，以表彰她在战争中所发挥的作用。在大多数记载中，它被描述为用一种山羊皮做成的，中间有一个戈尔工（Gorgon）人头像的武装装备。

was wet. Then cut he them up piecemeal, and made ready his supper. So he ate even as a mountain–bred lion, and ceased not, devouring entrails and flesh and bones with their marrow. And we wept and raised our hands to Zeus, beholding the cruel deeds; and we were at our wits' end. And after the Cyclops had filled his huge maw with human flesh and the milk he drank thereafter, he lay within the cave, stretched out among his sheep.

So I took counsel in my great heart, whether I should draw near, and pluck my sharp sword from my thigh, and stab him in the breast, where the midriff holds the liver, feeling for the place with my hand. But my second thought withheld me, for so should we too have perished even there with utter doom. For we should not have prevailed to roll away with our hands from the lofty door the heavy stone which he set there. So for that time we made moan, awaiting the bright Dawn.

Now when early Dawn shone forth, the rosy–fingered, again he kindled the fire and milked his goodly flocks all orderly, and beneath each ewe set her lamb. Anon when he had done all his work busily, again he seized yet other two men and made ready his mid-day meal. And after the meal, lightly he moved away the great door–stone, and drave his fat flocks forth from the cave, and afterwards he set it in his place again, as one might set the lid on a quiver. Then with a loud whoop, the Cyclops turned his fat flocks towards the hills; but I was left devising evil in the deep of my heart, if in any wise I might avenge me, and Athene grant me renown.

And this was the counsel that showed best in my sight. There lay by a sheep–fold a great club of the Cyclops, a club of olive wood, yet green, which he had cut to carry with him when it should be seasoned. Now when we saw it we likened it in size to the mast of a black ship of twenty oars, a wide merchant vessel that traverses the great sea gulf, so huge it was to view in bulk and length. I stood thereby and cut off from it a portion as it were a fathom's length, and set it by my fellows, and bade them fine it down, and they made it even, while I stood by and sharpened it to a point, and straightway I took it and hardened it in the bright fire. Then I laid it well away, and hid it beneath the dung, which was scattered in great heaps in the depths of the cave. And I bade my company cast lots among them, which of them should risk the adventure with me, and lift the bar and turn it about in his eye, when sweet sleep came upon him. And the lot fell upon those four whom I myself would have been fain to choose, and I appointed myself to be the fifth among them. In the evening he came shepherding his flocks of goodly fleece, and presently he drave his fat flocks into the cave each and all, nor left he any without in the deep courtyard, whether through some foreboding, or perchance that the god so bade him do. Thereafter he lifted the huge door–stone and set it in the mouth of the cave, and sitting down he milked the ewes and bleating goats, all orderly, and beneath each ewe he placed her young. Now when he had done all his work busily, again he seized yet other two and made ready his supper. Then I stood by the Cyclops and spake to him, holding in my hands an ivy bowl of the dark wine:

"Cyclops, take and drink wine after thy feast of man's meat, that thou mayest know what manner of drink this was that our ship held. And lo, I was bringing it thee as a drink offering, if haply thou mayest take pity and send me on my way home, but thy mad rage is past all sufferance. O hard of heart, how may another of the many men there be come ever to thee again, seeing that thy deeds have been lawless?"

So I spake, and he took the cup and drank it off, and found great delight in drinking the sweet draught, and asked me for it yet a second time:

"Give it me again of thy grace, and tell me thy name straightway, that I may give thee a stranger's gift, wherein thou mayest be glad. Yea for the earth, the grain–giver, bears for the Cyclôpes the mighty clusters of the juice of the grape, and the rain of Zeus gives them increase, but this is a rill of very nectar and ambrosia."

So he spake, and again I handed him the dark wine. Thrice I bare and gave it him, and thrice in his folly he drank it to the lees. Now when the wine had got about the wits of the Cyclops, then did I speak to him with soft words:

"Cyclops, thou askest me my renowned name, and I will declare it unto thee, and do thou grant me a stranger's gift, as thou didst promise. Noman is my name, and Noman they call me, my father and my mother and all my fellows."

So I spake, and straightway he answered me out of his pitiless heart:

"Noman will I eat last in the number of his fellows, and the others before him: that shall be thy gift."

Therewith he sank backwards and fell with face upturned, and there he lay with his great neck bent round, and sleep, that conquers all men, overcame him. And the wine and the fragments of men's flesh issued forth from his mouth, and he vomited, being heavy with wine. Then I thrust in that stake under the deep ashes, until it should grow hot, and I spake to my companions comfortable words, lest any should hang back from me in fear. But when that bar of olive wood was just about to catch fire in the flame, green though it was, and began to glow terribly, even then I came nigh, and drew it from the coals, and my fellows gathered about me, and some god breathed great courage into us. For their part they seized the bar of olive wood, that was sharpened at the point, and thrust it into his eye, while I from my place aloft turned it about, as when a man bores a ship's beam with a drill while his fellows below spin it with a strap, which they hold at either end, and the auger runs round continually. Even so did we seize the fiery-pointed brand and whirled it round in his eye, and the blood flowed about the heated bar. And the breath of the flame singed his eyelids and brows all about, as the ball of the eye burnt away, and the roots thereof crackled in the flame. And as when a smith dips an axe or adze in chill water with a great hissing, when he would temper it—for hereby anon comes the strength of iron—even so did his eye hiss round the stake of olive. And he raised a great and terrible cry, that the rock rang around, and we fled away in fear, while he plucked forth from his eye the brand bedabbled in much blood. Then maddened with pain he cast it from him with his hands, and called with a loud voice on the Cyclôpes, who dwelt about him in the caves along the windy heights. And they heard the cry and flocked together from every side, and gathering round the cave asked him what ailed him:

"What hath so distressed thee, Polyphemus, that thou criest thus aloud through the immortal night, and makest us sleepless? Surely no mortal driveth off thy flocks against thy will: surely none slayeth thyself by force or craft?"

And the strong Polyphemus spake to them again from out the cave: "My friends, Noman is slaying me by guile, nor at all by force."

And they answered and spake winged words: "If then no man is violently handling thee in thy solitude, it can in no wise be that thou shouldest escape the sickness sent by mighty Zeus. Nay, pray thou to thy father, the lord Poseidon."

On this wise they spake and departed; and my heart within me laughed to see how my name and cunning counsel had beguiled them. But the Cyclops, groaning and travailing in pain, groped with his hands, and lifted away the stone from the door of the cave, and himself sat in the entry, with arms outstretched to catch, if he might, any one that was going forth with his sheep, so witless, methinks, did he hope to find me. But I advised me how all might be for the very best, if perchance I might find a way of escape from death for my companions and myself, and I wove all manner of craft and counsel, as a man will for his life, seeing that great mischief was nigh. And this was the counsel that showed best in my sight. The rams of the flock were well nurtured and thick of fleece, great and goodly, with wool dark as the violet. Quietly I lashed them together with twisted withies, whereon the Cyclops slept, that lawless monster. Three together I took: now the middle one of the three would bear each a man, but the other twain went on either side, saving my fellows. Thus every three sheep bare their man. But as for me I laid hold of the back of a young ram who was far the best and the goodliest of all the flock, and curled beneath his shaggy belly there I lay, and so clung face upward, grasping the wondrous fleece with a steadfast heart. So for that time making moan we awaited the bright Dawn.

So soon as early Dawn shone forth, the rosy-fingered, then did the rams of the flock hasten forth to pasture, but the ewes bleated unmilked about the pens, for their udders were swollen to bursting. Then their lord, sore stricken with pain, felt along the backs of all the sheep as they stood up before him, and guessed not in his folly how that my men were bound beneath the breasts of his thick–fleeced flocks. Last of all the sheep came forth the ram, cumbered with his wool, and the weight of me and my cunning. And the strong Polyphemus laid his hands on him and spake to him, saying:

"Dear ram, wherefore, I pray thee, art thou the last of all the flocks to go forth from the cave, who of old wast not wont to lag behind the sheep, but wert ever the foremost to pluck the tender blossom of the pasture, faring with long strides, and wert still the first to come to the streams of the rivers, and first didst long to return to the homestead in the evening? But now art thou the very last. Surely thou art sorrowing for the eye of thy lord, which an evil man blinded, with his accursed fellows, when he had subdued my wits with wine, even Noman, whom I say hath not yet escaped destruction. Ah, if thou couldst feel as I, and be endued with speech, to tell me where he shifts about to shun my wrath; then should he be smitten, and his brains be dashed against the floor here and there about the cave, and my heart be lightened of the sorrows which Noman, nothing worth, hath brought me!"

Therewith he sent the ram forth from him, and when we had gone but a little way from the cave and from the yard, first I loosed myself from under the ram and then I set my fellows free. And swiftly we drave on those stiff–shanked sheep, so rich in fat, and often turned to look about, till we came to the ship. And a glad sight to our fellows were we that had fled from death, but the others they would have bemoaned with tears; howbeit I suffered it not, but with frowning brows forbade each man to weep. Rather I bade them to cast on board the many sheep with goodly fleece, and to sail over the salt sea water. So they embarked forthwith, and sate upon the benches, and sitting orderly smote the grey sea water with their oars.

II. Common Terms, Words and Phrases for the Text

Cyclôpes 诸库克洛普斯

Cyclops 库克洛普斯

Nymphs 宁芙

Zeus 宙斯

Cicones 基科涅斯人

Phoebus Apollo 福玻斯·阿波罗

Athene 雅典娜

Poseidon 波塞冬

III. Exercises and Thinking

1. Can you describe what the society of the Cyclôpes looks like?
2. How did Odysseus and his entourage blind the Cyclops?
3. How did Odysseus and his entourage escape from the Cyclops' cave?

IV. Further Readings and Internet Links

1. Further Readings

Homer, *The Odyssey*, Vol. 1, 2nd Ed., trans. by A. T. Murray, Harvard: Harvard University Press, 1995.

[古希腊]荷马:《荷马史诗·奥德赛》，王焕生译，人民文学出版社2003年版。

[古希腊]荷马:《奥德赛（第七至十二卷）》，罗念生、王焕生译，上海人民出版社 2012 年版。

2. Internet Links

Loeb Classical Library: https://www.loebclassics.com

The Project Gutenberg eBook of The Odyssey of Homer: https://www.gutenberg.org/cache/epub/1728/pg1728-images.html#chap12

Unit 11

Bihistun Inscription
《贝希斯敦铭文》

在古代伊朗，自古以来就有勒石为铭的传统，卢卢比国王阿奴巴尼曾经在伊朗西部克尔曼沙阿省的涯石上刻下了铭文与浮雕。此外，还发现了其他一些统治者的浮雕、铭文。可能从此开始，在伊朗地区形成了某种勒石为铭的传统。

在这些崖刻中，《贝希斯敦铭文》最负盛名。该铭文是波斯王大流士一世，命人在今伊朗西部克尔曼沙阿省的贝希斯敦山的一处悬崖峭壁上刻写的。该崖刻在离地面 105 米的悬崖之上，高 15 米、宽 25 米。该铭文由浮雕与铭文两部分组成，其中浮雕部分描绘了这样一幅场景：大流士一世手持象征王权的弓、左脚踩着高墨达，大流士的身后有两名侍从，前面站着九个双手被绑、脖子上套着绳子的人，他们代表被大流士一世打败的反叛者。在这些人的上面的中心位置，刻画了阿胡拉马兹达神明。而铭文部分是用古波斯语（5 栏 414 行）、埃兰语（8 栏 260 行）和巴比伦语（112 行）书写而成。这里选取的内容出自库特（Kuhrt）编纂的《波斯帝国：阿契美尼德时期文献集》英译本。

该铭文的主要内容是大流士一世夺取王位的过程，以及在其统治时期的对外征伐活动。在铭文中，大流士一世把镇压高墨达以及对外征伐的胜利，归因为阿胡拉马兹达的庇佑，由此可见，在波斯帝国的宗教生活中，阿胡拉马兹达占有非常突出的地位。从该铭文可以看出，在大流士统治时期，波斯帝国的领土非常大，伊朗、两河流域、亚美尼亚、小亚细亚、中亚、北非都在波斯帝国的疆域之内。该铭文对于了解波斯帝国初期的政治形势、领土状况、对外征伐有重要史料价值。

I. Text[①]

(col. I)

§ 1 I am Darius, the great king, king of kings,[②] king in Persia, king of peoples/countries[③], son of Vishtaspa (Gr. Hystaspes[④]), grandson of Arshama (Gr. Arsames), an Achaemenid.

§ 2 Darius the king proclaims: My father is Vishtaspa; Vishtaspa's father is Arshama; Arshama's father is Ariaramna (Gr. Ariaramnes); Ariaramna's father is Cishpish (Gr. Teispes); Cishpish's father is Hakhaimanish (Gr. Achaemenes).

§ 3 Darius the king proclaims: For this reason we are called Achaemenids. From long ago we are noble; from long ago we are royal.

§ 4 Darius the king proclaims: Eight of our family were kings before; I am the ninth; nine kings are we in succession.

§ 5 Darius the king proclaims: By the favour of Auramazda, I am king; Auramazda bestowed kingship upon me.

§ 6 Darius the king proclaims: These are the peoples/countries who obey me; by the favour of Auramazda, I was their king: Persia, Elam, Babylonia, Assyria, Arabia, Egypt, those of the sea, Lydia, Ionia, Media, Armenia, Cappadocia, Parthia, Drangiana, Areia, Chorasmia, Bactria, Sogdiana, Gandara, Scythia (Saca[⑤]), Sattagydia, Arachosia, Maka; in all twenty-three peoples/countries.

§ 7 Darius the king proclaims: These are the peoples who obeyed me; by the favour

---

① Am é lie Kuhrt, *The Persian Empire: A Corpus of Sources from the Achaemenid Period*, London and New York: Routledge, 2007, pp. 141－148.

② 该王衔最早为两河流域的中亚述国王采用，后来乌拉尔图的国王也采用，显然，波斯的王衔受到了两河流域的影响。

③ 该王衔最早为两河流域中亚述的国王使用，在此影响下波斯使用该王衔。其中，古波斯词语“*dahyu*-”有“国家、百姓”的意思，但是，从两河流域的王衔来看，此处意思当为“百姓”。

④ 此处为希腊文中的名字。

⑤ 萨卡（Saca）是被古典作家称为斯基泰人的民族，居住在中亚和俄罗斯南部的大草原上。

of Auramazda, they were my faithful subjects; they brought me "tribute" ; what was said to them by me, whether by night or by day, that they did.

§ 8 Darius the king proclaims: Among these peoples, the man who was loyal, him I rewarded; he who was faithless, I punished; by the favour of Auramazda, these peoples respected my law; in accordance with what was said to them by me, they acted.

§ 9 Darius the king proclaims: Auramazda bestowed this kingship on me; Auramazda gave me his help until I gained this kingship; by the favour of Auramazda, I possess this kingship.

§ 10 Darius the king proclaims: This is what was done by me after I became king:① the son of Cyrus, by name Cambyses, of our family, he was king here; this Cambyses had a brother, by name Bardiya; he had the same mother, the same father as Cambyses; then Cambyses killed that Bardiya; when Cambyses killed Bardiya, the people did not know that Bardiya had been killed; then, Cambyses went to Egypt. When Cambyses had gone to Egypt, then the people became disloyal; and the Lie grew among the people, both in Persia and Media and among the other peoples.

§ 11 Darius the king proclaims: Then there was a man, a magus②, Gaumata by name; he rebelled in Paishiyauvada③. A mountain, by name Arakadri④, from there—fourteen days of the month Viyakhna⑤ had gone (11 March 522), when he rebelled. He lied thus to the people: "I am Bardiya, son of Cyrus, brother of Cambyses." Then all the people became rebellious against Cambyses; they went over to him, both Persia and Media, as well as the other peoples. He seized the kingship; nine days of the month Garmapada⑥ had gone (1 July 522), then he seized the kingship. After that, Cambyses

---

① 下面叙述的是大流士一世登上王位时波斯的状况。

② 古代波斯祭司集团的成员的称呼。

③ Paishiyauvada 是法尔斯（Fars）的一个城镇，可能在帕萨加达（Pasargadae）附近，也可能是帕萨加达（Pasargadae）。

④ 阿拉卡德里山（Arakadri）是法尔斯的一座山，高墨塔的老巢。

⑤ 维亚赫那月（month Viyakhna），古波斯历第 12 月，相当于公历的 2—3 月。

⑥ 加尔马帕达月（month Garmapada），古波斯历第 4 月，相当于公历的 6—7 月。

died his own death.

§ 12 Darius the king proclaims: This kingship, which Gaumata the magus took away from Cambyses, this kingship had belonged for a long time to our family. After that, Gaumata the magus took it away from Cambyses; he took to himself Persia, Media, as well as the other peoples/countries; he made them his own, he became king.

§ 13 Darius the king proclaims: There was no man, neither a Persian, nor a Mede, nor anyone of our family, who could take the kingship away from that Gaumata the magus. The people were very much afraid of him, (thinking that) he would kill many people who had known Bardiya previously. Here is the reason that he might have killed people: "Lest they know that I am not Bardiya, son of Cyrus." No one dared to say anything about Gaumata the magus, until I came. Then I invoked Auramazda; Auramazda brought me help. Ten days of the month Bagayadi were past (29 September 522), then I, with a few men, killed that Gaumata the magus, and his foremost followers. A fortress, by name Sikayahuvati, a district by name Nisaya①, in Media, that is where I killed him. I took the kingship away from him; with the help of Auramazda, I became king; Auramazda granted me the kingship.

§ 14 Darius the king proclaims: The kingdom which had been taken away from our family, I re-established it, I put it back in its place. In accordance with what had been previously, I made the cult-centres, which Gaumata the magus destroyed. I restored to the people, the pastures and herds, the household slaves and the houses/domains, which Gaumata the magus took away from them. I re-established the people on its foundation, Persia, Media and the other peoples. In accordance with what had been previously, I brought back what had been taken away. By the favour of Auramazda, this is what I did. I strove until I had restored our house to its legitimate place, as (it was) before; with the help of Auramazda, I strove in such a way that Gaumata the magus did not make our

① 尼萨亚（Nisaya）是米底的一个地区，因产马而负有盛名。

house destitute.

§ 15 Darius the king proclaims: This is what I did after I became king.

§ 16 Darius the king proclaims: After I had killed Gaumata the magus, a man called Acina, son of Upadarma, rebelled in Elam. To the people, he declared this: "I am king in Elam." After that, the Elamites became rebellious; they went over to that Acina; he became king in Elam. And a man, a Babylonian, called Nadintabaira (Bab. Nidintu-Bel①), son of Ainaira (Bab. Kin-zer), rebelled in Babylon; he lied to the people thus: "I am Nebuchadnezzar, son of Nabonidus②." Then all the Babylonian people went over to that Nadintabaira; Babylonia became rebellious; he seized the kingship in Babylon.

§ 17 Darius the king proclaims: So then, I sent to Elam.③ That Acina was led to me as a prisoner; I killed him.

§ 18 Darius the king proclaims: After that, I went to Babylon, against that Nadintabaira, who called himself Nebuchadnezzar. The army of Nadintabaira held the Tigris. It took its stand there, and the water was not fordable④. So I placed my army on skins⑤; I placed one part on camels, for others I brought horses. Auramazda gave me help; by the favour of Auramazda, we crossed the Tigris. There I utterly defeated the army of Nadintabaira: twenty-six days of the month Aciyadiya⑥ had gone (13 December 522), when we fought the battle.

§ 19 Darius the king proclaims: After that, I went to (the city of) Babylon. But, when I had not yet reached Babylon, a town called Zazana, beside the Euphrates – there

① 此处为巴比伦文中的名字。

② 那伯尼杜（Nabonidus）是新巴比伦王国的末王。

③ 这句话不容易理解，在《贝希斯敦铭文》的巴比伦语、埃兰语版本中，这句话的意思是“我派使节到了埃兰”。

④ 原文的意思是“航行”，此处译者意译为“可涉水而过”。

⑤ 此处指的是用皮囊渡河。

⑥ 阿斯亚底亚月（month Aciyadiya），古波斯历第 9 月，相当于公历的 11—12 月。

this Nadintabaira, who called himself Nebuchadnezzar, came with an army against me to offer battle. Then we fought a battle; Auramazda helped me; by the favour of Auramazda, I utterly defeated the army of Nadintabaira. The remainder were thrown into the water. Two days of the month Anamaka had gone (18 December 522), when we fought that battle.

(col. II)

§ 20 Darius the king proclaims: Then Nadintabaira fled with a few horsemen. He went to Babylon. Then I went to Babylon. By the favour of Auramazda, I captured both Babylon and Nadintabaira. After that, I killed that Nadintabaira in Babylon.

§ 21 Darius the king proclaims: While I was in Babylon, these are the people/ countries who/which became rebellious against me: Persia, Elam, Media, Assyria, Egypt, Parthia, Margiana, Sattagydia, Scythia (Saca).

§ 22 Darius the king proclaims: A man called Martiya, son of Cincakhri – a town called Kuganaka[①], in Persia, was his home. He rebelled in Elam; he declared to the people, "I am Imanish, king in Elam."

§ 23 Darius the king proclaims: At that time, I was near Elam. Then the Elamites were afraid of me; they seized that Martiya, who was their chief, and killed him.

§ 24 Darius the king proclaims: A man called Fravartish, a Mede, rebelled in Media. He declared to the people, "I am Khshathrita, of the family of Uvakhshtra." After that, the Median army, which was in the royal house, rebelled against me. It went over to that Fravartish. He became king in Media.

§ 25 Darius the king proclaims: The Persian and Median army which was with me, was a small (force). Then I sent out an army. A Persian called Vidarna, my subject, I made their chief. I spoke to them thus, "Go, smite that Median army, which does not call itself mine." Then that Vidarna went with his army. When he

① 库加那卡（Kuganaka）在法尔斯。

reached Media—a town called Maru[①], in Media—there he fought with the Medes. He who was chief among the Medes was not there at that time. Auramazda helped me; by the favour of Auramazda, my army utterly defeated that rebellious army. Twenty-seven days of the month Anamaka had gone by (12 January 521), then the battle was fought by them. After that, my army—a district called Kampanda[②], in Media—there it waited for me until I arrived in Media.

§ 26 Darius the king proclaims: An Armenian called Dadarshi, my subject, I sent him to Armenia. I spoke to him thus, "Go! That rebellious army, which does not call itself mine, smite it!" Then Dadarshi marched away. When he arrived in Armenia, the rebels gathered together (and) marched against Dadarshi to join battle. A village called Zuza, in Armenia—there they joined battle. Auramazda helped me; by the favour of Auramazda, my army utterly defeated that rebel army. Eight days of the month Thuravahara[③] had gone by (21 May 521); then they fought the battle.

§ 27 Darius the king proclaims: For a second time the rebels gathered; they came out against Dadarshi to join battle. A fortress called Tigra[④], in Armenia—there they joined battle. Auramazda helped me; by the favour of Auramazda, my army utterly defeated that rebellious army. Eighteen days of the month Thuravahara had gone by (31 May 521); then they fought the battle.

§ 28 Darius the king proclaims: For a third time, the rebels gathered; they came out against Dadarshi to join battle. A fortress called Uyama[⑤], in Armenia—there they joined battle. Auramazda helped me; by the favour of Auramazda, my army utterly defeated that rebellious army. Nine days of the month Thaigarci[⑥] had gone by (21 June

---

① 马鲁（Maru），具体位置不详。

② 卡姆潘达（Kampanda），具体位置不详，推测它距离埃克巴塔那（Ecbatana）并不太远。

③ 苏拉瓦哈拉月（month Thuravahara），古波斯历第 2 月，相当于公历的 4—5 月。

④ 提格拉（Tigra），具体位置不详。

⑤ 乌亚马（Uyama），具体位置不详。

⑥ 塞加尔斯月（month Thaigarci），古波斯历第 3 月，相当于公历的 5—6 月。

521); then they fought the battle. Afterwards, Dadarshi waited for me until I arrived in Media.

§ 29 Darius the king proclaims: Afterwards a Persian called Vaumisa, my subject, I sent him to Armenia. I spoke to him thus: "Go! This rebellious army, which does not call itself mine, smite it!" Then Vaumisa marched away. When he arrived in Armenia, the rebels assembled; they came out against Vaumisa to join battle. A region called Izala①, in Assyria—there they joined battle. Auramazda helped me; by the favour of Auramazda, my army utterly defeated that rebellious army. Fifteen days of the month Anamaka had gone (31 December 522), then they fought the battle.

§ 30 Darius the king proclaims: For a second time the rebels gathered; they came out against Vaumisa to join battle. A region called Autiyara②, in Armenia—there they joined battle. Auramazda helped me; by the favour of Auramazda, my army utterly defeated that rebellious army. On the last day of the month Thuravahara (11 June 521)—then they fought the battle. Then Vaumisa waited for me in Armenia until I arrived in Media.

§ 31 Darius the king proclaims: Then I left Babylon; I went to Media. When I arrived in Media, a town called Kunduru③, in Media—there this Fravartish, who called himself king in Media, came with his army against me to join battle. Then we joined battle. Auramazda helped me; by the favour of Auramazda, I utterly defeated the army of Fravartish. Twenty–five days of the month Adukanaisha④ had gone (7 May 521)—then we fought that battle.

§ 32 Darius the king proclaims: Then this Fravartish fled with a few horsemen. A place called Raga⑤, in Media—he went there. Then I sent an army in pursuit. Fravartish

① 伊扎拉（Izala），可能位于阿布丁山（Tur Abdin）以西。
② 奥提亚拉（Autiyara），具体位置不详。
③ 昆都鲁（Kunduru），具体位置不详。
④ 阿杜卡奈沙月（month Adukanaisha），古波斯历第 1 月，相当于公历的 3—4 月。
⑤ 拉加（Raga），今伊朗的德黑兰（Tehran）附近。

was seized; he was brought before me. I cut off his nose, ears and tongue, and tore out one eye. He was held in fetters at my palace entrance; all the people saw him. After that, I impaled him at Ecbatana; and the men who were his foremost followers, those I hanged at Ecbatana in the fortress.

§ 33 Darius the king proclaims: A man called Cicantakhma, a Sagartian, rebelled against me; he said to the people: "I am king in Sagartia①, of the family of Uvakhshtra." Then I sent a Persian and Median army; a Mede called Takhmaspada, my subject—I made him their chief. I spoke to them thus: "Go forth; the rebel army which will not call itself mine—defeat it!" Then Takhmaspada went off with the army; he joined battle with Cicantakhma. Auramazda helped me; by the favour of Auramazda, my army defeated that rebel army and took Cicantakhma prisoner, brought him to me. After that I cut off his nose, ears, and tore out one eye. He was held in fetters at my palace entrance; all the people saw him. After that, I impaled him at Arbela②.

§ 34 Darius the king proclaims: This (is) what has been done by me in Media.

§ 35 Darius the king proclaims: Parthia and Hyrcania③ rebelled against me, called themselves (supporters) of Fravartish. Vishtaspa, my father, was in Parthia; the people abandoned him, became rebellious. Then Vishtaspa went forth with the army which was faithful to him. A place called Vishpauzati④, in Parthia—there he joined battle with the Parthians. Auramazda helped me; by the favour of Auramazda, Vishtaspa utterly defeated that rebel army; twelve days of the month Viyakhna had gone (8 March 521); then the battle was fought by them.

① 萨加尔提阿（Sagartia），具体位置不详。
② 阿尔贝拉（Arbela），今伊拉克的埃尔比勒（Erbil）。
③ 海尔卡尼阿（Hyrcania），可能指的是伊朗东北部地区。
④ 维什泡扎提（Vishpauzati），具体位置不详。

(col. III)

§ 36 Darius the king proclaims: After that, I sent a Persian army to Vishtaspa from Raga. When this army reached Vishtaspa, then Vishtaspa took that army (and) marched off. A place called Patigarbana①, in Parthia—there he joined battle with the rebels. Auramazda helped me; by the favour of Auramazda, Vishtaspa utterly defeated that rebel army. One day of the month Garmapada had gone (12 July 521), then they fought the battle.

§ 37 Darius the king proclaims: After that the country/people became mine. This (is) what has been done by me in Parthia.

§ 38 Darius the king proclaims: A country called Margiana② rebelled against me. A man called Frada, a Margian, they made chief. Then I sent against him a Persian called Dadarshi, my subject, satrap in Bactria. I spoke to him thus: "Go, defeat that army which does not call itself mine!" After that, Dadarshi marched out with the army; he joined battle with the Margians. Auramazda helped me; by the favour of Auramazda my army utterly defeated that rebel army. Twenty-three days of the month Aciyadiya had gone (10 December 522, or 28 December 521), then they fought the battle.

§ 39 Darius the king proclaims: After that the country became mine. This (is) what has been done by me in Bactria.

§ 40 Darius the king proclaims: A man called Vahyazdata—a place called Tarava, a region called Yutiya③, in Persia—there he lived. He revolted in Persia for the second time. He spoke to the people thus: "I am Bardiya, the son of Cyrus." Then the Persian army, which (was) in the palace (and had been summoned) from Anshan④ previously, became rebellious to me, joined that Vahyazdata; he became king in Persia.

---

① 帕提加尔卜巴那（Patigarbana），具体位置不详。

② 马尔加那（Margiana），今土库曼斯坦的梅尔夫大绿洲（the great oasis of Merv）地区。

③ 越提亚（Yutiya），具体位置不详。

④ 安山（Anshan），法尔斯地区的古城。

§ 41 Darius the king speaks thus: Then I sent forth the Persian and Median army which was with me. A Persian called Artavardiya, my subject, I made their chief. The other Persian army went behind me to Media. After that, Artavardiya went with his army to Persia. When he arrived in Persia—a place called Rakha[①], in Persia—there that Vahyazdata, who called himself Bardiya, came with an army against Artavardiya to join battle. After that they joined battle. Auramazda helped me; by the favour of Auramazda, my army utterly defeated that army of Vahyazdata. Twelve days of the month Thuravahara had gone (24 May 521), then they fought the battle.

§ 42 Darius the king proclaims: After that, this Vahyazdata fled with a few horsemen; he went to Paishiyauvada. From there, he got an army; again he marched against Artavardiya to join battle. A mountain called Parga[②]—there they joined battle. Auramazda helped me; by the favour of Auramazda, my army utterly defeated this army of Vahyazdata; five days of the month Garmapada had gone by (16 July 521), then they fought the battle, and they took that Vahyazdata prisoner, and they took his foremost followers prisoner.

§ 43 Darius the king proclaims: Then, that Vahyazdata and the men who were his foremost followers—a place called Huvadaicaya[③], in Persia—there I impaled them.

§ 44 Darius the king proclaims: This (is) what has been done by me in Persia.

§ 45 Darius the king proclaims: That Vahyazdata, who called himself Bardiya, had sent an army to Arachosia[④]—a Persian called Vivana, my subject, satrap in Arachosia—against him; he had made one man their chief. He spoke to them thus: "Go, defeat Vivana and that army which calls itself (that) of Darius the king!" After that, this army which Vahyazdata had sent, marched against Vivana to join battle. A fortress called

① 拉夏（Rakha），具体位置不详。

② 帕尔加（Parga），具体位置不详。

③ 胡瓦代卡亚（Huvadaicaya），冈比西斯时期的重要宗教中心，在大流士一世时期成为波斯波利斯（Persepolis）的一部分。

④ 阿拉寇斯阿（Arachosia），今阿富汗坎大哈周边地区。

Kapishkani—there they joined battle. Auramazda helped me; by the favour of Auramazda my army utterly defeated that rebel army. Thirteen days of the month Anamaka had gone by (29 December 522), then they fought the battle.

§ 46 Darius the king proclaims: Once more the rebels gathered, came out against Vivana to join battle. A district called Gandutava[①]—there they joined battle. Auramazda helped me; by the favour of Auramazda, my army utterly defeated that rebel army. Seven days of the month Viyakhna had gone by (21 February 521), then they joined battle.

§ 47 Darius the king proclaims: Then that man who was the chief of that army, which Vahyazdata had sent against Vivana, fled with a small number of horsemen (and) went off. A fortress called Arshada, in Arachosial—he came there. After that, Vivana marched with an army in pursuit; there he took him prisoner and slew the men who were his foremost followers.

§ 48 Darius the king proclaims: After that the region became mine.

§ 49 Darius the king proclaims: While I was in Persia and Media, again a second time, Babylonia revolted against me. A man called Arakha, an Armenian, son of Haldita—he rebelled in Babylon. A district called Dubala—from there he lied to the people thus: "I am Nebuchadnezzar, the son of Nabonidus." Then the Babylonians rebelled against me, went over to that Arakha. He seized Babylon; he became king in Babylon.

§ 50 Darius the king proclaims: After that I sent an army to Babylon. A Persian called Vindafarna, my subject—him I made chief of them. I said to him thus: "Go! Defeat that Babylonian army, which does not call itself mine." Then Vindafarna went to Babylon with the army. Auramazda helped me; by the favour of Auramazda, Vindafarna defeated that army and (placed) them in fetters. Twenty-two days of the month Varkazana had gone by (27 November 521), then he took prisoner that Arakha who had lyingly called

① 甘杜塔瓦（Gandutava），可能是今阿富汗的喀布尔以东的甘达马克（Gandamak）。

himself Nebuchadnezzar and the men who were his foremost followers. I gave the order: that Arakha and the men who were his foremost followers were impaled at Babylon.

(col. IV)

§ 51 Darius the king proclaims: This (is) what has been done by me in Babylon.

§ 52 Darius the king proclaims: This (is) what I have done, by the favour of Auramazda, in one and the same year, after I became king. I have fought nineteen battles. By the favour of Auramazda, I defeated them and took nine kings prisoner. One called Gaumata, a magus, lied, saying: "I am Bardiya, son of Cyrus" ; he made Persia rebellious. One called Acina, an Elamite, lied, saying: "I am king in Elam" ; he made Elam rebellious. One called Nadintabaira, a Babylonian, lied, saying: "I am Nebuchadnezzar, son of Nabonidus" ; he made Babylon rebellious. One called Martiya, a Persian, lied, saying: "I am Imani, king in Elam" ; he made Elam rebellious. One called Fravartish, a Mede, lied, saying: "I am Khshathrita, of the family of Uvakhshtra" ; he made Media rebellious. One called Cicantakhma, a Sagartian, lied, saying: "I am king in Sagartia, of the family of Uvakhshtra" ; he made Sagartia rebellious. One called Frada, a Margian, lied, saying: "I am king in Margiana" ; he made Margiana rebellious. One called Vahyazdata, a Persian, lied, saying: "I am Bardiya, son of Cyrus" ; he made Persia rebellious. One called Arakha, an Armenian, lied saying: "I am Nebuchadnezzar, son of Nabonidus" ; he made Babylonia rebellious.

II. Common Terms, Words and Phrases for the Text

Elam 埃兰

Persia 波斯

Babylonia 巴比伦尼亚

Assyria 亚述

Lydia 吕底亚

Ionia 爱奥尼亚

Media 米底

Parthia 帕提亚

magus 马古祭司

Cyrus 居鲁士

Cambyses 冈比西斯

Darius 大流士

Tigris 底格里斯河

Babylon 巴比伦

Ecbatana 埃克巴塔那

satrap 总督

Bactria 巴克特里亚

III. Exercises and Thinking

1. What did Gaumat do after the death of Camyses ?

2. According to §§ 1–52, How many rebels did Darius I defeat in the first year of his reign? Who were they?

3. According to Behistun Inscription, what were the territories of the Persian Empire under the reign of Darius I King?

IV. Further Readings and Internet Links

1. Further Readings

George G. Cameron, "The Old Persian Text of the Bisitun Inscription," *Journal of Cuneiform Studies*, Vol. 5, No. 2 (1951), pp. 47–54.

Herbert Cushing Tolman, *Ancient Persian Lexicon and the Texts of the Achaemenidan Inscriptions: Transliterated and Translated with Special Reference to Their Recent Re-Examination*, New York: American book company, 1908.

Herbert Cushing Tolman, *The Behistan inscription of King Darius: Translation and*

Critical Notes to The Persian Text with Special Reference to Recent Re–Examinations of The Rock, Nashville: Vanderbilt University, 1908.

2. Internet Links

OLD PERSIAN TEXTS: https://www.avesta.org/op/op.htm#db 1

Behistun, Persian Text: https://www.livius.org/sources/content/behistun–persian–text/

Unit 12

Annal of Muršili II

《穆尔西里二世年代记》

古代赫梯人重视历史叙述与书写，从古王国起就开始编撰年代记，一直持续到赫梯帝国时期。古代赫梯国王留下了众多年代记，如《哈图西里一世年代记》《图德哈里一世年代记》《阿尔努旺达一世年代记》《哈图西里三世年代记》《苏皮鲁流马一世事迹》《穆尔西里二世事迹》。这些年代记通常以第一人称或有时以第三人称叙述赫梯统治者的军事行动，把这些军事行动按照统治年代为序编排，对军事行动的叙述采取了程式化的语言：敌人对赫梯的敌对，赫梯国王对敌进行军事打击并取得胜利，敌方城市被毁灭，赫梯国王把战利品送回哈图萨。当然，这些年代记也会提及赫梯国王的政治、宗教活动。

从现有资料来看，《穆尔西里二世年代记》是赫梯年代记的代表作，该年代记共有五个抄本。这部年代记包括序言、正文、结语三部分，其中正文部分主要描述了穆尔西里二世统治前十年的军事行动，因此，该年代记别名为《穆尔西里二世的十年年代记》。该年代记对每一年发生事情的叙述比较程式化，对每一年事情的叙述，则以"在下一年"来开头，以"这是我在一年中做的事"这样的表述作总结。这就使得该年代记的时间顺序非常清晰，从而具有编年史的特征。

该年代记从穆尔西里二世即位写起，描述对卡什卡人、阿尔扎瓦、阿兹-哈亚萨、努哈什舍、卡迭什等国或族群的战争。其中描述了对阿尔扎瓦的胜利以及把阿尔扎瓦拆分成三个王国。这为解释赫梯与小亚细亚西部以及爱琴海地区的国家间关系提供了重要史料，还提及了赫梯对叙利亚国家卡迭什、努哈什舍的战争，对于了解赫梯与埃及在叙利亚地区的争夺有很大帮助。从穆尔西里二世的军事行动来看，卡什卡人给赫梯造成了很大麻烦，穆尔西里二世统治前十年，花了很大精力来对卡什卡作战。此外，该年代记的前言提及苏皮鲁流马一世、阿尔努旺达二世的死亡。这两个事件可以与《穆尔西里二世祈祷词》的内容联系起来，从而对于复原赫梯王国的史实有很大帮助。

I. Text[1]

[Thus speaks] My Majesty[2] Muršili[3], the Great King, King of the land of Ḫatti, the hero, son of Šuppiluliuma[4], Great King, the hero.

Before I sat down on my father's throne, all the enemy foreign lands began hostilities. When my father became a god,[5] Arnuwanda[6], my brother, sat on his father's throne. But, afterwards he, too, became sick.[7] When the enemy lands heard that my brother Arnuwanda was sick, the enemy lands began hostilities.

And when my brother Arnuwanda became a god, those enemy lands which had not yet begun hostilities, they too began hostilities. The enemy foreign lands said as follows: "His father, who was king of Ḫatti, was a heroic king. He kept the enemy lands defeated and he has become a god. His son who sat on his father's throne was also in the prime of life, and he got sick and he also became a god.

Now, the one who has sat down on his father's throne is a child.[8] He will not (be

① William W. Hallo, *The Context of Scripture*, Vol. 2, Leiden and Boston: Brill, 2003, pp. 85－87.

② 这是对赫梯文献中"我的太阳神"的意译。

③ 穆尔西里二世（Muršili II），赫梯国王，苏皮鲁流马一世的第三子，公元前 1330—前 1295 年在位。

④ 苏皮鲁流马一世（Šuppiluliuma I），赫梯国王，公元前 1370—前 1330 年在位。

⑤ 国王成神指的是国王去世。

⑥ 阿尔努旺达二世（Arnuwanda II），赫梯国王，约公元前 1330 年在位。

⑦ 赫梯国王苏皮鲁流马一世、阿尔努旺达二世可能死于瘟疫，这可以从穆尔西里二世的瘟疫祈祷文推断出来。

⑧ 虽然穆尔西里二世是一位年轻且缺乏经验的国王，但几乎可以肯定的是，他在登上赫梯王位时，已经是一个有能力独立统治国家的年轻人。

able to) save the borders of Ḫatti and Ḫatti itself."

Because my father was establishing garrisons in the land of Mitanni①, he tarried in a garrison, and the festivals of the Sungoddess of Arinna②, my lady, lapsed.

When I, My Majesty, sat on my father's throne, while I had not yet gone against any of the enemy foreign lands who were in a state of hostilities with me, I concerned myself with and performed the regular festivals of the Sungoddess of Arinna, my lady. I held up my hand to the Sungoddess of Arinna, my lady, and said as follows: "O Sungoddess of Arinna, my lady! The enemy foreign lands who have called me a child and belittled me, have begun seeking to take away the borders of the Sungoddess of Arinna, my lady. Stand by me, O Sungoddess of Arinna, my lady. Destroy those enemy foreign lands before me." The Sungoddess of Arinna heard my words and stood by me. After I sat down on my father's throne, in ten years I vanquished these enemy foreign lands and destroyed them.

Year 1

The Kaška③ of the land of Durmitta④ began hostilities with me and [came] for battle against me. Subsequently the (other) Kaška also came. They began to attack the land of Durmitta. I, My Majesty, went against them. I attacked the leading districts of the Kaška-Land — Ḫalila and Dudduška. I looted them including their transplantees⑤, cattle and sheep and brought them away to Ḫattuša. The towns of Ḫalila and Dudduška I burned down.

---

① 米坦尼（Mitanni）是公元前两千纪的从扎格罗斯山到地中海东岸的横跨两河流域北部与叙利亚的国家，该国后来被赫梯王苏皮鲁流马一世灭亡，该国的王子苏提瓦扎在赫梯的支持下重建王国，成为赫梯的藩属国，该藩属国后来被中亚述所灭。

② 阿利那的太阳女神（the Sungoddess of Arinna），是赫梯神话中最重要的女神，她是天气神塔尔浑那（Tarḫunna）的妻子。该女神的崇拜中心在阿利那，可能是现在的卡拉谢尔－胡尤克（Karaşehir Hüyük）。赫梯人把该女神称为“诸国之女王”，由此可见她在赫梯人心目中的地位。

③ 卡什卡（Kaška）是青铜时代一个松散的非印欧人的族群，他们生活在赫梯人生活的核心区与黑海之间的山区。

④ 杜尔米塔（Durmitta）是卡尼什以东的城市，在穆尔西里二世时期曾经被卡什卡人所占据。

⑤ 原文用表意符NAM.RA，在赫梯语中是*arnuwala*，意思是“俘虏”，译者鉴于学界多翻译为“被驱逐者（deportee）”，认为这些人被赫梯人迁移到赫梯国内而并非驱逐出小亚细亚，所以，采用了一个全新的词汇“移植者（transplantee）”来翻译该词。

When the Kaška heard about the destruction of Ḫalila and Dudduška, the whole land of the Kaška came to help and came for battle against me. I, My Majesty, fought them. The Sungoddess of Arinna, my lady, the victorious Stormgod①, my lord, Mezzulla② and all the gods ran before me. I defeated the levies of the Kaška and killed them. The Kaška of the land of Durmitta resubmitted and they began to give [me troops].

[Then] I, [My Majesty,] returned. Because the Kaška of the land of Išḫupitta③ had become hostile and ceased giving me troops, I, My Majesty, went to the land of Išḫupitta. I attacked the town of [...]ḫumiššena④. I looted it including its transplantees, cattle and sheep and brought them away to Ḫattuša⑤, while the town I burned down. I resubjugated the Kaška of the land of Išḫupitta. They began to give me troops. All this I did in one year.

Year 2

In the following year I went [to the Upper Land⑥,] because the district of Tipiya⑦ had become hostile and ceased giving me troops⑧. I, My Majesty, attacked Katḫaiduwa⑨. I brought its transplantees, cattle, and sheep back to Ḫattuša, [while the town I burned down.]

Then I [retur]ned [from Tipiya to Ḫattuša]. Because the land of Išḫupitta had [again]

---

① 暴风神（Stormgod），是赫梯的天气神塔尔浑那（Tarḫunna）。

② 美朱拉（Mezzulla），是赫梯神话中的一位女神。根据赫梯神话，她与阿利那的太阳女神有关联，她及其女儿与阿利那的太阳女神形成三女神组合。此外，她是阿利那的太阳女神与塔尔浑那（Tarḫunna）的女儿。

③ 伊苏皮塔（Išḫupitta），可能是古典文献中的 Amaseia、土耳其文献中的 Amasya，位于黑海海岸的群山中，坐落在叶希尔马克河（Yeşilırmak River）畔的山谷中。

④ 此词的部分组成受损，不可读。

⑤ 哈图萨（Ḫattuša）是赫梯的首都，今土耳其的博加兹卡莱（Boğazkale）。

⑥ 上地（the Upper Land），赫梯以所生活的哈里什河为中心，把东北地区称为上地，把西南地区称为下地。

⑦ 提皮亚（Tipiya）是卡什卡人在上地建立的一个定居点。

⑧ 在赫梯王苏皮鲁流马一世统治时期，与卡什卡人签订了条约，其中一项内容是卡什卡人要向赫梯提供作战人员，但是，在苏皮鲁流马一世时期以及阿尔努旺达二世短暂统治时期，卡什卡人停止向赫梯提供作战人员。

⑨ 卡特哈杜瓦（Katḫaiduwa）是卡什卡人在上地建立的另外一个定居点。

become hostile, [I sent ...] and he defeated it again a second time. Those who [had been the head of the rebellion] escaped there. Nunnata [and Pazzanna①, my servants ...–d②] and [I chased(?)] them [to Kammama③] in the land of the Kaška. [No one(?) esc]aped. [When I demanded those] people [who had been] the head of the rebellion, [they seized and killed] them. I, My Majesty, [made] Kammama [my servants again]. The [Sungoddess of Arinna,] my lady, [the victorious Stormgod, my lord,] Mezzulla, [and all] the gods [ran before me, and I defeated Palḫuišša④(?).I looted it including its transplantees,] cattle and sheep [and brought them] away [to Ḫattuša.] All this [I did in one year].

Year 3

In the following year [I did ... When Arnuwanda(?)], my brother, in [...], [the troops of the town of Attārimma], the troops of the town of Ḫuwaršanašša and the troops of the town of [Šuruda⑤ fled before him and went] to [Arzawa⑥. I sent a messenger] to Uḫḫa–ziti⑦. [I] wrote to him as follows: "People [who belong to me—the troops of Attārimma,] the troops of Ḫuwaršanašša [and the troops of Šuruda]—came [to you. Give them back to me.]" But Uḫḫa–ziti [wrote back] to me [as follows]: "[I will] not [give] any[one back] to you. [...] by force [...]" [He mustered] his troops [...]

[He stood] for battle behind the town of Tikkukkuwa⑧. I, [My Majesty] fought [him]. The Sungoddess of [Arinna, my lady, the] victorious [Stormgod], my lord, Mezzula [and

① 努那塔（Nunnata）与帕扎那（Pazzanna）是赫梯的臣民，在伊苏皮塔发动叛乱，为此穆尔西里二世出兵平叛。之后叛乱者逃到了卡什卡人的一处名为卡马马的地方，穆尔西里二世紧追而来，要求卡马马人交出两个叛乱者。最后，卡马马人屈服，杀掉了努那塔和帕扎那。

② 该词损毁严重，只能看到读音为"d"的楔形文字符号。

③ 卡马马（Kammama）是卡什卡人的一个地点，位置不详。

④ 帕尔胡伊沙（Palḫuišša）是卡什卡人的领导人，有学者认为在他领导下，卡什卡人逐渐形成了一个王国。

⑤ 阿塔里马（Attārimma）、胡瓦尔沙那沙（Ḫuwaršanašša）、苏鲁达（Šuruda）是赫梯与阿尔扎瓦接壤地区的三个城市。

⑥ 阿尔扎瓦（Arzawa），有广义与狭义之分，狭义是指小阿尔扎瓦国（Arzawa Minor），广义是指以小阿尔扎瓦为核心组成的联盟，主要成员是小阿尔扎瓦、米拉、维卢沙、塞哈河流域国家、哈帕拉。

⑦ 乌哈兹提（Uḫḫa–ziti），阿尔扎瓦末王，可能与赫梯王穆尔西里二世同时代。

⑧ 提库库瓦（Tikkukkuwa）是与一个名为达什马哈（Dasmaha）有关的地方，可能在今土耳其拉辛镇（Laçin）的东边。

all the god]s ran before me and [I defeated] the enemy and destroyed them. I burned down Tikkukkuwa [...]. I also burned the district of Dašma[ha ...]

[I went to ..].-ittakattaša, [and it ...] I attacked. [...], and I [...]-d [...] for the second time(?) [...]

Then I went forth to Išḫupitta. I attacked Palḫuišša. The Pišḫuruan① enemy stood behind Palḫuišša for battle against me. I fought them. The Sungoddess of Arinna, my lady, the victorious Stormgod, my lord, Mezzulla and all the gods ran before me. I destroyed the Pišḫuruan enemy behind Palḫuišša, then I burned down the town.

From Palḫuišša I came back to Ḫattuša. I set my infantry and horse-troops in motion and in that same year I went against Arzawa. I sent a messenger to Uḫḫa-ziti. I wrote to him as follows: "Because I asked you to return my subjects who came to you and you did not give them back and you kept calling me a child and you kept belittling me. Now, come, we will fight. Let the Stormgod, my lord, decide our lawsuit." ②

When I had gone and when I had arrived in Lawaša③, the victorious Stormgod, my lord, showed his divine power. He shot a lightning bolt. My troops saw the lightning bolt and the land of Arzawa saw it. The lightning bolt went and struck Arzawa. It struck Apāša (Ephesus?)④, the city of Uḫḫa-ziti. Uḫḫa-ziti fell on his knees and became ill. When Uḫḫa-ziti became ill, he did not subsequently come against me for battle. (Instead) he sent his son Piyama-^{d}LAMMA⑤ with infantry and horse-troops against me. He stood for battle against me at the Āštarpa River⑥ in Walma⑦. I, My Majesty fought him. The Sungoddess of Arinna, my lady, the victorious Stormgod, my lord, Mezzulla and all the

① 皮什胡鲁安（Pišḫuruan），具体不详。
② 在赫梯人的观念中，国家之间的矛盾是一场诉讼，当协商不成的时候，由神明来裁决。
③ 拉瓦沙（Lawaša）是小亚细亚西南部的一座山，可能是古典文献提及的拉特诺山（Latenos），具体位置不详。
④ 阿帕沙（Apāša），是小阿尔扎瓦的首都，可能是古典时代以弗所。
⑤ 有学者把表意符 ^{d}LAMMA 读作 Kurunta，库伦塔（Kurunta）是小亚细亚的某些族群所崇拜的神明。
⑥ 阿西塔尔帕河（Āštarpa River），可能是今土耳其西南部的米德尔河（Meander River）。
⑦ 瓦尔马（Walma）是阿西塔尔帕河流域的一个地方。

gods ran before me. I defeated Piyama–^{d}LAMMA, son of Uḫḫa–ziti, with his infantry and his horse–troops, and I destroyed them. Then I pursued him and I went across to Arzawa. I went to Apāša into the city of Uḫḫa–ziti. Uḫḫa–ziti did not resist me and fled before me. He went across into the sea by ship(??) to the islands(??). There he remained.

All the land of Arzawa fled. Some (potential) transplantees fled to Mt. Arinnanda① and they held Mt. Arinnanda. Other (potential) transplantees fled to the town of Puranda② and they held Puranda. Yet other (potential) tranplantees fled across into the sea with Uḫḫa–ziti. I, My Majesty, pursued the transplantees on Mt. Arinnanda. I battled Mt. Arinnanda. The Sungoddess of Arinna, my lady, the victorious Stormgod, my lord, Mezzulla and all the gods ran before me. I vanquished Mt. Arinnanda. The transplantees whom I, My Majesty, brought back for the royal estate numbered 15,500. Those whom the Hittite lords, infantry and horse–troops brought back were innumerable. Then I sent the tranplantees to Ḫattuša and they were led away.

When I vanquished Mt. Arinnanda, I returned to the Āštarpa river and at the Āštarpa river I built a walled military camp. There I celebrated the Festival of the Year. All this I did in one year.

Year 4

When it became Spring—as long as Uḫḫa–ziti was sick and was in the midst of sea (i.e. on an island) his sons were with him. Uḫḫa–ziti died in the midst of sea, but his sons split up. One son was still in the midst of the sea, but one, Tapalazunauli, returned from the sea. Since all (remaining) of Arzawa had gone [...] up to Puranda, Tapalazunauli (also) went up to Puranda. When I had taken care of the Festival of the Year, I went to Puranda for battle. Tapalazunauli came down from Puranda with infantry and horse–

① 阿里南达山（Mt. Arinnanda），可能是今小亚细亚的西海岸的米卡莱山（Mykale）。

② 普兰达（Puranda），可能是今小亚细亚西海岸的巴登吉吉丘（Bademgediği Tepe），位于今伊兹密尔东南 40 千米处。参见 Makale Bilgisi, "The Arzawa Lands. The Historical Geography of Izmir and Its Environs During Late Bronze Age in The Light of New Archaeological Research", *Turkish Academy of Sciences Journal of Archaeology*, Issue 27, 2020, pp. 151–157。

troops for battle against me. He stood for battle against me in his own territory①. I, My Majesty, fought him. The Sungoddess of Arinna, my lady, the victorious Stormgod, my lord, Mezzulla and all the gods ran before me. I defeated Tapalazunauli, [son of Uḫḫa-ziti,] and his infantry and horse-troops and destroyed him. Then I pursued him. I went and surrounded Puranda and shut it up; I took away its water.

[When] I had shut up Puranda, Tapalazunauli, son of Uḫḫa-ziti, who was up in Puranda, became afraid. He fled down from Puranda at night. He took charge of [his wife,] his children, and the (potential) transplantees together with (their) provisions; he led them down from Puranda. However, when I, My Majesty, heard: "Tapalazunauli fled down [at night] and he took charge of his wife, his children and the (potential) transplantees together with (their) provisions and led them down," I, My Majesty, sent my infantry and horse-troops after him. They harried Tapalazunauli on the road. They captured his wife, his children, and the transplantees and brought them back. Tapalazunauli escaped alone, a single person. The aforementioned infantry and horse-troops kept for themselves the transplantees whom they had ha[rried] on the road.

When it had come about that I had shut up Puranda for [x] days, I [attack]ed [Puranda. The Sungoddess of Arinna, my lady, the victorious Stormgod,] my [lord,] Mezzulla [and all the gods ran before me.] I vanquished Puranda. [The transplantees whom I, My Majesty, brought back for the royal estate] numbered 16, [X]00. Those [transplantees,] cattle and sheep [which the Hittite lords, infantry and horse-troops brought back] were [innumerable. Then I sent them to Ḫattuša and they] were led away.

[...] was in [the midst of the sea ...Piyama]- ^{d}LA[MMA,] son of Uḫḫa-ziti, [... departed] from the sea [and took refuge(?)] with the king of Aḫḫiyawa② [...] I, [My Majesty] sent [...] by ship, [...-ed ...] and they brought him away. [The transplantees

① 直译为：他的田地和草地。
② 阿黑亚瓦（Aḫḫiyawa），学界对于阿黑亚瓦的位置还有争议，但是，多数学者认为它可能是对古希腊的阿凯亚人（the Archaeans）所居住的土地的称呼。

with him] they also brought away. [The transplantees from ...] and the transplantees from Lipa① consisted of [ ] transplantees. I sent [them to Ḫattuša] and they were led away.

[When] I came back [to the Še]ḫa–[River Land②,] I would have fought [Manapa–Tarḫunta③ who] was [lord] in Šeha–River Land. However, when [Manapa–Tarḫunta] heard about me: "The Hittite king is coming," [he became] afraid and so [he did not] then [come] against me. He sent [to] me his mother and old men and old women. They came and [fell down] at my feet. Because the women fell down at my feet, I had mercy on the women and so I did [not] enter the Šeḫa–River Land. They handed over to me the Hittite transplantees who were in Šeḫa–River Land. There were 4,000 transplantees whom they handed over. I sent them back to Ḫattuša and they led them away. Manapa–Tarḫunta and Šeḫa–River Land I made into my subjects.

Then I went to Mirā ④. I gave Mirā to Mašḫuiluwa⑤; I gave Šeḫa–River Land to Manapa–Tarḫunta; and I gave Ḫapalla⑥ to Targašnalli⑦. I made these lands into my subjects where they were. I imposed military obligations on them and they began to give me troops. Because I wintered within Arzawa, in two years the Sungoddess of Arinna, my lady, the victorious Stormgod, my lord, Mezzulla and all the gods ran before me and I overcame Arzawa. Some (of Arzawa) I brought away to Ḫattuša and some I made into my subjects where they were. I imposed military obligations on them and they began to give me troops. The transplantees whom I, My Majesty, brought back for the royal estates, because I overcame all of Arzawa, numbered all together 66,000. Those whom the Hittite

① 利帕（Lipa）可能是赫梯国的一处地方。

② 塞哈河国（Šeha–River Land），晚期青铜时代小亚细亚西部的国家，位于米拉与维卢沙之间，是大阿尔扎瓦的组成部分之一。

③ 马那帕塔尔浑塔（Manapa–Tarḫunta）是塞哈河国的国王，公元前1322—前1290年在位。

④ 米拉（Mirā），晚期青铜时代小亚细亚西部的国家，位于小阿尔扎瓦以东地区，是大阿尔扎瓦的组成部分之一。

⑤ 马什晖鲁瓦（Mašḫuiluwa）是米拉的国王，公元前1330—前1300年在位。

⑥ 哈帕拉（Ḫapalla）是小亚细亚中部、西部的国家，是大阿尔扎瓦的组成部分之一。

⑦ 塔尔加西那里（Targašnalli）是哈帕拉的国王，公元前1319—前1310年在位。

lords, infantry and horse–troops brought back were innumerable. When I had overcome all of Arzawa, then I came away to Ḫattuša. All this I did in the one year since I had wintered in Arzawa.

Year 5

The next year I went to Mt. Ašḫarpaya①. Since the Kaška had possession of Mt. Ašḫarpaya, they had cut the Pala–roads②. I fought these Kaška of Mt. Ašḫarpaya. The Sungoddess of Arinna, my lady, the victorious Stormgod, my lord, Mezzulla and all the gods ran before me and I overcame Mt. Ašḫarpaya which the Kaška had held. I destroyed it. I emptied Mt. Ašḫarpaya and then departed. When I arrived in Šammaḫa, I entered Ziulila③.

While my father was in Mitanni, the Arawannan enemy by continually attacking Kiššiya④ kept it greatly oppressed. I, My Majesty, went to Arawanna⑤ and attacked Arawanna. The Sungoddess of Arinna, my lady, the victorious Stormgod, my lord, Mezzulla and all the gods ran before me and I overcame all Arawanna. The transplantees whom I brought back from Arawanna for the royal estates numbered 3,500. The transplantees, cattle and sheep that the Hittite lords, infantry and horse–troops brought back were innumerable. When I had overcome Arawanna, then I came back to Ḫattuša. All this I did in one year.

Year 6

The next year I went to Zimurriya⑥. The Kaška who had occupied Mt. Tarikarimu⑦ by force in the time of my grandfather, subsequently became a danger for Hittite

---

① 阿沙尔帕亚山（Mt. Ašḫarpaya），在哈里什河左岸延伸的山脉，在帕拉与沙马哈之间。
② 帕拉路（Pala–roads），可能指的是通往帕拉的道路。
③ 沙马哈（Šammaha）与兹乌里拉（Ziulila）是阿沙尔帕亚山附近的城市。
④ 凯西亚（Kiššiya），可能在今土耳其安卡拉附近。
⑤ 阿拉瓦那（Arawanna）可能是黑海边上的番红花城（Safranbolu）。
⑥ 兹姆里亚（Zimurriya），有学者把此地名读作兹哈里亚（Ziḫarriya），可能是卡什卡的一处地方。
⑦ 塔里卡里姆山（Mt. Tarikarimu），卡什卡人生活地区的山脉。

territory①. They came and attacked Hittite territory and they oppressed it greatly. I, My Majesty went and attacked Mt. Tarikarimu, which the Kaška had occupied. The Sungoddess of Arinna, my lady, the victorious Stormgod, my lord, Mezzulla and all the gods ran before me and I overcame the Kaška of Mt. Tarikarimu and destroyed them. I emptied Mt. Tarikarimu and burned the whole land of Zimurriya. Then I returned to Ḫattuša. All this I did in one year.

II. Common Terms, Words and Phrases for the Text

Great King 大王

Hatti 赫梯

Arzawa 阿尔扎瓦

Levy 征兵服役，应征入伍者

the Upper Land 上地

lightning bolt 闪电

Kaška 卡什卡

III. Exercises and Thinking

1. What was Manapa-Tarḫunta's response in the face of the Hittite army's attack?

2. After defeating Arzawa, how did Muršili II dismember Arzawa?

3. According to the Annal, which deities played a role in the victory of Muršili II's war?

IV. Further Readings and Internet Links

1. Further Readings

Philo H. J. Houwink Ten Cate, "Mursilis' Northwestern Campaigns-Additional Fragments of His Comprehensive Annals," *Journal of Near Eastern Studies*, Vol. 25, No.

① 直译为"哈图萨"，由于该年代记显然用哈图萨来指代赫梯，因此，译者意译为"赫梯的领土"。

3 (Jul., 1966) , pp. 162–191.

Trevor Bryce, *The Kingdom of the Hittites*, New Ed., Oxford and New York: Oxford University Press, 2005.

李政:《赫梯文明与外来文化》，江西人民出版社 1996 年版。

[澳] 特雷弗 · 布赖斯:《安纳托利亚勇士：赫梯人简史》，蒋家瑜译，商务印书馆 2022 年版。

2. Internet Links

The Hittite Grammar Homepage：https://www.assyrianlanguages.org/hittite/index_en.php?page=textes

Unit 13

The Histories
《通史》

古代希腊、罗马重视史学书写，先后出现了一批史学家，如希罗多德、修昔底德、李维、塔西佗等。罗马在地中海地区的扩张给古典史家以很大冲击，从而促使他们去思考记录历史的方式与内容。波利比乌斯（前 200—前 118）就是此类史家中的佼佼者。他的代表作《通史》是一部世界史，他把它称为“普遍的历史”。他说，“之前的世界历史都是分散的，因为所有的事件都没有形成统一的整体，换言之，从成因到结果，它们都是局部性的。但是，从现在开始，历史变成了有机的整体”。

波利比乌斯的《通史》共有 40 卷，现在残留 5 卷。在《通史》开篇，波利比乌斯申明他主要叙述公元前 220—前 168 年的历史，但是，事实上他从第一次布匿战争（爆发于公元前 264 年）开始写起。他之所以把公元前 220 年作为叙述起点，在于“意大利和利比亚的事件同希腊和亚洲的那些事件相勾连，所有的事件都通往一个单向的结果。这就是为什么我要从这个时间开始我的历史写作。因为，正是由于罗马人在这场汉尼拔战争中打败了迦太基人，罗马人方才开始相信，自己征服世界的计划迈出了最为关键和最为困难的一步，由此，他们第一次开始将自己的双手伸向其他地方和跨海挥军希腊与亚洲大陆”。具体而言，《通史》记录了公元前 3 世纪、前 2 世纪罗马在地中海的崛起的历史，详细记录了意大利、伊比利亚、希腊、马其顿、叙利亚、埃及和非洲发生的事件，并记载了布匿战争和马其顿战争等许多事件。

波利比乌斯的《通史》之所以重要，与波利比乌斯对罗马宪政的分析、研究是分不开的。波利比乌斯对罗马从蕞尔小邦发展成为地中海的主人惊异不已，为此试图探讨罗马称霸地中海的原因。他认为，罗马强盛起来的真正原因是罗马政治制度具有优越性。在《通史》第六卷中，波利比乌斯论述了罗马的政治制度，认为罗马共和国本质上是混合宪制，这是一种成熟、稳固且优良的政体制度，正是在这种制度下，罗马取得了一场又一场战争的胜利，最终成为地中海的霸主。有学者认为，波利比乌斯对罗马共和国政府权力分立、权力的制衡机制进行了探讨，对孟德斯鸠的《论法的精神》、洛克的《政府论》，以及美国宪法的制定者产生了影响。这里选取的内容出自波利比乌斯《通史》的佩顿（Paton）英译本。

I. Text①

11. From the crossing of Xerxes to Greece...② and for thirty years after this period, it was always one of those polities which was an object of special study, and it was at its best and nearest to perfection at the time of the Hannibalic war③, the period at which I interrupted my narrative to deal with it. Therefore now that I have described its growth, I will explain what were the conditions at the time when by their defeat at Cannae the Romans were brought face to face with disaster.

I am quite aware that to those who have been born and bred under the Roman Republic my account of it will seem somewhat imperfect owing to the omission of certain details. For as they have complete knowledge of it and practical acquaintance with all its parts, having been familiar with these customs and institutions from childhood, they will not be struck by the extent of the information I give but will demand in addition all I have omitted: they will not think that the author has purposely omitted small peculiarities,

---

① Polybius, *The Histories*, Volume III, trans. by W. R. Paton, Cambridge, Massachusetts: Harvard University Press, London: William Heinemann Ltd., 1923, pp. 293-311.

② 此处文字损毁。

③ 即第二次布匿战争。

but that owing to ignorance he has been silent regarding the origins of many things and some points of capital importance. Had I mentioned them, they would not have been impressed by my doing so, regarding them as small and trivial points, but as they are omitted they will demand their inclusion as if they were vital matters, through a desire themselves to appear better informed than the author. Now a good critic should not judge authors by what they omit, but by what they relate, and if he finds any falsehood in this, he may conclude that the omissions are due to ignorance; but if all the writer says is true, he should admit that he has been silent about these matters deliberately and not from ignorance.

These remarks are meant for those who find fault with authors in a cavilling rather than just spirit...

In so far as any view of a matter we form applies to the right occasion, so far expressions of approval or blame are sound. When circumstances change, and when applied to these changed conditions, the most excellent and true reflections of authors seem often not only not acceptable, but utterly offensive...

The three kinds of government that I spoke of above all shared in the control of the Roman state. And such fairness and propriety in all respects was shown in the use of these three elements for drawing up the constitution and in its subsequent administration that it was impossible even for a native to pronounce with certainty whether the whole system was aristocratic, democratic, or monarchical. This was indeed only natural. For if one fixed one's eyes on the power of the consuls, the constitution seemed completely monarchical and royal; if on that of the senate it seemed again to be aristocratic; and when one looked at the power of the masses, it seemed clearly to be a democracy. The parts of the state falling under the control of each element were and with a few modifications still are as follows.

12. The consuls, previous to leading out their legions, exercise authority in Rome over all public affairs, since all the other magistrates except the tribunes are under

them and bound to obey them, and it is they who introduce embassies to the senate. Besides this it is they who consult the senate on matters of urgency, they who carry out in detail the provisions of its decrees. Again as concerns all affairs of state administered by the people it is their duty to take these under their charge, to summon assemblies, to introduce measures, and to preside over the execution of the popular decrees. As for preparation for war and the general conduct of operations in the field, here their power is almost uncontrolled; for they are empowered to make what demands they choose on the allies, to appoint military tribunes, to levy soldiers and select those who are fittest for service. They also have the right of inflicting, when on active service, punishment on anyone under their command; and they are authorized to spend any sum they decide upon from the public funds, being accompanied by a quaestor who faithfully executes their instructions. So that if one looks at this part of the administration alone, one may reasonably pronounce the constitution to be a pure monarchy or kingship. I may remark that any changes in these matters or in others of which I am about to speak that may be made in present or future times do not in any way affect the truth of the views I here state.

13. To pass to the senate. In the first place it has the control of the treasury, all revenue and expenditure being regulated by it. For with the exception of payments made to the consuls, the quaestors are not allowed to disburse for any particular object without a decree of the senate. And even the item of expenditure which is far heavier and more important than any other—the outlay every five years by the censors on public works, whether constructions or repairs—is under the control of the senate, which makes a grant to the censors for the purpose. Similarly crimes committed in Italy which require a public investigation, such as treason, conspiracy, poisoning, and assassination, are under the jurisdiction of the senate. Also if any private person or community in Italy is in need of arbitration or indeed claims damages or requires succour or protection, the senate attends to all such matters. It also occupies itself with the dispatch of all embassies sent

to countries outside of Italy for the purpose either of settling differences, or of offering friendly advice, or indeed of imposing demands, or of receiving submission, or of declaring war; and in like manner with respect to embassies arriving in Rome it decides what reception and what answer should be given to them. All these matters are in the hands of the senate, nor have the people anything whatever to do with them. So that again to one residing in Rome during the absence of the consuls the constitution appears to be entirely aristocratic; and this is the conviction of many Greek states and many of the kings, as the senate manages all business connected with them.

14. After this we are naturally inclined to ask what part in the constitution is left for the people, considering that the senate controls all the particular matters I mentioned, and, what is most important, manages all matters of revenue and expenditure, and considering that the consuls again have uncontrolled authority as regards armaments and operations in the field. But nevertheless there is a part and a very important part left for the people. For it is the people which alone has the right to confer honours and inflict punishment, the only bonds by which kingdoms and states and in a word human society in general are held together. For where the distinction between these is overlooked or is observed but ill applied, no affairs can be properly administered. How indeed is this possible when good and evil men are held in equal estimation? It is by the people, then, in many cases that offences punishable by a fine are tried when the accused have held the highest office; and they are the only court which may try on capital charges. As regards the latter they have a practice which is praiseworthy and should be mentioned. Their usage allows those on trial for their lives when found guilty liberty to depart openly, thus inflicting voluntary exile on themselves, if even only one of the tribes that pronounce the verdict has not yet voted. Such exiles enjoy safety in the territories of Naples, Praeneste, Tibur, and other *civitates foederatae*. Again it is the people who bestow office on the deserving, the noblest reward of virtue in a state; the people have the power of approving or rejecting laws, and what is most important of all, they deliberate on the

question of war and peace. Further in the case of alliances, terms of peace, and treaties, it is the people who ratify all these or the reverse. Thus here again one might plausibly say that the people's share in the government is the greatest, and that the constitution is a democratic one.

15. Having stated how political power is distributed among the different parts of the state, I will now explain how each of the three parts is enabled, if they wish, to counteract or co–operate with the others. The consul, when he leaves with his army invested with the powers I mentioned, appears indeed to have absolute authority in all matters necessary for carrying out his purpose; but in fact he requires the support of the people and the senate, and is not able to bring his operations to a conclusion without them. For it is obvious that the legions require constant supplies, and without the consent of the senate, neither corn, clothing, nor pay can be provided; so that the commander's plans come to nothing, if the senate chooses to be deliberately negligent and obstructive. It also depends on the senate whether or not a general can carry out completely his conceptions and designs, since it has the right of either superseding him when his year's term of office has expired or of retaining him in command. Again it is in its power to celebrate with pomp and to magnify the successes of a general or on the other hand to obscure and belittle them. For the processions they call triumphs, in which the generals bring the actual spectacle of their achievements before the eyes of their fellow–citizens, cannot be properly organized and sometimes even cannot be held at all, unless the senate consents and provides the requisite funds. As for the people it is most indispensable for the consuls to conciliate them, however far away from home they may be; for, as I said, it is the people which ratifies or annuls terms of peace and treaties, and what is most important, on laying down office the consuls are obliged to account for their actions to the people. So that in no respect is it safe for the consuls to neglect keeping in favour with both the senate and the people.

16. The senate again, which possesses such great power, is obliged in the first place to pay attention to the commons in public affairs and respect the wishes of the people,

and it cannot carry out inquiries into the most grave and important offences against the state, punishable with death, and their correction, unless the *senatus consultum* is confirmed by the people. The same is the case in matters which directly affect the senate itself. For if anyone introduces a law meant to deprive the senate of some of its traditional authority, or to abolish the precedence and other distinctions of the senators or even to curtail them of their private fortunes, it is the people alone which has the power of passing or rejecting any such measure. And what is most important is that if a single one of the tribunes interposes, the senate is unable to decide finally about any matter, and cannot even meet and hold sittings; and here it is to be observed that the tribunes are always obliged to act as the people decree and to pay every attention to their wishes. Therefore for all these reasons the senate is afraid of the masses and must pay due attention to the popular will.

17. Similarly, again, the people must be submissive to the senate and respect its members both in public and in private. Through the whole of Italy a vast number of contracts, which it would not be easy to enumerate, are given out by the censors for the construction and repair of public buildings, and besides this there are many things which are farmed, such as navigable rivers, harbours, gardens, mines, lands, in fact everything that forms part of the Roman dominion. Now all these matters are undertaken by the people, and one may almost say that everyone is interested in these contracts and the work they involve. For certain people are the actual purchasers from the censors of the contracts, others are the partners of these first, others stand surety for them, others pledge their own fortunes to the state for this purpose. Now in all these matters the senate is supreme. It can grant extension of time; it can relieve the contractor if any accident occurs; and if the work proves to be absolutely impossible to carry out it can liberate him from his contract. There are in fact many ways in which the senate can either benefit or injure those who manage public property, as all these matters are referred to it. What is even more important is that the judges in most civil trials, whether public or private, are

appointed from its members, where the action involves large interests. So that all citizens being at the mercy of the senate, and looking forward with alarm to the uncertainty of litigation, are very shy of obstructing or resisting its decisions. Similarly everyone is reluctant to oppose the projects of the consuls as all are generally and individually under their authority when in the field.

18. Such being the power that each part has of hampering the others or co-operating with them, their union is adequate to all emergencies, so that it is impossible to find a better political system than this. For whenever the menace of some common danger from abroad compels them to act in concord and support each other, so great does the strength of the state become, that nothing which is requisite can be neglected, as all are zealously competing in devising means of meeting the need of the hour, nor can any decision arrived at fail to be executed promptly, as all are co-operating both in public and in private to the accomplishment of the task they have set themselves; and consequently this peculiar form of constitution possesses an irresistible power of attaining every object upon which it is resolved. When again they are freed from external menace, and reap the harvest of good fortune and affluence which is the result of their success, and in the enjoyment of this prosperity are corrupted by flattery and idleness and wax insolent and overbearing, as indeed happens often enough, it is then especially that we see the state providing itself a remedy for the evil from which it suffers. For when one part having grown out of proportion to the others aims at supremacy and tends to become too predominant, it is evident that, as for the reasons above given none of the three is absolute, but the purpose of the one can be counterworked and thwarted by the others, none of them will excessively outgrow the others or treat them with contempt. All in fact remains in *statu quo*, on the one hand, because any aggressive impulse is sure to be checked and from the outset each estate stands in dread of being interfered with by the others...①

① 此处文字损毁。

II. Common Terms, Words and Phrases for the Text

Xerxes 薛西斯

the Hannibalic war 汉尼拔战争

Cannae 坎尼

aristocratic 贵族制的

democratic 民主制的

monarchical 君主制的

consul 执政官

senate 元老院

masse 民众

legion 军团

magistrate 官员

tribune 保民官

military tribune 军事保民官

quaestor 行政官

monarchy 君主，王

kingship 王权，王政

treasury 国库

senatus consultum 元老院建议

statu quo 现状

III. Exercises and Thinking

1. What was the role of consuls in the Roman constitution?

2. How did the Roman Senate exert its influence over the governmental affairs?

3. How do the consuls, the senate, and the people in ancient Rome counterbalance each other's powers?

IV. Further Readings and Internet Links

1. Further Readings

F. W. Walbank, "Polybius on the Roman Constitution," *The Classical Quarterly*, Vol. 37, No. 3/4 (Jul. – Oct., 1943), pp. 73–89.

[古罗马]波利比乌斯:《通史》上卷，杨之涵译，上海三联书店 2021 年版。

晏绍祥:《希腊城邦民主与罗马共和政治》，人民出版社 2019 年版。

2. Internet Links

POLYBIUS, THE HISTORIES: https://www.perseus.tufts.edu/hopper/text?doc=Perseus:text:1999.01.0234

Unit 14

The Grand Scribe's Records

《史记》

《史记》是中国古代史学的一座丰碑，由西汉著名史学家司马迁所著，是中国历史上第一部纪传体通史。《史记》主要由本纪、表、书、世家和列传五部分组成，其中的“十二本纪”记录了历代帝王的事迹，“十表”系统地编排了历史事件，“八书”记载了各种制度的变化，“三十世家”叙述了诸侯国的历史，而“七十列传”则是对个人事迹的记载。这样的结构设计使得《史记》既详尽又系统，被后人誉为“史家之绝唱，无韵之离骚”。

《淮阴侯列传》是《史记》列传中比较重要的一篇，描述了韩信辉煌而又悲剧的一生。韩信早年穷困潦倒，后投身项羽麾下未被重用，之后韩信改投刘邦军中，最终被刘邦拜为大将军。在楚汉之争的过程中，韩信以其杰出的军事才能横扫魏、赵、代、燕、齐诸国，最终打败项羽，帮助刘邦统一天下。在此过程中，韩信的军事天赋发挥到了极致，在楚汉蒲坂之战中，他以声东击西之计拿下魏都安邑；在井陉之战中，背水一战，大破赵军；在潍水之战中，水淹齐楚联军，斩杀楚将龙且；在垓下之战中，布五军阵诱敌，击破项羽军，最终迫使项羽自刎于乌江。最后，韩信被吕后与萧何合谋杀死于长乐宫，并被诛三族。

在该列传中，除了刻画韩信的才能外，司马迁还对韩信的性格作了描述，比如，隐忍，年轻时受胯下之辱；居功自傲，在灭魏、徇赵、胁燕、定齐之后，派人向刘邦上书，挟制刘邦当上齐王；不知进退，韩信被贬为淮阴侯后，怨恨刘邦而常常装病不参加朝见或跟随出行；知恩图报，回报年少时帮助过他的南昌亭长与漂母。

I. Text[1]

When Xiang Liang (d. 208 B.C.) crossed the Huai River, [Han] Xin grasped his sword to follow him. He stayed [as a subordinate] under his banner [but] there was nothing for which his name could become known. After Xiang Liang was defeated and he then attached himself to Xiang Yü (232 B.C.–202 B.C.); [Xiang] Yü made him a Palace Attendant[2]. He approached Xiang Yü several times with strategies, but [Xiang] Yü did not employ them. When the King of Han entered Shu, [Han] Xin fled Chu and went over to Han. He was not yet able to make his name known and served as Marshal [Director of Guests][3]. He had broken the law and was about to be beheaded. The thirteen [other] people of his group had been beheaded. Next came [Han] Xin. Just then [Han] Xin looked up and saw the Magistrate of Teng[4]; he said, "Doesn't the Sovereign want to attain the world? Why does he behead a robust man?" The Magistrate of Teng, considering his words extraordinary and his appearance robust, set him free and did not behead him. He talked with him and was greatly pleased with him. He reported to the Sovereign and the Sovereign appointed him to be Chief Commandant of Millet[5]. The Sovereign still did not consider him extraordinary.

[Han] Xin spoke with Xiao He (d. 193 B.C.) several times and [Xiao] He considered him extraordinary. When they came to Nan-zheng[6], those commanders[7] who had fled on the way were several dozen. [Han] Xin speculated that "[Xiao] He and others must

---

① 本文选自 Ssm-ma Ch'en, *The Grand Scribe's Records*, Vol. VIII, Part I, ed. by William H. Nienhauser, Bloomington & Indianapolis: Indiana University Press, 2008, pp. 71–88。由于原文对于专有名词尤其是人名、地名采用了韦氏拼音，阅读起来多有不便，故改为汉语拼音，原文在人名、地名后面往往标注有中文繁体字词，出于练习英文的考虑，对其作了删除。

② 原文为“郎中”。

③ 原文为“连敖”。

④ 滕公，指的是汉朝开国功臣夏侯婴，他早年曾为滕县县令驾驶马车，人称“滕公”。

⑤ 原文为“治粟都尉”。

⑥ 南郑，今陕西省汉中市南郑。

⑦ 原文为“诸将”。

have talked [about me] to the Sovereign several times and the Sovereign did not employ me," thus he fled. When [Xiao] He heard that [Han] Xin had fled, he was not able to [let the Sovereign] know it in time and chased after him in person. There was a person who talked of this to the Sovereign, saying "Chancellor① He has fled." The Sovereign was enraged as if he had lost his left and right hands. Staying [away] for a day or two, [Xiao] He came to pay a visit to the Sovereign. The Sovereign, angry and pleased at the same time, reviled [Xiao] He: "You fled, why?" [Xiao] He said, "Your servant② dares not flee. Your servant chased after a person who fled." The Sovereign said, "Who was the person you chased after?" [Xiao] He said, "It was Han Xin." The Sovereign again reviled him: "The number of commanders who have fled numbered in the dozens and you did not chase any of them. [To claim] that you chased after [Han] Xin is deception." [Xiao] He said, "Commanders are easy to attain. As far as [Han] Xin is concerned, he is a warrior for the state③ with no match. [If] Your Majesty④ indeed wants to rule Han–zhong as a king for a long time, there is no reason to involve [Han] Xin in the affairs. [If] you indeed want to contend for the world, besides [Han] Xin, there is no one with whom [you] could plan affairs. It is merely a matter of what Your Majesty decides?" The King said, "I indeed want to go east. How can I stay here pent up for a long time?" [Xiao] He said, "As your Majesty plans that you indeed want to head east, if you can make good use of [Han] Xin, [Han] Xin will stay; if you cannot make good use of him, [Han] Xin will in the end flee." The King said, "I will make him a commander⑤ for your sake." [Xiao] He said, "Even if he becomes a commander, [Han] Xin surely will not stay." The King said, "I will make him Commander–in–chief⑥." [Xiao] He said, "This would be auspicious in the

① 原文为"丞相"。
② 原文为"臣"。
③ 原文为"国士"。
④ 原文为"王"。
⑤ 原文为"将"。
⑥ 原文为"大将"。

extreme!" At this the King intended to summon [Han] Xin and appoint him. [Xiao] He said, "Your Majesty has always been haughty and without social norms. Now, to appoint him Commander–in–chief is like calling a little child. This is why [Han] Xin left. If Your Majesty indeed wants to appoint him, choose an auspicious day, fast and purify yourself, set up the altar platform and provide the rituals, then it would be permissible." The King consented to it. The commanders were all pleased. Every person thought he himself would obtain the [position of] Commander–in–chief. When the time came to appoint the Commander–in–chief, and it was Han Xin, the entire army was all astonished.

When the ritual for appointing [Han] Xin was completed, he was seated at the place of honor. The King said, "The chancellor talked about you, General, several times. General, how will you teach us planning and strategy?" [Han] Xin was apologetic, taking advantage to ask the King, "Now isn't it the one who contends for the power of the world in the east districts King Xiang?" The King of Han said, "It is so." [Han] Xin said, "Great King, between King Xiang and yourself, whom do you consider more valiant, ferocious, benevolent and strong?" The King of Han kept silent for quite a while and [finally] said, "I am inferior to him." [Han] Xin knelt down, bowed his head twice and said approvingly, "Yes. I also think you, the Great King, are inferior [to him]. However, I used to serve him. I would like to tell you what kind of person King Xiang is. When King Xiang shouts furiously, a thousand people all crouch down. However, he cannot appoint and assign worthy commanders. This is just the courage of an ordinary man. When King Xiang receives someone, he is respectful and affectionate and his words are gentle. When people fall ill, he weeps and shares his food and drink. When it comes to people who are employed and possess merit and should be enfeoffed and ennobled, [he plays with] the seal [of office until] it is worn and cannot bear to give it away. This is what is called the benevolence of a woman. Although King Xiang holds hegemony over the world and has made subjects of the feudal lords[①], he does not reside within the passes but has made

① 原文为"诸侯"。

Peng-cheng[①] the capital. He violated the covenant with Yi di[②] (The Righteousness Emperor, d. 205 B.C.) and enthroned those who were on intimate terms with and were liked by him as kings. The feudal lords felt unjustified. When the feudal lords saw King Xiang move and expel Yi di, settling him in the south of the Jiang[③], they all returned to expel their masters and enthroned themselves as kings in good regions. None of the places King Xiang passed were not harmed or destroyed. The world resented it very much and the people did not attach [themselves] to him with affection, [but] were only forced by his might and strength. Although in name he is the Hegemon[④], in fact he has lost the hearts of the world. For this reason I say that his might is easily weakened. [If] now you, Great King, can really reverse his way: Appoint the martial and courageous people in the world, who could not be executed! Enfeoff meritorious vassals with cities and towns of the world, who could not be subdued! With [your] righteous soldiers, follow the officers longing to return east, who could not be routed! Furthermore, the kings of the Three-qin[⑤] were the commanders of Qin and had commanded the young men of Qin for several years. Those who have been killed and fled could not be counted. They further cheated their host to surrender to the feudal lords. On reaching Xin-an[⑥], King Xiang deceived and buried alive over 200,000 soldiers of Qin who had surrendered, with only [Zhang] Han, [Si-ma] Xin and [Dong] Yi able to be spared. The fathers and elder brothers of Qin resented these three persons so much that the pain penetrated into the marrow of their bones. Now Chu enthroned these three persons through its might; but none of the

---

① 彭城，今徐州一带。

② 义帝，是秦朝末年的政治人物、楚国宗室，楚怀王之孙，后受原楚国贵族项梁拥立为反秦的起义军领袖之一，他袭用祖父的称号“楚怀王”。秦亡后，项羽尊称他为楚义帝。

③ 原文为“江南”。

④ 原文为“霸”。

⑤ 项羽把陕西的关中和陕北一分为三：封秦降将章邯为雍王，都废丘（今东马坊村遗址），辖咸阳以西及甘肃东部地区；封司马欣为塞王，都栎阳（今西安阎良附近），辖咸阳以东；封董翳为翟王，都高奴（城址史有三说：富县、安塞、延安），辖陕北。这样，陕西有了“三秦”的称呼。

⑥ 新安，今洛阳以西 40 千米之处。

Qin people love them. When you, Great King, entered the Wu Pass[①], you did not harm even a single hair. You did away with the cruel laws of Qin, making an agreement with the Qin people and enacted legal system of three articles. There are none of the Qin people who do not want to have you, Great King, serve as the King of Qin. According to the agreement among the feudal lords, you, Great King, should be King of the land within the Passes, people of the land within the Passes all know it. When you lost the position and entered Han–zhong, there were none of the Qin people who did not regret it. Now, Great King, you rise up and move east, the Three–qin could be pacified with the delivery of a proclamation." At this, the King of Han was greatly pleased and thought to himself that he had been late in obtaining [Han] Xin. Then he followed [Han] Xin's plan, arranging and deploying what the commanders were about to attack.

In the eighth month, the King of Han raised troops and moved east out of Chen–cang[②], stabilizing the Three–qin.

In the second year of Han (205 B.C.), [the King of Han] went out through the [Han–gu] Pass[③] and took Wei and He–nan. The kings of Han[④] and Yin[⑤] both surrendered. [The King of Han] joined with Qi and Zhao to assault Chu together. In the fourth month, reaching Peng–cheng, the Han troops were defeated, dispersed and returned [to the west]. [Han] Xin further collected troops and joined the King of Han at Xing–yang[⑥], again assaulting and destroying Chu between Jing[⑦] and Suo[⑧]. For this reason, the Chu troops could not in the end move west.

---

① 武关，秦国的四大关之一，是关中通向南阳盆地的重要关口。
② 陈仓，今陕西宝鸡以东 8 千米处。从宝鸡到汉中的陈仓道，是古代连接关中与川蜀的重要通道。
③ 函谷关，秦国的四大关之一，今河南省三门峡市灵宝市函谷关镇王垛村。
④ 郑昌，本为秦会稽郡吴县的县令，后项羽杀死韩王成后，改立郑昌为韩王，令他对抗刘邦。
⑤ 司马卬，本为秦末赵王武臣的部将，后项羽分封十八路诸侯，因司马卬平定河内有功，而被封为殷王，封地河内郡，建都朝歌城。
⑥ 荥阳，即今荥阳，位于河南省郑州市西北 15 千米处。
⑦ 京，古代荥阳以南的县。
⑧ 索，古代荥阳以南的地方。

[When the King of] Han was defeated at and retreated from Peng–cheng. [Si–ma] Xin, the King of Sai, and [Dong] Yi, the King of Di, fled from Han and surrendered to Chu. Qi and Zhao also rebelled against Han and made peace with Chu. In the sixth month, [Wei] Bao①, the King of Wei, visited [the King of Han] and returned home to see to his parent's health. On reaching his state, he immediately cut off the pass on the He, rebelled against Han, and made a peace agreement with Chu. The King of Han sent Scholar Li② to persuade Bao, but he could not make him surrender. In its eighth month, [the King of Han] appointed [Han] Xin Chancellor of the Left③ to assault Wei. The King of Wei massed his troops at Pu–ban④, and blocked off [the He River at] Lin–jin⑤, [Han] Xin then gradually set up decoy troops, and displayed boats [as if he] intended to cross at Lin–jin, but his ambushing troops crossed [the River] at Xia–yang⑥ using wood jars⑦ and made a surprise attack on An–yi. Bao, the King of Wei, was surprised and led troops to meet [Han] Xin. [Han] Xin then captured [Wei] Bao and stabilized Wei as He–dong Commandery⑧. The King of Han dispatched Zhang Er⑨ to join together with [Han] Xin, to lead the troops and move east to assault Zhao and Dai⑩ in the north. In the intercalary month after the ninth month, they defeated the troops of Dai and caught Xia

---

① 魏豹，原魏国公子，其兄魏咎被陈胜尊为魏王，魏咎死后魏豹投靠项羽，后被项羽立为魏王。

② 原文为“郦生”，即郦食其，他是秦末楚汉时期儒生，多被称作“郦生”，自刘邦攻打陈留起追随刘邦，为刘邦灭楚建汉做出了重大贡献。

③ 原文为“左丞相”。

④ 蒲阪位于黄河东岸。

⑤ 临晋位于黄河西岸。

⑥ 夏阳，可能在黄河西岸的蒲阪以北的 80 千米处，在今陕西韩城市古少梁遗址。

⑦ 原文为“木罂缶”。

⑧ 原文为“河东郡”。

⑨ 张耳，少时为魏国信陵君的门客，后参加陈胜、吴广起义，被任命为校尉，与陈馀共立武臣为赵王，自任丞相。公元前 206 年，项羽分封诸侯时，张耳被立为常山王，定都襄国。公元前 205 年，因受陈馀、田荣的袭击，遂归附汉王刘邦。公元前 204 年，张耳和韩信攻破赵国井陉，在泜水河畔杀死陈馀，追杀赵王歇。公元前 203 年，汉王封张耳为赵王。次年，张耳逝世，谥号景王。

⑩ 陈馀打败张耳后，占据了赵地，立赵歇为赵王，赵歇封陈馀为代王。

Yüe① at Yü-yü②. As soon as [Han] Xin subdued Wei and defeated Dai, [The King of] Han sent someone to collect his picked troops, to go to Xing-yang to resist Chu.

[Han] Xin and Zhang Er, with tens of thousands of soldiers, intended to move east to go down Jing-xing Mountain③ and attack Zhao. The King of Zhao and Chen Yü④, the Lord of Cheng-an⑤, learning that Han was about to make a surprise attack on them, gathered troops at the Jing-xing Pass⑥ and claimed to have 200,000 soldiers. Li Zuo-che⑦, the Lord of Guang-wu, tried to persuade the Lord of Cheng-an, saying, "I have heard that Han Xin, a general of Han, waded across the Western He, took the King of Wei prisoner, caught Xia Yüe, and recently spilled blood at Yü-yü. Now, aided by Zhang Er, he discusses intending to subdue Zhao. In this [situation], having left his own state and fighting far from home, following up on a victory, his vanguard could not be resisted. I have heard that if provisions are transported from a distance of a thousand *li*⑧, the soldiers will have a look of hunger on their faces, and if they cook only after chopping firewood and cutting grass, the troops will not go to sleep with full stomachs. Now on the road through Jing-xing, two carriages cannot move alongside each other and cavalry cannot ride abreast. Advancing for hundreds of *li*, the circumstances will be such that the provisions must be following after them [the army]. I hope you, Honorable Sir⑨, will lend me 30,000 ambuscaders and from an unfrequented route I will cut off his supplies and gear. You, Honorable Sir, dig deep trenches, construct high barricades, strengthen the camp and do not give them battle. They will not be able to fight when they advance and

---

① 夏说，楚汉之争时陈馀的属下，曾经成功说服齐王田荣协助陈馀击败常山王张耳，后被陈馀派到代国做相国，在韩信击垮代军后，他被韩信俘虏。
② 阏与，可能在今山西省晋中市和顺县一带。
③ 今河北石家庄西北的井陉。
④ 陈馀，秦末大梁（今河南开封）人，代王兼赵国太傅，井陉之战失败后，被韩信杀死。
⑤ 原文为“成安君”。
⑥ 井陉口，为太行八陉的第五陉的东出口。
⑦ 李左车，赵国名将李牧之孙。秦末天下大乱，李左车辅佐赵王歇，因赫赫战功被赵王封为广武君。
⑧ 原文为“千里”。
⑨ 原文为“足下”。

not able to return [to their base] when they retreat. My ambuscaders will cut off their rear, leaving nothing in the fields to be plundered. In less than ten days, the heads of the two commanders could be presented under your banners. I hope Your Lordship① will give heed to my plan. Otherwise, you will for sure be caught by [those] two men." The Lord of Cheng-an was a *ju* scholar② and had always claimed that righteous troops should not employ deceptive strategies and plans for ambush. He said, "I have heard that in military precepts [if one's troops are] ten times [the enemy's], then besiege them; if double, then fight them. Now Han Xin's troops are said to be tens of thousands. In fact, they are no more than several thousand. They have come a thousand *li* to attack us and must be extremely exhausted. Now if we avoid them and do not attack like this, later when there will be a larger force, how can we overcome it? Then the feudal lords③ will consider me cowardly and will readily launch an attack against me." He did not listen to the plan of the Lord of Guang-wu; the Lord of Guang-wu's plan was not used.

When Han Xin sent someone to spy on them, he learned that it [the plan] was not being used and returned to report this. Greatly pleased, only then did [Han Xin] venture to lead [his] troops down [out of Zhao]. When they were still thirty *li* from the Mouth of Jing-xing [Pass], they stopped and rested. In the middle of the night the command to set out was transmitted. He chose two thousand light cavalry, the men each holding a red guidon. They took a backroad and hid in the hills, looking down at the troops of Zhao. [Han Xin] instructed them saying, "Once [the troops of] Zhao see us retreat, they will definitely vacate their barricades and pursue us. You enter the barricades of Zhao quickly, pull out the guidons of Zhao and set up the red guidons of Han." He ordered his adjutant general④ to pass out light meals⑤ and said, "Today we will defeat Zhao

① 原文为"君"。
② 原文为"儒者"。
③ 原文为"诸侯"。
④ 原文为"裨将"。
⑤ 原文为"飧"。

and feast together!" None of the various commanders believed him, but pretended to by reply, "Right!" [Han Xin] said to the military officials, "Zhao has already taken the advantageous location to be their barricades. Furthermore, they have not seen the flags and drums of [your] Commander–in–chief and they will not assault the vanguard of our troops out of fear that we, on reaching defiles and obstacles, would return [to Zhao]." [Han] Xin then sent ten thousand men to advance first; they went out [of the Jing–xing Pass] and drew up in array with their backs against the river[①]. The troops of Zhao looked out and saw this and laughed uproariously. At dawn, [Han] Xin set up the flags and drums of Commander–in–chief and marched out of the Jing–xing Pass to the beating of drums. [The troops of Zhao] opened their barricades and assaulted them, fighting violently for a long time. At this, [Han] Xin and Zhang Er pretended to abandon their drums and flags and ran to the troops beside the river. The troops at the river opened [the barricades] and let them enter. They fought fiercely again [with the troops of Zhao]. As expected, [the troops of] Zhao vacated their barricades, contested for the drums and flags of Han and pursued Han Xin and Zhang Er. Han Xin and Zhang Er had already joined the army beside the river. The army fought desperately and could not be defeated. The two thousand horsemen waiting in ambush dispatched by Han Xin, waited together until the troops of Zhao vacated their barricades to pursue the trophies, riding into the barricades of Zhao, they pulled out all of their flags and set up two thousand red guidons of Han. The Zhao army had already lost a victory and could not catch [Han] Xin and the others. They wanted to withdrew and return to their barricades; their barricades were filled with the red guidons of Han. They were shocked and believed Han had already caught all the commanders of the King of Zhao. Then the soldiers fell into disorder and ran in flight. Although the commanders of Zhao cut down some, they could not stop them. At this, the soldiers of Han attacked from both sides, completely defeating and taking captive the

① 这里的河是绵蔓河，是滹沱河的支流。

troops of Zhao. They beheaded the Lord of Cheng-an at the Zhi River① and captured Xie, the King of Zhao.

[Han] Xin then ordered the army not to kill the Lord of Guang-wu. He would pay a thousand [pieces of] gold to buy him from anyone who caught him alive. At this, there was someone who tied up the Lord of Guang-wu and presented him under the banners. [Han] Xin then loosened his fetters, had the Lord of Guang-wu sit facing east. He himself sat facing west and treated him like a teacher.

After the various commanders presented the heads [of the enemies] and the captives, they all offered their congratulations. They took the advantage to ask [Han] Xin and said, "The *Art of War* says 'keep the hills to your right and your back; keep the waters to the front or at your left.' Now you, General, on the contrary ordered your subjects to draw up in array with our backs against the river and said, 'We will defeat Zhao and feast together.' Your servants were not convinced. However, we won with this in the end. What strategy was this?" [Han] Xin said, "This is in *The Art of War*, however, you gentlemen did not notice it. Doesn't *The Art of War* say 'They will survive after being trapped in a fatal situation and will live on after being placed in a hopeless position?' Furthermore, I do not have well-trained officers. This is what is called 'drive the street rabble and have them fight.' The circumstances were that I had to put them in a fatal situation and made every person fight for his life. If I had put them in a safe situation, they would have had already run away. How could they have been held and employed?" The various commanders were all convinced and said, "Well put. It is of [a level] that we could not reach."

At this, [Han] Xin asked the Lord of Guang-wu and said, "Your humble servant② wants to go north and attack Yan③ and go east to attack Qi. How can I attain merit?"

---

① 原文为"泜水"，这是滹沱河的另外一条支流，即泜河。

② 原文为"仆"。

③ 公元前206年，项羽把原燕国一分为二，立臧荼为燕王，改封原燕王韩广为辽东王。

The Lord of Guang–wu declined and said, "I have heard that a commander of a defeated army was not eligible to discuss bravery and a minister of a subjugated state was not eligible to plan for its survival. Now I am a captive of defeat and subjugation. How can I be eligible to weigh important issues?" [Han] Xin said, "Your humble servant heard that when Bai–li Xi stayed in Yü, Yü was destroyed; but when he was in Qin, Qin became the Hegemon. It is not that he was foolish in Yü but wise in Qin. It is a matter of being made use of and listened to or not. If the Lord of Cheng-an had indeed listened to your plan, Honorable Sir, people like me would also have had been taken captives. Since he did not employ you, Honorable Sir, I could wait on you." [Han Xin] took advantage to question him insistently, "I will follow your plan wholeheartedly. I hope you, Honorable Sir, will not decline [to advise me]." The Lord of Guang-wu said, "I have heard there must be one error among a thousand ideas of a wise man and there must be one inspiration among a thousand ideas of a fool. For this reason it is said, 'A sagacious man chooses even from the words of a madman.' However, I am afraid my plan is not truly worth employing, I would like humbly to contribute my loyalty. Although the Lord of Cheng-an had plans of achieving a hundred victories in a hundred battles, in a single morning he lost it [his plans], his troops were defeated beneath the city wall of Hao①, and he himself died on Zhi River. Now you, General, waded across the Xi He (Western River)②, took the King of Wei captive, caught Xia Yüe at Yü–yü, at a single stroke descended from Jing-xing, defeated a multitude of over 200,000 men of Zhao, and executed the Lord of Cheng-an. Your fame is known to all within the seas and your awe–inspiring force causes the world to tremble. All the farmers have stopped their tilling, laid down their plows, put on beautiful clothes and feasted on delicious food. They are inclining their ears to wait for your commands. [A situation] like this is to the General's advantage. However, the people are wearied and soldiers exhausted. They, in fact, would be difficult to make

① 原文为"鄗下"，鄗在春秋时是晋邑，战国时是战国的赵邑，今河北柏乡县北 10.5 千米固城店镇。
② 龙门河。

use of. Now you want to raise the tired and weary soldiers and halt them at the foot of the solid wall of Yan. You want to fight, but are afraid that your strength will not be sufficient to take the city as time passes. Your condition becomes manifest and your situation will worsen. Your provisions will run out as time drags on. Yet weak Yan will not submit and Qi is certain to defend its borders and strengthen itself. As long as Qi and Yan hold out and do not submit, the power between Liu [Bang] and Xiang [Yü] will be indistinguishable. [A situation] like this is to the General's disadvantage. In the opinion of your foolish servant, I privately think it is also a mistake. For this reason, a person who is good at employing troops will not attack advantage with disadvantage, but will instead attack disadvantage with advantage." Han Xin said, "If so, what should I follow?" The Lord of Guang–wu replied, "Right now, let me make a plan for you, General. It will be better to put aside armor, rest the troops, stabilize Zhao, and comfort its orphans. Within a hundred *li*, serve wine and meat everyday to feast the officers and feed the soldiers. Face the roads to Yan in the north, and after that dispatch an eloquent persuader to take a curt letter to Yan, disclosing your advantage to them. They definitely dare not disobey. Once Yan has submitted, send your propagandists east to inform Qi. Qi is sure to follow the prevailing wind and submit once they hear the news. Even if there are wise men, they will not know how to plan for Qi. [Once things are] like this, then you can plan matters of the world. In military [strategy] from the beginning making noise precedes taking action. This [plan] is what [military strategy] dictates." Han Xin said, "Well put." He followed his plan and sent an envoy to visit Yan. Yan followed the prevailing wind and submitted. [Han Xin] then dispatched an envoy to report to [the King of] Han. He took advantage to request to install Zhang Er as the King of Zhao so as to stabilize and comfort the state. The King of Han consented to it and then installed Zhang Er as the King of Zhao.

Chu had sent ambuscaders to cross the He and attack Zhao several times. [Zhang] Er, the King of Zhao, and Han Xin traveled back and forth to go to Zhao's aid. They took advantage to stabilize the cities and towns of Zhao on the way and sent out troops to reach Han. Chu had just put the King of Han in dire straits by besieging him at Xing-yang; the King of Han escaped to the south and went to the area between Wan[①] and Ye[②]. He obtained Jing Bu[③] and fled to Cheng-gao[④] where Chu again put them in dire straits by besieging them. In the sixth month, the King of Han went out from Cheng-gao, moved east to cross the He and followed Zhang Er's troops to Xiu-wu[⑤] in the company of only the Magistrate of Teng. Upon his arrival, [the King of Han] stayed in the post station. In the morning he claimed himself to be the envoy of Han and galloped into the barricades of Zhao. Zhang Er and Han Xin had not yet arisen. [The King of Han] immediately seized the seals from their sleeping quarters, summoned the various commanders with the banners and shifted their positions. When [Han] Xin and [Zhang] Er arose, they then learned the King of Han had come and were greatly astonished. The King of Han seized the troops of these two men. He then ordered Zhang Er to defend the territories of Zhao and appointed Han Xin to become Chancellor[⑥], collecting the soldiers of Zhao who had not yet been sent out to attack Qi.

[Han] Xin led the troops east. Before he crossed [the He] at the Ping-yuan [Ford][⑦], he heard that the King of Han had sent Li Yi-ji to Qi and he had already persuaded Qi to submit. Han Xin intended to stop. Kuai Tong[⑧], a rhetorician from Fan-yang, tried to persuade him [to go on] by saying, "General, you received a decree to attack Qi. However, [the King of] Han had only sent a secret envoy to subdue Zhao. Is there a

---

① 宛，今河南南阳，在荥阳西南 250 千米处，秦朝时由南阳郡管辖。
② 叶，荥阳以南 190 千米处，秦朝时由南阳郡管辖。
③ 黥布，本名英布，因受秦律被黥而又称黥布。他是秦末汉初名将，项羽把他封为九江王，后叛楚归汉，与韩信、彭越并称汉初三大名将。汉朝建立后，他被封为淮南王，后起兵反汉，被刘邦击败，逃亡时被妻舅吴臣命乡民刺杀而死。
④ 成皋，今荥阳西南 25 千米处的黄河南岸。
⑤ 修武，今河南省新乡以西 16 千米处的黄河北岸。
⑥ 原文为“相国”。
⑦ 平原津，今山东省平原以北 8 千米处。
⑧ 蒯通，本名蒯彻，为避汉武帝的讳而被司马迁改为通，秦末汉初谋士。

decree to stop you, General? How could you not go on? Furthermore Master Li[①], [though] only a rhetorician, by leaning upon the crossbar of his carriage and wagging his three-inch tongue, has subdued seventy some cities of Qi. You, General, command a host of tens of thousands, but after more than a year have only subdued fifty some cities of Zhao. You have been a commander for several years. Is that not equal to the merit of a *ju* scholar-whelp[②]?" At this, [Han] Xin believe he [Kuai Tong] was right, followed his plan, and finally crossed the He. Qi had already listened to Master Li and kept him to indulge in wine. They dismissed the defenses prepared against Han. [Han] Xin took advantage to make a surprise attack on the army of Qi at Li-xia[③], finally reaching Lin-zi. The King of Qi, Tian Guang, thought Scholar Li had sold him out and then boiled him alive, fleeing to Gao-mi and sending an envoy to go to Chu requesting aid. When Han Xin had already stabilized Lin-zi, he then went east to pursue [Tian] Guang, reaching [a point] west of Gao-mi. Chu also sent Long Jü[④] to command [troops], said to be 200,000 soldiers, to come to the aid of Qi.

[Tian] Guang, the King of Qi, and Long Jü combined their armies to give [Han] Xin battle. Before [the armies] joined [in battle], someone tried to persuade Long Jü, saying, "The troops of Han are fighting far away [from home] and will fight fiercely. Their vanguards cannot be resisted. The troops of Qi and Chu fight in the own territory they live in, and they will be easily defeated and to scattered. It would be better to deepen the entrenchments and asked the King of Qi to send his trusted subjects to rally the lost cities. When the lost cities hear that their king is still alive and Chu has come to their aid, they will definitely rebel against Han. The soldiers of Han live two thousand *li* away from home, if the cities of Qi all rebel against them, the situation will be that there is

---

① 原文为“郦生”。
② 原文为“竖儒”。
③ 历下，今山东省济南市以西8千米处。
④ 龙且，部分文献中又记作“龙苴”“龙沮”。他是秦汉之际楚国将领，起初隶属于项梁，任职司马，项梁战死后，投奔项羽。

no place to get food and [they will] surrender without fighting." Long Jü said, "All my life I have known what kind of person Han Xin is. He is easy to deal with. Furthermore, as to coming to the aid of Qi and subduing it without fighting, what merit will I have? Now [if] I fight with him and win, I can obtain half of Qi. Why should I stop?" Then he [prepared for] battle. He and [Han] Xin arrayed [their troops] on opposite sides of the Wei River①. Han Xin then ordered people by night to make ten thousand some bags and fill them with sand. He blocked the river upper stream, led the troops halfway across to attack Long Jü. Pretending to be defeated, they turned and fled. Long Jü was pleased as expected and said, "I knew indeed that [Han] Xin was cowardly." Then he pursued [Han] Xin and crossed the river. [Han] Xin sent people to break open the barrier of [sand] bags and the water rushed down. Most of Long Jü's troops were not able to cross. Then [Han Xin] quickly attacked them and killed Long Jü. Long Jü's troops on the east side of the river scattered and ran. The King of Qi, [Tian] Guang, fled. Then [Han] Xin pursued him northward, reaching Cheng-yang② and took all the soldiers of Chu captives.

In the fourth year of Han (203 B.C.), [Han Xin] finally subdued and pacified all of Qi. He sent a person to speak to the King of Han, saying, "Qi is false and deceitful and is a state that often revolts and changes sides. It borders Chu in the south. If an acting king③ is not installed to guard it, the situation will not be stabilized. I would like to serve as the acting king for the convenience [of the State]. Just at this time, Chu had put the King of Han in dire straits by besieging him at Xing-yang. When the envoy sent by Han Xin arrived, [the King of Han] opened the letter. The King of Han was enraged and cursed loudly, "I am in difficulties here, day and night expecting you to come to aide me. Yet you want to enthrone yourself as a king!" Zhang Liang and Chen Ping stepped on the King of Han's foot and accordingly leaned to his ear and said, "Right now Han is

---

① 潍河，古称潍水，山东省最长和流域面积最广的河流。
② 城阳，可能是西汉的城阳郡，治所在今山东省莒县城阳镇。
③ 原文为"假王"。

at a disadvantage. How can you prohibit [Han] Xin from being a king. It would be better to take advantage to install him, treat him well and make him defend [Qi] for himself. Otherwise a crisis will be born." The King of Han also realized this and accordingly again cursed loudly: "This real man has stabilized the feudal lords, then he should serve as a real king. Why should he be an acting one?" Thus he dispatched Zhang Liang to go and enthrone [Han] Xin as the King of Qi and collected his troops to attack Chu.

II. Common Terms, Words and Phrases for the Text

memoir 列传

Huai River 淮河

Palace Attendant 郎中

Magistrate 公

Chief Commandant of Millet 治粟都尉

Chancellor 丞相

Your servant 臣

commander 将军

warrior for the state 国士

Commander-in-chief 大将

auspicious day 吉日

the place of honor 上位

feudal lords 诸侯

Three-qin 三秦

Wu Pass 武关

don't harm even a single hair 秋毫不犯

Chancellor of the Left 左丞相

Commandery 郡

Lord 君

ambuscader 奇兵

Jing-xing Pass 井陉关

guidon 旗帜

adjutant general 裨将，副官

light meal 飧，简单的饭食

Art of War 兵法

persuader 辩士

curt letter 咫尺之书

follow the prevailing wind 从风，跟风

rhetorician 辩士

three-inch tongue 三寸不烂之舌

whelp 竖子

boil someone alive 把……烹杀

the acting king 假王，代理的王

King Xiang 项王

III. Exercises and Thinking

1. How did Han Xin eventually gain recognition and rise to a position of power?

2. According to Han Xin, what advantages did Liu Bang have over Xiang Yü in the struggle for power?

3. How did Han Xin achieve victory in the Battle of Jing-xing?

IV. Further Readings and Internet Links

1. Further Readings

Sima Qian, *Records of the Grand historian: Han Dynasty I*, Rivised Ed., translated by Burton Watson, Hong Kong and New York: Columbia University Press, 1993.

John De Francis, "Biography of The Marquis of Huai-yin," *Harvard Journal of*

Asiatic Studies, Vol. 10, No. 2 (Sep., 1947), pp. 179–215.

[汉]司马迁撰、[南朝宋]裴骃集解、[唐]司马贞索隐、[唐]张守节正义：《史记》，点校本二十四史修订本，中华书局 2014 年版。

2. Internet Links

Chinese Text Project: https://ctext.org/shiji/ens

Part III

Medieval History of the World

世界中古史

世界中古史是封建社会的形成、发展和衰落的历史，是人类发展史的重要组成部分。中古时期是一个充满活力、不断进步、对人们极富吸引力的阶段。法国著名史学家雅克·勒高夫在《中世纪文明》序言中称西方中世纪“是一个具有特别的创造力和为西方文明奠基的时期”。尽管这是对西方中世纪的评价，但同样适用于这一时期的非西方地区。

本编共选取七篇文献。其中五篇为欧洲法律文献，包括《狄奥多西法典》《萨利克法兰克人法典》《大宪章》《庄园法庭判例选编》《君士坦丁赠礼》，一篇为中古阿拉伯帝国盛期阿维森纳《医典》节选，一篇为中国唐朝中期陆羽的《茶经》节选。

《狄奥多西法典》是日耳曼人入侵西罗马帝国时，由东罗马帝国在5世纪初期编纂的，同时在东西罗马帝国生效的统一法典，对欧洲历史发展影响深远。《萨利克法兰克人法典》是西欧中世纪早期诸日耳曼法典中比较有代表性的法律文献，直到9世纪初，查理大帝还对其进行了修订和完善。英国的《大宪章》和《庄园法庭判例选编》分别从上层和下层反映了英国的封建制度。《君士坦丁赠礼》形成于8世纪中叶至9世纪中叶的西欧，反映了当时西欧社会政治与宗教错综复杂的关系，旨在为扩大教宗权力提供法律依据。《医典》不仅是阿拉伯帝国科学家伊本·西拿（欧洲人称其为阿维森纳）个人智慧的结晶，而且是东西方医学文明交流融合的成果，成为11—18世纪欧洲人参考的重要医学著作。中国唐朝陆羽的《茶经》不仅是关于中国茶文化的经典，而且也是世界上第一部茶学专著，是古代中国劳动人民经济社会生活发展的重要文明成果。

从总体上看，本编所选文献史料旨在展现世界中古时期亚欧大陆诸区域和国家经济社会发展的文明成果。尤其是尝试选取中古时期亚洲高度发达的阿拉伯帝国和中国唐朝的文明成就，在一定程度上体现了亚欧不同文明之间相互交往、交流、交融的历程。

Unit 15

The Theodosian Code
《狄奥多西法典》

公元 395 年，罗马帝国因狄奥多西一世去世而被其两子平分，正式分裂成东罗马帝国与西罗马帝国。此后，西罗马帝国面临着日益严峻的蛮族入侵浪潮，日益名存实亡。476 年日耳曼雇佣兵首领奥多亚克废黜西罗马帝国皇帝，正式宣告西罗马帝国灭亡。

在日耳曼人入侵和西罗马帝国衰亡过程中，东西罗马帝国皇帝试图通过法律手段维持局面。当时为了适应帝国多民族、多阶层日益复杂的法律生活，罗马法吸收了各地习惯而日益通俗化、简约化。429 年，东罗马皇帝狄奥多西二世与西罗马皇帝瓦伦蒂尼阿努斯三世也遵循罗马法的发展趋势，共同下令汇编从君士坦丁至狄奥多西二世统治期间诸皇帝所颁布的所有法令，经过 9 年努力，438 年终于编纂出了《狄奥多西法典》。该法典收录了 313—438 年皇帝颁布的所有法令，后来又接着编纂了 438—468 年东西罗马帝国皇帝的法令，为《查士丁尼法典》的编纂奠定了基础。这也是日耳曼人入侵时所面对的西罗马帝国通行的法律，并由此开始了西欧多元一体的法律建构历程。[①]

《狄奥多西法典》的编纂完成，与狄奥多西二世个人息息相关。他喜爱读书，朝政主要由其亲属和大臣掌控，自己则亲自参与 425 年创立君士坦丁堡大学的工作，并参与了该法典的编纂。这是深受其姐帕尔切丽娅影响的结果。她一方面掌握宫廷大权，另一方面教育狄奥多西二世，目的是把狄奥多西二世培

---

① 参见张乃和：《中世纪西欧法律的多元一体建构》，《中国社会科学》2022 年第 10 期。

养成为一位宽厚、庄严、温和而又文雅的君主。该法典的编纂在一定意义上就是其个人形象的展现。

《狄奥多西法典》共3000多条，分为16卷，卷之下分章，各章内容按日期排列。第1—5卷为市民法，属于私法内容；其后各卷均为公法内容。其中，第6—8卷为行政法，第9卷为刑法，第10和11卷为财政法，第12—15卷为地方法，最后一卷为宗教法。该法典在欧洲西部一直使用到12世纪，在东罗马帝国则被后来的《查士丁尼法典》所取代。这里选取的内容出自克莱德·法尔（Clyde Pharr）编纂的《狄奥多西法典》英译本。

I. Excerpt from *The Theodosian Code*①

BOOK II

TITLE 22: Claims for Inheritances

1. Emperor Constantine Augustus and the Caesar to Maximus, Prefect of the City.

If a man should lose the dignity of Roman citizenship and thereby become a Latin and if he should depart from the boon of light while in the said status, his entire peculium shall be vindicated by his patron or by those children or grandchildren of the patron who have in no way lost the right of agnation.

The children shall not be permitted to undertake a suit as though it were a controversy over an inheritance, since the nature of the status of the deceased rather must be considered—not the status which he received as his lot through the benefit of the freedom which was granted to him, but that status in which he departed from the boon of light.

Given on the third day before the kalends of February at Sofia (Serdica) in the year of the seventh consulship of the Augustus Himself and the consulship of the Caesar. ——January 30, 326, 320.

① Clyde Pharr ed., *The Theodosian Code and Novels, and the Sirmondian Constitutions, A Translation with Commentary, Glossary, and Bibliography*, New Jersey: The Lawbook Exchange, Ltd., 2012, pp. 55–451.

BOOK III

TITLE 1: Contracts of Purchase

1. Emperor Constantine Augustus to Profuturus, Prefect of the Annona.

It is not at all fitting that the good faith of sale and purchase should be broken, when no duress was exerted through fraud. For a contract that has been executed without any flaw must not be disturbed by a litigious controversy because of the sole complaint that the price was too cheap.

Posted on the ides of August in the year of the fifth consulship of Constantine Augustus and the consulship of Licinius Caesar.

2. The same Augustus to Gregorius.

The purchaser shall assume the tax assessment of property that is purchased, and no person shall be permitted either to buy or sell property without its tax assessment.

Moreover, in accordance with this law, there must henceforth be a public or fiscal inspection, so that if any property should be sold without its tax assessment and this fact should be reported by another, the seller, indeed, shall lose the landholding, and the purchaser for his part shall lose the price that he has paid, since the fisc shall vindicate both.

It is also Our pleasure that no person shall engage in the sale of anything whatsoever unless at the time when the contract between the seller and the buyer is formally executed, a certain and true ownership is proved by the neighbors. To such an extent shall the precaution prescribed by this law be observed that even if "benches," or strips of land, as they are commonly called, are sold, the proof of showing ownership shall be fulfilled.

2. Nor shall the formalities between the buyer and the seller be solemnized in hidden corners, but fraudulent sales shall be completely buried and shall perish.

Given on the day before the nones of February at Constantinople in the year of the consulship of Felicianus and Titianus.—February 4, 337.

BOOK IV

TITLES 4: Testaments and Codicils

1. Emperor Constantine Augustus to Constantius, Praetorian Prefect.

In the case of codicils not preceded by a testament, just as in the case of wills in testamentary form, the presence of seven or of five witnesses must not be lacking, for thus it will come about that the provisions of testators for succession will be preserved without any trickery. Therefore, if ever the required number of witnesses should be lacking, the codicillary instrument shall be held invalid. It is Our pleasure that this rule shall be observed in all other kinds of wills also.

Given on the eleventh day before the kalends of January in the year of the seventh consulship of Constantine Augustus and the consulship of Constans Caesar.—December 22, 326.

BOOK V

TITLE 1: Statutory Inheritances

Emperor Constantine Augustus to Bassus, Prefect of the City.

It is Our pleasure that although a mother should not have the rights that accrue to parents on account of their children, a third portion of the entire estate of a child shall devolve upon her whenever she comes to the inheritance on intestacy, even though there should come between a paternal uncle of the decedent or the others to whom unimpaired rights of agnation are extended successively, and who will be the next following agnates by whom the mother could have been formerly excluded from the inheritance by right of consanguinity. Also by a like benefit, although a mother should have the rights that accrue to parents on account of their children, a third portion of such estate shall devolve upon a paternal uncle of the decedent or upon the uncle's son or finally his grandson, even when the tie of agnation is broken, as if, perchance, the right of consanguinity has been destroyed by the emancipation of anyone. Not without cause is it Our pleasure that when the mother is supported by the aforementioned privilege and the ties of agnation have been destroyed, Our benefit shall not be extended beyond the degree of grandson, for otherwise, if many persons were called to the inheritance, too much would appear to be taken from the mother and too little bestowed. 1. Therefore, whether one or several paternal uncles survive, or one or more sons of such paternal uncles, or even grandsons or granddaughters, no more than one third of all the goods shall devolve upon all of them together or upon individuals, in each case according to their degree of kinship. 2. In like manner, if there should be several persons by whom the mother can be excluded, no more than one third of the goods shall accrue to the mother as against them all. 3. Therefore, We decree that if persons of the aforesaid kinship should survive as agnates in unlimited number, the mother's interests shall be supported against them all, although such aid shall not be granted against the mother to all such kinsmen, but only to certain persons included above. Without a petition for possession of the goods— for the benefit rests upon this law and not upon action of the praetor—they shall immediately obtain the full ownership of the portion accruing to them, when the day for the accrual of such portion has arrived, by simple entry, that is, by the appropriation of any piece of property whatsoever, or by the disclosure of their intention. As long as they live they shall have the perpetual right of entry upon the portion of the inheritance granted to them. 4. Indeed, if the inheritance should not be first acquired thus by those persons whom the plan of Our indulgence embraces, We order that nothing shall pass to their successors, but the property shall remain in the possession of those persons who would have been able to retain it before the issuance of this law.

Given on the fourteenth day before the kalends of January at Rome in the year of the second consulship of Crispus and Constantine Caesars.—December (May) 19, 321; 317–319.

BOOK IX

TITLE 26: On the Julian Law on Corrupt Solicitation

1. Emperors Arcadius and Honorius Augustuses to Caesarius, Praetorian Prefect.

If any person should corruptly solicit the illustrious rank of a dignitary of Our palace or if anyone should attempt to ascend by corrupt solicitation to those honors which are not conferred except by Our decision on men approved by Us, whatever may be his station, class, or dignity, his goods shall be forfeited and vindicated at once to Our fisc, and he shall be punished by the exile of deportation. No person shall think that there is any difference between an attempted and an effectuated act of corrupt solicitation, since the laws punish by the same penalty both the crime and the intention to commit the crime.

Given on the fourteenth day before the kalends of March at Constantinople in the year of the consulship of Caesarius and Atticus.— February 16, 397.

3. The same Augustuses and Theodosius Augustus to Strategius, Vicar of Africa.

Offices already held once are not sought again without the disadvantage of rending asunder the public interest. Wherefore, by the authority of this regulation We decree that no person shall be admitted a second time to the same offices by surreptitious supplications to the Emperor, but appointments which have been impetrated in this manner shall be annulled. Such petitioners shall be compelled first of all to pay whatever they owe, and in the future those persons who violate this law shall receive the penalty of deportation.

Given on the third day before the kalends of June at Ravenna in the year of the first consulship of Theodosius Augustus and the consulship of Rumoridus.—May 30, 403.

TITLE 27: On the Julian Law on Extortion by Public Officials

Emperors Gratian, Valentinian, and Theodosius Augustuses to Neoterius, Praetorian Prefect.

Judges who have been convicted of having polluted themselves with thefts and other crimes shall be deprived of the insignia which had been conferred upon them by imperial letters patent, they shall be stripped of high rank and shall be rated among the people of lowest degree and plebeians. Nor shall they flatter themselves thereafter with that honor of which they have judged themselves unworthy.

Given on the eighteenth day before the kalends of February at Thessalonica in the year of the fifth consulship of Gratian Augustus and the first consulship of Theodosius Augustus.—January 15, 380.

2. The same Augustuses to Eutropius, Praetorian Prefect.

Those persons who have criminally conducted themselves in the service of the State shall know that all dignities, whether statutory or honorary, are forever closed to them. Wherefore, We order that Your Illustrious Magnificence shall permit no person at all to enter the provinces who at a former time has been accused on a charge of the crime of maladministration, but you shall refer their cases to Us.

Given on the fifteenth day before the kalends of July at Thessalonica in the year of the fifth consulship of Gratian Augustus and the first consulship of Theodosius Augustus.—June 17, 380.

3. The same Augustuses to Matronianus, Duke and Governor of Sardinia.

In order that the punishment of one person may cause fear in many, We order Natalis, the former duke, to go, under custody of members of the imperial bodyguard, to the province which he despoiled, that he may repay fourfold, even though unwillingly, not only that which—I shall not say—his confidential adviser and his soldiery and his personal aide received, but also that which he himself seized and carried away from Our provincials.

Given on the day before the ides of June at Constantinople in the year of the consulship of Antonius and Syagrius.—June 12, 382.

TITLE 28 The Crime of Peculation

Emperors Theodosius, Arcadius, and Honorius Augustuses to Rufinus, Praetorian Prefect.

Formerly it had been established that those judges who had shattered their provinces by peculation should be liable to the payment of a fine. But since this penalty is not adequate for the crime or the punishment equal to the offense, it is Our pleasure that the sentence of punishment shall be so severe that, although punishment can scarcely be found equal to these disgraceful crimes and so great evil cannot be expiated by suitable tortures, We command that this shall be a capital offense and that it shall be restrained by the most severe punishment.

Given on the fourth day before the ides of September at Constantinople in the year of the second consulship of Arcadius Augustus and the consulship of Rufinus.—September 10, 392.

2. Emperors Honorius and Theodosius Augustuses to Aurelianus, Praetorian Prefect for the second time.

It is not a work of sanctity to offer protection for rapine and plunder, since indeed these crimes, like the contagion of some deadly disease, must be avoided. For to rob and to keep spoils for a robber are not dissimilar crimes.

Given on the third day before the nones of March at Constantinople in the year of the tenth consulship of Honorius Augustus and the sixth consulship of Theodosius Augustus.—March 5, 415.

BOOK XVI

TITLE 2: Bishops, Churches, and Clerics

1. Emperor Constantine Augustus.

We have learned that clerics of the Catholic Church are being so harassed by a faction of heretics that they are being burdened by nominations and by service as tax receivers, as public custom demands, contrary to the privileges granted them. It is Our pleasure, therefore, that if Your Gravity should find any person thus harassed, another person shall be chosen as a substitute for him and that henceforward men of the aforesaid religion shall be protected from such outrages.

Given on the day before the kalends of November in the year of the third consulship of Constantine Augustus and of Licinius Caesar.—October 31, 313.

2. The same Augustus to Octavianus, Governor of Lucania and of Bruttium.

Those persons who devote the services of religion to divine worship, that is, those who are called clerics, shall be exempt from all compulsory public services whatever, lest, through the sacrilegious malice of certain persons, they should be called away from divine services.

Given on the twelfth day before the kalends of November in the year of the fifth consulship of Constantine Augustus and the consulship of Licinius Caesar.—October 21, 319; 313.

TITLE 5: Heretics

1. Emperor Constantine Augustus to Dracilianus.

The privileges that have been granted in consideration of religion must benefit only the adherents of the Catholic faith. It is Our will, moreover, that heretics and schismatics shall not only be alien from these privileges but shall also be bound and subjected to various compulsory public services.

Posted on the kalends of September at Gerastus in the year of the seventh consulship of Constantine Augustus and the consulship of Constantius Caesar.—September 1, 326.

5. Emperors Gratian, Valentinian, and Theodosius Augustuses to Hesperius, Praetorian Prefect.

All heresies are forbidden by both divine and imperial laws and shall forever cease. If any profane man by his punishable teachings should weaken the concept of God, he shall have the right to know such noxious doctrines only for himself but shall not reveal them to others to their hurt. If any person by a renewed death should corrupt bodies that have been redeemed by the venerable baptismal font, by taking away the effect of that ceremony which he repeats, he shall know such doctrines for himself alone, and he shall not ruin others by his nefarious teaching. All teachers and ministers alike of this perverse superstition shall abstain from the gathering places of a doctrine already condemned, whether they defame the name of bishop by the assumption of such priestly office, or, that which is almost the same, they belie religion with the appellation of priests, or also if they call themselves deacons, although they may not even be considered Christians. Finally, the rescript that was recently issued at Sirmium shall be annulled, and there shall remain only those enactments pertaining to Catholic doctrine which were decreed by Our father of eternal memory and which We ourselves commanded by an equally manifold order, which will survive forever.

Given on the third day before the nones of August at Milan.— August 3. Received on the thirteenth day before the kalends of September in the year of the consulship of Auxonius and Olybrius.— August 20, 379.

II. Common Terms, Words and Phrases for the Text

contract 合同，契约，合约

prefect（城市）行政长官

peculium 特有产，私产

patron（罗马法）保护人，庇主，恩主

agnation 父系亲属关系

tax assessment of property 财产税价评估

vindicate 证明，维护

formality 法律手续；法律形式

testament 遗嘱

statutory inheritances 法定遗嘱

intestacy 无遗嘱死亡

right of consanguinity 血亲权利

devolve（财产、权利、责任）转移

corrupt solicitation 贪污腐败的诱惑

dignitary 显要人物，（教会法）高级教士

vicar 代理人

surreptitious 秘密的，鬼鬼祟祟的，偷偷摸摸的

insignia 徽章，纹章，荣誉

imperial letters patent（由帝国或皇帝授予的）任命状

peculation 挪用公款，挪用公共财产

heretic 异教徒，异端分子

sacrilegious 亵圣的

rescript（罗马法）（罗马皇帝对法律问题的）解答敕令

III. Exercises and Thinking

1. Please briefly describe the relationship between testamentary inheritances and statutory one.

2. How does *the Theodosian code* deal with criminal public officials?

3. Please discuss the relationship between the church and the empire in the reign of Theodosius II.

IV. Further Readings and Internet Links

1. Further Readings

Clyde Pharr, *The Theodosian code and novels, and the Sirmondian Constitutions, A Translation with Commentary, Glossary, and Bibliography,* New Jersey: the Lawbook Exchange, Ltd., 2012.

徐家玲、林英、陈志强:《拜占庭帝国大通史（330—610）》，江苏人民出版社 2023 年版。

2. Internet Links

不列颠百科全书网站：https://www.britannica.com/topic/Theodosian-Code

Unit 16

The Laws of the Salian Franks

《萨利克法兰克人法典》

《萨利克法兰克人法典》是萨利克法兰克人的法律汇编。传统上认为其最初由法兰克国王克洛维（Clovis I，r. 481—511）在 507—511 年颁布。克洛维继任法兰克国王后，不断开疆拓土，形成疆域较为辽阔的王国。为了更好地治理其王国，克洛维命人将法兰克人的法律习惯以及国王的政令文件汇编起来。这就是法兰克人历史上第一部成文的法典——《萨利克法兰克人法典》(以下简称《法典》)。

继克洛维之后,《法典》增补了新的法令。到了 7—8 世纪，随着萨利克法兰克人经济社会的变迁，在罗马法与基督教的影响下,《法典》不断得到补充和修订。8 世纪中叶出现了包括上述《法典》内容在内的共计 100 个主题的《法律书》(*Lawbook*)。查理大帝在其基础上于 798 年颁布了学界所称的《萨利克法典（修订本）》(*Lex Salica Emendata*)。不久之后，查理大帝颁布了第二个修订本，这个修订本被学界称作《加洛林萨利克法典》(*Lex Salica Karolina*)。这部法典增补了 6 世纪晚期颁布的法令。在《加洛林萨利克法典》颁布之后，此前更古老版本的《法典》却并未被取代，至于它们在实践中是否同时具有法律效力，则不甚清楚。

在诸多版本中，克洛维颁布的《法典》最为重要，它较为翔实地反映了 5 世纪末 6 世纪初甚至更早时期法兰克人的经济社会状况，是研究法兰克王国早期历史的珍贵文献史料。

从《法典》中提及的各种牲畜家禽来看，当时畜牧业、养蜂业等在经济中仍和从前一样重要。农业经济则发展迅速，法兰克人不仅种植谷类作物，还播种大豆、豌豆、兵豆和芜菁，种植亚麻。法兰克人已经使用牛耕，熟练使用犁、耙，知晓施肥、除草，甚至还出现了三圃制。当时马尔克已处于衰落状态，出现了农奴，土地乃至宅旁园地都已私有化，法兰克人社会正处在经济社会转型阶段，阶级进一步分化，不平等现象进一步加剧，王权得到强化，教会的特权地位更加突出。不过，当时法兰克人社会还保留着氏族时代的不少原始遗风，主要表现为血缘关系还比较浓厚。根据《法典》，寡妇再嫁，其外甥、外孙、舅父比前夫亲属享有取得聘礼的优先权，杀死某人时须向其亲族支付偿命金，替贫穷亲族支付一部分杀人偿命金，等等。

其中的继承法影响深远。这主要体现在女性长期被排除在王位继承人之外。卡佩王朝末年面临王位继承问题时就参照了这一原则，王位传给了卡佩家族支系的瓦卢瓦家族。16 世纪，该法典文本被王权拥护者视为王国的基本法。1593 年，该法典被援引用于拒绝承认西班牙未成年的伊莎贝拉为法国国王候选人。直至 1883 年它在法国还有法律效力。

I. Excerpt from *The Laws of the Salian Franks* ①

III. CONCERNING THE THEFT OF CATTLE

2. He who steals a yearling calf shall be liable to pay six hundred denarii (i.e., fifteen solidi) in addition to return of the animal [or its value] plus a payment for the time its use was lost.

3. He who steals a two-year-old animal and it is proved against him shall be liable to pay six hundred denarii (i.e., fifteen solidi) in addition to return of the animal [or its value] plus a payment for the time its use was lost.

4. He who steals a cow with calf and it is proved against him shall be liable to pay

① Katherine Fischer Drew ed., *The Laws of the Salian Franks*, Philadelphia: University of Pennsylvania Press, 1991, pp. 68–126.

fourteen hundred denarii (i.e., thirty–five solidi) in addition to return of the animals [or their value] plus a payment for the time their use was lost.

IV. CONCERNING THE THEFT OF SHEEP

1. He who steals a nursing lamb and it is proved against him shall be liable to pay seven denarii (i.e., one–half a triens [one–third of a solidus]) in addition to return of the animal [or its value] plus a payment for the time its use was lost.

2. He who steals a one– or two–year–old wether and it is proved against him shall be liable to pay one hundred twenty denarii (i.e., three solidi) in addition to return of the animal [or its value] plus a payment for the time its use was lost.

V. CONCERNING THE THEFT OF GOATS

1. He who steals three goats and it is proved against him shall be liable to pay one hundred twenty denarii in addition to return of the animals [or their value] plus a payment for the time their use was lost.

2. He who steals more than three goats shall be liable to pay six hundred denarii in addition to return of the animals [or their value] plus a payment for the time their use was lost.

VI. CONCERNING THE THEFT OF DOGS

2. He who steals a dog that is a tracking hound *(canem agutoriutri)* shall be liable to pay six hundred denarii (i.e., fifteen solidi) in addition to return of the animal [or its value] plus a payment for the time its use was lost.

3. He who after sunset kills a dog that is usually tied up shall be treated as stated above: he shall be liable to pay six hundred denarii (i.e., fifteen solidi) in addition to payment of the dog's value plus a payment for the time its use was lost.

4. He who steals or kills a herd dog and it is proved against him shall be liable to pay one hundred twenty denarii (i.e., three solidi) in addition to return of the animal [or its value] plus a payment for the time its use was lost.

IX. CONCERNING DAMAGE TO A CULTIVATED FIELD OR SOME OTHER ENCLOSURE

1. He who finds a cow or horse or other animal in his field should do it no grievous harm. If he does do so and confesses it, he must restore the full value of the animal to its owner and keep for himself the weakened animal that he had struck. But if he does not confess it and it is proved against him, he shall be liable to pay six hundred denarii (i.e., fifteen solidi) in addition to return of the animal [or its value] plus a payment for the time its use was lost.

2. He who brands an animal, horse, or mare that he has stolen shall be liable to pay six hundred denarii (i.e., fifteen solidi) in addition to return of the animal [or its value] plus a payment for the time its use was lost.

3. He who finds in his field another man's animals that do not have a herder and shuts them up by force and makes it known to no one, and some of the animals die, must restore the full value of the animals to their owner and in addition be liable to pay fourteen hundred denarii (i.e., thirty-five solidi) [plus a payment for the time their use was lost].

5. If a man's pigs or other animals that are being watched run into someone else's field and, although he denies it, it is proved against him, he shall be liable to pay six hundred denarii (i.e., fifteen solidi).

XII. CONCERNING THEFTS OR BREAKING-IN COMMITTED BY SLAVES

1. The slave who steals something worth two denarii outside a house and it is proved against him shall, in addition to return of the object stolen [or its value] plus a payment for the time its use was lost, receive stretched out one hundred twenty lashes or shall pay one hundred twenty denarii (i.e., three solidi) to spare his back.

2. The slave who steals something worth forty denarii shall be castrated or pay two hundred forty denarii (i.e., six solidi). The lord of the slave who committed the theft shall return the object stolen [or its value] to its owner plus a payment for the time its use was lost.

XIII. CONCERNING THE ABDUCTION OF FREEMEN OR FREE WOMEN

1. If three men take a free girl from her house or workroom, the three shall be liable to pay twelve hundred denarii (i.e., thirty solidi).

2. If there are more than three involved, each one of them [over three] shall be liable to pay two hundred denarii (i.e., five solidi).

3. Each one of those who carried arrows shall [in addition] be liable to pay one hundred twenty denarii (i.e., three solidi).

4. The abductor shall be liable to pay twenty–five hundred denarii (i.e., sixty–two and one–half solidi).

5. If the girl was taken from a locked room or workroom, the penalty should be imposed as in the previous case.

XIV. CONCERNING WAYLAYING OR PILLAGING

1. He who robs a freeman by waylaying him and it is proved against him shall be liable to pay twenty–five hundred denarii (i.e., sixty–two and one–half solidi) [plus return of the objects taken in addition to a payment for the time their use was lost].

2. If a Roman robs a Salic barbarian *(barbarum Salicum)* and it is not certainly proved against him, he can clear himself with twenty–five oath–helpers, half of whom he has chosen. If he cannot find the oathhelpers he shall go to the ordeal of boiling water or it should be observed as in the case preceding [i.e., pay sixty–two and one–half solidi in addition to return of the objects taken or their value plus a payment for the time their use was lost].

3. If a Frank robs a Roman and it is not certainly proved, he shall clear himself with twenty oathhelpers, half of whom he has chosen. If he cannot find the oathhelpers, if it is proved, he shall be liable to pay twelve hundred denarii (i.e., thirty solidi) [in addition to return of the objects taken or their value plus a payment for the time their use was lost].

XVI CONCERNING ARSON

2. He who sets fire to a building (*salina*) made of wattling (*detem*) and it is proved

against him shall be liable to pay twenty–five hundred denarii (i.e., sixty–two and one–half solidi).

3. He who sets fire to a barn (*sficarium*) or granary (*machalum*) with grain in it and it is proved against him shall be liable to pay twenty–five hundred denarii (i.e., sixty–two and one–half solidi) [plus the value of the grain involved].

XXIII. ON MOUNTING A HORSE WITHOUT THE CONSENT OF ITS OWNER

He who mounts another man's horse without the consent of its owner and rides it around, and it is proved against him, shall be liable to pay twelve hundred denarii (i.e., thirty solidi).

XXVIII. CONCERNING SECRET HIRINGS

1. He who secretly tries to hire someone to kill a man and that one accepts the price for this but does not kill [the one intended] and this is proved against him [i.e., the hirer], he [the hirer] shall be liable to pay twenty–five hundred denarii (i.e., sixty–two and one–half solidi).

[1. He who secretly tries to hire someone to kill a man and that one accepts the price for this shall be liable to pay four thousand denarii (i.e., one hundred solidi).]

2. If he who was hired accepts the money and tries to kill the man designated but does not do it and it is proved against him, he [the man hired] shall be liable to pay twenty–five hundred denarii (i.e., sixty–two and one–half solidi).

3. If he who was hired transfers the job to a third man and it is proved against that one, that man shall be liable to pay twenty–five hundred denarii (i.e., sixty–two and one–half solidi): thus the giver, the receiver, and the transferer shall each of them be liable to pay sixty–two and one–half solidi.

XXXVIII. CONCERNING THE THEFT OF HORSES OR MARES

1. He who steals a horse that pulls a cart and it is proved against him shall be liable to pay eighteen hundred denarii (i.e, forty–five solidi) in addition to return of the animal [or its value] plus a payment for the time its use was lost.

2. He who steals a stallion *(admissarium)* from a Frank, and it is proved against him, shall be liable to pay eighteen hundred denarii (i.e., forty–five solidi) [in addition to return of the animal plus a payment for the time its use was lost].

4. He who steals a stallion *(wamnionem)* belonging to the king shall be liable to pay ninety solidi in addition to return of the animal [or its value] plus a payment for the time its use was lost.

XLI. ON THE KILLING OF FREEMEN

1. He who kills a free Frank or other barbarian who lives by Salic law, and it is proved against him, shall be liable to pay eight thousand denarii (i.e., two hundred solidi).

2. If he throws him into a well or holds him under water, he shall be liable to pay twenty–four thousand denarii (i.e., six hundred solidi). And for concealing it, he shall be liable as we have said before.

3. If he does not conceal his crime, he shall be liable to pay eight thousand denarii (i.e., two hundred solidi).

4. If he covers him over with sticks or bark or hides him with something to conceal him and it is proved against him, he shall be liable to pay twenty–four thousand denarii (i.e., six hundred solidi).

XLII. CONCERNING HOMICIDES COMMITTED BY A BAND OF MEN

1. He who with a band of men attacks a freeman in his house and kills him there shall be liable to pay twenty–four thousand denarii (i.e., six hundred solidi). And if the man killed was one of the king's sworn antrustions, he who is proved to have killed him shall be liable to pay eighteen hundred solidi.

5. If a man robs another man's villa and seizes property there, but nevertheless there is no certain proof, he may absolve himself of the crime with twenty–five oath–helpers, half of whom have been selected by himself. If he cannot find the oath–helpers, he shall be liable to pay twenty–five hundred denarii (i.e., sixty–two and one–half solidi).

LIV. ON THE KILLING OF A COUNT

1. He who kills a count shall be liable to pay twenty–four thousand denarii (i.e., six hundred solidi).

2. He who kills a sagibaron (*sacebaronem*) or count (*obgrafionem*) who is a servant (*puer*) of the king and it is proved against him shall be liable to pay twelve thousand denarii (i.e., three hundred solidi).

3. If anyone kills a sagibaron who is a freeman and has established himself or another as sagibaron, he shall be liable to pay twenty–four thousand denarii (i.e., six hundred solidi).

4. There should not be more than three sagibarons in each court and if they have said something final about a case that has been submitted to them, they shall make this secure and the case may not be removed to the count.

LVI. CONCERNING THE MAN WHO REFUSES TO COME TO COURT

1. If a man refuses to come to court or delays in carrying out what was judged against him by the rachimburgi, if he will not give security (*fidem*) for the composition or for the ordeal or for other penalty, he should be remanded to the presence of the king.

2. There should be twelve witnesses there who offer oath three at a time that they were present when the rachimburgi gave their judgment that he should go to the ordeal or give a pledge for the amount of the composition, and he neglected to do so.

3. Three others should then offer oath that they were present on that day when the rachimburgi gave their judgment that he should go to the ordeal or pay composition, that is, on that day forty days from the time that a day had formally been set again for him in court, and he was still unwilling to comply with the law.

4. Then let him be summoned to come before the king in fourteen days and three witnesses should offer oath that they had been there when he was summoned and had a day formally set for him. And if he has not come then, all nine witnesses, having been sworn, shall give their testimony as stated above.

5. Likewise on that day, if he has not come, another day should formally be set for him and there should be three witnesses there when the day is set. Then if he who calls the man to court fulfills all these things and he who was called to court still will not come to court or carry out the law, then the king before whom he was summoned shall place him outside his protection *(extra sermonem suum).*

LVIII. CONCERNING THE CHRENECRUDA (i.e., INVOLVING THE KIN IN THE PAYMENT OF COMPOSITION FOR HOMICIDE)

1. If anyone kills a man and, having given up all his property, he still does not have enough to pay the total composition, let him offer twelve oath–helpers [who will support his oath] that neither above the earth nor below the earth does he have more property than he has already given.

2. Afterwards he should enter his house and in his hand collect dust from its four corners, and then he should stand on the *duropdlo,* that is, on the threshold, looking into the house, and then with his left hand he should throw the earth over his shoulders onto him who is his nearest relative.

3. If his mother and brother have already paid [and the composition is still not fully paid], then he should throw the earth over the sister of his mother or her children. If there are none of these, then he should throw the earth over three from the maternal kin and three of the paternal kin who are next most nearly related.

4. And afterwards without a shirt and barefoot, with stick in hand, he should go jump over his fence [i.e., abandon his house?] and those three from the maternal side shall pay half of whatever is the value of the composition or the judgment set; and those others who come from the paternal side should do the same [i.e., pay the other half].

5. If any of these does not have that with which to pay his full share, let him who is poor throw the *chrenecruda* over him who has more so that he pays the entire judgment.

LIX. CONCERNING ALLODIAL LANDS *(de alodis)*

1. If a man dies and leaves no children, and if his father or mother survives him,

this person shall succeed to the inheritance.

2. If there is no father or mother but he leaves a brother or sister, they shall succeed to the inheritance.

3. If none of these is living, then the sister of the mother shall succeed to the inheritance.

4. If none of the mother's sisters live, then the sisters of the father will succeed to the inheritance.

5. If there is no father's sister, after these kindred whoever is closest who comes from the father's kin shall succeed to the inheritance.

6. But concerning Salic land (*term Salica*), no portion or inheritance is for a woman but all the land belongs to members of the male sex who are brothers.

LXII. CONCERNING THE COMPOSITION FOR HOMICIDE (i.e., BY WHAT MEANS THE RELATIVES OF A FATHER SHALL DIVIDE THE COMPOSITION AMONG THEMSELVES)

1. If a man who is a father is killed, his children shall collect half of the composition and those relatives who are closest to his father and to his mother shall divide the other half among them.

2. If there is no relative on one side, either the paternal or maternal, that portion of the composition will be collected by the fisc or by him to whom the fisc wishes to give it.

LXV. CONCERNING THE DESTRUCTION OF PROPERTY

If anyone destroys the fruit of another's land and will not restore it, if he is summoned to court and is convicted, he shall be liable to pay six hundred denarii (i.e., fifteen solidi)

II. Common Terms, Words and Phrases for the Text

The Laws of the Salian Franks《萨利克法兰克人法典》

a yearling calf 1岁龄牛犊

a denarius（拉丁语）古罗马的小银币；1个罗马帝国的金币，值25个小银币

a solidus（罗马帝国）金币，公元312年首次铸造和发行的钱币，重量为4.55克

a triens（罗马法）价值为1阿斯（as，古罗马货币单位，相当于12盎司）的1/3

wether 阉羊

a herd dog 牧羊犬

confess 承认，供认，坦白

abduction 诱拐，劫持，绑架

waylaying 拦路抢劫，埋伏

oath-helpers 助誓人

granary 谷仓，粮仓

designated 指定的

a stallion 种马，成年公马

a free Frank 法兰克自由民

barbarian 蛮族人

conceal 隐藏，隐匿，隐瞒

antrustion（法语，源自拉丁语 antrustio）心腹大臣，心腹奴仆

villa（意大利语，源自拉丁语）村庄，（乡村）庄园，别墅

sagibaron（欧洲古法中由国王任命的）法官

count 伯爵

servant（国人的）仆人

rachimburgi（欧洲古法）法官

security 担保，担保物，担保人

oath 宣誓，誓言，誓言陈述

ordeal 神明裁判

composition（日耳曼法）补偿金，抵偿金

summon 传唤

witness 证人

chrenecruda（萨利克法）掷草仪式

homicide 杀人

threshold 门槛，门口

the maternal kin 母系亲属

the paternal kin 父系亲属

allodial lands 自主保有的地产

succeed to the inheritance 继承遗产

destruction of property 破坏财产

convict 定罪；（经审判）证明……有罪；宣判……有罪

III. Exercises and Thinking

1. Please summarize the general characteristics of The Laws of the Salian Franks.

2. Please briefly describe Frankish social circumstances according to the Laws.

3. What influence did these laws have on later times?

IV. Further Readings and Internet links

1. Further Readings

Ian Wood, *The Merovingian Kingdoms, 450–751*, New York: Longman Publishing, 1994.

Katherine Fischer Drew, *The Laws of the Salian Franks*, Philadelphia: University of Pennsylvania Press, 1991.

《世界著名法典汉译丛书》编委会辑：《萨利克法典》，法律出版社2000年版。

2. Internet Links

不列颠百科全书网站：https://www.britannica.com/

Unit 17

The Donation of Constantine

《君士坦丁赠礼》

《君士坦丁赠礼》是中世纪时期一份伪造的君士坦丁大帝授权文件。主要内容是授予罗马教宗西尔维斯特一世（Sanctus Silvester PP.I，r. 314—335）及其继任者对其他四个宗主教区（君士坦丁堡、亚历山大里亚、安提阿和耶路撒冷），对一切宗教信仰事务的管辖权，以及对罗马城市和整个西罗马帝国的世俗统治权。目前，学界公认其创作时间为 8 世纪中叶至 9 世纪中叶，具体而言又有多个时间节点，其中 752—757 年说被学界大多数人所接受。它的创作地点大致有两种较为可信的说法，一是罗马，二是巴黎的圣丹尼斯修道院，还有学者认为是拜占庭。至于其作者，学界大多认为是罗马教廷的文书或无名的教士。

现存最早的《君士坦丁赠礼》手稿产生于 9 世纪，先后被汇编入《伪教令集》及格拉蒂安的《教令集》。尽管《君士坦丁赠礼》在 9—12 世纪被视为真实可靠的文件，但是在这期间并非无人质疑。大约在 1000 年，神圣罗马帝国皇帝奥托三世及其支持者对该文件的真实性表示过怀疑。12—13 世纪的民法学家频繁地质疑它的真实性。意大利人文主义先驱但丁（1265—1321）在《论世界帝国》中，从法理上质疑这份文件的真实性。[①] 1440 年，意大利人文主义者洛伦佐 · 瓦拉彻底地证明了《君士坦丁赠礼》是一份伪造的文件。这最终被教俗界认同。

迄今为止，学界对于伪造《君士坦丁赠礼》的目的大致有以下不同的说法。一是支持罗马教宗对意大利乃至对西罗马帝国至高无上统治权的主张；二是旨

① ［意］但丁：《论世界帝国》，朱虹译，商务印书馆 1986 年版，第 56-88 页。

在保护新的西方帝国即加洛林帝国免受拜占庭的攻击，进而证明查理曼帝国的合法性，消除拜占庭帝国在罗马的影响，获取对东正教会的至高权。另外，还有少数学者认为伪造《君士坦丁赠礼》仅为了颂扬罗马教宗西尔维斯特一世和君士坦丁大帝。目前，学界多支持前两种说法。这是因为在 8 世纪法兰克王国经历了由墨洛温王朝向加洛林王朝的更迭、教皇国的诞生、800 年查理被加冕为罗马人的皇帝、查理的加洛林帝国正式诞生。

这份伪造的文件客观上对西欧历史发展产生了重要影响。9 世纪中叶，罗马教宗尼古拉一世援引它来主张教宗的至高权威。11 世纪中叶，在罗马教会与东正教会的分裂冲突过程中，罗马教宗利奥九世（r.1049—1054）利用伪造的《君士坦丁赠礼》反对东正教的权力，并进一步主张对君士坦丁堡牧首的至高权威。在西欧政教冲突中，罗马教宗也利用了这份伪造的文件。13 世纪初，罗马教宗英诺森三世（r.1198—1216）甚至利用这份伪造的文件来主张教宗对世俗国家与统治者的至上权威。罗马教宗英诺森四世（r.1243—1254）任职期间在政教冲突中也利用了这份伪造的文件。到了 15 世纪中叶，《君士坦丁赠礼》彻底被证伪之后，多位罗马教宗仍援引它为在“地理大发现”过程中西班牙和葡萄牙两国产生的纠纷进行仲裁。

I. Excerpt from *The Donation of Constantine*①

2. Our most gracious serenity desires, in clear discourse, through the page of this our imperial decree, to bring to the knowledge of all the people in the whole world what things our Saviour and Redeemer the Lord Jesus Christ, the Son of the most High Father, has most wonderfully seen fit to bring about through his holy apostles Peter and Paul and by the intervention of our father Sylvester, the highest pontiff and the universal pope. First, indeed, putting forth, with the inmost confession of our heart, for the purpose of instructing the mind of all of you, our creed which we have learned from the aforesaid

① Johannes Fried ed., *Donation of Constantine and Constitutum Constantini*, Berlin: Walter de Gruyter, 2007, pp. 138–145.

most blessed father and our confessor, Sylvester the universal pontiff; and then at length announcing the mercy of God which has been poured upon us.

3. For we wish you to know, as we have signified through our former imperial decree, that we have gone away, from the worship of idols, from mute and deaf images made by hand, from devilish contrivances and from all the pomps of Satan; and have arrived at the pure faith of the Christians, which is the true light and everlasting life. Believing, according to what he—that same one, our revered supreme father and teacher, the pontiff Sylvester—has taught us, in God the Father, the almighty maker of Heaven and earth, of all things visible and invisible; and in Jesus Christ, his only Son, our Lord God, through whom all things are created; and in the Holy Spirit, the Lord and vivifier of the whole creature. We confess these, the Father and the Son and the Holy Spirit, in such way that, in the perfect Trinity, there shall also be a fulness of divinity and a unity of power. The Father is God, the Son is God, and the Holy Spirit is God; and these three are one in Jesus Christ. There are therefore three forms but one power.

5. For this is our orthodox creed, placed before us by our most blessed father Sylvester, the supreme pontiff. We exhort, therefore, all people, and all the different nations, to hold, cherish and preach this faith; and, in the name of the Holy Trinity, to obtain the grace of baptism; and, with a devout heart, to adore the Lord Jesus Christ our Saviour, who with the Father and the Holy Spirit, lives and reigns through infinite ages; whom Sylvester our father, the universal pontiff, preaches.

9. Hereupon that same most blessed Sylvester our father, bishop of the city of Rome, imposed upon us a time of penance-within our Lateran palace, in the chapel, in a hair garment—so that I might obtain pardon from our Lord God Jesus Christ our Saviour by vigils, fasts, and tears and prayers, for all things that had been impiously done and unjustly ordered by me. Then through the imposition of the hands of the clergy, I came to the bishop himself; and there, renouncing the pomps of Satan and his works, and all idols made by hands, of my own will before all the people I confessed: that I believed

in God the Father almighty, maker of Heaven and earth, and of all things visible and invisible; and in Jesus Christ, His only Son our Lord, who was born of the Holy Spirit and of the Virgin Mary. And, the font having been blessed, the wave of salvation purified me there with a triple immersion. For there, I being placed at the bottom of the font, saw with my own eyes a band from Heaven touching me; whence rising, clean, know that I was cleansed from all the squalor of leprosy. And, I being raised from the venerable font–putting on white raiment, be administered to me the sign of the seven–fold holy Spirit, the unction of the holy oil; and he traced the sign of the holy cross on my brow, saying: God seals thee with the seal of His faith in the name of the Father and the Son and the Holy Spirit, to signalize thy faith. All the clergy replied: "Amen." The bishop added, "peace be with thee."

10. And so, on the first day after receiving the mystery of the holy baptism, and after the cure of my body from the squalor of the leprosy, I recognized that there was no other God save the Father and the Son and the Holy Spirit; whom the most blessed Sylvester the pope doth preach; a trinity in one, a unity in three. For all the gods of the nations, whom I have worshipped up to this time, are proved to be demons; works made by the hand of men; inasmuch as that same venerable father told to us most clearly how much power in Heaven and on earth He, our Saviour, conferred on his apostle St. Peter, when finding him faithful after questioning him He said: "Thou art Peter, and upon this rock (petram) shall I build My Church, and the gates of bell shall not prevail against it." Give heed ye powerful, and incline the ear of your hearts to that which the good Lord and Master added to His disciple, saying: "And I will give thee the keys of the kingdom of Heaven; and whatever thou shalt bind on earth shall be bound also in Heaven, and whatever thou shalt loose on earth shall be loosed also in Heaven." This is very wonderful and glorious, to bind and loose on earth and to have it bound and loosed in Heaven.

11. And when, the blessed Sylvester preaching them, I perceived these things, and

learned that by the kindness of St. Peter himself I had been entirely restored to health: I together with all our satraps and the whole senate and the nobles and all the Roman people, who are subject to the glory of our rule—considered it advisable that, as on earth he (Peter) is seen to have been constituted vicar of the Son of God, so the pontiffs, who are the representatives of that same chief of the apostles, should obtain from us and our empire the power of a supremacy greater than the earthly clemency of our imperial serenity is seen to have had conceded to it,—we choosing that same prince of the apostles, or his vicars, to be our constant intercessors with God. And, to the extent of our earthly imperial power, we decree that his holy Roman church shall be honoured with veneration; and that, more than our empire and earthly throne, the most sacred seat of St. Peter shall be gloriously exalted; we giving to it the imperial power, and dignity of glory, and vigour and honour.

12. And we ordain and decree that he shall have the supremacy as well over the four chief seats Antioch, Alexandria, Constantinople and Jerusalem, as also over all the churches of God in the whole world. And he who for the time being shall be pontiff of that holy Roman church shall be more exalted than, and chief over, all the priests of the whole world; and, according to his judgment, everything which is to be provided for the service of God or the stability of the faith of the Christians is to be administered. It is indeed just, that there the holy law should have the seat of its rule where the founder of holy laws, our Saviour, told St. Peter to take the chair of the apostleship; where also, sustaining the cross, he blissfully took the cup of death and appeared as imitator of his Lord and Master; and that there the people should bend their necks at the confession of Christ's name, where their teacher, St. Paul the apostle, extending his neck for Christ, was crowned with martyrdom. There, until the end, let them seek a teacher, where the holy body of the teacher lies; and there, prone and humiliated, let them perform I the service of the heavenly king, God our Saviour Jesus Christ, where the proud were accustomed to serve under the rule of an earthly king.

14. For let all the people and the nations of the races in the whole world rejoice with us; we exhorting all of you to give unbounded thanks, together with us, to our Lord and Saviour Jesus Christ. For He is God in Heaven above and on earth below, who, visiting us through His holy apostles, made us worthy to receive the holy sacrament of baptism and health of body. In return for which, to those same holy apostles, my masters, St. Peter and St. Paul; and, through them, also to St. Sylvester, our father,—the chief pontiff and universal pope of the city of Rome,—and to all the pontiffs his successors, who until the end of the world shall be about to sit in the seat of St. Peter: we concede and, by this present, do confer, our imperial Lateran palace, which is preferred to, and ranks above, all the palaces in the whole world; then a diadem, that is, the crown of our head, and at the same time the tiara; and, also, the shoulder band,—that is, the collar that usually surrounds our imperial neck; and also the purple mantle, and crimson tunic, and all the imperial raiment; and the same rank as those presiding over the imperial cavalry; conferring also the imperial sceptres, and, at the same time, the spears and standards; also the banners and different imperial ornaments, and all the advantage of our high imperial position, and the glory of our power.

16. We also decreed this, that this same venerable one our father Sylvester, the supreme pontiff, and all the pontiffs his successors, might use and bear upon their heads—to the Praise of God and for the honour of St. Peter—the diadem; that is, the crown which we have granted him from our own head, of purest gold and precious gems. But he, the most holy pope, did not at all allow that crown of gold to be used over the clerical crown which he wears to the glory of St. Peter; but we placed upon his most holy head, with our own hands, a tiara of gleaming splendour representing the glorious resurrection of our Lord. And, holding the bridle of his horse, out of reverence for St. Peter we performed for him the duty of groom; decreeing that all the pontiffs his successors, and they alone, may use that tiara in processions in imitation of our own imperial dignity.

17. In order that the supreme pontificate may not deteriorate, but may rather be adorned with dignity and glory even more than is the dignity of the terrestrial Empire: behold, we confer to the frequently mentioned most blessed pontiff, our father Sylvester, the universal pope, as well our palace, as has been said, as also the city of Rome, all provinces, places and cities of Italy and the western regions and we—by our firm imperial will through this our godlike, holy and imperial constitution—relinquish them to his and his successors' power and rule, and we decree that they shall remain under the law of the holy Roman church.

18. Wherefore we have perceived it to be fitting that our empire and the power of our kingdom should be transferred and changed to the regions of the East; and that, in the province of Byzantium, in a most fitting place, a city should be built in our name; and that our empire should there be established. For, where the supremacy of priests and the bead of the Christian religion has been established by a heavenly ruler, it is not just that there an earthly ruler should have jurisdiction.

19. We decree, moreover, that all these things which, through this our imperial charter and through other godlike commands, we have established and confirmed, shall remain uninjured and unshaken until the end of the world. Wherefore, before the living God, who commanded us to reign, and in the face of his terrible judgment, we conjure, through this our imperial decree, all the emperors our successors, and all our nobles, the satraps also and the most glorious senate, and all the people in the whole world now and in all times previously subject to our rule: that no one of them, in any way allow himself to oppose or disregard, or in any way seize, these things which, by our imperial sanction, have been conceded to the holy Roman church and to all its pontiffs. If anyone, moreover,—which we do not believe—prove a scorner or despiser in this matter, he shall be subject and bound over to eternal damnation; and shall feel that the holy chiefs of the apostles of God, Peter and Paul, will be opposed to him in the present and in the future life. And, being burned in the nethermost hell, he shall perish with the devil and all the impious.

20. The page, moreover, of this our imperial decree, we, confirming it with our own hands, did place above the venerable body of St. Peter chief of the apostles; and there, promising to that same apostle of God that we would preserve inviolably all its provisions, and would leave in our commands to all the emperors our successors to preserve them, we did hand it over, to be enduringly and happily possessed, to our most blessed father Sylvester the supreme pontiff and universal pope, and, through him, to all the pontiffs his successors—God our Lord and our Saviour Jesus Christ consenting.

II. Common Terms, Words and Phrases for the Text

serenity 平静，宁静

the Saviour 救主，救世主（耶稣基督）

the Redeemer 救世主，耶稣基督

the Creed（基督教）信经

Pontiff 罗马教皇 / 教宗

the worship of idols 偶像崇拜

revered 尊敬的，崇敬的

God the Father 上帝圣父

the Son, our Lord, Jesus Christ 圣子，我们的主，耶稣基督

the Holy Spirit 圣灵

the Trinity（基督教）三位一体（圣父、圣子及圣灵合为上帝）

orthodox creed 正统的信条

exhort 规劝，敦促，告诫

baptism（基督教的）洗礼，浸礼

penance 补赎，悔罪

renounce 声明放弃，宣布放弃

salvation（基督教）得救，救恩，救世

squalor 肮脏，邋遢

leprosy 麻风病

venerable 令人尊重的，值得敬重的，受敬佩的

the unction of the holy oil 涂圣油（礼）

thee 你，汝，尔（旧时用词，现亦用于诗歌或宗教类语境，用作宾格）

thou 与 thee 同义

ye 你们，汝等

clergy（统称）圣职人员，神职人员

demon 魔鬼

clemency（对受惩罚的人表现出的）仁慈，慈悲，宽恕，宽容

intercessor 调解人，仲裁者

the Throne 王位，王权，帝位

martyrdom 殉难，殉道

unbounded（似）无限的，无尽的，无穷的

diadem 王冠，冕

the purple mantle 紫色披风

sceptre（象征王权的）节杖，权杖

tiara 冠状头饰；（罗马教宗戴的）三重冠

the Pope 罗马教宗

relinquish （正式）（尤指不情愿地）放弃

III. Exercises and Thinking

1.What was the primary purpose of *The Donation of Constantine*? Please explain your reasons.

2. Please contemplate the profound influence of *The Donation of Constantine.*

3. Please analyze the relationship between this text and the political situation of Western Europe in the eighth and ninth centuries.

IV. Further Readings and Internet Links

1. Further Readings

Johannes Fried, *Donation of Constantine and Constitutum Constantini*, Berlin: Walter de Gruyter, 2007.

[意]洛伦佐·瓦拉:《〈君士坦丁赠礼〉伪作考》,陈文海译,商务印书馆2022年版。

[意]洛伦佐·瓦拉:《〈君士坦丁赠礼〉辨伪》,李婧敬编译,商务印书馆2023年版。

2. Internet Links

不列颠百科全书网站:https://www.britannica.com/

Unit 18

The Canon of Medicine
阿维森纳《医典》

阿维森纳（Avicenna, 980—1037），阿拉伯文学家、音乐理论家、天文学家、政治家，杰出的医学家、哲学家，可谓百科全书式学者。原名伊本·西拿，西方人习惯将其称为阿维森纳。生于伊朗的布哈拉城（Bukhara，今属乌兹别克斯坦）附近的阿夫沙纳镇（Afshana，今属乌兹别克斯坦）的一个伊斯玛仪派伊斯兰教家庭，1037 年卒于哈马丹（Hamadan，今属伊朗）。父亲是萨曼王朝的一名税务官员。萨曼王朝首都布哈拉是伊斯兰东部世界的经济、文化中心，建有规模庞大的图书馆，藏书丰富。阿维森纳曾在自传中描述过该馆藏书的盛况。

据记载，阿维森纳智力超群，记忆力非凡。10 岁时，他就已经完成语言（母语为波斯语）和文学的学习，并能背诵《古兰经》。在其父之友，身为著名教师的伊斯玛仪什叶派拥护者——纳蒂利的指导下学习希腊逻辑学和数学。在自然科学和医学方面，他通过自学成为一名教师和执业医生。他因医术水平高而被召进宫廷为努赫·伊本·曼苏尔（即埃米尔努赫二世）治病，后者病愈后欣然允许他自由出入藏书丰富的萨曼王朝的宫廷图书馆。

在阿维森纳 22 岁时，其父亲去世，他迫于生计进入萨曼政府工作。在萨曼王朝被加兹尼王朝（又译伽色尼王朝）征服后，阿维森纳离开故乡，余生在波斯各城市度过，开启了作为宫廷医生或者偶尔作为政府文书的旅行生活。最终，他接受了白益王朝一位名叫沙姆斯·道拉（Shams al-Dawla）的王子的邀请，前往波斯西部的哈马丹城。在那里，他成为首席宫廷医生，两度官至维齐尔（vizier，宰相）。1022 年，白益王子沙姆斯去世，阿维森纳度过了一段艰难岁月

（包括被囚禁）后，被迫逃离哈马丹，前往伊斯法罕。在伊斯法罕，阿维森纳受到统治者阿拉·道拉（Ala al-Dawlah）及其宫廷的敬重，并在此享受着成年生活中最后也是最长的一段相对安宁稳定的时期，达 14 年之久。正是在这一时期，除了作为宫廷医生行医，阿维森纳还有规律地在一所矗立于伊斯法罕旧城的学校教书，并撰写大部分著作。1037 年，阿维森纳在陪同统治者道拉进行的一次军事行动中病倒，不久在哈马丹去世。

阿维森纳著作留存下来的逾 100 部。其中，最重要的医学著作就是《医典》。这部著作继承了古希腊医学家希波克拉底和盖伦的成就，同时吸收古代中国、印度、波斯等国家的医学成就，成为阿拉伯医学的集大成之作。《医典》全书共分为 5 卷，约 100 万字，代表了当时医学的最高成就，一经问世就在伊斯兰世界传播开来，并很快传至欧洲，受到伊斯兰世界和欧洲医学界推崇。在 12 世纪到 18 世纪中叶的 600 多年间，《医典》被西方多所大学用作医学教科书，被欧洲医生作为行医指南。

《医典》是一部系统的医学百科全书，曾有西方著名医学史家称之为医学"圣经"，对东西方医学影响巨大而深远。阿维森纳是中古阿拉伯一位享誉世界的医学巨擘，在欧洲赢得"医学王子"的美誉，在东方也家喻户晓，其人其事是波斯、阿拉伯、土耳其和印度穆斯林民间文学的重要来源，是东西方医学文化交流互鉴互融的杰出代表。这里选取的内容出自格鲁纳（Gruner）编纂的《医典》英译本。

I. Excerpt from *The Canon of Medicine of Avicenna*①

6. Medicine is the science by which we learn, (a) the various states of the human body, (i) in health, (ii) when not in health, (b) the means by which, (i) health is likely to be lost, and (ii) when lost, is likely to be restored to health. In other words, it is the art

① Avicenna ed., *A Treatise on The Canon of Medicine of Avicenna, Incorporating a Translation of the First Book,* by O. Cameron Gruner, London: Luzac & Co., 1930, pp. 25–540.

whereby health [the beauty of the body—long hair, clear complexion, fragrance and form (Chahar Maqala)] is conserved and the art whereby it is restored, after being lost.

11. To medicine pertains the (study of the) human body—how its health is maintained; how it loses health. To know fully about each of these we must ascertain the causes of both health and sickness.

12. Now as health and sickness and their causes are sometimes evident to the senses and sometimes only perceived by means of the evidence afforded by the various symptoms, we must in medicine gain a knowledge of the symptoms of health and sickness.

It is a dictum of the exact sciences that knowledge of a thing is attained only through a knowledge of the causes and the origins of the causes—assuming there to be causes and origins. Consequently our knowledge (of health and sickness) cannot be complete without an understanding both of symptoms and of the principles of being.

95. Galen regards the blood as the only normal body-fluid, for he considers that all others are excrementitious and quite useless. But if the blood were the only nourisher of the various organs of the body, it would be as much as saying they are all alike in temperament and nature. Bone would not be harder than flesh were it not for the hardness in the atrabilious humour present in the blood. Brain would not be softer than the flesh were it not for the presence in the blood of the soft serous humour which nourishes the brain. So we conclude that in the blood there are other humours, which leave it (in the various organs).

139. The natural or vegetative faculty is twofold, and includes (i) the nutritive faculty, which is concerned with the welfare and preservation of the individual, and secures nourishment to it to the end of life. This faculty resides in the liver, and its functions emerge therefrom; (ii) the reproductive faculty, which ensures the propagation of the race. This subserves the process of generation, and separates the substance of the sperm from the humours of the body and fashions the new body according to the decree

of Allah. The seat of this faculty is the generative organs, and its functions proceed from them.

196. There are three states of the human body, according to Galen:—

(i) Health—a state in virtue of which the human body presents that particular temperament and configuration whereby all its functions shall proceed unembarrassed.

(ii) Disease—a state which is exactly contrary to (i).

(iii) A third state which is neither health nor disease. There are three variants of this: (a) the health is not perfect and yet there is no actual illness. Ex.: the state in old persons, and in juveniles, and in those convalescent from illness. (b) Both states occur simultaneously in the same member: either in two quite different respects (as when the temperament of a person is normal, but there is compositional abnormality); or in two respects which are related to one another (as when a person is healthy in form, but there is error in size or position of a member; he may be healthy in regard to two passive qualities, but not in regard to two active ones). (c) Both states occur in one person, but at different times of the year (as when a person is well in winter but ill in spring).

452. By means of the symptoms and signs of the three main states of the body (health, illness, neutrality), we obtain information as to the present, the past and the future of the patient's state. Knowledge of his present state, says Galen, is of advantage to the patient alone, showing him what he must do; knowledge of the past is advantageous to the physician alone, as proving him to excel in his art, so that his advice becomes worthy of respect (because reliable) ; knowledge of the future serves both purposes—it is advantageous to the patient because it guides him along the road he should follow, and it is advantageous to the physician in showing him to excel in his art.

678. In the first part of this book it was stated that Medicine comprises two parts, one theoretical, and one practical, though both are really simply speculative science. That which is specially named "theory" relates to the formation of opinions and the showing of the evidence upon which they are based, without reference to the mode

of acting upon them. Thus this part deals with the temperaments, the humours, the faculties; and with the forms, the symptoms, and the causes of disease. That which is specially named "practical" relates to the mode of acting upon this knowledge, and the prescription of a regimen.

For instance, it is that part of Medicine which helps us to understand how the health of the body is to be maintained in this or that state, and by what means we can heal the diseases with which the body is afflicted. "Practical" does not refer to the performance of surgical operations. It is the *art* which teaches us *in what way* to procure healing—the "healing" art.

Having expounded in the first and second parts of this work the various matters pertaining to this theoretical part of Medicine, we now proceed to the study of the two subjects pertaining to the practical part—dealing with them in a general manner.

The two parts which belong to the practical side of Medicine are (1) The science of regulating the healthy body, so as to maintain it in health. The science of hygiene.

(2) The science of ruling the sick body so as to enable it to return to a state of health. The science of healing.

In this part then, the third, we write down fully how the health is to be maintained.

736. Since the regimen for maintaining health consists essentially in the regulation of (1) exercise, (2) food and (3) sleep, we may begin our discourse with the subject of (gymnastic) exercise. We may define exercise as voluntary movement entailing deep and hurried respiration.

Once we direct the attention towards regulating exercise as to amount and time, we shall find there is no need for such medicaments as are ordinarily required for remedying diseases dependent on [abnormal] matters, or diseases of temperament consequent upon such. This is true provided the rest of the regimen is appropriate and proper.

737. We know that this must be so when we reflect how, in regard to nutriment, our health depends on the nutriment being appropriate for us and regulated in quantity

and quality. For not one of the aliments which are capable of nourishing the body is converted into actual nutriment in its entirety. In every case digestion leaves something untouched, and nature takes care to have that evacuated. Nevertheless, the evacuation which nature accomplishes is not a complete one. Hence at the end of each digestion there is some superfluity left over. Should this be a frequent occurrence, repetition would lead to further aggregation until something measurable has accumulated. As a result, harmful effete substances would form and injure various parts of the body. When they undergo decomposition, putrefactive diseases arise (Bacterial infections). Should they be strong in quality, they will give rise to an intemperament; and if they should increase in quantity they would set up the symptoms of plethora which have already been described. Flowing to some member, they will result in an inflammatory mass, and their "vapours" will destroy the temperament of the substantial basis of the breath.

816. *Physiological effects of sleep.* At the present, we may say that sleep in moderation (1) assists the vegetative faculties in their functions, and (2) brings the sensitive faculties into repose and in so doing (3) renews and restores them, and thereby (4) arrests the dissipation of the breath (the vital power). Hence (1) the digestion of the food in the several stages we have named is accomplished. Sleep also (3) remedies the weakness due to the dispersal of the breath (vital power) in various ways; namely, by bodily fatigue, by coitus, by anger or violent emotional disturbance, and the rest.

Furthermore, a moderated amount of sleep brings about an equilibrium in regard to quantity and quality of the humours, and therefore it has a humectant and warming action, which is specially advantageous for the aged, who need their moisture preserving and renewing. That is why Galen said "every night I partake of a little packet of herbs—lettuce combined with aromatics; the former because they induce sleep, the latter because they rectify the coldness of the lettuce." And he said, "I am now careful to obtain sleep because I am an old man, and the humidity which sleep brings is beneficial to me."

818. *Conditions to observe regarding sleep.* Healthy persons should pay attention to the subject of sleep: it must be moderate, properly timed, and excess must be avoided. And on the other hand they must avoid the injury resulting to mental and all other faculties from remaining awake too long.

However a person is often driven to keep awake, and refrain from sleep owing to a dread of syncope and loss of strength.

The best sleep is that which is deep; and that which occurs after the food has passed on from the upper part of the intestine, and after the flatulences and eructations which may have followed have subsided; for to sleep on this is detrimental in many ways, though the person himself may not know of it; it keeps him turning from side to side in his sleep; it hinders digestion; and it does injury. For this reason, if the passage of the food out of the stomach is delayed, he should take a walk for a little while, and then retire to sleep.

It is also bad to go to sleep on an empty stomach, as this is weakening. It is bad to go to sleep after repletion, before the food has left the stomach, because sleep cannot be deep under such circumstances, and the sleeper will keep turning from one side to the other all the time. For when the natural faculties are busy with the work of digestion at a time when it is accustomed to be asleep, the fact of being prevented from waking up is disturbing to the natural faculties; so they become dulled and the process of digestion is disorganized.

It is also bad to go to sleep during the day, for in this case illnesses depending on humidity and catarrhal states are brought about; the colour of health passes off, the spleen becomes heavy, the nerves lose their tone; lack of vim and a poor appetite are noticed, and inflammatory conditions and fevers often appear.

854. In brief, the regimen appropriate for old people consists in giving those forms of aliment, drink, and baths which render the body warm and moist (i.e. moistening, calefacient food; warm or hot soft water baths). There should be plenty of sleep, and the

time spent on the couch should be liberal — more than is legitimate for adults. The flow of urine should be continually assisted by diluents; the mucus should be helped out of the stomach by way of the bowels and urine. The nature is too soft, and this needs correcting.

Massage: massage with oil, moderated both in quantity and quality so as to fall short of occasioning lassitude, is beneficial.

Exercise: Walking or horse–riding is taken after the massage. The choice depends on which is too fatiguing. If both forms of exercise are fatiguing, repeat the massage once or twice (instead).

Sleep: the air of the room: some pleasantly redolent aromatic should be used to perfume the air which is breathed, using one which is moderately "hot" .

After sleep, the body should be anointed with oil in order to stimulate the sensitive faculties. After this the horse–riding or walking exercise may be taken.

860. The wine which is best for elderly persons is old, red, with warming effect, and diuretic. New and white sweet wine should be avoided, unless a bath is taken after a meal at which such wine is taken, and unless there is thirst. In that case it is allowable to take white wine which is light without much body in it, thus taking the place of plain water.

Elderly persons must shun sweet wines which are likely to prove oppilative [but wines prepared with honey may be allowed even in cases where gout is threatened: Aeg].

872. The regimen which will reduce obesity. (1) Procure a rapid descent of the food from the stomach and intestines, in order to prevent completion of absorption by the mesentery. [One may take saltish things of laxative nature: Rhazes.] (2) Take food which is bulky but feebly nutritious. (3) Take the bath before food, often. [Take not food immediately after the bath, and a short sleep; follow up the bath with massage; make a long stay in the bath: Haly Abbas.] (4) Hard exercise. (5) Resolvent oils. [Rub in oil containing root of wild cucumber, marshmallows, gentian, all–heal root, birthwort root, poley, and centaury; volatile ointments; oil of dill: Aegineta.] (6) Electuaries: the lesser myrobalan electuary; electuary of lacca; "theriac." (7) Take vinegar, and salt, while

fasting.

905. The subject of treatment comprises three headlines: that of the regimen and diet, that of the use of medicines, and that of manual or operative interference.

By the word "regimen" we understand the systematic management of the several factors which we have enumerated as being essential to health, and among them diet has an (important) place. The prescription of a regimen is based upon data pertaining to the qualities of the nutrients to be selected, as well as those belonging to the qualities which determine the choice of medicines.

906. Treatment with food. In regard to *diet*, the first question to decide is as to the quantity of each article of food which should be allowed. Sometimes a given article of food is to be forbidden; sometimes lessened; sometimes no change need be made; sometimes the amount taken is to be increased.

The physician only forbids a food, or all food, if he intends that the digestive faculties [throughout the body] shall be left entirely free to complete the maturation of the humours. He prescribes a lessened amount of a food, if he wishes the digestive powers to be conserved. The very fact of taking nutriment is a tax on the digestive faculties; therefore the withdrawal of a certain amount of food means a corresponding alleviation for them.

The physician must also be watchful in regard to two dangers—one, that the natural powers should become too enfeebled; the second, that an illness should become too grave.

1105. *Action of wine on emotions and on breath.*—This is shown in the instance of those who drink excellent wine, for in such persons gladness increases to such a pitch that onlookers wonder how they can be jovial without reason. Such a thing, of course, cannot be. No impression is possible without an impressor.

But the fact is that when wine is taken in moderation, it gives rise to a large amount of breath, whose character is balanced, and whose luminosity is strong and brilliant. Hence wine disposes greatly to gladness, and the person is subject to quite trivial exciting agents. The breath now takes up the impression of agents belonging to the present time more easily than it does those which relate to the future; it responds to agents conducive to delight rather than those conducive to a sense of beauty. It also takes up an impression from agents which are prone to evoke conjecture rather than from those which are concerned with real understanding. The explanation of this is that normally the power of the mind brings about an act in the brain such as will expel the breath (when it is in the phase of having a mild degree of moisture); the brain thus becomes able to obey the motions of the thought and the exercise of the faculty of understanding. In inebriety, however, there is a very great inclination towards excess of moisture (which is incompatible with obedience to the understanding), owing to admixture with ascending and overflowing vapours, which render it too humid. 'This moisture prevents it from obeying the intellectual faculty and the tendencies of the thought, except in respect of very material and corporeal topics. It cannot serve in respect of very delicate spiritual matters. Whether stable or agitated, moisture cannot take part in the formation or presentation of spiritual affairs; it can only respond to corporeal ones.

II. Common Terms, Words and Phrases for the Text

dictum 名言，格言

Galen（古希腊医学家）盖仑

excrementitious 粪便的，排泄物的

temperament 气质，性格，禀性

humour 体液（旧时认为存在于人体内，有四种，可影响健康和性格）

the atrabilious humour 黑胆汁

the soft serous humour 柔软的黏液

the natural or vegetative faculty 自然本能或植物本能

the propagation of the race 种族繁衍

subserve 促进，有助于

sperm 精子，精液

the decree of Allah 安拉的旨意

convalescent 康复期的，正康复的，渐愈的

juvenile（正式或法律）少年

abnormality（身体、行为等）异常，反常，畸形，变态

neutrality 中立，中立状态；中间状态

regimen（医学或正式的）养生法

expound 详解，详述，阐述

the science of hygiene 卫生学，保健学

the science of healing 治疗学，康复学

gymnastic 体操的，体育的

respiration 呼吸

medicament 药剂，医药

nutriment 营养物

evacuate 排泄（粪便）

superfluity 多余物，残留物

effete 衰弱的，衰败的

decomposition 分解

physiological effect 生理作用，生理影响

lettuce 莴苣，生菜

aromatics 芳香料，芳香剂

rectify 矫正，纠正，改正

intestine 肠

flatulence（肠胃）气胀

eructation 打嗝（行为），喷出物

vim 精力，活力，力量

inflammatory（医学）炎性的，发炎的

aliment 营养物，滋养品

moistening, calefacient food 湿性食品，暖性食品

diluent 稀释剂，稀释液

mucus 黏液

urine 尿，小便

massage 按摩

lassitude 疲乏，无精打采，倦怠

diuretic（医学）利尿的；利尿药

oppilative 便秘的

resolvent 分解的，有溶解力的；溶解物，溶剂

mesentery（解剖）肠系膜

electuary （药学）药糖剂

fasting（因宗教或健康原因）节食，禁食，斋戒

enfeeble 使衰弱，使虚弱，使无力

luminosity 发光，发亮

III. Exercises and Thinking

1. Please provide a new understanding of health.

2. Which achievements did *The Canon of Medicine of Avicenna* absorb？

3. Please discuss the health and wellness for seniors.

4. Please illustrate your understanding on treatments of medicine and food.

IV. Further Readings and Internet Links

1.Further Readings

Avicenna, *A Treatise on The Canon of Medicine of Avicenna, Incorporating a Translation of the First Book,* by O. Cameron Gruner, London: Luzac & Co., 1930.

[阿拉伯]阿维森纳编著:《阿维森纳医典》，朱明主译，人民卫生出版社2010年版。

2.Internet Links

南京医科大学医学史研究中心：https://yxs.njmu.edu.cn/2024/0612/c11160a265802/page.htm

不列颠百科全书网站：https://www.britannica.com/

Unit 19

Magna Carta
《大宪章》

《大宪章》是中世纪英国历史上一份重要的法律文件。最初由约翰王（King John, r. 1199—1216）于1215年被迫盖章，后经英格兰国王多次确认。它的产生是英格兰国内外一系列因素共同作用的结果。约翰统治时期王室财政负担沉重。约翰与罗马教宗英诺森三世在坎特伯雷大主教人选上发生激烈冲突，又与国内贵族互不信任，矛盾不断激化。约翰在位期间与法国冲突不断，以失败告终，最终加剧了约翰与贵族之间的矛盾，进而促成1215年《大宪章》的诞生。

《大宪章》的诞生与三位重要人物息息相关，他们分别是坎特伯雷大主教斯蒂芬·兰顿、彭布罗克伯爵威廉·马歇尔、罗马教宗英诺森三世。兰顿出生于林肯郡一个中等家庭，受过良好的教育，少年时在巴黎学习人文学科与神学。在巴黎学习期间，兰顿就与当时还未曾担任罗马教宗的英诺森三世相识。1206年，兰顿成为枢机主教，卷入了约翰王与英诺森三世选任坎特伯雷大主教的圣职推荐权之争。兰顿也卷入贵族反对约翰王的斗争中并支持贵族，成为反对派的精神领袖，在与国王谈判和草拟《大宪章》过程中发挥了重要作用。彭布罗克伯爵威廉是国王忠实的顾问，年轻时曾被其父送到诺曼底服役，后来得到英王的信任与重用，成为第一代彭布罗克伯爵。作为约翰王的顾问，威廉利用自己的声望赢得了国王和贵族的信任，在草拟并促使双方接受《大宪章》过程中起着关键作用。后来威廉成为年轻的亨利三世的摄政、王国的监护人，为再次确认和颁布1217年《大宪章》起到了极为重要的作用。教宗英诺森三世出生于罗马的一个贵族之家，曾在罗马圣安德里亚修道院接受教育，少年时到巴黎学习人文学科与神学，后在博洛尼亚大学学习法律；1198年被选为罗马教宗。为加强教宗权威，英诺森三世加剧了政教之争，尤其是在英国坎特伯雷大主教人选上与约翰王发生冲突，最终以约翰屈服而告终。在英诺森三世支持下，兰顿担任了坎特伯雷大主教。

《大宪章》诸多条款出自1100年亨利一世加冕时颁布的《权利特许状》。1214年约翰发布的《教会自由选举特许状》是另一渊源。所谓的《无名自由宪章》因附加在亨利一世《自由特许状》之后而引起了《大宪章》起草者的注意。尽管《男爵条例》发布日期不明，但其中的13项条款重现于《大宪章》的最终版本。

1215年6月15日约翰王签署的《大宪章》共计63章，按主题可以分为6类。第一类与教会权利相关。第二类是约翰与男爵关系的条款。第三类涉及行政事务，还包括刑事诉讼程序。第四类是授予城镇权利的条款。第五类涉及为保证国王承诺履行而创立的执行机制。第六类则提出了诸多持久且重要的政治法律思想观念与原则。1216、1217年先后重新颁布了《大宪章》，1225年第三次重新颁布后，其成为最终版本的《大宪章》，此后又经历多次确认。1225年，《大宪章》成为较早被抄写进大多数私人法律书手稿的一部法律文献。在19世纪和20世纪的法律改革运动中，《大宪章》诸多条款被废除。目前，英国议会承认的是1297年爱德华一世确认的版本，共计37条，其中第1、9、29、37条至今仍然有效。这里选取的内容出自哈里·罗斯威尔（Hary Rothwell）编纂的《英国历史文献汇编》英文版。

I.Excerpt from *Magna Carta*①

1. In the first place have granted to God, and by this our present charter confirmed for us and our heirs for ever that the English church shall be free, and shall have its rights undiminished and its liberties unimpaired; and it is our will that it be thus

① Harry Rothwell ed, *English Historical Documents*, vol. 3, London: Eyre & Spottiswoode, 1975, pp. 317–323.

observed; which is evident from the fact that, before the quarrel between us and our barons began, we willingly and spontaneously granted and by our charter confirmed the freedom of elections which is reckoned most important and very essential to the English church, and obtained confirmation of it from the lord pope Innocent III; the which we will observe and we wish our heirs to observe it in good faith for ever. We have also granted to all free men of our kingdom, for ourselves and our heirs for ever, all the liberties written below, to be had and held by them and their heirs of us and our heirs.

2. If any of our earls or barons or others holding of us in chief by knight service dies, and at his death his heir be of full age and owe relief he shall have his inheritance on payment of the old relief, namely the heir or heirs of an earl £100 at most, for a whole earl's barony, the heir or heirs of a baron £100 for a whole barony, the heir or heirs of a knight 100s, for a whole knight's fee; and he who owes less shall give less according to the ancient usage of fiefs.

3. If, however, the heir of any such be under age and a ward, he shall have his inheritance when he comes of age without paying relief and without making fine.

4. The guardian of the land of such an heir who is under age shall take from the land of the heir no more than reasonable revenues, reasonable customary dues and reasonable services, and that without destruction and waste of men or goods; and if we commit the wardship of the land of any such to a sheriff, or to any other who is answerable to us for its revenues, and he destroys or wastes what he has wardship of, we will take compensation from him and the land shall be committed to two lawful and discreet men of that fief, who shall be answerable for the revenues to us or to him to whom we have assigned them; and if we give or sell to anyone the wardship of any such land and he causes destruction or waste therein, he shall lose that wardship, and it shall be transferred to two lawful and discreet men of that fief, who shall similarly be answerable to us as is aforesaid.

5. Moreover, so long as he has the wardship of the land, the guardian shall keep in repair the houses, parks, preserves, ponds, mills and other things pertaining to the land

out of the revenues from it; and he shall restore to the heir when he comes of age his land fully stocked with ploughs and the means of husbandry according to what the season of husbandry requires and the revenues of the land can reasonably bear.

6. Heirs shall be married without disparagement, yet so that before the marriage is contracted the nearest in blood to the heir shall have notice.

7. A widow shall have her marriage portion and inheritance forthwith and without difficulty after the death of her husband; nor shall she pay anything to have her dower or her marriage portion or the inheritance which she and her husband held on the day of her husband's death; and she may remain in her husband's house for forty days after his death, within which time her dower shall be assigned to her.

8. No widow shall be forced to marry so long as she wishes to live without a husband, provided that she gives security not to marry without our consent if she holds of us, or without the consent of her lord of whom she holds, if she holds of another.

9. Neither we nor our bailiffs will seize for any debt any land or rent, so long as the chattels of the debtor are sufficient to repay the debt; nor will those who have gone surety for the debtor be distrained so long as the principal debtor is himself able to pay the debt; and if the principal debtor fails to pay the debt, having nothing wherewith to pay it, then shall the sureties answer for the debt; and they shall, if they wish, have the lands and rents of the debtor until they are reimbursed for the debt which they have paid for him, unless the principal debtor can show that he has discharged his obligation in the matter to the said sureties.

13. And the city of London shall have all its ancient liberties and free customs, as well by land as by water. Furthermore, we will grant that all other cities, boroughs, towns, and ports shall have all their liberties and free customs.

16. No one shall be compelled to do greater service for a knight's fee or for any other free holding than is due from it.

17. Common pleas shall not follow our court, but shall be held in some fixed place.

18. Recognitions of *novel disseisin, of mort d'ancestor,* and of *darrein presentment* shall not be held elsewhere than in the counties to which they relate, and in this manner —we, or, if we should be out of the realm, our chief justiciar, will send two justices through each county four times a year, who, with four knights of each county chosen by the county, shall hold the said assizes in the county and on the day and in the place of meeting of the county court.

19. And if the said assizes cannot all be held on the day of the county court, there shall stay behind as many of the knights and freeholders who were present at the county court on that day as are necessary for the sufficient making of judgments, according to the amount of business to be done.

20. A free man shall not be amerced for a trivial offence except in accordance with the degree of the offence, and for a grave offence he shall be amerced in accordance with its gravity, yet saving his way of living; and a merchant in the same way, saving his stock-in-trade; and a villein shall be amerced in the same way, saving his means of livelihood—if they have fallen into our mercy: and none of the aforesaid amercements shall be imposed except by the oath of good men of the neighbourhood.

21. Earls and barons shall not be amerced except through their peers, and only in accordance with the degree of the offence.

22. No clerk shall be amerced in respect of his lay holding except after the manner of the others aforesaid and not according to the amount of his ecclesiastical benefice.

23. No vill or individual shall be compelled to make bridges at river banks, except those who from of old are legally bound to do so.

24. No sheriff, constable, coroners, or others of our bailiffs, shall hold pleas of our crown.

26. If anyone holding a lay fief of us dies and our sheriff or bailiff shows our letters patent of summons for a debt that the deceased owed us, it shall be lawful for our sheriff or bailiff to attach and make a list of chattels of the deceased found upon the lay fief to

the value of that debt under the supervision of law—worthy men, provided that none of the chattels shall be removed until the debt which is manifest has been paid to us in full; and the residue shall be left to the executors for carrying out the will of the deceased. And if nothing is owing to us from him, all the chattels shall accrue to the deceased, saving to his wife and children their reasonable shares.

28. No constable or other bailiff of ours shall take anyone's corn or other chattels unless he pays on the spot in cash for them or can delay payment by arrangement with the seller.

29. No constable shall compel any knight to give money instead of castle–guard, if he is willing to do the guard himself or through another good man, if for some good reason he cannot do it himself; and if we lead or send him on military service, he shall be excused guard in proportion to the time that because of us he has been on service.

30. No sheriff, or bailiff of ours, or anyone else shall take the horses or carts of any free man for transport work save with the agreement of that freeman.

31. Neither we nor our bailiffs will take, for castles or other works of ours, timber which is not ours, except with the agreement of him whose timber it is.

32. We will not hold for more than a year and a day the lands of those convicted of felony, and then the lands shall be handed over to the lords of the fiefs.

33. Henceforth all fish–weirs shall be cleared completely from the Thames and the Medway and throughout all England, except along the sea coast.

34. The writ called *Praecipe* shall not in future be issued to anyone in respect of any holding whereby a free man may lose his court.

35. Let there be one measure for wine throughout our kingdom, and one measure for ale, and one measure for corn, namely "the London quarter"; and one width for cloths whether dyed, russet or halberget, namely two ells within the selvedges. Let it be the same with weights as with measures.

36. Nothing shall be given or taken in future for the writ of inquisition of life or

limbs; instead it shall be granted free of charge and not refused.

37. If anyone holds of us by fee–farm, by socage, or by burgage, and holds land of another by knight service, we will not, by reason of that fee–farm, socage, or burgage, have the wardship of his heir or of land of his that is of the fief of the other; nor will we have custody of the fee–farm, socage, or burgage, unless such fee–farm owes knight service. We will not have custody of anyone's heir or land which he holds of another by knight service by reason of any petty serjeanty which he holds of us by the service of rendering to us knives or arrows or the like.

38. No bailiff shall in future put anyone to trial upon his own bare word, without reliable witnesses produced for this purpose.

39. No free man shall be arrested or imprisoned, or disseised or outlawed or exiled or in any way victimised, neither will we attack him or send anyone to attack him, except by the lawful judgment of his peers or by the law of the land.

40. To no one will we sell, to no one will we refuse or delay right or justice.

41. All merchants shall be able to go out of and come into England safely and securely and stay and travel throughout England, as well by land as by water, for buying and selling by the ancient and right customs free from all evil tolls, except in time of war and if they are of the land that is at war with us. And if such are found in our land at the beginning of a war, they shall be attached, without injury to their persons or goods, until we, or our chief justiciar, know how merchants of our land are treated who were found in the land at war with us when war broke out; and if ours are safe there, the others shall be safe in our land.

43. If anyone who holds of some escheat such as the honour of Wallingford, Nottingham, Boulogne, Lancaster, or of other escheats which are in our hands and are baronies dies, his heir shall give no other relief and do no other service to us than he would have done to the baron if that barony had been in the baron's hands; and we will hold it in the same manner in which the baron held it.

44. Men who live outside the forest need not henceforth come before our justices of the forest upon a general summons, unless they are impleaded or are sureties for any person or persons who are attached for forest offences.

45. We will not make justices, constables, sheriffs or bailiffs save of such as know the law of the kingdom and mean to observe it well.

46. All barons who have founded abbeys for which they have charters of the kings of England or ancient tenure shall have the custody of them during vacancies, as they ought to have.

47. All forests that have been made forest in our time shall be immediately disafforested; and so be it done with river-banks that have been made preserves by us in our time.

54. No one shall be arrested or imprisoned upon the appeal of a woman for the death of anyone except her husband.

56. If we have disseised or kept out Welshmen from lands or liberties or other things without the legal judgment of their peers in England or in Wales, they shall be immediately restored to them; and if a dispute arises over this, then let it be decided in the March by the judgment of their peers—for holdings in England according to the law of England, for holdings in Wales according to the law of Wales, and for holdings in the March according to the law of the March. Welshmen shall do the same to us and ours.

60. All these aforesaid customs and liberties which we have granted to be observed in our kingdom as far as it pertains to us towards our men, all of our kingdom, clerks as well as laymen, shall observe as far as it pertains to them towards their men.

II. Common Terms, Words and Phrases for the Text

heir 继承人

the English church 英格兰教会

undiminished 未减少的；未衰的；未减弱的

unimpaired 未被损坏的；未毁坏的

baron 男爵（贵族爵位中最低一级）

earl 伯爵

knight service 骑士役

barony 男爵爵位，男爵领地

guardian 监护人

sheriff（英格兰）郡长

fief 领地，封地，庄园，采邑

wardship 监护，保护

husbandry 农牧业

bailiff 执达员，执达官

distrain 扣押

novel disseisin（拉丁语）新近发生的强占土地行为

mort d'ancestor 死去先人占有权

darrein presentment（英格兰古法）最终推荐权（之诉）

justiciar 法官，首席政法官，摄政官

freeholder 自由地产保有人

villein（英格兰）维兰，农奴

ecclesiastical benefice 教会圣俸

vill 村邑，村庄，乡村

constable 治安官员；警察，警官

coroner 郡验尸官

chattel 动产

executor 遗嘱执行人

castle-guard（封建法）保卫城堡保有（骑士役土地保有方式的一种）

felony（普通法上的）重罪

fish-weir 鱼梁，鱼堰

Praecipe（拉丁语，英格兰古法）指令令状

selvedge （布的）织边；布边

serjeanty 百户区长；警官，治安官；管家

victimise （不正当地）使受害，使受苦

escheat 土地复归

vacancy 空缺，空职，空额

disafforest 将已变为森林的土地恢复至普通土地，使其成为不受森林法约束的普通土地

peer 同等地位的人，侪辈，同侪

the March 边境，边疆，边地

III. Exercises and Thinking

1. Please discuss the background of the birth of *Magna Carta*.

2. Who do you think played the most important role in creating *Magna Carta*?

3. Please analyze great significance of *Magna Carta* from different perspectives.

IV. Further Readings and Internet Links

1. Further Readings

[英]威廉·夏普·麦克奇尼：《大宪章的历史导读》，李红海编译，中国政法大学出版社 2016 年版。

Ralph V. Turner, *Magna Carta, Through the Ages,* London: Pearson Education Limited, 2003.

2. Internet Links

不列颠百科全书网站：https://www.britannica.com/search?query=Magna+Carta

Unit 20 *Select Cases in Manorial Courts, 1250—1550*

《庄园法庭判例选编(1250—1550年)》

中世纪英国的庄园法庭从理论上说可以划分为三类，即刑事法庭（the Court Leet）用于维护国王的和平，男爵法庭（the Court Baron）和习惯法庭（the Customary Court）则处理庄园日常事务。[①] 这里的庄园法庭是指其中的习惯法庭，主要涉及领主对其佃户行使的民事管辖权。它通常由领主本人或其管家主持，一般三四周开庭一次，也有一些庄园法庭一年开庭一两次，甚至更久才开庭一次。庄园法庭处理的事务非常庞杂，主要包括维护领主权益、解决庄民纠纷和处理公共事务等。[②] 庄园法庭在17世纪就已经衰落了。1867年的《郡法院法》（*County Courts Act*）实际上废止了庄园法庭。

庄园法庭审理案件记录形成了庄园法庭卷宗，自13世纪开始保存下来，记载了庄园条田的分配，佃户之间的土地转让，各类农民的契约合同，以及乡村的犯罪与刑罚，等等。这些案件记录也是当时各地习惯法的重要内容，是英国普通法的重要组成部分，因而它们是研究中世纪英国法律史、地方史和经济社会史的宝贵资料。早在19世纪末，英国法律史学家梅特兰就曾关注到了这些资料，并整理出版了《庄园及其他领主法庭诉讼选编》。[③] 20世纪末，美国天主教大学历史学教授普斯与杜兰大学法学教授邦菲尔德共同编纂了《庄园法庭案例

---

① 赵文洪：《庄园法庭、村规民约与中世纪欧洲“公地共同体”》，《历史研究》2007年第4期。

② 李云飞：《中世纪英格兰庄园法庭探微》，《世界历史》2005年第2期。

③ 参见 F. W. Maitland, *Select Pleas in Manorial and Other Seignorial Courts*, Vol. 1, London: Dernard Quaritch, 1889。

选编（1250—1550年）》。这里选读的文献就出自他们编纂的版本。

普斯与邦菲尔德共选编了225个案例。他们根据案件涉及的内容分为两大类：财产法案例与家庭法案例。前者又细分为三种类型，即遗产与执行、土地保有、寡妇地产与寡妇公簿地产。后者细分为四种类型：婚姻、私生、监护（权）、遗嘱检验。不过，这样的划分并非绝对，因为归为某一类的案例也可能因涉案情况的多重性而归于其他类。从总体上看，这些案例反映了中世纪英格兰庄园的经济社会生活情况。

I. Excerpt from *Select Cases in Manorial Courts, 1250–1550*①

5. b. CROWLE, at Luddington, 21 May 1319

Fine 20s.

This enrolment attests that whereas dispute was moved between Cicely Sadde, plaintiff, and Adam the son of William de Amcotes of Garthorpe, tenant, concerning one messuage with the appurtenances in Garthorpe as appears above in the preceding court, together they are agreed in this form, that the said Cicely in open court surrenders, releases and quit – claims to the said Adam, to hold in bondage of the lord abbot. And he gives the lord abbot 20s. as a fine.

6. BURNHAM THORPE (Norfolk), 7 December 1321

Amercement 3d.

Philip Seward of Brisley, by Thomas Page his attorney, seeks against Joan Cokeman half of one messuage and of six acres of land with the appurtenances in Burnham Overy as his right etc., and whereof Margaret, the daughter of Emma the daughter and heir of Robert le Barker, and the kinswoman of the said Philip, was seised etc. And from the same Margaret, fee and demesne reverted to Seward de Brisley, the brother of Robert the

① L. R. Poos and Lloyd Bonfield eds., *Select Cases in Manorial Courts, 1250–1550, Property and Family Law*, London: Selden Society, 1998, pp. 8–158.

father of Emma the mother of Margaret. And from Seward, fee and demesne descended to the aforesaid Philip who now seeks as son and heir. And this he is ready to verify etc.

And the said Joan comes and denies etc. And she says that the aforesaid tenement was given to Robert le Barker and Margaret his wife and the heirs issuing of their bodies. And she prays that this be inquired into.

And because it was found by inquest that the said tenement was given to the said Robert and Margaret and the heirs issuing of their bodies, and that issue is lacking in the third degree, it was decided that the said Philip should take nothing etc., but be in mercy for false claim, and the said Joan should withdraw quit.

14. a. LITTLE DUNMOW (Essex), 18 November 1328

Fine 40d.

Juliana la Reves held of the lord one messuage and five customary lands for the term of her life, after whose death Geoffrey Frankeleyn and Maud his wife come and pray to be admitted to the aforesaid tenement as to the right and inheritance of the said Maud. And because it was found by the whole homage that the said Maud is the daughter and next heir of the same Juliana, and that Denise, the sister of the same Maud, can claim nothing in the aforesaid tenements according to the custom of the manor because she was married outside the homage by a fine made formerly in the same court, therefore seisin therein was granted to the same Geoffrey and Maud, to hold at the lord's will by the services and customs etc. And they give for entry etc. And they did fealty.

54. a. WITCHAM RECTORY (Cambridgeshire), 20 November 1316

Fine half a mark

Thomas Payn came into court and rendered into the lord's hand one cottage with the appurtenances. And John Smith came and received that cottage, to have and hold to himself and his issue according to the custom of the manor, saving the right of each. And he gives the lord half a mark for entry. Pledge, Thomas the reeve. And the aforesaid John will provide reasonable maintenance for the aforesaid Thomas for the entire life of the same Thomas, and one bushel of wheat each year and one meal at each Christmas, and for the said meal the aforesaid Thomas will work one day in autumn with the aforesaid John. And William Payn came and rendered his entire right into the lord's hands, if he should have anything of right in the said cottage, for the benefit of the aforesaid John, excluding himself and his heirs from every action and claim for ever etc.

54. b. WITCHAM RECTORY, 10 September 1336

Plea

At the complaint of Maud Payn, John Smith of Babraham was summoned to answer in a plea of covenant. And thereof she says that at a certain day and year it was agreed between them that the said John would provide for the same Maud for the term of her life a certain chamber in which she could dwell, and he would give the same Maud yearly one bushel of wheat at the feast of All Saints, which same covenant he utterly broke toward her etc., to the same Maud's damage 20s. etc. And therein she produces etc. And the said John denies etc. And he says that he broke no covenant toward her as etc. And he prays that this be inquired into etc. And the other likewise etc. Therefore it was ordered that the bailiff should cause a good inquest to come at the next [*court*] etc.

It was ordered | inquest

54. c. WITCHAM RECTORY, 28 April 1337

Amercement | nothing because poor

It was found by inquest between Maud Payn and John Smith that the said Maud has nothing of right in her claim, because the rolls of the court of the tenth [*year*] [1316–17] of King Edward father of the present [*king*] bar her from every action. But the said John Smith by his grace granted to her half a bushel of wheat, to be received from him yearly henceforth for the term of her life. And because the said Maud falsely made claim of the said John, therefore she is in mercy, and let the said John go without day therein.

121. METHLEY (Yorkshire WR), 29 October 1364

John Halyman and John Cok complain of Hugh Couper and Ellen his wife in a plea of covenant. And thereof they say that whereas the said Ellen , when she was single, demised to them fourteen acres of land in Houghton , along with the reversion of one acre of land there which Magote Sperling held in dower , to hold to the same John and John from the feast of St Peter ad Vincula [1 August 1362] in the thirty-sixth year of the reign of King Edward the third until the end of six years then next following and fully completed , the aforesaid Hugh and Ellen withhold the aforesaid reversion of one acre of land aforesaid from the aforesaid John Halyman and John Cok and against the aforesaid covenant to their damage 10s. And therein they produce their suit.

And the aforesaid Hugh and Ellen deny etc., and they say that the said Ellen demised to the aforesaid John Halyman and John Cok fourteen acres of land, but without any reversion of any land. And thereof they pray the record of the rolls, and the aforesaid John and John likewise.

And the rolls having been searched there in open court, it was found by the same that the said Ellen demised to them fourteen acres, but without any reversion of any land etc. And because the aforesaid John Halyman and John Cok believed that this was the fault of the clerk, because he enrolled the aforesaid covenant badly, the same John and John give the lord 2s. to have an inquest.

Whereof an inquest was taken by the oath of William Dughti, John Duffan, John Knyght, Thomas Knyght, John Nundy, Roger Storor, Hugh Storor, Thomas de Carleton, Roger de Whitley, Michael Scot, Henry de Idel and Robert le Warde, who say upon their oath that the said Ellen demised to the aforesaid John Halyman and John Cok fourteen acres only, without any reversion of the one acre of land aforesaid. And they say that that acre of land belongs to the same Hugh and Ellen as the right of the same Ellen, because the said Magote who held it in dower is now married, for which same acre the aforesaid Hugh and Ellen will perform for the lord the services owed and accustomed for so much land. And so it was found by the aforesaid inquest that the aforesaid Hugh and Ellen did not break any covenant toward the aforesaid John and John, as they counted against them. Therefore it was decided that the aforesaid John Halyman and John Cok should take nothing by their complaint, but be in mercy for false claim.

Fine to have an inquest 2s. | *amercement 3d.*

143. HINDERCLAY (Suffolk), 24 July 1296

Amercement 3d.

Sarah who was the wife of Thomas Botun comes into court and seeks against John Burgeys one and a half roods of land in Hinderclay as her right and inheritance, in which same land the aforesaid John Burgeys does not have entry except through Thomas Botun her husband, whom she could not gainsay in his life. And that it be her right and inheritance she prays that it be inquired into etc.

And the aforesaid John Burgeys comes and denies force etc. where and when etc. And he says that she ought not to be heard in her petition, because the aforesaid Sarah came into open court along with Thomas Botun her husband, and they surrendered the said land jointly into the lord's hands etc., and that his father received the said land in open court etc. And he says that the usual custom of the manor is that when a man and his wife together should surrender any tenement, although it be of the wife's inheritance and right, after the man's death the wife loses any action to seek the aforesaid tenement, because they surrendered together etc.

And the aforesaid Sarah says that the custom is not such. And she says that her husband could do his will of her and her body etc. And she sues her action and prays that her right be inquired into etc. And John puts himself upon an inquest etc.

And an inquest was made therein by Reginald the son of Walter, William the son of Adam, Adam Belsent, Richard Archer, Ralph Kempe, Nicholas le Reve, Gilbert Shepherd, John le Noble, Nicholas le Wodeward, Simon Osbern. Robert atte Crop, William le Carter, Roger Shepherd and William le Cupere, who say upon their oath that the aforesaid Sarah does not have right in the said land, because along with Thomas Botun her husband she came into open court and surrendered the aforesaid land etc. And therefore it was decided by the court that the aforesaid Sarah should recover nothing, but be in mercy for false complaint, and the aforesaid John should go without day therein against her, by the pledge of Walter Gilbert and Walter Botun.

184. WHITTLESFORD (Cambridgeshire), 22 May 1391

Next [court]

And that Alice, lately daughter of Richard le Reve, a neif of the lord, fornicated and gave birth to a certain daughter, but with whom the said Alice fornicated they do not know. Therefore it was ordered that they inquire better at the next [court]etc.

186. WEST KEAL (Lincolnshire), 8 October 1287

Fine 26s. 8d.

Richard Fox , neif of the lord , who held one messuage and one oxgang of land in Keal, is dead . And thereupon Maud the wife of the same Richard came and took the aforesaid messuage and oxgang of land to the use of Nicholas, the son and heir of the same Richard. And it was granted to her by the lady for 26s. 8d., to be paid in the two years next following at the four principal terms of the year in equal portions, the term beginning at the Christmas next following. Moreover it was granted to the said Maud that she may hold the aforesaid land until the lawful age of the said heir and have the profit to her own use, performing the services owed therein. Pledges, Peter in le Hirn, Salver the son of Perman, John the son of Richard and William Wetherhogg, both for doing all the aforesaid and for sustaining the said heir during his minor age.

190. GREAT WALTHAM AND HIGH EASTER (Essex), 24 October 1332

Fine 66s. 8d.

Maud Pondeluyt, who held in free bench of the inheritance of John Pondeluyt half a yardland of land and half a quarter of molland, is dead, whereby Alice who was the wife of the aforesaid John prays that she may have the aforesaid land, to hold until the full age of Richard the son of the aforesaid John, who is three years of age. And because it is not the custom of the manor that she may hold the aforesaid land, because she was married outside and without licence, therefore the said land was delivered to a certain Henry le Blake, to whom the said land can in no way descend in the name of inheritance, to hold of the lord until the lawful age of the said Richard by the services owed therein. And he will maintain and sustain the buildings and all other things pertaining to the aforesaid tenements. And he will provide for the aforesaid Richard all necessaries, both in food and in clothing, for the entire time aforesaid. And he gives a fine, as appears. Pledges, all the customers.

198. METHLEY (Yorkshire WR), 8 October 1352

Custody and fine 13s. 4d.

Robert the son of Adam Sumay of Methley, who held of the lord one messuage and one oxgang of land with the appurtenances in Methley, was not of sound memory nor of sound mind, whereby the said tenements came into the lord's hands as his escheat. And afterwards the custody of the body of the said Robert and of the aforesaid land was granted to Cicely de Croston for his entire life, which same Cicely has ended her last day, after whose death the custody of the aforesaid body and lands came another time into the lord's hand, which same custody of the aforesaid body and lands was granted to Christine the daughter of Adam Sumay as nearer kinswoman of the same Robert, to hold for the entire life of the same Robert by the services and customs etc., and for providing reasonable sustenance yearly to the aforesaid Robert. And she gives the lord 3s. 4d. for custody etc. And also she gives the lord 10s. as a fine for entry of the aforesaid lands.

213. a. FORDINGTON (Dorset), 24 November 1351

Law

John Gouges (essoined) and Alice his wife, executrix of the testament of Henry Knyves, are at law against John Couke and Richard Couke, executors of the testament of the said Henry, that they have not performed a covenant with them to acquit all the debts of the said Henry, to have the chamber and pots of the said Henry, nor did they break any covenant therein with them to the damages of 5s. nor of any money. Pledge of law [*blank*].

213. b. FORDINGTON, 14 February 1352

Amercement 3d.

John Gouges and Alice his wife, executrix of the testament of Henry Knyves, are in mercy because they failed in what they waged against John Couke and Richard Couke in a plea of debt, a plea of broken covenant [*sic*], to the damages of 3s. 6d.

II. Common Terms, Words and Phrases for the Text

stipulate 约定，规定

term 开庭期

plaintiff 原告，起诉人

messuage 宅院，住宅

seisin 占有

demesne 自有地，自主地，自用地

inheritance 遗产

custom of the manor 庄园习惯

tenement 保有物

fealty 效忠

reeve 执达官

bushel 蒲式耳（谷物和水果的容量单位，相当于 8 加仑）

amercement 罚金，惩罚

plea 答辩，诉状

dower 寡妇地产

reversion 复归权，土地复归权，财产复归权

inquest 死因审理；验尸；勘验；调查

rood 路得（面积单位，相当于 1/4 英亩）

petition　申诉；申请

right　权利

fornicate　私通；通奸

neif　农奴

oxgang　12—15 英亩土地，约相当于一头牛一年内能耕的土地

custody　监护，监管，保管

executrix of the testament　女遗嘱执行人

covenant　盖印合同，盖印契约；合同，协议

III. Exercises and Thinking

1. Please summarize the main functions of manor courts in medieval England.

2. Please write an overview of manorial land tenure in medieval England.

3. Please briefly describe the marriage of the tenants of a manor in medieval England.

IV. Further Readings and Internet Links

1. Further Readings

[英] 贝内特：《英国庄园生活：1150—1400 年农民生活状况研究》，龙秀清等译，侯建新校，上海人民出版社 2005 年版。

L. R. Poos and Lloyd Bonfield, *Select Cases in Manorial Courts, 1250–1550, Property and Family Law*, London: Selden Society, 1998.

F. W. Maitland, *Select Pleas in Manorial and Other Seignorial Courts, vol. 1, Reigns of Henry III and Edward I*, London: Bernard Quaritch, 15 Piccadilly, 1889.

2. Internet Links

不列颠百科全书网站：https://www.britannica.com/

Unit 21

The Classic of Tea

《茶经》

中国是世界上最早种茶、饮茶的国家。古巴蜀地区是茶树的原产地，这在考古发掘、植物分类学研究以及文献记载等方面均已经得到证实。唐代之前，北方不常饮茶，南方则从长江上游的四川，逐渐发展到中下游的荆楚吴越一带。饮茶之风，逐渐传遍大江南北，甚至及于塞外，则始于唐代。

唐代的种茶、制茶与饮茶比较昌盛，为"茶圣"陆羽撰写《茶经》奠定了基础。陆羽（733—804），生于复州竟陵城（今湖北省天门市），804年病逝于湖州，葬于杼山。幼年时陆羽遭遗弃，后被龙盖寺（后更名西塔寺）住持智积禅师收养，取名为陆羽。智积禅师擅长品茶，对陆羽影响巨大。陆羽少年时，智积禅师开始教其习文识字，习诵佛经，并教其煮茶问汤，但陆羽不喜念经修行，不肯削发为僧，744年逃离龙盖寺，到戏班当优伶。746年，竟陵太守李齐物在一次州人聚饮中看到陆羽出众的表演，十分欣赏其才华，将其收为养子，亲自在府中教授陆羽诗文，并修书推荐他到隐居于火门山（今湖北天门市的天门山）的邹夫子处读书。七年之后，陆羽习成下山，开始了四处游历，考察茶事生活，长期与官吏、文士和方士为友。752年，陆羽与竟陵司马崔国辅相识。在无锡结识诗人皇甫冉（717—770）。在吴兴结识皎然和尚。773年，陆羽结识湖州刺史颜真卿。780年，在颜真卿、皎然等友人帮助下，陆羽的《茶经》问世。

陆羽的《茶经》是中国也是世界上第一部茶学专著。《茶经》总结了古代有关茶事的知识，对茶的起源、种类、特征、制法、烹蒸、茶具、水的品第以及饮茶风俗、名茶产地等有全面论述。在陆羽之前，尽管我国南方一些地区种茶、饮茶的历史久远，但还未有人撰刊过一本茶学的专著。茶之有书，自陆羽著述开始。《茶经》全面论述了唐及唐以前的茶事，成为中国茶文化形成的标志。自陆羽《茶经》之后，有关茶之书籍不断被撰写并出版，一时风行大唐王朝。后世有关的著作更是数不胜数。

茶文化是世界文明百花园中璀璨的明珠。它发源于我国，渐次传播到世界各地。朝鲜和日本较早接受了中国的茶文化。日本空海和尚（774—835）、学问僧永忠（743—816）、最澄大师（767—822）等接受中国的茶文化以后，逐渐在日本形成了茶道。9 世纪以降，茶叶成为与中亚游牧部落主要的贸易商品。欧洲最早提到茶的是威尼斯人 G. B. 拉穆西奥。但是，茶叶输入欧洲却是在 17 世纪。1658 年，茶叶首次在伦敦加拉威的咖啡馆公开出售。17 世纪中叶，饮茶在荷兰蔚然成风。18 世纪以降，饮茶成为欧洲人生活中不可或缺的一部分。

I. Excerpt from *The Classic of Tea*①

No. 1, The Beginnings of Tea

Tea is from a grand tree in the South. The tree may grow from one or two feet to as much as twelve. In the rivers and gorges of the Province of Szechwan are trees whose girth is such that it requires two men to embrace them. Those trees must be felled for plucking.

Its trunk is suggestive of the gourd and its leaves, of the gardenia. The flower is like that of the wild red rose turned white. The seeds are like those of the coir palm. The leaves have the fragrance of cloves while the roots are as those of the walnut. The character for tea, which we call ch'a, is sometimes made with "herb" as the significant element, sometimes "tree" and sometimes both. Its common name is varied with *chia*, shê, *ming* or *ch'uan*.

① Lu Yü, *The Classic of Tea, Origins & Rituals,* Translated and Introduced by Francis Ross Carpenter and Demi Hitz, New Jersey: The Ecco Press, 1974, pp. 59-150.

Tea is of a cold nature and may be used in case of blockage or stoppage of the bowels. When its flavor is at its coldest nature, it is most suitable as a drink. If one is generally moderate but is feeling hot or warm, given to melancholia, suffering from aching of the brain, smarting of the eyes, troubled in the four limbs or afflicted in the hundred joints, he may take tea four or five times. Its liquor is like the sweetest dew of Heaven.

No. 4 The Équipage

THE CAULDRON The cauldron is made of pig iron although some of today's craftsmen use the so–called puddled–iron process to make them. They are usually made from old plowshares or scrap chains.

Clay is spread over the inside and gravelly earth over the outside. The cauldron is polished on the inside to make it easy to clean but is allowed to remain rough on the outside to absorb more of the flames.

The ears are squared for stability and the lips flared to facilitate spreading the leaves. The bowl is extended to protect the center. When the bowl is thus extended, the center will be agitated. When the center is agitated, it is easy to toss the leaves. When leaves can be tossed without hindrance, then the taste will be pure and unadulterated.

In Hung Chou the cauldrons are made of tile and in Lan Chou, of stone. Both the tile and stone ones are exquisite utensils, but by their nature they lack stability and are hard to manage. For long usage, cauldrons should be made of silver, as they will yield the purest tea. Silver is somewhat extravagant, but when beauty is the standard, it is silver that is beautiful. When purity is the standard, it is silver that yields the purity. For constancy and long use, one always resorts to silver.

THE TEA BOWL Yüeh Chou ware is best. Ting Chou ware is next best. After that come the bowls of Wu Chou, Yüeh Chou, Shou Chou, and Hung Chou.

There are those who argue that the bowls of Hsing Chou are superior to Yüeh ware. That is not at all the case. It is proper to say that if Hsing ware is silver, then Yüeh ware is jade. Or if the bowls of Hsing Chou are snow, then those of Yüeh are ice. Hsing ware, being white, gives a cinnabar cast to the tea. Yüeh ware, having a greenish hue, enhances the true color of the tea. That is yet a third way to describe Yüeh Chou's superiority to Hsing Chou in the way of tea bowls. In his poem on tea, Tu Yü speaks of the équipage and of a moistly glossy bowl that originated in the East. The bowl was Yüeh ware. Hence for him Yüeh Chou made the best of bowls.

The lip does not curl over, but the base is round and shallow and will hold fewer than eight ounces.

Stoneware from both the Yüeh Chous is of a bluegreen shade. Being so it intensifies and emphasizes the color of the tea. If the tea is of a light red color, it will appear as red in the white bowls of Hsing Chou. If the tea is red, it will look a rusty brown in Shou Chou bowls, they being of a yellow glaze. Because Hung Chou ware is brown, the tea will look black.

All of those are unworthy of tea.

No. 5, The Brewing of Tea

Water from the slow–flowing streams, the stone–lined pools or milk–pure springs is the best of mountain water. Never take tea made from water that falls in cascades, gushes from springs, rushes in a torrent or that eddies and surges as if nature were rinsing its mouth. Over usage of all such water to make tea will lead to illnesses of the throat.

Of the many other streams that flow through mountain and valley, there are those that are clear and pure but which sink into the ground and are absorbed before finding an outlet. From the hot season to the time of frost, the dragon may be sequestered and noxious poisons will accumulate within them. One taste of the water will tell you if it is all right. If the evil genius of a stream makes the water bubble like a fresh spring, pour it out.

When the water is boiling, it must look like fishes' eyes and give off but the hint of a sound. When at the edges it chatters like a bubbling spring and looks like pearls innumerable strung together, it has reached the second stage. When it leaps like breakers majestic and resounds like a swelling wave, it is at its peak. Any more and the water will be boiled out and should not be used.

When the boiling water is in its first stage, you may add a measure of salt in accordance with the amount of water. You can tell when to stop by sampling it.

During the second stage of the boiling, draw off a ladle full of water and stir around the center of the boil with your bamboo pincers. If you judge that it is not yet right, lower the pincers into the center of the boil and do it with force. If it still leaps up making waves and splashing into a froth, pour back some of the water you have drawn off. That will stop it from overboiling while encouraging its essential virtue.

When you draw off the water during the first boil, allow it to stand. If on the surface of the froth there is a lining like a black cloud, do not drink it, for the flavor will be untrue.

The first cup should have a haunting flavor, strange and lasting. There are those who allow it to continue simmering to nourish the elegance and retain the froth even through a first, second and third cup. After the third cup, one should not drink more than a fourth or fifth cup unless he is very thirsty.

At every brewing, one pint of water should be used for five cups of tea. Take the tea cups one after the other so that the heavy impurities will remain at the bottom and the choicest froths float across the top like patches of thin ice. Then the delicate virtues of the tea will be retained throughout. But when you drink it, sip only. Otherwise, you will dissipate the flavor.

Moderation is the very essence of tea. Tea does not lend itself to extravagance. If a tea is insipid and bland, it will lose its flavor before even half a cup has disappeared. How much more so in the case of extravagance in its use. The vibrance will fade from the color and the perfection of its fragrance will melt away.

When tea has a sweet flavor, it may be called chia. If it is less than sweet and of a bitter or strong taste, it is called ch'uan. If it is bitter or strong when sipped but sweet when swallowed, it is called ch'a.

NO.6, Drinking the Tea

Born to this earth are three kinds of creatures. Some are winged and fly. Some are furred and run. Still others stretch their mouths and talk. All of them must eat and drink to survive.

There are times, nonetheless, when the meaning of "drink" becomes obscure. If one would merely slake his thirst, then he can drink water. Should melancholy, sadness or anger strike, he can turn to wine to drink. But if one would dispel an evening's unproductive lassitude, the meaning of "drink" is tea.

Now tea, used as a drink, was first discovered by the Emperor Shen Nung. Among other great tea drinkers, we have heard that in the State of Lu there was the Duke of Chou while the State of Ch'i had Yen Ying. During the Han Dynasty there were Yang Hsiung and Ssu–Ma Hsiang–ju. During the Wu, there was Wei Yao. During the Chin there were Liu Kun, as well as Chang Ts'ai, my distant ancestor Lu Na and Hsieh An among others pulled out of memory at random. All of them drank tea.

Tea has been traditionally taken so extensively that it is immersed in our customs and flourishes in the present Dynasty both North and South. From Ching to Yü, it is the common drink of every household.

Thus with tea. There are nine ways by which man must tax himself when he has to do with tea.

He must manufacture it.

He must develop a sense of selectivity and discrimination about it.

He must provide the proper implements.

He must prepare the right kind of fire.

He must select a suitable water.

He must roast the tea to a turn.

He must grind it well. He must brew it to its ultimate perfection.

He must, finally, drink it.

There are no short cuts. Merely to pick tea in the shade and dry it in the cool of the evening is not to manufacture it. To nibble it for flavor and sniff at it for fragrance is not to be discriminating. To bring along a musty tripod or a bowl charged with nose–insulting odors is not to provide the proper implements. Resinous firewood and old kitchen charcoal are not the stuff for a seemly fire. Water from turbulent rapids or dammed–up flood water is not a suitable water. Tea cannot be said to be roasted when it is heated on the outside and left raw underneath. Reducing it to jade powder and green dust is not grinding tea. Manipulating the instruments awkwardly and transitions from instrument to instrument that attract attention are not brewing tea. Finally, taking prodigious amounts of tea in summer and none at all in winter are not drinking tea.

For exquisite freshness and vibrant fragrance, limit the number of cups to three. If one can be satisfied with less than perfection, five are permissible. If one's guests number up to five rows, it will be necessary to use three bowls. If seven, then five bowls will be required. If there are six guests or fewer, do not economize on the number of bowls.

But if even one guest is missing from the assemblage, then the haunting and lasting flavor of the tea must take his place.

No. 7 Notations of Tea

The Book of Chin, "Chung Hsing Period" : Lu Na was prefect of Wu Hsing. The General Hsieh An frequently expressed the wish to visit Na. Na's nephew, Lu Shu, blamed his uncle because no preparations had been made. Not daring to raise the question with him, he privately stored up provisions for several scores of guests. When the general arrived, all that was set out for him was tea and fruit. But suddenly Shu appeared bearing provisions and delicacies and punctiliously served them in the proper utensils. As soon as An left, Na caned Shu, giving him forty strokes and said, "You have never been able to do anything to make the life of your father's younger brother brighter or more profitable. Why then must you complicate even my simplest affairs?"

Liu Kun wrote to his nephew Liu Yen, Governor of the southern part of Yen Chou, and said, "I have already received from An Chou one catty each of dried ginger, cassia and skullcap. They are the things I needed, but I continue sluggish and am the captive of melancholy. I seem to think of nothing but some real tea. Do you think you might arrange it?"

Tso Ssu has a poem "*Gracious Ladies*."

There is a gracious lady in my home.
Her complexion is surpassing white dazzling white, glistening white.
She was called Wan Su—White silk finely spun.
Each part—the mouth, her teeth, her nose—is fine and true.
Her younger sister is Hui Fang: Gentle Fragrance.
With eyes and eyebrows that are living paintings.

The Wild Duck soars and then hovers over my garden orchard.
The fruit has fallen, fresh, and ready to pick.
I long for flowers that bend with the wind and rain.
In my mind I write a play about Tea.
The wind breathes and sighs among the tripods and cauldrons.

"*Climbing the Tower in Ch'eng Tu*" by Chang Meng-yang:

...

While fragrant Tea stills the six passions,
And its encompassing flavors fill the nine provinces.
Our lives are of small account—we rest in peace.
This is a land to be savored.

The Poems of Wang Wei:

Silently, silently I steal into my chambers.

Deserted.

Deserted and barren is the grand hall.

Waiting.

Waiting for a man who will not return.

Resigned, I go to my tea.

Pao Ling-hui, younger sister of Pao Chao, wrote a poem called "Scented Tea."

T'ao Hung-ching in *the Records of Miscellany*: When bitter tea is too light, it should be mixed with other juices. In olden times, Tan Ch'iu-tzu, the Lord of Yellow Mountain, used it.

The Records of the Later Wei: Wang Su of Lan Yeh took office in the South. He was a lover of tea and even had his special blend. But when he returned to the North, he preferred mutton and curds to tea. Someone, wanting to know how tea compared to curds, inquired about it from him and he replied, "Tea is unworthy to be a slave to curds."

According to *the Comprehensive Map of the Empire*, one hundred forty li east of the District of Lin Sui, there is a stream called Tea Brook.

The Records of Wu Hsing of Shan Chien: There is a Mt. Wen twenty li west of Wu Ch'eng from which is produced tea for the Court.

According to *the Atlas of I Ling*, tea has been produced in the mountains of Wang Chou, Nv Kuan, Ching Mén and Huang Niu.

In *the Atlas of Yung Chia*, there is a mountain called White Tea Mountain three hundred li east of Yung Chia. Also there is an area called Tea Slopes about two hundred li south of Shan Yang according to *the Atlas of Huai Yin*.

The Atlas of Ch'a Ling says: Ch'a Ling derives its name from the hills and valleys there that produce tea.

According to the section on *"Trees" in the Pên–ts'ao*, its tea, if bitter, is called *ming* but if it has a sweet taste, it is called *ch'a*. If the bitterness is only very subtle and if it is of a cold nature, it will be harmless. Such tea is good for sores and ulcers, enhances urination and helps get rid of phlegm. If the liquor is taken exceeding hot, it will help one to sleep but little. It should be picked in the fall.

If it is bitter, it dissipates hunger and cheers the downcast. The Commentary adds: The bitter tea is picked in the spring.

In the section on "Herbs" in the *Pên-ts'ao*, it is said that bitter *t'u* is also called *ch'a* and that the names were used interchangeably.

Tea will flourish in the winter and on sand banks, along rivers, in mountains, hills and along the roadsides. Even in the coldest of winters it will not die. Pick and dry it on the third day of the third month. The Commentary adds: "One wonders if modern–day 'tea' is indicated by the text." On tea that helps keep one awake, the Commentary to the *Pên-ts'ao* states: "It is said in the *Book of Songs*, 'Who says that t'u is bitter? and again, *T'u* from yellow soil is like sugar.' All of them are herbs." T'ao, however, says that bitter tea is of the tree family and is not to be counted an herb. He says that if tea is picked in the spring, it is called "bitter tea."

No. 9 Generalities

Concerning the preparation and utensils: If it is that time of spring when there is a ban on fires and one has nevertheless plucked some tea out in the wilds, or perhaps from a Monastery or a mountain garden or coppice; and if he has already steamed, ground, roasted and dried it by fire, he may dispense with some seven steps. That is to say, he need not shave it; pound it; dry it with charcoal over a drying hole; string it, hang it in a drying shed; tie it or put it in a storage container. All those steps and the related equipment may be ignored.

Concerning the équipage for brewing tea: If among the pines, there is a rock on which one can sit, he may omit the utensil rack.

If he is using dry firewood and a tripod frame, then the brazier, cinder receptacle, stoker, fire tongs and the stand can be eliminated.

Should one be lucky enough to discover a clear spring or happen upon a fast-running stream, he need not use the water dispenser, the scouring box or the water filter.

If there are only five guests or fewer and the host selects the very quintessence of teas for tasting, he may dispense with the netting to strain the tea.

II. Common Terms, Words and Phrases for the Text

the Province of Szechwan 四川省

gorge 峡，峡谷

girth 围长，干围，腰围

gardenia 栀子（花）

clove 丁香

walnut 核桃（树，木），胡桃（树，木）

cauldron 大锅

pig iron 生铁，铸铁

agitate 搅动，摇动（液体等）

unadulterated 纯的，不掺杂质的，完全的，十足的，不折不扣的

exquisite utensils 精美器具

the Tea Bowl 茶碗

the Brewing of Tea 茶之煮

cascade 小瀑布（尤指一连串瀑布中的一支）

torrent 急流，激流，湍流，洪流

eddy （水或空气的）涡流，漩涡

a bubbling spring 涌泉

pincer 钳子

simmer 用文火炖，煨

pint 品脱（容量单位，为 ⅛ 加仑，在英国等国家约合 0.568 升）

slake 缓和（口渴），解（渴）

melancholy 忧郁，伤悲

selectivity 选择性

nibble 小口咬，一点点地咬（食物）

prodigious 巨大的，伟大的

assemblage（人、物的）集聚，聚集

notations of tea 茶之事

punctiliously 一丝不苟地，循规蹈矩地

cassia 肉桂，桂皮

dried ginger 干姜块

Gracious Ladies《娇女》

Climbing the Tower in Ch'eng Tu《登成都楼》

savor 口味，细品，享用

"Trees" in the Pên-ts'ao《本草·木部》

dissipate（使）消散，消失；驱散

monastery 隐修院，修道院，寺院

III. Exercises and Thinking

1. Please outline the significant reasons for the development of tea industry in Tang Dynasty.

2. What can you learn from Lu Yü?

3. Please discuss the relationship between drinking tea and history of daily social life.

IV. Further Readings and Internet Links

1. Further Readings

Lu Yü, *The Classic of Tea, Origins & Rituals,* Translated and Introduced by Francis

Ross Carpenter and Demi Hitz, New Jersey: The Ecco Press, 1974.

[唐]陆羽:《茶经》，沈冬梅译注，中华书局 2010 年版。

吴觉农 主编:《茶经述评》(第二版)，中国农业出版社 2005 年版。

2. Internet Links

JSTOR 过刊数据库：https://www.jstor.org/action/doBasicSearch?Query=chinese+tea&so=rel

Part IV

Modern History of the World

世界近代史

从某种程度上说，世界近代史是资本主义的兴衰史，也是资本主义向全球侵略扩张和世界各地人民反抗资本主义侵略扩张的斗争史。资本主义的兴起和演变是一条纵向发展的主线。在欧洲，虽然资本主义萌芽产生于14、15世纪的意大利北部城市，但直到16世纪资本主义时代才真正开始。世界历史也由此开启了由农本向重商的转变。

在文艺复兴、宗教改革的基础上，大航海、科学革命、资产阶级革命、工业革命等为18世纪中期开启的工业革命作了系统性的铺垫。本编重点关注世界近代史中科学技术的发展和传播，兼顾近代全球化趋势下政治经济格局，节选了近代科技领域的重要著述，涉及的培根、牛顿、卡特赖特都为人类文明进步作出过贡献。在世界近代史中，科学革命和政治革命是二元革命。在政治方面，本编节选了《人权宣言》，它是法国大革命时期的纲领性文件；还选取了《威斯特伐利亚和约》，它是近代欧洲宗教改革背景下的成果，突出反映了宗教改革对欧洲政局的冲击和重组。由此可见，宗教改革对欧洲新思想、新发现的刺激作用甚大。《威斯特伐利亚和约》在近代国际法以及现代国际法中也具有重要意义。《法兰西内战》分析了巴黎公社的发展过程和历史意义，总结了巴黎公社的经验与教训。此外，近代还有一个重要部分，即殖民主义，本篇节选了《不列颠在印度的统治的未来结果》。它有助于我们理解近代欧洲殖民主义的本质。另外，本篇还节选了《筹办夷务始末》，这份珍贵的史料向我们呈现了清朝在西方殖民者入侵后，面临更先进的技术和舰炮时的应对之策。从近代开始，中国在世界上曾一度陷入被动，后发愤图强，逐渐走到改革开放的今天。

16世纪以来，人类的科技进步、社会进步和文明交流互鉴，有目共睹，但人类的大分裂、大毁灭、大转折，也不能视而不见。大航海、大发现带来的时空革命，使人类的命运首次联结在一起，世界成为地球村。本篇挖掘世界近代史中科技创新和发展的经验，研究实验科学何以战胜西方传统哲学和经院哲学，研究牛顿数学和力学原理如何应用于机械工业，研究近代科技影响力向全球传导的历史。

Unit 22

Novum Organum
培根《新工具》

16 世纪和 17 世纪的西欧正经历宗教改革和启蒙运动带来的社会思想变革，同时欧洲的经济也因殖民扩张及海外贸易拓展发生了质的变化，西欧社会一系列的发展推动科学领域产生新发现、新理论和新观点。彼时西欧天文学、数学、医学、机械力学等方面都突破了传统的认知，有伽利略、牛顿、威廉·哈维等著名人物。弗朗西斯·培根（Francis Bacon，1561—1626）的《新工具》正是在此时代背景中应运而生。

培根是英国著名的哲学家，首创科学归纳法，开启了近代认识论转向。马克思、恩格斯称赞培根为“英国唯物主义和整个现代实验科学的真正始祖”[①]。培根的《新工具》一书于 1620 年出版，书名来自亚里士多德的《工具论》，但书中充满了批判精神和实践精神。培根认为，逻辑学应是产生知识的理论，而古希腊哲学、经院哲学长于思辨性的认知，却不能指导人们探索自然与真理。培根的批判是切中要害的，他指出了经院哲学的空洞性，指出亚里士多德三段论“只是就命题迫人同意，而抓不住事物的本身”[②]。培根据理批驳，为时人厘清了哲学认知，为实验科学奠定了逻辑基础。

培根创立的科学归纳法，叙述了应用科学归纳法的原则和操作程序，要求通过观察和实验搜集材料，然后对所得材料加以分析和整理，运用排斥法推导出事物的真正原因或形式。培根的科学归纳法为近代实验科学提供了有效的逻

---

① 《马克思恩格斯文集》第 1 卷，人民出版社 2009 年版，第 331 页。

② ［英］培根：《新工具》，许宝骙译，商务印书馆 1984 年版，第 10 页。

辑工具，因而受到近代众多哲学家和科学家的肯定，如笛卡尔、康德。培根的《新工具》也被引入其他国家，作为宣传科学、励精图治的读物。清末康有为曾向光绪皇帝介绍培根，康氏认为培根创新理论是英国改革和新政的开始，力荐培根的著作。

培根开创的实验科学方法有利于近代科学发展，但是也受时代所限而带有局限性，如归纳分析法也带有经验主义、形而上的弊端。当代读者应更多地从历史的角度去欣赏《新工具》所蕴含的智慧。这里选取的内容出自迪维（Devey）编纂的《新工具》英文版。

I. Excerpt from *Novum Organum*①

The present system of logic rather assists in confirming and rendering inveterate the errors founded on vulgar notions than in searching after truth, and is therefore more hurtful than useful.

The syllogism is not applied to the principles of the sciences, and is of no avail in intermediate axioms, as being very unequal to the subtilty of nature. It forces assent, therefore, and not things.

The syllogism consists of propositions; propositions of words; words are signs of notions. If, therefore, the notions (which form the basis of the whole) be confused and carelessly abstracted from things, there is no solidity in the superstructure. Our only hope, then, is in genuine induction.

We have no sound notions either in logic or physics; substance, quality, action, passion, and existence are not clear notions; much less weight, levity, density, tenuity, moisture, dryness, generation, corruption, attraction, repulsion, element, matter, form, and the like. They are all fantastical and ill-defined.

① Lord Bacon, "Novum Organum", in Joseph Devey ed., *A Library of Universal Literature in Four Parts Comprising Science, Biography, Fiction and the Great Orations*, New York: P. F. Collier and Son, 1901, pp.13–22.

The notions of less abstract natures, as man, dog, dove, and the immediate perceptions of sense, as heat, cold, white, black, do not deceive us materially, yet even these are sometimes confused by mutability of matter and the intermixture of things. All the rest which men have hitherto employed are errors, and improperly abstracted and deduced from things.

There is the same degree of licentiousness and error in forming axioms as in abstracting notions, and that in the first principles, which depend on common induction; still more is this the case in axioms and inferior propositions derived from syllogisms.

The present discoveries in science are such as lie immediately beneath the surface of common notions. It is necessary, however, to penetrate the more secret and remote parts of nature, in order to abstract both notions and axioms from things by a more certain and guarded method.

There are and can exist but two ways of investigating and discovering truth. The one hurries on rapidly from the senses and particulars to the most general axioms, and from them, as principles and their supposed indisputable truth, derives and discovers the intermediate axioms. This is the way now in use. The other constructs its axioms from the senses and particulars, by ascending continually and gradually, till it finally arrives at the most general axioms, which is the true but unattempted way.

The understanding when left to itself proceeds by the same way as that which it would have adopted under the guidance of logic, namely, the first; for the mind is fond of starting off to generalities, that it may avoid labor, and after dwelling a little on a subject is fatigued by experiment. But those evil are augmented by logic, for the sake of the ostentation of dispute.

The understanding, when left to itself in a man of a steady, patient, and reflecting disposition (especially when unimpeded by received doctrines), makes some attempt in the right way, but with little effect, since the understanding, undirected and unassisted, is unequal to and unfit for the task of vanquishing the obscurity of things.

Each of these two ways begins from the senses and particulars, and ends in the greatest generalities. But they are immeasurably different; for the one merely touches cursorily the limits of experiment and particulars, while the other runs duly and regularly through them—the one from the very outset lays down some abstract and useless generalities, the other gradually rises to those principles which are really the most common in nature.

There is no small difference between the idols of the human mind and the ideas of the Divine mind—that is to say, between certain idle dogmas and the real stamp and impression of created objects, as they are found in nature.

Axioms determined upon in argument can never assist in the discovery of new effects; for the subtilty of nature is vastly superior to that of argument. But axioms properly and regularly abstracted from particulars easily point out and define new particulars, and therefore impart activity to the sciences.

The axioms now in use are derived from a scanty handful, as it were, of experience, and a few particulars of frequent occurrence, whence they are of much the same dimensions or extent as their origin. And if any neglected or unknown instance occurs, the axiom is saved by some frivolous distinction, when it would be more consistent with truth to amend it.

We are wont, for the sake of distinction, to call that human reasoning which we apply to nature the anticipation of nature (as being rash and premature), and that which is properly deduced from things the interpretation of nature.

Anticipations are sufficiently powerful in producing unanimity, for if men were all to become even uniformly mad, they might agree tolerably well with each other.

Anticipations again, will be assented to much more readily than interpretation, because being deduced from a few instances, and these principally of familiar occurrence, they immediately hit the understanding and satisfy the imagination; while, on the contrary, interpretations, being deduced from various subjects, and these widely dispersed, cannot suddenly strike the understanding, so that in common estimation they must appear difficult and discordant, and almost like the mysteries of faith.

In sciences founded on opinions and dogmas, it is right to make use of anticipations and logic if you wish to force assent rather than things.

If all the capacities of all ages should unite and combine and transmit their labors, no great progress will be made in learning by anticipations, because the radical errors, and those which occur in the first process of the mind, are not cured by the excellence of subsequent means and remedies.

It is in vain to expect any great progress in the sciences by the superinducing or ingrafting new matters upon old. An instauration must be made from the very foundations, if we do not wish to revolve forever in a circle, making only some slight and contemptible progress.

The ancient authors and all others are left in undisputed possession of their honors; for we enter into no comparison of capacity or talent, but of method, and assume the part of a guide rather than of a critic.

To speak plainly, no correct judgment can be formed either of our method or its discoveries by those anticipations which are now in common use; for it is not to be required of us to submit ourselves to the judgment of the very method we ourselves arraign.

Nor is it an easy matter to deliver and explain our sentiments; for those things which are in themselves new can yet be only understood from some analogy to what is old.

Alexander Borgia said of the expedition of the French into Italy that they came with chalk in their hands to mark up their lodgings, and not with weapons to force their passage. Even so do we wish our philosophy to make its way quietly into those minds that are fit for it, and of good capacity; for we have no need of contention where we differ in first principles, and in our very notions, and even in our forms of demonstration.

We have but one simple method of delivering our sentiments, namely, we must bring men to particulars and their regular series and order, and they must for a while renounce their notions, and begin to form an acquaintance with things.

Our method and that of the sceptics' agree in some respects at first setting out, but differ most widely, and are completely opposed to each other in their conclusion; for they roundly assert that nothing can be known; we, that but a small part of nature can be known, by the present method; their next step, however, is to destroy the authority of the senses and understanding, while we invent and supply them with assistance.

The idols and false notions which have already preoccupied the human understanding, and are deeply rooted in it, not only so beset men's minds that they become difficult of access, but even when access is obtained will again meet and trouble us in the instauration of the sciences, unless mankind when forewarned guard themselves with all possible care against them.

Four species of idols beset the human mind, to which (for distinction's sake) we have assigned names, calling the first Idols of the Tribe, the second Idols of the Den, the third Idols of the Market, the fourth Idols of the Theatre.

The formation of notions and axioms on the foundation of true induction is the only fitting remedy by which we can ward off and expel these idols. It is, however, of great service to point them out; for the doctrine of idols bears the same relation to the interpretation of nature as that of the confutation of sophisms does to common logic.

The idols of the tribe are inherent in human nature and the very tribe or race of man; for man's sense is falsely asserted to be the standard of things; on the contrary, all the perceptions both of the senses and the mind bear reference to man and not to the universe, and the human mind resembles those uneven mirrors which impart their own properties to different objects, from which rays are emitted and distort and disfigure them.

The idols of the den are those of each individual; for everybody (in addition to the errors common to the race of man) has his own individual den or cavern, which intercepts and corrupts the light of nature, either from his own peculiar and singular disposition, or from his education and intercourse with others, or from his reading, and the authority acquired by those whom he reverences and admires, or from the different impressions produced on the mind, as it happens to be preoccupied and predisposed, or equable and tranquil, and the like; so that the spirit of man (according to its several dispositions), is variable, confused, and as it were actuated by chance; and Heraclitus said well that men search for knowledge in lesser worlds, and not in the greater or common world.

There are also idols formed by the reciprocal intercourse and society of man with man, which we call idols of the market, from the commerce and association of men with each other; for men converse by means of language, but words are formed at the will of the generality, and there arises from a bad and unapt formation of words a wonderful obstruction to the mind. Nor can the definitions and explanations with which learned men are wont to guard and protect themselves in some instances afford a complete remedy—words still manifestly force the understanding, throw everything into confusion, and lead mankind into vain and innumerable controversies and fallacies.

Lastly, there are idols which have crept into men's minds from the various dogmas of peculiar systems of philosophy, and also from the perverted rules of demonstration, and these we denominate idols of the theatre: for we regard all the systems of philosophy hitherto received or imagined, as so many plays brought out and performed, creating fictitious and theatrical worlds. Nor do we speak only of the present systems, or of the philosophy and sects of the ancients, since numerous other plays of a similar nature can be still composed and made to agree with each other, the causes of the most opposite errors being generally the same. Nor, again, do we allude merely to general systems, but also to many elements and axioms of sciences which have become inveterate by tradition, implicit credence, and neglect. We must, however, discuss each species of idols more fully and distinctly in order to guard the human understanding against them.

II. Common Terms, Words and Phrases for the Text

atomist 原子论者

cosmology 宇宙论

empiricism 经验主义，经验论

dogmatize 教条化，武断地提出

natural philosophy 自然哲学

system of logic 逻辑体系

syllogism 三段论

dialectics 辩证法

methodological 方法论的，方法的

inductive method 归纳法

axiom 公理，格言

generality 概论，普遍性

ostentation 卖弄，虚有其表，虚饰

doctrine 教义，信条

subtilty 狡诈，微妙

particulars 详情，细节

unanimity 同意，全体一致

dogmas 教条

superinduce 增添，引起

ingraft 灌输，嫁接

instauration 恢复，建立

analogy 比拟，类比

sentiment 观点，情绪

contention 观点，争论，争夺

sceptic 怀疑论者，无神论者

sophism 诡辩

reverence 尊敬，尊敬的阁下

Democritus 德谟克利特

Heraclitus 赫拉克利特

fallacy 谬论，谬误性

sui generis 独一无二的

astrology 占星术，星座

heterogeneous 参差的，多相的，不均一的

infinity 无限，无穷

tincture 酊，色泽，迹象，染色

III. Exercises and Thinking

1. What did Bacon criticize in the *Novum Organum*?

2. Try to figure out the logic by which Bacon argued and presented his theory.

3. Read and induce contemporary philosophers' views on Bacon's theory.

IV. Further Readings and Internet Links

1. Further Readings

余丽嫦:《培根及其哲学》，人民出版社 1987 年版。

胡景钊、余丽嫦:《十七世纪英国哲学》，商务印书馆 2006 年版。

[英]弗兰西斯·培根:《培根随笔集》，曹明伦译，人民文学出版社 2006 年版。

[法]克里斯托夫·多米诺:《培根》，陈惠儿译，上海译文出版社 2003 年版。

[英]威廉·R. 索利:《英国哲学史》，段德智译，商务印书馆 2017 年版。

2. Internet Links

中国社会科学院哲学研究所：http://philosophy.cass.cn/

上海社会科学院哲学研究所：https://ip.sass.org.cn/main.htm

清华大学哲学系：https://www.phil.tsinghua.edu.cn/

Faculty of Philosophy, University of Oxford: https://www.philosophy.ox.ac.uk/

Unit 23

The Treaty of Westphalia

1648年《威斯特伐利亚和约》

1618—1648年，欧洲各国尤其是神圣罗马帝国饱受战争之苦。从16世纪开始，路德教、加尔文教等新教出现，并逐渐在一些地区获得支持，这使原本松散的神圣罗马帝国因宗教改革而更加分裂。帝国各个大小不一的邦国、城市、领地政治分裂、社会冲突加剧。另有强敌环伺，神圣罗马帝国面临着法国和奥斯曼土耳其帝国威胁。新教诸侯与天主教诸侯各自联合欧洲其他强国使得战争局面错综复杂。漫长的战乱和分裂使得各方都有了和谈的意愿，尽管和谈过程中仍然冲突不断，但最终欧洲各国还是以和约的方式结束了三十年战争。

1648年《威斯特伐利亚和约》是三十年战争中各方签署的一系列和约的总称，目的就是恢复神圣罗马帝国的和平与秩序，其内容确立了帝国内部各诸侯的权力和利益问题，主张以宗教宽容原则处理教派矛盾、宗教财产争议等问题。1648年，神圣罗马帝国与法国、瑞典等国签署《奥斯纳布吕克和约》和《明斯特和约》，意在解决交战国间的领土争端、战争赔偿等问题。

《威斯特伐利亚和约》的重要意义不仅在于它结束了三十年之久的欧洲战争，也因它是众国战后和约而具有国际关系领域的里程碑式意义。历史学、国际关系学、国际法等领域都有对《威斯特伐利亚和约》的深入解读，《威斯特伐利亚和约》在历史学、国际关系学中皆反映出全球化叙事的发展趋势。学者们将《威斯特伐利亚和约》视为近代欧洲史的重要节点，从中演绎出国家主权、领土权、国际体系等具有普遍世界性意义的概念。关于《威斯特伐利亚和约》的现实约束力和有效性、它是否确立了主权国家为国际行为体的国际关系基本原则、威斯特伐利亚体系是否存在等问题，学术界众说纷纭。因此，回归史料本身有益于反思性的学术探讨。

I. Excerpt from *The Treaty of Westphalia*①

The Articles of the Treaty of Peace, Signed and Sealed, at Munster, in Westphalia, The 24th of October, 1648, By the Ambassadors, Plenipotentiaries, of their Sacred, Imperial, and Most Christian Majesties, and the Extraordinary Deputies, Electors, Princes, and States of the Sacred Roman Empire.

Article I

That there shall be a Christian and Universal Peace, and a Perpetual, True, and Sincere Amity, between the Sacred Imperial Majesty, and the Sacred Most Christian Majesty; as also, between all and each of the Allies, and Adherents of the said Imperial Majesty, the House of Austria, and its Heirs, Successors; but chiefly between the Electors, Prince and States of the Empire on the one side, and all and each of the Allies of the said Christian Majesty, and all their Heirs and Successors, chiefly between the most Serene Queen and Kingdom of Sweedland, the Electors respectively, the Princes and States of the Empire on the other part. That this Peace and Amity be observed and cultivated with such a sincerity, and such zeal, each Party shall endeavour to procure the benefit, honour, and advantage of each other, that thus on all sides they may see flourish the good of this peace and this friendship in the Roman Empire, and the Kingdom of France, by entertaining a good faithful neighbourhood.

II

That there shall be on the one side and the other, a perpetual oblivion, Amnisty, or Pardon of all what has been committed since the beginning of these troubles, in what

① *The Articles of the Treaty of Peace, Signed and Sealed at Munster in Westphalia, the 24th of October, 1648*, London: Printed by W. Onley, 1697, pp. 4-11.

place, or what manner soever the hostilities have been practised, in such a manner, that under no pretext soever, any one shall practise any acts of Hostility against the other, they shall give each other no Enmity, or cause any trouble; neither as to persons, neither to them, or to their effects and security; and that neither of themselves, or by others, neither privately nor openly, neither directly or indirectly, neither under the colour of Right, nor by the way of Deed, neither within or without the extent of the Empire, notwithstanding all Covenants made before to the contrary: that they all not act, or permit to be acted, any wrong or injury to any whatsoever; but that all that has passed on the one side, and the other, as well before, as during the War, in words, writings, and outragious actions, in violences, hostilities, damages and expences, without any respect to persons or things, shall be entirely abolished, in such a manner, that all which might be demanded, or pretended of each other on that behalf, shall be buried in an eternal oblivion.

III

And that the Riciprocal Amity between the Emperour and the most Christian King, the Electors, Princes and States of the Empire, might be maintained so much the more firm and sincere (without touching as yet that Article of Assurance, which will be mentioned hereafter) the one shall never assist the present or future Enemies of the other, under what title and pretence it may be, neither with Arms, Money, Soldiers, or any fort of munitions; nor shall permit retire through his countries, or sojourn any Enemies troops of any of the Treating, and who is Members of this pacification.

IV

That the Circle of Burgundy shall be and continue a Member of the Empire, after the disputes between France and Spain (comprehended in this Treaty) shall be terminated. That, nevertheless, neither the Emperour, nor any of the States of the Empire, shall meddle with the Wars which are now agitating. That if for the future any dispute arises between the two kingdoms, notwithstanding that the necessity of the abovesaid reciprocal obligation, which is not to aid each others enemies, shall always continue firm between the Empire and the Kingdom of France, yet it shall be free to the States to succour without the bounds of the Empire, such or such Kingdoms; but that nevertheless, according to the Constitutions of the Empire.

V

That the controversie touching Lorrian, shall be referred to Arbitrators nominated by both sides, or it shall be terminated by a Treaty between France and Spain, or by some other Friendly Means; and it shall be free as well for the Emperour as Electors, Princes and States of the Empire, to aid and advance this Accord by an amicable Interposition, and by other Offices of Pacification, without using arms and means of war.

VI

According to this foundation of reciprocal amity, and a general amity, all and every one of the Electors of the Sacred Roman Empire, the Princes and States (therein comprehended the nobility, which depend immediately from the Empire) their Vassals, Subjects, Citizens, Inhabitants, to whom on the occasion of the Bohemian, or German Troubles, or Alliances contracted here and there, might have been caused from the one Party or the other, any Prejudice, or Damage in what manner, or under what pretence it may be, as well in their Lordships, their Fiefs, Underfeifs, Allodations, as in their dignities, immunities, rights, and priviledges, shall be fully re–establish'd on the one side and the other, in the Ecclesiastick or Laick–State, which they enjoyed, or could lawfully enjoy, notwithstanding all Alterations which have been made in the mean time to the contrary.

VII

If the possessors of Estates, which are to be restored, think they have lawful exceptions, yet it shall not hinder the Restitution; which done, the reason and exception may be examined before competent Judges, in order to be disposed of.

VIII

And tho' by the precedent General Rule it may be easily judged who those are, and how far the Restitution extends; nevertheless, at the instance, and by the favour of some following cases of the great importance, it has been thought fit to make a particular mention without, that thereby those who are not in express Terms named, shall be exempted, or forgot.

IX

Since the Arrest the Emperour had made to be given formerly in the Provincial–Assembly, against the moveable effects belonging to the Prince Elector of Treves, and transported into the Dutchy of Luxembourg, tho' released and abolished, yet at the instance of some, has been renewed; to which has been added a sequestration, which the said assembly has made of the Jurisdiction of Burch, belonging to the Arch–bishoprick, and of the Moiety of the Lordship of St. John, belonging to John Reinhard of Soeteren, which is contrary to the Concordats drawn up at Ausburg in the year 1548, by the Publick Interposition of the Empire, between the Elector of Treves, and the Dutchy of Burgundy: It has been agreed, that the abovesaid arrest and sequestration shall be taken away with all speed from the Assembly of Luxembourg, that the said Jurisdiction, Lordship, and Electoral, and Patrimonial Effects, with the sequestered revenues, shall be released and rendred to the Lord Elector, and if by accident some things should be strayed, it shall be fully restored to him, the petitioners being referred for the obtaining the administration of their Rights to the Judge of the Prince Elector, who is competent in the Empire.

X

As for what concerns the Castles of Ehenbrestein, and of Hamestein, the Emperour shall draw, or cause the Garrisons to be drawn off in the time and manner limitted here underneath in the Article of Execution, and shall return those Castles to the Lord Elector of Treves, and to his Metropolitan Chapter, for to be in the Guard of the Empire, and the Electorate; for which end, the Captain, and the new Garrison which shall be put in there by the Elector, shall also take the Oaths of Fidelity to him and his Chapter.

XI

After which the Assembly of Munster and Osnabrug has brought the Palatinate–Cause to these Terms, that the dispute which has been debated for so long at time, has been terminated in the manner following:

XII

And in the first place, as to what concerns the House of Bavaria, the Electoral Dignity, and the Electors Palatine have hitherto had with all their Regales, Offices, Precedencies, Arms and Rights whatever they be belonging to this Dignity, without excepting any, as also all the higher Palatinate and the County of Cham shall remain as for the time past, also for the future, with all their Appurtenances, Regales and Rights, with the Lord Maximilian, Count Palatine of the Rhine, Duke of Bavaria, and with his children, and with all the Line of William, whilst there shall be any Male–Children.

XIII

Reciprocally the Lord Elector of Bavaria, renounces entirely for himself and his heirs and successors the Debt of thirteen millions, as also all his pretensions in Upper Austria, and shall deliver to his Imperial Majesty immediately after the Publication of the Peace, all Acts and Arrests obtained for that end, in order to be made void and annulled.

XIV

As for what regards the Palatinate House, the Emperor and the Empire, for the benefit of the Pulick Tranquility, they consent, that by virtue of this present Agreement, there be established and Eighth Electorate; which the Lord Charles Lewis, Count Palatine of the Rhine, shall enjoy for the future, and his heirs and paternal Relations descending from the Branch of Rudolphe, pursuant to the Order of Succession, set forth in the golden Bull; and that by this Investiture, the Lord Charles Lewis, nor his Successors shall have no right upon what has been attributed with the Electoral Dignity, to the Lord Elector of Bavaria, and all the Branch of William.

XV

Afterwards, that all the Lower Palatinate, with all and each of Ecclesiastical and Secular Lands, Rights and Appurtenances, which the Electors and Princes Palatines enjoyed before the Troubles of Bohemia, shall be fully restored to him; as also all the ducuments, registers and papers belonging thereto; and that by the emperor's Authority, annulling all what might have been done to the contrary, so that neither the Catholick King, nor any other who possess any thing thereof, can any ways oppose this Restitution.

XVI

And by reason that certain Jurisdictions of the Bergstract, belonging anciently to the Elector of Mayence, were in the Year 1463, Mortgaged to the Palatines for a certain Sum of Money; upon Condition of Perpetual Redemption, it has been agreed that the same Jurisdictions shall remain with the present Lord Elector of Mayence, and provided the Mortgage be paid in ready Money, within a limited time after the Execution of the Peace concluded; and that he satisfies the other conditions, which he is bound to by the tenor of the letters of mortgage.

XVII

It shall also be free to the Elector of Treves, as well in the Quality of Bishop of Spires, as Bishop of Worms, to demand before competent Judges, the Rights he pretends upon certain Ecclesiastical Lands, scituated in the territories of the Lower Palatinate, if so be those Princes make not a friendly composition among them.

XVIII

That if it should happen that the male branch of William should be entirely extinct, the Palatine still subsisting, not only in the Upper Palatinate, but also the Electoral Dignity of the Dukes of Bavaria shall come back to the said surviving Palatines, and in the mean time enjoy the investiture; but then the eighth Electorate shall be entirely suppressed. But, in such case, nevertheless, of the return of the Upper Palatinate to the surviving Palatines, the Heirs of any Allodian Lands of the Bavarian Electors shall remain in Possession of the Rights and Benefices, which may lawfully appertain to them.

XIX

That the contracts of Family made between the Electoral House of Heidelberg, and Nieuburg, touching the succession to the Electorate, confirmed by the precedent Emperors; as also all the Rights of the Rudolphine Branch, for as much as they are not contrary to this Disposition, shall be conserved and maintained entire.

XX

Moreover, if any Fiefs in Juliers shall be found open by lawful means, the Question shall be decided in favour of the Palatines.

XXI

Further, to deprive the Lord Charles Lewis, in some manner, of the Troubles of providing his Brothers with Appenages, his Imperial Majesty will ordain that there be paid Forty Thousand Rixdollars to the said Brothers, in the four ensuing Years; the first commencing the first from the Year 1649. The payment is to be made of ten thousand Rixdollars Yearly, with Five per Cent. Interest.

XXII

Further, that all the Palatinate House, with all and each of them, who have been, or in any manner are tyed to him; and above all, the Ministers who have served him in this Assembly, or who have formerly served him; as also all those who are exiled out of the Palatinate, shall enjoy the general Amnisty here above promised, with the same Rights as those who are comprehended therein, or of whom has been made a more particular and ampler mention in the Article of Grievance.

XXIII

Reciprocally the Lord Charles Lewis and his Brothers shall render Obedience, and keep Fidelity to His Imperial Majesty, like the other Electors and Princes of the Empire, and shall renonuce to the pretensions of the Upper Palatinate, as well for them as their heirs; whilest any male and lawful heir of the Branch of William shall continue alive.

XXIV

And upon the mention, which has been made to give a dowry and a Pention to the Mother, Dowager of the said Prince, and to his sisters, his sacred Imperial Majesty, (according to the affection he has for the Palatinate House) has promised to the said Mother Dowager, for them Maintainance and Subsistance, to pay once for all, twenty thousand Rixdollars; and to each of the sisters of the said Lord Charles Lewis, when they shall marry, ten thousand Rixdollars, the said Prince Charles Lewis being bound to disburse the overplus.

XXV

That the said Lord Charles Lewis shall give no troubles to the Counts of Leiningen, and of Daxburg, nor to their successors in the Lower Palatinate, but he shall let them peaceably enjoy their rights obtained many ages ago, and confirmed by the Emperors.

XXVI

That he shall leave inviolably the Free Nobility of the Empire, which are in Franconia, Swabia, and all along the Rhine, and in his Appurtenances in the State they are.

II. Common Terms, Words and Phrases for the Text

treaty of peace 和平条约

Westphalia 威斯特伐利亚

ambassador 大使，使节

The Sacred Roman Empire 神圣罗马帝国

plenipotentiary 全权大使

Arch-Duke 大公

vassal 诸侯，封臣

ecclesiastic 教士，教会的

Prince Elector 选帝侯

archbishopric 大主教的管区，大主教之职

Bohemia 波西米亚

Bavaria 巴伐利亚

Burgundy 勃艮第

Luxembourg 卢森堡

Lorrain 洛林

dowry 嫁妆，亡夫遗产

dowager 爵位遗孀，贵妇

Marquis（Marquess）侯爵

confiscation 没收，征用

Prince Lewis XlV 路易十四

Prince Charles II 查理二世

garrison 要塞，卫戍部队

bailiwick 管辖范围、职责范围

lordship 贵族身份，阁下，统治

nomination 推荐，任命，被提名的人

obedience 顺从，服从

restitution 恢复，归还，赔偿

reimbursement 赔付，赔偿

Treaty of Aix-La-Chapelle《亚琛条约》

priory 小修道院

jurisdiction 司法权，审判权

ordinance 条例，法令，圣餐礼

III. Exercises and Thinking

1. What was the course of the Thirty Years' War?

2. What were the impacts of Westphalia Treaty of Peace on the Sacred Roman

Empire?

3. What were the historical meaning of the Westphalian System?

IV. Further Readings and Internet Links

1. Further Readings

[英] 塞缪尔·罗森·加德纳:《三十年战争史：1618—1648》，王晋瑞译，华文出版社 2019 年版。

李明倩:《〈威斯特伐利亚和约〉与近代国际法》，商务印书馆 2018 年版。

翟楚:《近代欧洲之政治与外交》，商务印书馆 1946 年版。

李祖训:《神圣罗马帝国》，商务印书馆 1964 年版。

2. Internet Links

中国社会科学院欧洲研究所：http://ies.cass.cn

中国法学网（中国社会科学院国际法研究所、国际法研究所主办）：http://iolaw.cssn.cn

外交学院国际关系研究所：https://iir.cfau.edu.cn

International Law Commission, The United Nations: https://legal.un.org/ilc/research.shtml

Unit 24 First Charter of the Royal Society of London

1662 年英国皇家学会特许状

英国皇家学会历史悠久，深受世界其他科学群体和科学机构的关注。英国皇家学会创立的背景可追溯到文艺复兴和英国宗教改革，直至 17 世纪英国出现了像培根这样突破传统思想倡导实验科学的哲学家。当时英国的天文学、物理学、几何学、神学等都有了新的发展。学者们通过相互交流使新科学成果和新思想得到传播，英国皇家学会正是在这样的学术氛围中逐步创立的。1640 年前后，英国政治局势动荡，英国学者们仍然一心治学，他们不定期地举办学术集会，探讨各自的研究进展，交流欧洲学术动态。他们开展学术讨论的地点并不固定，有时在格雷山姆学院，有时在酒馆，有时在学者的住处。1660 年 11 月，在格雷山姆学院，学者们提议建立促进数学、物理、实验的学院。1662 年，查理二世颁发特许状，正式批准成立皇家学会。在特许状中，英国国王表达了对自然哲学和促进实用技艺的科学的重视。

英国皇家学会成立后，逐渐完善其组织机制，转型成更专业的现代科学学会。英国政府与皇家学会的关联也更紧密，不只是在口号上提出借助科学壮大帝国，还向皇家学会划拨资助经费。皇家学会本身在经营资本和投资方面的成效也是它得以延续和成功的重要因素。所以皇家学会的制度设计、经费保障、科学创新等方面都在不断完善和发展。英国皇家学会历任会长亦功不可没，如我们熟知的牛顿。他采取了包括规定会员会费在内的一系列措施来保障学会的运转。英国皇家学会广纳领先科学人才，后来又设有名誉会员，进一步扩大了其影响力。

英国皇家学会在英国工业革命和海外殖民扩张中都发挥了重要作用。詹姆斯·瓦特就是英国皇家学会的会员。英国为殖民扩张而构建出“社会达尔文主义”的理论，其源头就是皇家学会会员达尔文所著的《物种起源》。由于英国皇家学会的历史角色复杂，研究皇家学会的著述不断涌现，从其创立之初便有史册记录，各国学者对其进行了广泛探讨，因此本篇也予以关注。

I. Excerpt from First Charter of the Royal Society of London①

First Charter, Granted to the President, Council, and Fellows of the Royal Society of London, By King Charles the Second, A.D. 1662.

Charles the Second, by the grace of God King of England, Scotland, France, and Ireland, Defender of the Faith, &c., to all to whom these present Letters shall come, greeting.

We have long and fully resolved with Ourself extend not only the boundaries of the Empire, but also the very arts and sciences. Therefore we look with favour upon all forms of learning, but with particular grace we encourage philosophical studies, especially those which by actual experiments attempt either to shape out a new philosophy or to perfect the old. In order, therefore, that such studies, which have not hitherto been sufficiently brilliant in any part of the world, may shine conspicuously amongst our people, and that at length the whole world of letters may always recognise us not only as the Defender of the Faith, but also as the universal lover and patron of every kind of truth:

Know ye that we, of our special grace and of our certain knowledge and mere motion, have ordained, established, granted, and declared, and by these presents for us, our heirs, and successors do ordain, establish, grant, and declare, that from henceforth

① Royal Society (Great Britain), *The Record of the Royal Society of London*, London: Harrison and Sons, Printers in Ordinary to Her Majesty, 1897, pp. 31–43.

for ever there shall be a Society, consisting of a President, Council, and Fellows, which shall be called and named The Royal Society; And for us, our heirs, and successors we do make, ordain, create, and constitute by these presents the same Society, by the name of The President, Council, and Fellows of the Royal Society, one body corporate and politic in fact, deed, and name, really and fully, and that by the same name they may have perpetual succession; and that they and their successors (whose studies are to be applied to further promoting by the authority of experiments the sciences of natural things and of useful arts), by the same name of The President, Council, and Fellows of the Royal Society aforesaid, may and shall be in all future times persons able and capable in law to have, acquire, receive, and possess lands and tenements, meadows, feedings, pastures, liberties, privileges, franchises, jurisdictions, and hereditaments whatsoever, to themselves and their successors in fee and perpetuity, or for term of life, lives, or years, or otherwise in whatsoever manner, and also goods and chattels, and all other things, of whatsoever kind, nature, sort, or quality they may be; and also to give, grant, demise, and assign the same lands, tenements, and hereditaments, goods and chattels, and to do and execute all acts and things necessary of and concerning the same, by the name aforesaid; And that by the name of The President, Council, and Fellows of the Royal Society aforesaid they may henceforth for ever be able and have power to plead and be impleaded, to answer and be answered, to defend and be defended, in whatsoever Courts and places, and before whatsoever Judges and Justices and other persons and officers of us, our heirs, and successors, in all and singular actions, pleas, suits, plaints, causes, matters, things, and demands whatsoever, of whatsoever kind, nature, or sort they may or shall be, in the same manner and form as any of our lieges within this our Realm of England, being persons able and capable in law, or as any body corporate or politic within this our Realm of England, may be able and have power to have, acquire, receive, possess, give, and grant, to plead and be impleaded, to answer and be answered, to defend or be defended; And that the same President, Council, and Fellows of the

Royal Society aforesaid, and their successors, may have for ever a Common Seal, to serve for transacting the causes and affairs whatsoever of them and their successors; and that it may and shall be good and lawful to the same President, Council, and Fellows of the Royal Society aforesaid, and to their successors for the time being, to break, change, and make anew that Seal from time to time, according as it shall seem most expedient to them.

And that our royal intention may obtain the better effect, and for the good rule and government of the aforesaid Royal Society from time to time, we will, and by these presents for us, our heirs, and successors do grant to the same President, Council, and Fellows of the Royal Society aforesaid, and to their successors, that henceforth for ever the Council aforesaid shall be and consist of twenty–one persons (of whom we will the President to be always one); And that all and singular other persons who within one month next following after the date of these presents shall be received and admitted by the President and Council, and in all time following by the President, Council, and Fellows, into the same Society, as Members of the Royal Society aforesaid, and shall have been noted in the Register by them to be kept, shall be and shall be called and named Fellows of the Royal Society aforesaid: whom, the more eminently they are distinguished for the study of every kind of learning and good letters, the more ardently they desire to promote the honour, studies, and advantage of this Society, the more they are noted for integrity of life, uprightness of character, and piety, and excel in fidelity and affection of mind towards us, our Crown, and dignity, the more we wish them to be especially deemed fitting and worthy of being admitted into the number of the Fellows of the same Society.

And for the better execution of our will and grant in this behalf, we have assigned, nominated, constituted, and made, and by these presents for us, our heirs, and successors do assign, nominate, constitute, and make, our very well beloved and trusty William, Viscount Brouncker, Chancellor to our very dear consort, Queen Catherine, to be and become the first and present President of the Royal Society aforesaid; willing that the aforesaid William, Viscount Brouncker, shall continue in the office of President of the Royal Society aforesaid from the date of these presents until the feast of St. Andrew next following after the date of these presents, and until one other of the Council of the Royal Society aforesaid for the time being shall have been elected, appointed, and sworn to that office in due manner, according to the ordinance and provision below in these presents expressed and declared (if the aforesaid William, Viscount Brouncker, shall live so long); having first taken a corporal oath well and faithfully to execute his office in and by all things touching that office, according to the true intention of these presents, before our very well-beloved and very trusty Cousin and Councillor Edward, Earl of Clarendon, our Chancellor of England: to which same Edward, Earl of Clarendon, our Chancellor aforesaid, we give and grant full power and authority, to administer the oath aforesaid in these words following, that is to say:—

I, William, Viscount Brouncker, do promise to deal faithfully and honestly in all things belonging to the trust committed to me as President of this Royal Society, during my employment in that capacity. So help me God!

We have also assigned, constituted, and made, and by these presents for us, our heirs, and successors do make, our beloved and trusty Robert Moray, Knight, one of our Privy Council in our Realm of Scotland; Robert Boyle, Esquire; William Brereton, Esquire, eldest son of the Baron de Brereton; Kenelm Digby, Knight, Chancellor to our very dear mother, Queen Maria; Paul Neile, Knight, one of the Gentlemen of our Privy Chamber; Henry Slingesby, Esquire, another of the Gentlemen of our aforesaid Privy Chamber; William Petty, Knight; John Wallis, Doctor in Divinity; Timothy Clarke, Doctor in Medicine and one of our Physicians; John Wilkins, Doctor in Divinity; George Ent, Doctor in Medicine; William Aerskine, one of our Cup-bearers; Jonathan Goddard, Doctor in Medicine and Professor of Gresham College; Christopher Wren, Doctor in Medicine, Saville Professor of Astronomy in our University of Oxford; William Balle, Esquire; Matthew Wren, Esquire; John Evelyn, Esquire; Thomas Henshawe,

Esquire; Dudley Palmer, of Grey's Inn, in our County of Middlesex, Esquire; and Henry Oldenburg, Esquire, together with the President aforesaid, to be and become the first and present twenty–one of the Council of the Royal Society aforesaid; to be continued in the same offices from the date of these presents until the aforesaid feast of Saint Andrew the Apostle next following, and thenceforth until other fitting and able and sufficient persons shall have been elected, appointed, and sworn into the offices aforesaid (if they shall live so long, or shall not have been amoved for any just and reasonable cause); first taking corporal oaths before the President of the aforesaid Royal Society, well and faithfully to execute their offices in and by all things touching those offices, according to the form and effect of the aforesaid oath, *mutatis mutandis*, to be administered to the President of the Royal Society aforesaid by our Chancellor of England; (to which same President for the time being, for us, our heirs, and successors, we give and grant by these presents full power and authority to administer the oaths aforesaid;) And that the same persons, so as it is aforesaid elected, appointed, and sworn, and hereafter to be elected, appointed, and sworn from time to time, to the Council of the aforesaid Royal Society, shall be and become aiding, counselling, and assistant in all matters, business, and affairs touching or concerning the better regulation, government, and direction of the aforesaid Royal Society, and of every Member of the same.

And further we will, and by these presents for us, our heirs, and successors do grant to the aforesaid President, Council, and Fellows of the Royal Society aforesaid, and to their successors, that the President, Council, and Fellows of the Royal Society aforesaid for the time being (of whom we will the President for the time being to be one) may and shall have from time to time in all future times for ever power and authority to nominate and elect, and that they may be able and have power to elect and nominate, every year, on the aforesaid feast of St. Andrew, one of the Council of the aforesaid Royal Society for the time being, who may and shall be President of the Royal Society aforesaid until the feast of St. Andrew the Apostle thereafter next following (if he shall live so long, or shall not be amoved meanwhile for any just and reasonable cause), and thenceforth until another shall have been elected, appointed, and nominated to the office of President of the Royal Society aforesaid; and that he, after that he shall so have been elected and nominated, as it is aforesaid, to the office of President of the Royal Society aforesaid, before he be admitted to that office, shall take a corporal oath before the Council of the same Royal Society, or any seven or more of them, rightly, well, and faithfully to execute that office in all things touching that office, according to the form and effect of the aforesaid oath, mutatis mutandis (to which same Council, or to any seven or more of them, we give and grant by these presents for us, our heirs, and successors, full power and authority to administer the aforesaid oath from time to time, as often as it shall be necessary); and that after having so taken such oath, as it is aforesaid, he may be able and have power to execute the office of President of the Royal Society aforesaid until the feast of St. Andrew the Apostle thereafter next following; And if it shall happen that the President of the Royal Society aforesaid for the time being, at any time, so long as he shall be in the office of President of the same Royal Society, shall die or be amoved from his office, that then and so often it may and shall be good and lawful to the Council and Fellows of the aforesaid Royal Society, or to any seven or more of them (of whom we will the President of the Council aforesaid to be always one at such an election), to elect and appoint another of the aforesaid number of the Council aforesaid as President of the Royal Society aforesaid; and that he so elected and appointed may have and exercise that office during the residue of the same year, and until another shall have been in due manner elected and sworn to that office, first taking a corporal oath in the form last specified; and so as often as the case shall so happen.

And further we will, that whenever it shall happen that any one or any of the Council of the Royal Society aforesaid for the time being shall die, or be amoved from that office, or retire (which same [members] of the Council of the Royal Society aforesaid, and every one of them, we will to be amoveable for misbehaviour or any other reasonable cause, at the good pleasure of the President and of the rest of the Council aforesaid surviving and remaining in that office, or of the major part of the same, of whom we will the President for the time being to be one), that then and so often it may and shall be good and lawful to the aforesaid President, Council, and Fellows of the Royal Society aforesaid, or to the major part of the same (of whom we will the President of the Royal Society aforesaid for the time being to be one), to nominate, elect, and appoint one other or several others of the Fellows of the Royal Society aforesaid, in the place or places of him or them so dead, retired, or amoved, to fill up the aforesaid number of twenty–one persons of the Council of the Royal Society aforesaid; and that he or they so elected and appointed in that office may have the same office until the feast of St. Andrew the Apostle then next following, and thenceforth until one other or several others shall have been elected, appointed, and nominated; first taking a corporal oath before the President and Council of the Royal Society aforesaid, or any seven or more of them for the time being, well and faithfully to execute that office in and by all things touching that office, according to the true intention of these presents.

And further we will, and by these presents for us, our heirs, and successors do grant to the aforesaid President, Council, and Fellows of the aforesaid Royal Society, and to their successors, that they and their successors, every year, on the aforesaid feast of St. Andrew the Apostle, may and shall have full power and authority to elect, nominate, appoint, and change ten of the Fellows of the Royal Society aforesaid, to fill up the places and offices of ten of the aforesaid number of twenty–one of the Council of the Royal Society aforesaid; for we do declare it to be our royal pleasure, and by these presents for us, our heirs, and successors we do grant, that ten of the aforesaid Council, and no more, shall be annually changed and amoved by the President, Council, and Fellows of the Royal Society aforesaid.

We will also, and for us, our heirs, and successors do grant to the aforesaid President, Council, and Fellows of the aforesaid Royal Society, and to their successors, that if it shall happen that the President of the same Royal Society for the time being is detained by sickness or infirmity, or is employed in the service of us, our heirs, or successors, or is otherwise occupied, so that he shall not be able to attend to the necessary affairs of the same Royal Society touching the office of President, that then and so often it may and shall be good and lawful to the same President so detained, employed, or occupied, to nominate and appoint one of the Council of the aforesaid Royal Society for the time being to be and become the Deputy of the same President; which same Deputy, so to be made and appointed in the office of Deputy of the President aforesaid, may and shall be the Deputy of the same President from time to time, as often as the aforesaid President shall happen to be so absent, during the whole time in which the aforesaid President shall continue in the office of President; unless in the meanwhile the aforesaid President of the Royal Society aforesaid for the time being shall have made and appointed one other of the aforesaid Council his Deputy; And that every such Deputy of the aforesaid President so to be made and appointed, as it is aforesaid, may be able and have power to do and execute all and singular things which pertain or ought to pertain to the office of President of the aforesaid Royal Society, or which are limited and appointed to be done and executed by the aforesaid President, by virtue of these our Letters Patent, from time to time, as often as the aforesaid President shall so happen to be absent, during such time as he shall continue the Deputy of the aforesaid President, by force of these our Letters Patent, as fully, freely, and wholly, and in as ample manner and form, as the aforesaid President, if he were present, would be able and have power and do and execute those things; of a corporal oath first to be taken by such Deputy upon the holy Gospels of God, in the form and effect last specified, well and faithfully to execute all and singular things which pertain to the office of President, before the aforesaid Council of the aforesaid Royal Society, or any seven or more of them; and so as often as the case shall so happen: to which same Council, or to any seven or more of them, for the time being, we do give and grant by these presents power and authority to administer the oath aforesaid as often as the case shall so happen, without procuring or obtaining any writ, commission, or further warrant in that behalf from us, our heirs, or successors.

And further we will, and by these presents for us, our heirs, and successors do grant to the aforesaid President, Council, and Fellows of the Royal Society aforesaid, and to their successors, that they and their successors henceforth for ever may and shall have one Treasurer, two Secretaries, one Clerk, and two Serjeants–at–Mace, who may from time to time attend upon the President; and that the aforesaid Treasurer, Secretaries, Clerk, and Serjeants–at–Mace, to be elected and nominated, before they be admitted to execute their several and respective offices, shall take their corporal oaths in the form and effect last specified, before the President and Council of the same Royal Society, or any seven or more of them, rightly, well, and faithfully to execute their several and respective offices then in all things touching the same; and that after having so taken such oaths, as it is aforesaid, they may exercise and use their respective offices; to which same President and Council, or to any seven or more of them, we do give and grant by these presents full power and authority to administer the oaths aforesaid from time to time to the aforesaid several and respective officers and their successors: And we have assigned, nominated, chosen, created, appointed, and made, and by these presents for us, our heirs, and successors do assign, nominate, choose, create, appoint, and make, our beloved subjects William Balle, Esquire, to be and become the first and present Treasurer, and the aforesaid John Wilkins and Henry Oldenburg to be and become the first and present Secretaries, of the aforesaid Royal Society; to be continued in the same offices until the aforesaid feast of St. Andrew the Apostle next following after the date of these presents: And that from time to time and at all times on the aforesaid feast of Saint Andrew the Apostle (unless it shall be Sunday, and if it be Sunday, then on the day next following) the President, Council, and Fellows of the aforesaid Royal Society for the time being, or the major part of the same (of whom we will the President for the time being to be one), may be able and have power to elect, nominate, and appoint other upright and discreet men, from time to time, as Treasurer, Secretaries, Clerk, and Serjeants-at-Mace of the aforesaid Royal Society; and that those who shall so have been elected, appointed, and sworn to the aforesaid several and respective offices, as it is aforesaid, may be able and have power to exercise and enjoy those respective offices until the aforesaid feast of St. Andrew then next following, their aforesaid oaths, as it is aforesaid, first to be taken; and so as often as the case shall so happen. And if it shall happen that any one or any of the officers aforesaid of the same Royal Society shall die, or be amoved from their respective offices, that then and so often it may and shall be good and lawful to the President, Council, and Fellows of the aforesaid Royal Society, or to the major part of the same (of whom we will the President for the time being to be one), to elect and appoint another or others to the office or offices of those persons so deceased or amoved; and that he or they so elected and appointed may have and exercise the respective offices aforesaid during the residue of the same year, and until another or others shall have been in due manner elected and sworn to those respective offices; and so as often as the case shall so happen.

And moreover we will, and of our special grace and of our certain knowledge and mere motion do grant to the aforesaid President, Council, and Fellows of the Royal Society aforesaid, and to their successors, that the President and Council of the aforesaid Royal Society for the time being, and the major part of the same (of whom we will the President for the time being to be one), may be able and have power to meet together and assemble in a College or other public place or Hall within our City of London, or in any other convenient place within ten miles of our same City; and that they so met together and assembled shall and may have full authority, power, and faculty from time to time to draw up, constitute, ordain, make, and establish such laws, statutes, acts, ordinances, and constitutions as shall seem to them, or to the major part of them, to be good, wholesome, useful, honourable, and necessary, according to their sound discretions, and to do and perform all other things whatsoever belonging to the affairs and matters of the Royal Society aforesaid; all and singular which laws, statutes, acts, ordinances, and constitutions so to be made as it is aforesaid, we will, and by these presents for us, our heirs, and successors, firmly enjoining, do order and command, that they shall be inviolably observed from time to time, according to the tenor and effect of the same, so nevertheless that the aforesaid laws, statutes, acts, ordinances, and constitutions so to be made as it is aforesaid, and every one of them, be reasonable, and not repugnant or contrary to the laws, customs, acts, or statutes of this our Realm of England.

And further, of our more ample special grace and of our certain knowledge and mere motion, we have given and granted, and by these presents for us, our heirs, and successors do give and grant to the aforesaid Council and Fellows of the aforesaid Royal Society, and to their successors, full power and authority from time to time to elect, nominate, and appoint one or more Typographers or Printers, and Chalcographers or Engravers, and to grant to him or them, by a writing, sealed with the Common Seal of the aforesaid Royal Society, and signed by the hand of the President for the time being, faculty to print such things, matters, and affairs touching or concerning the aforesaid [Royal] Society, as shall have been committed to the aforesaid Typographer or Printer, Chalcographer or Engraver, or Typographers or Printers, Chalcographers or Engravers, from time to time, by the President and Council of the aforesaid Royal Society, or any seven or more of them (of whom we will the President for the time being to be one); their corporal oaths first to be taken, before they be admitted to exercise their offices, before the President and Council for the time being, or any seven or more of them, in the form and effect last specified; to which same President and Council, or to any seven or more of them, we do give and grant by these presents full power and authority to administer the oaths aforesaid.

And further, in order that the aforesaid President, Council, and Fellows of the aforesaid Royal Society may obtain the better effect in their philosophical studies, of our more ample special grace and of our certain knowledge and mere motion, we have given and granted, and by these presents for us, our heirs, and successors, do give and grant, to the aforesaid President, Council, and Fellows of the aforesaid Royal Society, and to their successors, that they and their successors from time to time may and shall have full power and authority from time to time, and at such seasonable times, according to their discretion, to require, take, and receive the bodies of such persons as have suffered death by the hand of the executioner, and to anatomize them, in such ample form and manner, and to all intents and purposes, as the College of Physicians and the Corporation of Surgeons of our City of London have used or enjoyed, or may be able and have power to use or enjoy, the same bodies.

And further, for the improvement of the experiments, arts, and sciences of the aforesaid Royal Society, of our more abundant special grace and of our certain knowledge and mere motion, we have given and granted, and by these presents for us, our heirs, and successors do give and grant, to the aforesaid President, Council, and Fellows of the aforesaid Royal Society, and to their successors, that they and their successors from time to time may and shall have full power and authority, by letters or epistles under the hand of the aforesaid President, in the presence of the Council, or of any seven or more of them, and in the name of the Royal Society, and sealed with their Common Seal aforesaid, to enjoy mutual intelligence and knowledge with all and all manner of strangers and foreigners, whether private or collegiate, corporate or politic, without any molestation, interruption, or disturbance whatsoever: Provided nevertheless, that this our indulgence, so granted as it is aforesaid, be not extended to further use than the particular benefit and interest of the aforesaid Royal Society in matters or things philosophical, mathematical, or mechanical.

And further we have given and granted, and by these presents for us, our heirs, and successors do give and grant to the aforesaid President, Council, and Fellows of the Royal Society aforesaid, and to their successors, full power and authority to erect, build, and construct, or to make or cause to be erected, built, and constructed, within our City of London, or ten miles of the same, one or more College or Colleges, of whatsoever kind or quality, for the habitation, assembly, and meeting of the aforesaid President, Council, and Fellows of the aforesaid Royal Society, and of their successors, for the ordering and arranging of their affairs and other matters concerning the same Royal Society.

And further we will, and by these presents for us, our heirs, and successors do ordain, constitute, and appoint, that if any abuses or differences hereafter shall arise and happen concerning the government or other matters or affairs of the aforesaid Royal Society, whereby any injury or hindrance may be done to the constitution, stability, and progress of the studies, or to the matters and affairs, of the same; that then and so often, by these presents, for us, our heirs, and successors, we do authorise, [ordain,] nominate, assign, and appoint our aforesaid very well-beloved and very trusty Cousin and Councillor Edward, Earl of Clarendon, our Chancellor of our Realm of England, by himself during his life, and, after his death, then the Archbishop of Canterbury, the Chancellor or Keeper of the Greet Seal of England, the Treasurer of England, the Bishop of London, the Keeper of the Privy Seal, and the two Principal Secretaries for the time being, or any four or more of them, to reconcile, compose, and adjust the same differences and abuses.

And further we will, and by these presents, for us, our heirs, and successors, firmly enjoining, do order and command all and singular the Justices, Mayors, Aldermen, Sheriffs, Bailiffs, Constables, and other officers, ministers, and subjects whomsoever of us, our heirs, and successors, that they be from time to time aiding and assistant to the aforesaid President, Council, and Fellows of the Royal Society aforesaid, and to their successors, in and by all things, according to the true intention of these our Letters Patent.

Although express mention of the true yearly value or of the certainty of the premises, or of any of them, or of other gifts or grants before these times made by us or by any of our progenitors or predecessors to the aforesaid President, Council, and Fellows of the Royal Society, is not made in these presents; or any statute, act, ordinance, provision, proclamation, or restriction to the contrary thereof heretofore had, made, enacted, ordained, or provided, or any other thing, cause, or matter whatsoever, in any wise notwithstanding.

In witness whereof we have caused these our Letters to be made Patent. Witness Ourself, at Westminster, the fifteenth day of July, in the fourteenth year of our reign.

By the King himself.

Howard.

II. Common Terms, Words and Phrases for the Text

Royal Society of London 伦敦皇家学会

Council of the Royal Society 皇家学会理事会

hereditament 可继承财产

piety 虔诚

Viscount Brouncker 布朗克子爵

Feast of St. Andrew 圣安德鲁节

corporal oath 基督教的宣誓仪式（手触摸着《圣经》宣誓）

Earl of Clarendon 克拉伦登伯爵

Privy Council 枢密院

chancellor 名誉校长、大法官

Privy Chamber 枢密室

Doctor in Divinity 神学博士

apostle 使徒

mutatis mutandis 类似的情况下作相应的调整，已作必要的修改

infirmity 病弱、病症、缺点

pertain 适用、从属、生效

letters patent 专利特许证

writ 令状

treasurer 财务主管，会计，司库

residue 剩余物，剩余遗产

discretion 自行决定权，谨慎

repugnant 不得人心，使嫌恶，与……矛盾

typographer 印刷商，印刷工人

chalcographer 铜版雕刻专家

engraver 雕刻师

the common seal 通用印章

executioner 行刑者

anatomize 解剖，仔细分析

molestation 妨害，折磨等

indulgence 特赦，延期付款，放纵等

Archbishop of Canterbury 坎特伯雷大主教

The Great Seal of England 英格兰国玺

Lord Privy Seal 掌玺大臣

III. Exercises and Thinking

1. What was the historical background of the establishment of the Royal Society?

2. What were contributions made by the Royal Society of London in the British Scientific and Industrial Revolution?

3. Research on how did the Royal Society build its international reputation since its foundation.

IV. Further Readings and Internet Links

1. Further Readings

[英] 阿德里安·泰尼斯伍德:《英国皇家学会：现代科学的起点》，王兢译，

北京燕山出版社2020年版。

罗兴波：《17世纪英国科学研究方法的发展：以伦敦皇家学会为中心》，中国科学技术出版社2012年版。

英国皇家学会著：《科学：开放的事业》，何巍等译，上海交通大学出版社2015年版。

刘贵华：《人文主义与近代早期英国大学教育》，中国社会科学出版社2016年版。

2. Internet Links

The Royal Society: https://royalsociety.org/

The Royal Historical Society: https://royalhistsoc.org/

Royal Society Publishing: https://royalsocietypublishing.org/journal/rsnr

Unit 25 The Mathematical Principles of Natural Philosophy
牛顿《自然哲学的数学原理》

英国科学家艾萨克·牛顿（Isaac Newton，1642—1727）曾被埃德蒙·哈雷（Edmond Halley）赞誉为“缪斯垂青的人”“比任何一个凡人更接近神的人”①。他为物理学和数学作出杰出贡献，他的成就主要体现在力学、光学和微积分运算方法等方面。1687年，牛顿的《自然哲学的数学原理》（以下简称《原理》）首次出版，书中提出了力学的三大运动定律和万有引力定律。牛顿通过《原理》建立起经典力学体系，并将其运用于解释地球上的物理现象以及天体运动。牛顿的力学为18世纪的工业革命及其后的机器生产准备了科学理论。

对于《原理》这本书以及牛顿的自然哲学思想，最有争议的当数“总释”部分。牛顿在“总释”中解释了撰写《原理》的起因，回应了学界的质疑，并且谈到上帝与自然哲学的关系。正因“总释”部分让读者了解到牛顿的信仰，学者们纷纷阐释和评价起“理性的牛顿”和“神学家的牛顿”。关于“总释”部分的探讨延续至今。

《原理》这本书被介绍到中国始于清末。李善兰曾翻译过《原理》的一部分。20世纪30年代，郑太朴翻译的《原理》出版，但这个版本如今很难看到了。现在能找到的中译本主要有王克迪、赵振江、曾琼瑶等译者的译本。中国从清末对物理学、数学、自然哲学日益重视。《原理》一书对于历史学专业学生

---

① ［英］牛顿：《自然哲学的数学原理》，赵振江译，商务印书馆2011年版，“序言”。

而言内容难免有些高深晦涩，我们需要借助中译本来阅读英文原本。然而，中译本仅能供我们作参照，原因有两个：一是不同版本的中译本翻译有所出入，需要读者评判其准确度；二是我们从历史学专业角度读《原理》，自然不限于读懂原文，更在于读懂其思想的源头和历史价值。这里选取的内容出自莫特（Motte）1729年编纂的《原理》英文版。

I. Excerpt from *The Mathematical Principles of Natural Philosophy*①

Since the ancients (as we are told by Pappus) made great account of the science of mechanics in the investigation of natural things; and the moderns, laying aside substantial forms and occult qualities, have endeavoured to subject the phenomena of nature to the laws of mathematics; I have in this treatise cultivated Mathematics, so far as it regards Philosophy. The ancients considered Mechanics in a twofold respect; as rational, which proceeds accurately by demonstration, and practical. To practical Mechanics all the manual arts belong, from which Mechanics took its name. But as artificers do not work with perfect accuracy, it comes to pass that Mechanics is so distinguished from Geometry, that what is perfectly accurate is called Geometrical, what is less so is called Mechanical. But the errors are not in the art, but in the artificers. He that works with less accuracy, is an imperfect Mechanic, and if any could work with perfect accuracy, he would be the most perfect Mechanic of all. For the description of right lines and circles, upon which Geometry is founded, belongs to Mechanics. Geometry does not teach us to draw these lines, but requires them to be drawn. For it requires that the learner should first be taught to describe these accurately, before he enters upon Geometry; then it shews how by these operations problems may be solved. To describe right lines and circles are problems, but not geometrical problems. The solution

---

① Sir Isaac Newton, *The Mathematical Principles of Natural Philosophy, Volume I*, Translated into English by Andrew Motte, London: Printed for Benjamin Motte, at Middle–Temple–Gate, in Fleetstreet, 1729, pp. 1–9.

of these problems is required from Mechanics; and by Geometry the use of them, when so solved, is shewn. And it is the glory of Geometry that from those few principles, fetched from without, it is able to produce so many things. Therefore Geometry is founded in mechanical practice, and is nothing but that part of universal Mechanics which accurately proposes and demonstrates the art of measuring. But since the manual arts are chiefly conversant in the moving of bodies, it comes to pass that Geometry is commonly referred to their magnitudes, and Mechanics to their motion. In this sense Rational Mechanics will be the Science of motions resulting from any forces whatsoever and of the forces required to produce any motions, accurately proposed and demonstrated. This part of Mechanics was cultivated by the ancients in the Five Powers which relate to manual arts, who considered gravity (it not being manual power) no otherwise than as it moved weights by those powers. Our design not respecting arts but philosophy, and our subject, not manual but natural powers, we consider chiefly those things which relate to gravity, levity, elastic force, the resistance of fluids, and the like forces whether attractive or impulsive. And therefore we offer this work as mathematical principles of philosophy. For all the difficulty of philosophy seems to consist in this, from the phenomena of motions to investigate the forces of Nature, and then from these forces to demonstrate the other phenomena. And to this end, the general propositions in the first and second book are directed. In the third book we give an example of this in the explication of the System of the World. For by the propositions mathematically demonstrated in the first books, we there derive from the celestial phenomena, the forces of Gravity with which bodies tend to the Sun and the several Planets. Then from these forces by other propositions, which are also mathematical, we deduce the motions of the Planets, the Comets, the Moon, and the Sea. I wish we could derive the rest of the phenomena of Nature by the same kind of reasoning from mechanical principles. For I am induced by many reasons to suspect that they may all defend upon certain forces by which the particles of bodies, by some causes hitherto unknown, are either mutually impelled towards each other and cohere in regular figures, or are repelled and recede from each other; which forces being unknown, Philosophers have hitherto attempted the search of Nature in vain. But I hope the principles here laid down will afford some light either to that, or some truer, method of Philosophy.

In the publication of this Work, the most acute and universally learned Mr. Edmund Halley not only assisted me with his pains in correcting the press and taking care of the schemes, but it was to his solicitations that its becoming publick is owing. For when he had obtained of me my demonstrations of the figure of the celestial orbits, he continually pressed me to communicate the same to the Royal Society; who afterwards by their kind encouragement and entreaties, engaged me to think of publishing them. But after I had begun to consider the inequalities of the lunar motions, and had entered upon some other things relating to the laws and measures of gravity, and other forces; and the figures that would be described by bodies attracted according to given laws; and the motion of several bodies moving among themselves; the motion of bodies in resisting mediums; the forces, densities, and motions of mediums; the orbits of the Comets, and such like; I put off that publication till I had made a search into those matters, and could put out the whole together. What relates to the Lunar motions (being imperfect) I have put all together in the corollaries of prop. 66. to avoid being obliged to propose and distinctly demonstrate the several things there contained in a method more prolix than the subject deserved, and interrupt the series of the several propositions. Some things found out after the rest, I chose to insert in places less suitable, rather than change the number of the propositions and the citations. I heartily beg that what I have here done may be read with candour, and that the defects I have been guilty of upon this difficult subject may be, not so much reprehended, as kindly supplied, and investigated by new endeavours of my readers.

Definition I

The Quantity of Matter is the measure of the same, arising from its density and bulk conjunctly.

Thus air of a double density, in a double space, is quadruple in quantity; in a triple space, sextuple in quantity. The same thing is to be understood of snow, and fine dust or powders, that are condensed by compression or liquefaction; and of all bodies that are by any causes whatever differently condensed. I have no regard in this place to a medium, if any such there is, that freely pervades the interstices between the parts of bodies. It is this quantity that I mean hereafter every where under the name of Body or Mass. And the same is known by weight of each body: For it is proportional to the weight, as I have found by experiments on pendulums, very accurately made, which shall be shewn hereafter.

Definition II

The quantity of Motion is the measure of the same, arising from the velocity and quantity of matter conjunctly. The motion of the whole is the Sum of the motions of all parts; and therefore in a body double in quantity, with equal velocity, the motion is double; with twice the velocity, it is quadruple.

Definition III

The Vis Insita, or Innate Force of Matter is a power of resisting, by which every body, as much as in it lies, endeavours to persevere in its present state, whether it be of rest, or of moving uniformly forward in a right line.

This force is ever proportional to the body whose force it is; and differs nothing from the inactivity of the Mass, but in our manner of conceiving it. A body from the inactivity of matter, is not without difficulty put cut of its state of rest or motion. Upon which account, this Vis Insita, may, by a most significant name, be called Vis Inertia, or Force of Inactivity. But a body exerts this force only, when another force impressed upon it, endeavours to change its conditions; and exercise of this force may be considered both as resistance and impulse: It is resistance in so far as the body, for maintain its present state withstands the force impressed; it is impulse, in so far as the body, by not easily giving way to the impressed force of another, endeavours to change the state of that other.

Resistance is usually ascribed to bodies at rest, and impulse to those in motion: But motion and rest, as commonly conceived, are only relatively distinguished; nor are those bodies always truly at rest, which commonly are taken to be so.

Definition IV

An impressed force is an action exerted upon a body, in order to change its state, either of rest, or of moving uniformly forward in a right line. This force consists in the action only; and remains no longer in the body, when the action is over. For a body maintains every new state it acquires, by its Vis Inertia only. Impressed forces are of different origines; as from percussion, from pressure, from centripetal force.

Definition V

A Centripetal force is that by which bodies are drawn or impelled, or any way tend, towards a point as to a centre. Of this sort is Gravity by which bodies tend to the centre of the Earth; Magnetism, by which iron tends to the loadstone; and that force, whatever it is, by which the Planets are perpetually drawn aside from the rectilinear motions, which otherwise they would pursue, and made to revolve in curvilinear orbits. A stone, whirled about in a fling, endeavours to recede from the hand that turns it; and by that endeavour, distends the fling, and that with so much the greater force, as it is revolved with the greater velocity and as soon as ever it is let go, flies away. That force which opposes it self to this endeavour, and by which the fling perpetually draws back the stone towards the hand, and retains it in its orbit, because it is directed to the hand as centre of the orbit, I call the Centripetal force. And the same thing is to be understood of all bodies, revolved in any orbits. They all endeavour to recede from the centres of their orbits; and were it not for the opposition of a contray force which restrains them to, and detains them in their orbits, which I therefore call Centripetal, would fly off in right lines, with an uniform motion. A projectile, if it was not for the force of gravity, would not deviate towards the Earth, but would go off from it in a right line and that with an uniform motion, if the resistance of the Air was taken away. It is by its gravity that it is drawn aside perpetually from its rectilinear course, and made to deviate towards the Earth, more or less, according to the force of its gravity, and the velocity of its motion. The lees its gravity is, for the quantity of its matter, or the greater the velocity with which it is projected, the less will it deviate from a rectilinear course, and the farther it will go. If a leaden ball projected from the top of a mountain by the force of gun–powder with a given velocity, and in a direction parallel to the horizon, is carried in a curve line to the distance of two miles before it falls to the ground; the same, if the resistance of the Air was took away, with a double or decuple velocity, would fly twice or ten times as far. And by increasing the velocity, we may at pleasure increase the distance to which it might be projected, and diminish the curvature of the line, which it might describe, till at last it should fall at the distance of 10, 30, or 90 degrees, or even might go quite round the whole Earth before it falls; or lastly, so that it might never fall to the Earth, but go forwards into the Celestial Spaces, and proceed in its motion in infinitum. And after the same manner, that a projectile, by the force of gravity, may be made to revolve in an orbit, and go round the whole Earth, the Moon also, either by the force of gravity, if it is endued with gravity, or by any other force, that impels it towards the Earth, may be perpetually drawn aside towards the Earth, out of the rectilinear way, which by its innate force it would pursue; and be made to revolve in the orbit which it now describes: nor could the Moon without some such force, be retained in its orbit. If this force was too small, it would not sufficiently turn the Moon out of a rectilinear course: if it was too great, it would turn it too much, and draw down the Moon from its orbit towards the Earth. It is necessary, that the force be of a just quantity, and it belongs to the Mathematicians to find the force, that may serve exactly to retain a body in a given orbit, with a given velocity; and vice vera, to determine the curvilinear way, into which a body projected from a given place, with a given velocity, may be made to deviate from its natural rectilinear way, by means of a given force. The quantity of any Centripetal Force may be considered as of three kinds, Absolute, Accelerative, and Motive.

Definition VI

The absolute quantity of a centripetal force is the measure of the same, proportional to the efficacy of the cause that propagates it from the centre, through the spaces round about. Thus the magnetic force is greater in one load–stone and less in another, according to their sizes and strength.

Definition VII

The accelerative quantity of a centripetal force is the measure of the same, proportional to the velocity which it generates in a given time. Thus the force of the same load–stone is greater at a less distance, and less at a greater: also the force of gravity is greater in valleys, less on tops of exceeding high mountains; and yet less (as shall be hereafter shewn) at greater distances from the body of the Earth; but at equal distances, it is the same every where because (taking away, or allowing for, the resistance of the Air) it equally accelerates all falling bodies, whether heavy or light, great or small.

Definition VIII

The motive quantity of a centripetal force, is the measure of the same, proportional to the motion which it generates in a given time. Thus the Weight is greater in a greater body, less in a less body; it is greater near to the Earth, and less at remoter distances. This sort of quantity is the centripetency, or propension of the whole body towards the centre, or as I may say, its Weight; and it is ever known by the quantity of a force equal and contrary to it, that is just sufficient to hinder the descent of the body.

These quantities of Forces, we may for brevity's sake call by the names of Motive, Accelerative and Absolute force; and for distinction sake consider them, with respect to the Bodies that tend to the centre; to the Places of those bodies; and to the Centre of force towards which they tend: That is to say, I refer the Motive force to the Body, as an endeavour and propensity of the whole towards a centre, arising from the propensities of the several parts taken together; the Accelerative force to the Place of the body, as a certain power or energy diffused from the centre to all places around to move the bodies that are in them; and the Absolute force to the Centre, as indued with some cause, without which those motive forces would not be propagated through the spaces round about; whether that cause is some central body, (such as is the Load Stone, in the centre of the force of Magnetism, or the Earth in the centre of the gravitating force) or any thing else that does not yet appear. For I here design only to give a Mathematical notion of those forces, without considering their Physical causes and seats.

Wherefore the Accelerative force will stand in the same relation to the Motive, as celerity does to motion. For the quantity of motion arises from the celerity, drawn into the quantity of matter; and the motive force arises from the accelerative force drawn into the same quantity of matter. For the sum of the actions of the Accelerative force, upon the several particles of the body, is the Motive force of the whole. Hence it is, that near the surface of the Earth, where the accelerative gravity, or force productive of gravity in all bodies is the same, the motive gravity or the Weight is as the Body: but if we should ascend to higher regions, where the accelerative gravity is less, the Weight would be likewise diminished, and would always be as product of the Body, by the Accelerative gravity. So in those regions, where the accelerative gravity is diminished in to one half, the Weight of a body two or three times less, will be four or six times less.

I likewise call Attractions and Impulses, in the same sense, Accelerative, and Motive; and use the words Attraction, Impulse or Propensity of any sort towards a centre, promiscuously, and indifferently, one for another; considering those forces not Physically but Mathematically: Wherefore, the reader is not to imagine, that by those words, I any where take upon me to define the kind, or the manner of any Action, the causes or the physical reason thereof, or that I attribute Forces, in a true and Physical sense, to certain centres (which are only Mathematical points); when at any time I happen to speak of centres at attracting or as endued with attractive powers.

II. Common Terms, Words and Phrases for the Text

Isaac Newton 艾萨克·牛顿

Mathematical principles 数学原理

Pappus 帕普斯（古希腊数学家）

Science of Mechanics 力学

laws of Mathematics 数学定律

occult 神秘的，超自然的等

manual arts 手工艺

Geometry 几何学

motion 运动，动作，议案等

Rational Mechanics 理性力学

Edmund Halley 埃德蒙·哈雷（英国天文学家）

solicitation 请求，征求，教唆等

celestial orbits 天体轨道

the Lunar motion 月球运动

orbits of the Comets 彗星轨道

the quantity of matter 物质的量

quadruple 成四倍，四倍的数量等

triple 三倍的，三人的等

sextuple 六倍，六倍增长等

condense 冷凝，压缩，浓缩

compression 压紧，压缩

liquefaction 液化，溶解

pendulum 钟摆，变化不定等

velocity 速率，快速，周转率

Vis Inertia 惯性力

centripetal force 向心力

rectilinear motion 直线运动

curvilinear orbit 曲线轨道

projectile 抛射体，炮弹等

deviate 偏离，违背等

curvature 弯曲，曲率

infinitum 无限的，无休止的

vice versa 反之亦然

motive force 原动力

absolute force 绝对力

accelerative force 加速力

efficacy 功效，效力

magnetic force 磁力

propensity 倾向，习性

III. Exercises and Thinking

1. Try to analyze the historical and academic background of the publishment of *The Mathematical Principles of Natural Philosophy*.

2. What did Newton contribute to the development of the Royal Society?

3. Study on how were Newton's works introduced to China?

IV. Further Readings and Internet Links

1. Further Readings

[英] 牛顿:《自然哲学的数学原理》，赵振江译，商务印书馆 2006 年版。

庞雪晨:《郭嵩焘与近代西方天文学》，人民出版社 2019 年版。

潘际坰:《牛顿》，商务印书馆 1965 年版。

吴燕:《科学、利益与欧洲扩张》，中国社会科学出版社 2013 年版。

2. Internet Links

中国科学院自然科学史研究所：www.ihns.ac.cn/

中国科学技术大学科技哲学系：https://sts.ustc.edu.cn/main.htm

Collections of the Correspondence of Isaac Newton: https://www.cambridge.org/core/publications/collections/the-correspondence-of-isaac-newton

Unit 26 Cartwright's Narrative Concerning His Invention

卡特赖特发明自述

英国是世界上最早完成工业革命的国家，对人类社会发展的意义不言而喻。我们时常思考当下的科技变革会给国家和人类带来怎样的巨变，这样的巨变可能会怎样演进，这类问题的答案或许可以在以往的工业革命中找到线索。人类第一次工业革命发生在 18 世纪中期至 19 世纪 40 年代。围绕第一次工业革命，学界探讨的问题主要有：为何工业革命首先出现在英国；科技变革与英国社会转型如何实现协同演进；英国工业革命如何影响世界经济格局。这三个问题的真相是复杂的，我们有必要花更多时间去释读工业革命期间的历史文献。

埃德蒙·卡特赖特（Edmund Cartwright，1743—1823）是英国工业革命期间杰出的发明家，以其对纺织机械领域的贡献而著名。青年时期的卡特赖特曾在牛津大学学习，后来他在约克郡和兰开斯特郡担任过教区牧师。1785 年，卡特赖特完成了水利织布机的发明和专利申请，1792 年又发明了羊毛精梳机。在他的自述中，卡特赖特详细记录了改良纺织机的过程，包括应用中曲折的试验过程。该动力织布机的发明改变了他个人的命运并改变了英国纺织业的发展轨迹。1821 年，卡特赖特因其发明对科技的贡献而得到皇家学会的认可，当选为皇家学会会员。他的发明改变了英国纺织行业，新技术的应用也改变了英国工人阶级的状况。对其他国家来说，正如其自述中所言，英国纺织业冲击了印度等国家的传统纺织业，提升了近代英国在全球资源市场的地位，美洲和非洲被迫成为英国棉纺织业原料和劳动力供应地。随着英国对外殖民侵略扩张，世界上更广阔的区域也被卷入英国工业化资本体系中，成为其廉价纺织品的销售市场。

一个行业的技术变革，引起了从微观到宏观层面的巨变。

通过卡特赖特的自述，我们可以了解一项技术变革的发生和发展过程，以及 18 世纪英国社会应对科技变革的机制。这里选取的卡特赖特发明自述内容出自 1843 年英文版的《动力织布机发明者的回忆录：埃德蒙·卡特赖特的生平、著述与机械发明》。

I. Excerpt from Cartwright's Narrative Concerning His Invention①

It has been already stated, that Dr. Cartwright, even during the existence of his patent right, had retained but little expectation of deriving any pecuniary advantage from his invention of weaving; and when his latest patent had been several years expired, the prospect of remuneration appeared entirely hopeless. He might be aware that his loom was coming into use, but he had now so little communication with the manufacturing districts, that he could form no idea of the extent to which it was adopted. Weaving by machinery was, however, beginning to make considerable progress, and was even then preparing for him the only compensation that he ever received for years of anxiety, and great pecuniary loss. This progress was connected with the circumstances of the times, by which an extraordinary impulse had been given to the British manufactures in general, and which rendered the beginning of the present century a far more favourable period for the introduction of machine weaving than that in which Dr. Cartwright had first attempted it. The great improvements that had been effected in the art of spinning, had, with other causes, occasioned a vast accumulation of cotton yarn, which on account of the disturbed state of the Continent, could no longer be disposed of in the foreign market, neither could hands (which, in consequence of a long protracted war, were become less numerous than they had been) be found sufficient to work it up at home. At the same time, the

① Mary Strickland, *A Memoir of the Life, Writings, and Mechanical Inventions of the Edmund Cartwright, Inventor of the Power Loom, Etc. Etc.*, London: Saunders and Otley, 1843, pp. 213–240.

demand for English cotton piece goods was greatly increasing, and the manufacturers found themselves called upon to devise some means of answering a demand which want of hands and want of looms prevented their being able to supply. The only expedient that seemed to present itself, was the adoption of the hitherto rejected power–loom: thus literally justifying the hypothetical suggestion of its author, in that remarkable conversation which had first turned his attention to the subject of mechanics. From the year 1792, when Messrs. Grimshaw's mill had been destroyed, and Mr. Cartwright's establishment, at Doncaster, as well as some others connected with it, was abandoned, it does not appear that any manufacturer had ventured openly to employ his loom, liable as he would in that case have been to a payment for its use during the existence of the patent right.

The machine, however, had not been lost sight of, and on its becoming open to the public by the expiration of the patent; several manufacturers sought to adapt it to their own purposes. Great improvements doubtless did receive from that ingenuity and spirit of enterprise, which were called into action by the circumstances of the times, but rather unfairly towards Dr. Cartwright, some of these improvers assumed to themselves the whole merit of the invention, and though his machine formed the basis, as it still does, of all the power–looms that have hitherto been found effective, his claim to the original invention was far from being generally recognised. In some instances the invention had been ascribed to persons who had formerly worked looms under a licence from Dr. Cartwright, but who, either from want of capital, or the then unfavourable state of the trade, had not succeeded in their undertakings, and yet had retained so decided a conviction of the value of the machine as to be induced to revive it under more encouraging auspices.

The improved quality of the yarn had also contributed to render machine weaving less difficult, as well as the fabric produced by it, of a more perfect quality than when Dr. Cartwright first undertook it. The extraordinary advances that had been made in the application of mechanical power, by improvements in the steam–engine &c., doubtless facilitated the extension of the power–loom; but in justice to a most ingenious man, it must be acknowledged that Mr. Radcliffe's admirable contrivance for dressing the warp before it is put into the loom, by which means time and attendance are saved, contributed probably beyond any other improvement to render it completely available.

About the year 1806, Dr. Cartwright was induced to make some inquiries respecting the state of the cotton manufacture in general, but more especially in the neighbourhood and town of Manchester, and found that machine–weaving was already practised to a much greater extent than he had anticipated, and that considerable profit was accruing, not only to individuals, but to the country at large; from discoveries which to him had been productive of nothing but loss and disappointment. In a letter to his friend Dr. Bardsley, senior, an eminent physician in Manchester, he could not refrain from expressing the bitterness of his feelings on the subject, and this letter being communicated to some highly respectable and influential gentlemen of that place, they were so much struck by the hardship of Dr. Cartwright's case, as to express their willingness to concur in any application to Parliament that he or his friends should think proper to make, for the purpose of obtaining some remuneration from the public. In consequence of the encouragement given by these gentlemen, Dr. Bardsley, with a warmth of friendship most truly appreciated by him in whose favour it was exerted, applied himself to obtain the information that was required, in order to shew the grounds on which Dr. Cartwright might have a claim to public gratitude, and also what was no less material, to satisfy the minds of the manufacturers that he really was the original inventor of the machine in question, which so many of them were in the habit of using.

The result of these inquiries tended to shew, that the power loom was already employed to a considerable extent, and that its use was rapidly increasing; but no stronger proof could be required of the importance that was attached to its progress by those best acquainted with, and most deeply concerned in the trade, than the fact, that a memorial, in Dr. Cartwright's favour, was signed by fifty of the most respectable and influential gentlemen of the town and neighbourhood of Manchester, and presented to Government in August, 1807. This memorial was followed, in the spring of 1808, by a petition from Dr. Cartwright, to the House of Commons; and the house having agreed to take his claims into consideration, a committee was appointed to that effect; and on the 4th and 7th March, and on the 12th April, evidence was examined in support of his allegations.

He was fortunately enabled to bring forward a very material witness in Mr. Joseph Taylor, who had not only been his own engineer at the outset of his mechanical career, but had also been the superintendant at Messrs. Grimshaw's factory, at Knott Mill, at the time when its destruction by fire had given so severe a check to the introduction of the power–loom. In Mr. Baines's interesting History of the Cotton Manufacture, is a passage relative to Messrs. Grimshaw's connection with Dr. Cartwright, which might lead to a very different inference from what really was the fact, and which can only have found a place in a work of so much candour and liberality, in consequence of some defective information. It is here stated, that " about 1790, Messrs. Grimshaw, of Gorton, under a licence from Dr. Cartwright, erected a weaving factory at Knott Mills, Manchester, and attempted to improve the power–loom, at great cost to themselves. They did not succeed, and the factory being burnt down, they abandoned the undertaking."

Now, Messrs. Grimshaw had certainly been at a great expense, but that was incurred in erecting a factory, which was to contain 500 of Dr. Cartwright's looms; and as only about four–and–twenty of the looms were actually set to work, before the mill was destroyed, no just estimate could be formed of the probable success of the undertaking, although it appears from Taylor's evidence, that the looms (which there is no ground whatever for supposing Messrs. Grimshaw had been at any cost to improve,) were found to do their work remarkably well.

The substance of Mr. Taylor's evidence was to this effect. He stated, that he was acquainted with Dr. Cartwright's invention, in 1784, even before the first patent was taken out; that he had then seen a trial of it, and, in his judgment, it was calculated to answer the purpose of weaving. In 1791, he had accompanied Mr. Grimshaw, who was a master check-manufacturer, in great business, to Doncaster, where he then witnessed the improvement Mr. Cartwright had effected since the taking out of his first patent. Mr. Grimshaw having entered into an agreement to employ a certain number of Mr. Cartwright's looms, proceeded to build a large mill for that purpose; the expense of which, independently of the steam-engine and machinery, which would be nearly 3000*l*. additional, was estimated at 5700*l*. Of the four-and-twenty looms that were completed, twelve were set to work, at weaving check, which had been Mr. Grimshaw's peculiar line of business.

These looms worked exceedingly well; they wrought the work for half the amount of wages which they were then paying to hand weavers; the weavers, in consequence, threatened to destroy the mill, and the owners received anonymous letters to that effect. On receiving these letters, a considerable part of the property, especially the yarn, was removed out of the mill; and in about a month afterwards, in March, 1792, it was burnt down. From the rapidity with which the building was consumed, it probably was fired in different places, and Mr. Taylor was confirmed, in his conviction, of its being by design, from the circumstance of there not having been, to his personal knowledge as manager, any fire employed within the mill during three preceding days.

Messrs. Grimshaw, who had ensured their property to the amount of 12,000*l*., did not venture to re-build their mill at Manchester, and had tried in vain in other places. It also appeared in evidence, that the alarm, in consequence of this untoward event, and continued threats on the part of the hand-weavers, had become so general, that no one ventured openly to use the loom within the period of Dr. Cartwright's patent right.

One passage in Mr. Taylor's evidence seems particularly deserving of notice, as it shews, if his opinion be correct, that this machine is not necessarily chargeable with all the evils that have fallen on the hand-loom weavers, and that if they had availed themselves of its advantages, instead of obstinately setting themselves against it, the great manufacturers might not have been driven to adopt the mill system to the extent they have done: and that the hand-weavers might still have retained such a portion of business in their own hands as would have enabled them better to meet those fluctuations which every description of trade and manufactures is liable to, and which legislative interference cannot prevent, and only very imperfectly remedy.

On being desired to state to the committee whether the unavoidable effect of this invention is to crowd the persons together who are employed in it, Mr. Taylor replied, that " the machinery may be worked with equal advantage without crowding people together, by the weaver having looms in his own family and turning them by hand; six looms may be turned by one man, by which means he may employ little children, and superintend them himself, and will have six looms at once, instead of one, and every loom would do as much work as one weaver would do at a common loom."

It was also stated by Mr. Taylor, that cloth, woven by machinery, was of a better quality and bore a higher price than that woven by hand; a statement fully confirmed by the fact, that cloth woven by hand is frequently stamped as power-loom cloth, and sold as such to all parts of the world.

The next evidence was that of Mr. William Radcliffe, of Stockport, a gentleman of great practical experience and knowledge in every branch of the cotton trade, and whose opinion as to the probable increase of the use of the power-loom, has been completely justified by the event. Until applied to by Dr. Cartwright's solicitors, it does not appear that Mr. Radcliffe knew who was the inventor of the power-looms, though he had himself employed them; but the circumstance of these looms being known by the name of the Doncaster loom, sufficiently identified the inventor, and Mr. Radcliffe came forward, with the utmost liberality and candour, to do justice to their merit. His evidence, in the first place, went to shew that the inveterate opposition of the hand-weavers had been the means of deterring the manufacturers from adopting the use of machinery, until the trade had now become such that the hand–weavers themselves were interested in producing a sufficient supply of cotton goods at home to answer the increasing demand for them, as well as to work up the surplus quantity of yarn. "During a period of about nine years," Mr. Radcliffe said, "from 1793 to 1802, the machinery for spinning cotton yarn, with the ingenuity, practical knowledge, and persevering industry of the persons concerned in this branch, became so perfect as to enable the spinners to produce more yarn than could possibly be made into cloth by all the weavers Great Britain could collect for the purpose. The demand for cotton cloth was equal, during this period, to take off the whole produce of the spindle, if weavers could have been found to have made it into cloth; but this being impossible, the spinners began to export the surplus to the manufacturers abroad—into France, Germany, Russia, Switzerland, Holland, Spain, Portugal, Denmark, Sweden, &c., countries possessing a multitude of weavers formerly employed in weaving linen, silk, stuffs, &c. &c., whose labour was to be had at half the price which was paid for such labour in this country. The consequence of which has been, that these foreign manufacturers began to furnish their neighbours with such cotton cloths as heretofore they could only obtain from this country: hence, by degrees, the British manufacturers and the East India Company lost nearly all their trade for piece goods to those countries before mentioned, which is the sole cause of all the distress which is now heard of in the cotton trade." Mr. Radcliffe proceeded to state, that "this invention of Dr. Cartwright's, coupled with some other improvements that have been lately discovered for preparing and dressing the cotton twist ready for the loom, is particularly calculated to remedy this evil speedily, by working up a great part of their surplus yarn, and that not into fabrics that will interfere with the cotton goods heretofore made by our weavers, but into vast quantities of strong stout cotton goods for shirting, sheeting, &c." He also stated, that he knew many spinners who were ready to appropriate part of their mills to weaving by machinery, on Dr. Cartwright's principles, when any demand for piece goods should spring up; and that if it should be generally adopted, the trade for piece goods would immediately revive, and by degrees the markets would not only open again for cotton goods manufactured in Great Britain, but also for those imported by the East India Company, who had suffered very greatly by the foreigners making from our twist, goods similar to what they used to purchase at the Company's sales, which had answered their purpose abroad as a substitute for India cloth." Mr. Radcliffe added, "that he considered the invention of Dr. Cartwright as so important to the prosperity of the Manchester trade, that were it suppressed, or its application no further extended, the cotton trade would be chiefly confined to spinning, and the weavers on the continent, in the end, become the sole manufacturers."

On being asked what were the number of mills in which these looms were set up, he replied that he knew of twenty–eight, or thirty, and there might be more of which he did not know; and also gave it as his opinion, that it had been necessary for Dr. Cartwright to establish a manufactory, and to have a number of looms actually at work, in order to shew their operation, and to try different experiments for the purpose of bringing them to perfection.

We cannot close this portion of our subject without some expression of sympathy for the hard lot of the unfortunate Mr. Radcliffe. His great ingenuity and services to the country deserved a better return than the neglect and discouragement he experienced; and he, alas! was one of those instances of unrewarded talents that have solely contributed to the aggrandizement of others. The author was in correspondence, some years since, with Mr. Radcliffe, on the subject of this memoir; and was much gratified by the candour and liberality with which he did ample justice to the value of Dr. Cartwright's invention. It was painful to learn that he had himself reaped so little advantage from improvements that had greatly facilitated the use of the power–loom; and it was no less painful to feel conscious of the utter inability to forward and assist his claims to national remuneration.

From other evidence brought forward, it appeared that Dr. Cartwright had expended between thirty and forty thousand pounds in prosecuting and bringing his mechanical inventions to perfection.

In the following year, a grant of ten thousand pounds was made, on the part of His Majesty's government, to Dr. Cartwright, "for the good service he had rendered the public by his invention of weaving."

It cannot be inconsistent with a liberal economy for a government to encourage ingenuity, which for want of support might be lost to the public; at the same time a government ought not to be called upon to indemnify individuals for losses and expenditure incurred in speculations, which (though eventually advantageous to the public) had been undertaken solely with a view of profit to themselves. But in the instance of Dr. Cartwright, compensation, rather than remuneration, was the principle on which he sought the attention of the legislature. A system of intimidation, against which the laws of his country had failed to protect him, had, for a series of years, prevented a fair trial being made of his machinery for weaving; and, in addition to the disappointment of his reasonable expectations of gain, a prejudice had also been created against the invention itself, which nothing but an extraordinary combination of circumstances could finally have overcome. This prejudice had a tendency to deprive him of the credit of the invention. It had been hastily concluded that the machine was inefficient, because it had not been adopted; and when, on being tried, it was found to succeed, its success was attributed wholly to the alterations engrafted upon it. Indeed, there is great reason to believe, that but for this public recognition from the legislature, Dr. Cartwright's claim, even to the invention of the power-loom, would not have been generally admitted, although at the time of his application to parliament there does not appear to have been the slightest attempt made to invalidate his claim to originality on the part of those to whom the chief merit of the invention has subsequently been ascribed.

Admitting, however, that the grant to Dr. Cartwright was conferred as a reward to ingenuity, it ought, in justice to those members of His Majesty's Government who proposed it, to be observed, that it was not incautiously or lightly made. It was not until two years after the presentation to the first lord of the Treasury, of the memorial from Manchester, that Mr. Perceval proposed in the House of Commons any remuneration to Dr. Cartwright; and he, in the meantime, had been required to produce satisfactory evidence in support of his allegations, whilst to his rivals, or opponents, ample opportunity had been given to rebut them.

The gratitude with which Dr. Cartwright received this act of justice, was heightened by the reflection that he owed it to the liberal feelings of a ministry, to whose leading members he was personally unknown, but to whom it was not unknown that his principal associates and connexions were chiefly amongst their political opponents.

The event has more than justified the view which the legislature of 1809 was led to form of the importance of the invention of the power–loom. The warmest advocate for mechanical enterprise, the most sanguine believer in its success, could hardly have anticipated that more than one hundred thousand power–looms should be employed in the island of Great Britain alone. Yet such, at the present time, is the astonishing fact; and these looms, now brought, by the incessant application of ingenuity, to an extreme degree of perfection, are producing yearly millions of pieces of almost every variety of fabric that can be applied to the useful or ornamental clothing of mankind.

II. Common Terms, Words and Phrases for the Text

patent right 专利权

pecuniary advantage 钱财上的好处

remuneration 薪酬，赔偿

cotton yarn 棉纱

protracted war 持久战

power–loom 动力织机

auspices 赞助，保护，预兆

mechanical power 机械动力

steam-engine 蒸汽机

contrivance 发明，计谋等

mill 工厂，磨坊等

hand weaver 手工织布者

the East India Company 东印度公司

spindle 纺锤，锭子等

ingenuity 精巧的装置，心灵手巧等

rebut 反驳，揭露等

III. Exercises and Thinking

1. What were the effects after Carwright's inventions applied to manufacture?

2. Try to do some research on the British patent system in the Eighteenth Century.

3. Why did the Industrial Revolution start in the England first?

IV. Further Readings and Internet Links

1. Further Readings

[英]H. J. 哈巴库克、[英]M.M. 波斯坦主编:《工业革命及其以后的经济发展：收入、人口及技术变迁》,《剑桥欧洲经济史》(第六卷)，经济科学出版社 2002 年版。

[英]查尔斯·辛格等主编:《工业革命 1750—1850》,《技术史》(第四卷)，辛元欧、刘兵主译，上海科技教育出版社 2004 年版。

2. Internet Links

天津纺织博物馆：http://www.tjtextile.com/ttm/

Unit 27 *The Future Results of British Rule in India*
《不列颠在印度的统治的未来结果》

《不列颠在印度的统治的未来结果》是马克思著名经典文献之一，揭示了英国对印度的侵略真相，是理解近代欧洲殖民主义历史主线的重要文献。

1600年，英国成立东印度公司，开始了对印度的殖民入侵。1757年，英国在普拉西战役中取胜，为英国在印度的殖民统治奠定了基础。此后，英国通过四次侵略迈索尔的战争和三次侵略马拉塔的战争，占领了印度的南部和中部。1849年，英国吞并旁遮普，完成了对印度的全部占领。印度完全沦为英国的殖民地。

马克思揭露了英国在印度进行殖民统治的本质。他在1853年6月10日撰写的《不列颠在印度的统治》一文中提出："但是，不列颠人给印度斯坦带来的灾难，与印度斯坦过去所遭受的一切灾难比较起来，毫无疑问在本质上属于另一种，在程度上要深重得多。我在这里所指的还不是不列颠东印度公司在亚洲式专制的基础上建立起来的欧洲式专制，这两种专制结合起来要比萨尔塞达庙里任何狰狞的神像都更为可怕。"① 7月22日，马克思用英文写出了《不列颠在印度的统治的未来结果》。8月8日，该文章发表在《纽约每日论坛报》(*New York Daily Tribune*)，更加全面彻底地揭露了英国的侵略本质。该文提出英国在印度要完成的双重使命：一个是破坏的使命，即消灭旧时的亚洲式的社会；另一个是重建的使命，即在亚洲为西方式的社会奠定物质基础。但马克思所说的

① 《马克思恩格斯选集》第1卷，人民出版社2012年版，第849页。

这种“双重使命”并非给英国殖民侵略唱赞歌，而是揭示其内在不可调和的矛盾和必然灭亡的命运，更是在讽刺和批判“资产阶级文明的极端伪善和它的野蛮本性”①。

《不列颠在印度的统治的未来结果》是历史领域学生学习马克思著名经典的必读历史文献，对学生理解近代欧洲的殖民主义本质，把握马克思历史唯物主义科学内涵具有重要意义。

I. Excerpt from *The Future Results of British Rule in India*②

I propose in this letter to conclude my observations on India.

How came it that English supremacy was established in India? The paramount power of the Great Mogul was broken by the Mogul Viceroys. The power of the Viceroys was broken by the Mahrattas. The power of the Mahrattas was broken by the Afghans, and while all were struggling against all, the Briton rushed in and was enabled to subdue them all. A country not only divided between Mahommedan and Hindoo, but between tribe and tribe, between caste and caste; a society whose framework was based on a sort of equilibrium, resulting from a general repulsion and constitutional exclusiveness between all its members. Such a country and such a society, were they not the predestined prey of conquest? If we knew nothing of the past history of Hindostan, would there not be the one great and incontestable fact, that even at this moment India is held in English thraldom by an Indian army maintained at the cost of India? India, then, could not escape the fate of being conquered, and the whole of her past history, if it be anything, is the history of the successive conquests she has undergone. Indian society has no history at all, at least no known history. What we call its history, is but the history of the successive intruders who founded their empires on the passive basis of that unresisting and unchanging society. The question, therefore, is not whether the English

① 张乃和：《英国殖民印度并非“仁慈专制”》，《历史评论》2020 年第 4 期。

② Karl Marx and Frederick Engels, *Collected Works*, vol. 12, New York:International Publishers, 1979, pp. 217－221.

had a right to conquer India, but whether we are to prefer India conquered by the Turk, by the Persian, by the Russian, to India conquered by the Briton.

England has to fulfill a double mission in India: one destructive, the other regenerating—the annihilation of old Asiatic society, and the laying the material foundations of Western society in Asia.

Arabs, Turks, Tartars, Moguls, who had successively overrun India, soon became *Hindooized*, the barbarian conquerors being, by an eternal law of history, conquered themselves by the superior civilization of their subjects. The British were the first conquerors superior, and therefore, inaccessible to Hindoo civilization. They destroyed it by breaking up the native communities, by uprooting the native industry, and by levelling all that was great and elevated in the native society. The historic pages of their rule in India report hardly anything beyond that destruction. The work of regeneration hardly transpires through a heap of ruins. Nevertheless it has begun.

The political unity of India, more consolidated, and extending farther than it ever did under the Great Moguls, was the first condition of its regeneration. That unity, imposed by the British sword, will now be strengthened and perpetuated by the electric telegraph. The native army, organized and trained by the British drill-sergeant, was the *sine qua non* of Indian self-emancipation, and of India ceasing to be the prey of the first foreign intruder. The free press, introduced for the first time into Asiatic society, and managed principally by the common offspring of Hindoos and Europeans, is a new and powerful agent of reconstruction. The Zemindari and Ryotwar themselves, abominable as they are, involve two distinct forms of private property in land — the great desideratum of Asiatic society. From the Indian natives, reluctantly and sparingly educated at Calcutta, under English superintendence, a fresh class is springing up, endowed with the requirements for government and imbued with European science. Steam has brought India into regular and rapid communication with Europe, has connected its chief ports with those of the whole south-eastern ocean, and has revindicated it from the isolated position which was the prime law of its stagnation. The day is not far distant when, by a combination of railways and steam-vessels, the distance between England and India, measured by time, will be shortened to eight days, and when that once fabulous country will thus be actually annexed to the Western world.

The ruling classes of Great Britain have had, till now, but an accidental, transitory and exceptional interest in the progress of India. The aristocracy wanted to conquer it, the moneyocracy to plunder it, and the millocracy to undersell it. But now the tables are turned. The millocracy have discovered that the transformation of India into a reproductive country has become of vital importance to them, and that, to that end, it is necessary, above all, to gift her with means of irrigation and of internal communication. They intend now drawing a net of railroads over India. And they will do it. The results must be inappreciable.

It is notorious that the productive powers of India are paralysed by the utter want of means for conveying and exchanging its various produce. Nowhere, more than in India, do we meet with social destitution in the midst of natural plenty, for want of the means of exchange. It was proved before a Committee of the British House of Commons, which sat in 1848, that

"when grain was selling from 6/ a quarter to 8/ a quarter at Khandesh, it was sold at 64/ a quarter to 70/ a quarter at Poona, where the people were dying in the streets of famine, without the possibility of gaining supplies from Khandesh, because the clay-roads were impracticable." ①

The introduction of railroads may be easily made to subserve agricultural purposes by the formation of tanks, where ground is required for embankment, and by the conveyance of water along the different lines. Thus irrigation, the *sine qua non* of farming in the East, might be greatly extended, and the frequently recurring local famines, arising

① J. Dickinson, *The Government of India under a Bureaucracy*, London and Manchester: Simms & Dinham, 1853, pp. 81–82.

from the want of water, would be averted. The general importance of railways, viewed under this head, must become evident, when we remember that irrigated lands, even in the districts near Ghauts, pay three times as much in taxes, afford ten or twelve times as much employment, and yield twelve or fifteen times as much profit, as the same area without irrigation.

Railways will afford the means of diminishing the amount and the cost of the military establishments. Col. Warren, Town Major of the Fort St. William, stated before a Select Committee of the House of Commons:

"The practicability of receiving intelligence from distant parts of the country, in as many hours as at present it requires days and even weeks, and of sending instructions, with troops and stores, in the more brief period, are considerations which cannot be too highly estimated. Troops could be kept at more distant and healthier stations than at present, and much loss of life from sickness would by this means be spared. Stores could not to the same extent be required at the various depots, and the loss by decay, and the destruction incidental to the climate, would also be avoided. The number of troops might be diminished in direct proportion to their effectiveness."

We know that the municipal organization and the economical basis of the village communities has been broken up, but their worst feature, the dissolution of society into stereotype and disconnected atoms, has survived their vitality. The village isolation produced the absence of roads in India, and the absence of roads perpetuated the village isolation. On this plan a community existed with a given scale of low conveniences, almost without intercourse with other villages, without the desires and efforts indispensable to social advance. The British having broken up this self-sufficient *inertia* of the villages, railways will provide the new want of communication and intercourse. Besides,

"one of the effects of the railway system will be to bring into every village affected by it such knowledge of the contrivances and appliances of other countries, and such means of obtaining them, as will first put the hereditary and stipendiary village artisanship of India to full proof of its capabilities, and then supply its defects." (Chapman, *The Cotton and Commerce of India* [pp. 95–97].) ①

I know that the English millocracy intend to endow India with railways with the exclusive view of extracting at diminished expenses the cotton and other raw materials for their manufactures. But when you have once introduced machinery into the locomotion of a country, which possesses iron and coals, you are unable to withhold it from its fabrication. You cannot maintain a net of railways over an immense country without introducing all those industrial processes necessary to meet the immediate and current wants of railway locomotion, and out of which there must grow the application of machinery to those branches of industry not immediately connected with railways. The railway–system will therefore become, in India, truly the forerunner of modern industry. This is the more certain as the Hindoos are allowed by British authorities themselves to possess particular aptitude for accommodating themselves to entirely new labor, and acquiring the requisite knowledge of machinery. Ample proof of this fact is afforded by the capacities and expertness of the native engineers in the Calcutta mint, where they have been for years employed in working the steam machinery, by the natives attached to the several steam engines in the Burdwan② coal districts, and by other instances. Mr. Campbell himself, greatly influenced as he is by the prejudices of the East India Company, is obliged to avow

"that the great mass of the Indian people possesses a great industrial energy, is well fitted to accumulate capital, and remarkable for a mathematical clearness of head, and talent for figures and exact sciences." "Their intellects," he says, "are excellent." ③

---

① John Chapman, *The Cotton and Commerce of India*, London: John Chapman, 1851, pp. 95–97.

② 《纽约每日论坛报》中误为"Hurdwar"。

③ George Campbell, *Modern India:a Sketch of the System of Civil Government*, London: John Murray, 1852, pp. 59–60.

Modern industry, resulting from the railway system, will dissolve the hereditary divisions of labor, upon which rest the Indian castes, those decisive impediments to Indian progress and Indian power.

All the English bourgeoisie may be forced to do will neither emancipate nor materially mend the social condition of the mass of the people, depending not only on the development of the productive powers, but on their appropriation by the people. But what they will not fail to do is to lay down the material premises for both. Has the bourgeoisie ever done more? Has it ever effected a progress without dragging individuals and people through blood and dirt, through misery and degradation?

The Indians will not reap the fruits of the new elements of society scattered among them by the British bourgeoisie, till in Great Britain itself the now ruling classes shall have been supplanted by the industrial proletariat, or till the Hindoos themselves shall have grown strong enough to throw off the English yoke altogether. At all events, we may safely expect to see, at a more or less remote period, the regeneration of that great and interesting country, whose gentle natives are, to use the expression of Prince Soltykov, even in the most inferior classes, "*plus fins et plus adroits que les Italiens*," whose submission even is counterbalanced by a certain calm nobility, who, notwithstanding their natural langor, have astonished the British officers by their bravery, whose country has been the source of our languages, our religions, and who represent the type of the ancient German in the Jat, and the type of the ancient Greek in the Brahmin.

I cannot part with the subject of India without some concluding remarks.

The profound hypocrisy and inherent barbarism of bourgeois civilization lies unveiled before our eyes, turning from its home, where it assumes respectable forms, to the colonies, where it goes naked. They are the defenders of property, but did any revolutionary party ever originate agrarian revolutions like those in Bengal, in Madras, and in Bombay? Did they not, in India, to borrow an expression of that great robber, Lord Clive himself, resort to atrocious extortion, when simple corruption could not keep pace with their rapacity? While they prated in Europe about the inviolable sanctity of the national debt, did they not confiscate in India the dividends of the rajahs①, who had invested their private savings in the Company's own funds? While they combatted the French revolution under the pretext of defending "our holy religion," did they not forbid, at the same time, Christianity to be propagated in India, and did they not, in order to make money out of the pilgrims streaming to the temples of Orissa and Bengal, take up the trade in the murder and prostitution perpetrated in the temple of Juggernaut? These are the men of "Property, Order, Family, and Religion."

II. Common Terms, Words and Phrases for the Text

Mahrattas 马拉塔人

Great Mogul 大莫卧儿

caste 种姓

Tartars 鞑靼人

Zemindari 柴明达尔制

Ryotwar 莱特瓦尔制

village communities 农村公社

Jat 贾特（印度北部的一个种姓集团）

Brahmin 婆罗门

Juggernaut 札格纳特庙

III. Exercises and Thinking

1. How do you understand Marx's "Dual mission"？

2. Please discuss on the historical role of colonization.

① Rajah, title of the Indian princes. In the Middle Ages, it was given to Hindu feudal lords and in British India to certain big landowners.

IV. Further Readings and Internet Links

1. Further Readings

《马克思恩格斯选集》第 1 卷，人民出版社 2012 年版。

Karl Marx, *The Political Writings*, London and New York: Verso, 2019.

2. Internet Links

《不列颠在印度的统治的未来结果》英文版全文：https://marxists.architexturez.net/archive/marx/works/1853/07/22.htm

Unit 28 Declaration of the Rights of Man and of the Citizen

《人权和公民权宣言》

《人权和公民权宣言》简称《人权宣言》，是法国大革命时期颁布的重要文献，是法国大革命的一面旗帜，不仅影响了法国的历史进程，而且对世界历史发展影响深远。

1789 年 8 月 26 日，法国制宪议会通过了《人权宣言》，宣布了对旧制度的否定和新制定的原则，将启蒙运动宣传的政治学说以法律形式确定了下来。《人权宣言》是人类历史上第一部正式的人权宣言。它集中论述了“自然的、不可剥夺的神圣的人权”。它强调天赋人权，提出：“在权利方面，人生来是而且始终是自由平等的。”所谓权利，“就是自由、财产、安全和反抗压迫”。此外，它还提出了主权的根源在于国民的人民主权原则。《人权宣言》突出法律的作用，规定“法律是公共意志的体现”，公民都有参与制定法律的权利和遵守法律的义务，而法律是高于一切的。《人权宣言》为公民规定了言论、出版、信仰等自由权利。《人权宣言》最后强调纳税平等和财产权的不可侵犯。

《人权宣言》共确立了十七条权利，发表后，被印刷成各种各样的传单和小册子，激发了民众的革命热情，成为大革命时期有力的革命武器。1791 年，制宪议会制定了宪法，把《人权宣言》作为宪法的序言。《人权宣言》将启蒙思想发扬光大，并以法律的形式固定了下来，起到承前启后的巨大作用，对欧美的资产阶级革命或改革，产生了广泛而深远的影响。它还推动了包括中国辛亥革命在内的亚洲民族解放运动的思想解放。

I. Excerpt from *Declaration of the Rights of Man and of the Citizen*①

The representatives of the French people, organized as a National Assembly, believing that the ignorance, neglect, or contempt of the rights of man are the sole cause of public calamities and of the corruption of governments, have determined to set forth in a solemn declaration the natural, unalienable, and sacred rights of man, in order that this declaration, being constantly before all the members of the Social body, shall remind them continually of their rights and duties; in order that the acts of the legislative power, as well as those of the executive power, may be compared at any moment with the objects and purposes of all political institutions and may thus be more respected, and, lastly, in order that the grievances of the citizens, based hereafter upon simple and incontestable principles, shall tend to the maintenance of the constitution and redound to the happiness of all. Therefore the National Assembly recognizes and proclaims, in the presence and under the auspices of the Supreme Being, the following rights of man and of the citizen:

Articles:

1. Men are born and remain free and equal in rights. Social distinctions may be founded only upon the general good.

2. The aim of all political association is the preservation of the natural and imprescriptible rights of man. These rights are liberty, property, security, and resistance to oppression.

3. The principle of all sovereignty resides essentially in the nation. No body nor individual may exercise any authority which does not proceed directly from the nation.

4. Liberty consists in the freedom to do everything which injures no one else; hence the exercise of the natural rights of each man has no limits except those which assure to

---

① Brian Bonhomme Editor in Chief, Cathleen Boivin Consulting Editor, *Milestone Documents in World History*, vol. 2, Dallas:Schlager Group, 2010, pp. 819–820.

the other members of the society the enjoyment of the same rights. These limits can only be determined by law.

5. Law can only prohibit such actions as are hurtful to society. Nothing may be prevented which is not forbidden by law, and no one may be forced to do anything not provided for by law.

6. Law is the expression of the general will. Every citizen has a right to participate personally, or through his representative, in its foundation. It must be the same for all, whether it protects or punishes. All citizens, being equal in the eyes of the law, are equally eligible to all dignities and to all public positions and occupations, according to their abilities, and without distinction except that of their virtues and talents.

7. No person shall be accused, arrested, or imprisoned except in the cases and according to the forms prescribed by law. Any one soliciting, transmitting, executing, or causing to be executed, any arbitrary order, shall be punished. But any citizen summoned or arrested in virtue of the law shall submit without delay, as resistance constitutes an offense.

8. The law shall provide for such punishments only as are strictly and obviously necessary, and no one shall suffer punishment except it be legally inflicted in virtue of a law passed and promulgated before the commission of the offense.

9. As all persons are held innocent until they shall have been declared guilty, if arrest shall be deemed indispensable, all harshness not essential to the securing of the prisoner's person shall be severely repressed by law.

10. No one shall be disquieted on account of his opinions, including his religious views, provided their manifestation does not disturb the public order established by law.

11. The free communication of ideas and opinions is one of the most precious of the rights of man. Every citizen may, accordingly, speak, write, and print with freedom, but shall be responsible for such abuses of this freedom as shall be defined by law.

12. The security of the rights of man and of the citizen requires public military forces. These forces are, therefore, established for the good of all and not for the personal

advantage of those to whom they shall be intrusted.

13. A common contribution is essential for the maintenance of the public forces and for the cost of administration. This should be equitably distributed among all the citizens in proportion to their means.

14. All the citizens have a right to decide, either personally or by their representatives, as to the necessity of the public contribution; to grant this freely; to know to what uses it is put; and to fix the proportion, the mode of assessment and of collection and the duration of the taxes.

15. Society has the right to require of every public agent an account of his administration.

16. A society in which the observance of the law is not assured, nor the separation of powers defined, has no constitution at all.

17. Since property is an inviolable and sacred right, no one shall be deprived thereof except where public necessity, legally determined, shall clearly demand it, and then only on condition that the owner shall have been previously and equitably indemnified.

II. Common Terms, Words and Phrases for the Text

national assembly 国民会议

rights 权利

the legislative power 立法权

the executive power 行政权

the general will 公共意志

III. Exercises and Thinking

1. Through reading, please briefly answer the historical status and significance of *Declaration of the Rights of Man and of the Citizen*.

2. Please discuss about historical limitations of the document and its era.

IV. Further Readings and Internet links

1. Further Readings

Frank Maloy Anderson ed., *The Constitution and Other Select Documents Illustrative of the History of France, 1789–1907*, New York: Russell, 1908.

张芝联主编:《法国通史》,北京大学出版社 2009 年版。

2. Internet Links

徐明龙:关于法国《人权宣言》第一条的中译文:http://iwh.cssn.cn/xscg/sjdqgbs/201203/t20120322_5225298.shtml

《人权宣言》英文全文:https://avalon.law.yale.edu/18th_century/rightsof.asp

Unit 29

The Civil War in France
《法兰西内战》

19 世纪 60 年代末，法国基本完成了工业革命，资本主义经济迅速发展。法国资产阶级与无产阶级的矛盾也随之日益激化。普法战争前后，法国国内矛盾深重，政治动荡，马克思呼吁欧洲工人阶级联合起来，反对战争，建立工人阶级的政权。《法兰西内战》发表于 1871 年 5 月 30 日，马克思在这本书中叙述了法国战败后巴黎公社的实践。这部著作的重要性不仅在于它是研究普法战争前后法国史的重要文献，而且在于它是研究马克思无产阶级政治理论的重要文献。

《法兰西内战》的主要内容包括：国际工人协会总委员会关于普法战争的两篇宣言；无产阶级政权巴黎公社的措施与实践经验；马克思对国防政府和法国资产阶级政要的批判。《法兰西内战》不仅是马克思对巴黎公社斗争经验的分析和总结，更是对无产阶级革命理论的丰富和发展。它对于后来的无产阶级革命运动产生了深远的影响，为工人阶级争取自身权益、推翻资产阶级统治提供了重要的思想武器。同时，《法兰西内战》也为我们理解社会主义革命和建设提供了有益的启示。

中国对《法兰西内战》的了解始于五四运动之后。1938 年，延安解放社出版了吴黎平、刘云翻译的中译本，此后陆续出版多个中文全文翻译的《法兰西内战》。《法兰西内战》的传播史，也是马克思主义中国化的重要组成部分。学生阅读英文版的《法兰西内战》，可赏析马克思的文笔风采，置身于历史中体会马克思在资产阶级政治压迫下展现出的无畏革命精神。这里选取的内容出自外文出版社 1970 年版《法兰西内战》英文单行本。

I. Excerpt from *The Civil War in France*[①]

To The Members of The International Working Men's Association in Europe and The United States

In the Inaugural Address of the *International Working Men's Association*, of November, 1864, we said: "If the emancipation of the working classes requires their fraternal concurrence, how are they to fulfil that great mission with a foreign policy in pursuit of criminal designs, playing upon national prejudices, and squandering in piratical wars the people's blood and treasure?" We defined the foreign policy aimed at by the International in these words: "Vindicate the simple laws of morals and justice, which ought to govern the relations of private individuals, as the laws paramount of the intercourse of nations."

No wonder that Louis Bonaparte, who usurped his power by exploiting the war of classes in France, and perpetuated it by periodical wars abroad, should from the first have treated the International as a dangerous foe. On the eve of the plebiscite, he ordered a raid on the members of the Administrative Committees of the International Working Men's Association throughout France, at Paris, Lyons, Rouen, Marseilles, Brest, etc., on the pretext that the International was a secret society dabbling in a complot for his assassination, a pretext soon after exposed in its full absurdity by his own judges. What was the real crime of the French branches of the International? They told the French people publicly and emphatically that voting the plebiscite was voting despotism at home and war abroad. It has been, in fact, their work that in all the great towns, in all the industrial centres of France, the working class rose like one man to reject the plebiscite. Unfortunately the balance was turned by the heavy ignorance of the rural districts. The stock exchanges, the cabinets, the ruling classes and the press of Europe celebrated the

① Karl Marx, *The Civil War in France*, Peking: Foreign Languages Press, 1970, pp. 19—25.

plebiscite as a signal victory of the French emperor over the French working class; and it was the signal for the assassination, not of an individual, but of nations.

The war plot of July, 1870, is but an amended edition of the coup d'état of December, 1851. At first view, the thing seemed so absurd that France would not believe in its real good earnest. It rather believed the deputy denouncing the ministerial war talk as a mere stock jobbing trick. When, on July 15th, war was at last officially announced to the Corps L é gislatif, the whole opposition refused to vote the preliminary subsidies, even Thiers branded it as "detestable" ; all the independent journals of Paris condemned it, and, wonderful to relate, the provincial press joined in almost unanimously.

Meanwhile, the Paris members of the International had again set to work. In the Réveil of July 12th, they published their manifesto "to the workmen of all nations," from which we extract the following few passages.

"Once more," they say, "on the pretext of the European equilibrium, of national honour, the peace of the world is menaced by political ambitions. French, German, Spanish workmen! Let our voices unite in one cry of reprobation against war! ... War for a question of preponderance or a dynasty, can, in the eyes of workmen, be nothing but a criminal absurdity. In answer to the warlike proclamations of those who exempt themselves from the impost of blood, and find in public misfortunes a source of fresh speculations, we protest, we who want peace, labour and liberty! ... Brothers of Germany! Our division would only result in the complete triumph of despotism on both sides of the Rhine. ... Workmen of all countries! Whatever may for the present become of our common efforts, we, the members of the International Working Men's Association, who know of no frontiers, we send you as a pledge of indissoluble solidarity the good wishes and the salutations of the workmen of France."

This manifesto of our Paris section was followed by numerous similar French addresses, of which we can here only quote the declaration of Neuilly-sur-Seine, published in the Marseillaise of July 22nd: "The war, is it just?—No! The war, is it national?—No! It is merely dynastic. In the name of humanity, of democracy, and the true interests of France, we adhere completely and energetically to the protestation of the International against the war."

These protestations expressed the true sentiments of the French working people, as was soon shown by a curious incident. *The Band of the 10th of December*, first organized under the presidency of Louis Bonaparte, having been masqueraded into blouses and let loose on the streets of Paris, there to perform the contortions of war fever, the real workmen of the Faubourgs came forward with public peace demonstrations so overwhelming that Pietri, the Prefect of Police, thought it prudent to at once stop all further street politics, on the plea that the feal Paris people had given sufficient vent to their pent–up patriotism and exuberant war enthusiasm.

Whatever may be the incidents of Louis Bonaparte's war with Prussia, the death knell of the Second Empire has already sounded at Paris. It will end as it began, by a parody. But let us not forget that it is the governments and the ruling classes of Europe who enabled Louis Bonaparte to play during eighteen years the ferocious farce of the Restored Empire.

On the German side, the war is a war of defence, but who put Germany to the necessity of defending herself? Who enabled Louis Bonaparte to wage war upon her? Prussia! It was Bismarck who conspired with that very same Louis Bonaparte for the purpose of crushing popular opposition at home, and annexing Germany to the Hohenzollern dynasty. If the battle of Sadowa had been lost instead of being won, French battalions would have overrun Germany as the allies of Prussia. After her victory, did Prussia dream one moment of opposing a free Germany to an enslaved France? Just the contrary. While carefully preserving all the native beauties of her old system, she superadded all the tricks of the Second Empire, its real despotism and its mock democratism, its political shams and its financial jobs, its high–flown talk and its low legerdemains. The Bonapartist regime, which till then only flourished on one side of the

Rhine, had now got its counterfeit on the other. From such a state of things, what else could result but war?

If the German working class allow the present war to lose its strictly defensive character and to degenerate into a war against the French people, victory or defeat will prove alike disastrous. All the miseries that befell Germany after her war of independence will revive with accumulated intensity.

The principles of the International are, however, too widely spread and too firmly rooted amongst the German working class to apprehend such a sad consummation. The voices of the French workmen have re-echoed from Germany. A mass meeting of workmen, held at Brunswick on July 16th, expressed its full concurrence with the Paris manifesto, spurned the idea of national antagonism to France, and wound up its resolutions with these words: "We are enemies of all wars, but above all of dynastic wars. ...

With deep sorrow and grief we are forced to undergo a defensive war as an unavoidable evil; but we call, at the same time, upon the whole German working class to render recurrence of such an immense social misfortune impossible by vindicating for the peoples themselves the power decide on peace and war, and making them masters of their own destinies."

At Chemnitz, a meeting of delegates representing 50,000 Saxon workers adopted unanimously a resolution to this effect: "In the name of the German Democracy, and especially of the workmen forming the Democratic Socialist party, we declare the present war to be exclusively dynastic. ... We are happy to grasp the fraternal hand stretched out to us by the workmen of France. ... Mindful of the watchword of the International Working Men's Association:

Proletarians of all countries, unite, we shall never forget that the workmen of all countries are our friends and the despots of all countries our enemies." The Berlin branch of the International has also replied to the Paris manifesto: —"We," they say, "join with heart and hand your protestation. ... Solemnly we promise that neither the sound of the trumpet, nor the roar of the cannon, neither victory nor defeat shall divert us from our common work for the union of the children of toil of all countries."

Be it so!

In the background of this suicidal strife looms the dark figure of Russia. It is an ominous sign that the signal for the present war should have been given at the moment when the Moscovite government had just finished its strategical lines of railway and was already massing troops in the direction of the Pruth. Whatever sympathy the Germans may justly claim in a war of defence against Bonapartist aggression, they would forfeit at once by allowing the Prussian government to call for, or accept, the help of the Cossack. Let them remember that, after their war of independence against the first Napoleon, Germany lay for generations prostrate at the feet of the Czar.

The English working class stretch the hand of fellowship to the French and German working people. They feel deeply convinced that whatever turn the impending horrid war may take, the alliance of the working classes of all countries will ultimately kill war. The very fact that while official France and Germany are rushing into a fratricidal feud, the workmen of France and Germany send each other messages of peace and goodwill; this great fact, unparalleled in the history of the past, opens the vista of a brighter future. It proves that in contrast to old society, with its economical miseries and its political delirium, a new society is springing up, whose International rule will be Peace, because its national ruler will be everywhere the same—Labour! The Pioneer of that new society is the International Working Men's Association.

II. Common Terms, Words and Phrases for the Text

the International Working Men's Association 国际工人协会

inaugural address 就职演说

Louis Bonaparte 路易·波拿巴

plebiscite 公民投票，全民公决

complot 共谋，图谋

despotism 专制统治，独裁制

denounce 谴责，告发

detestable 可憎的

menace 威胁，危险的人或物等

reprobation 反对，谴责

Rhine 莱茵河

patriotism 爱国主义，爱国精神

Prussia 普鲁士

Bismarck 俾斯麦

The Hohenzollern Dynasty 霍亨索伦王朝

The Battle of Sadowa 萨多瓦战役

legerdemain 骗术，花招

Paris Manifesto《巴黎宣言》

Cossack 哥萨克，哥萨克人

Czar 沙皇，独裁者

III. Exercises and Thinking

1. What was Marx's resolution for the European Crisis in the 1870s in the first General Council of the International Working Men's Association?

2. Why France was defeated in the Franco-Prussian War?

3. What were Marx's opinions on Thiers's government after the Franco-Prussian War?

IV. Further Readings and Internet Links

1. Further Readings

北京大学国际政治系编：《巴黎公社》，商务印书馆 1974 年版。

朱庭光：《巴黎公社史》，中国社会科学出版社 1982 年版。

吴机鹏：《普法战争》，商务印书馆 1972 年版。

[美] 杰弗里·瓦夫罗：《普法战争：1870—1871 德国对法国的征服》，林国荣译，社会科学文献出版社 2020 年版。

郭华榕：《法兰西第二帝国史》，北京大学出版社 1991 年版。

Karl Marx, *The Paris Commune*, Bombay: People's Pub. House, 1944.

2. Internet Links

中共中央党史和文献研究院：https://www.dswxyjy.org.cn/

中央编译出版社数据库云平台：https://www.cctpbooks.com/

马克思主义研究网：http://marxism.cass.cn

Unit 30

The Management of Barbarian Affairs
《筹办夷务始末》

《筹办夷务始末》也称为《三朝筹办夷务始末》。它是清政府将道光、咸丰、同治三朝外交档案分别编纂的大型汇编，书中档案时间始于道光十六年四月（1836 年 6 月），止于同治十三年十二月（1875 年 1 月）。鸦片战争失败后，清政府在与西方侵略者交涉时感到需要借鉴以往经验，于是咸丰皇帝同意将道光朝外交档案挑选，抄录，汇编成书。咸丰元年（1851 年）开始编纂《道光朝筹办夷务始末》，咸丰六年九月完成。《道光朝筹办夷务始末》载录了从道光十六年四月清政府禁止鸦片的议政，到道光二十九年禁止英国人进入广州城通商。同治帝继位后编纂《咸丰朝筹办夷务始末》，载录的外交档案时间从道光三十年正月（1850 年 2 月）到咸丰十一年七月（1861 年 8 月）。光绪皇帝继位后沿袭旧制，编纂《同治筹办夷务始末》，载录的外交档案时间从咸丰十一年七月到同治十三年十二月。

《筹办夷务始末》是清末存留下来的重要官方文献史料，成为研究中国近代史和近代中国国际关系史必读文献。自西方入侵中国以来，清王朝给世人的印象是被迫抵抗、屈辱签约，殊不知清政府在应对过程中也积极制定了长远的制夷方略。本章摘取《道光朝筹办夷务始末》的一部分，其内容涉及清政府对美国的对华企图以及美国与其他西方国家关系的认知和判断，清政府希望借助美国人的力量抵制英国人对华侵略的野心。字里行间反映出清政府对西方的认知程度，以及清政府在鸦片战争失败之后反思教训的积极态度和谋定对抗列强的策略。

I. Excerpt from *The Management of Barbarian Affairs*①

The Chinese documents of this period, February 6, 1841 to December 12, 1842, comprise twenty-one memorials and thirteen edicts. The documents indicate a fairly lively interest in the problem of the United States on the part of the emperor. There are no formal or casual endorsements but there are three specific comments by the emperor and seven instances of interlinear or marginal notations in the emperor's hands. The memorialists are the coastal officials and generals involved in the First Opium War, then in its last stages in Canton, on the eastern seaboard, and the Yangtze valley. The period also covers the conclusion and initial operation of *the Treaty of Nanking*, concluded with Great Britain in August, 1842. Curiously enough, the one anti-Western memorialist during this period is a court official who was not personally involved in the war. Of the thirteen edicts, ten are addressed to the grand councillors, that is, they are important edicts involving state policy, either military or civil; three are of a routine character addressed to the Grand Secretariat. Two of these involve appointments and one involves denunciation and punishment of officials. As will be noted hereafter from time to time, the function of the Grand Secretariat during this period, insofar as it affects foreign relations, appears to be limited to the appointment, removal, and punishment of personnel. The grand secretaries are not concerned with the formulation or execution of foreign policy.

In content, the documents of this period deal with the trade and activities of Americans during the hostilities, and the status of the United States as a neutral. The discovery of the possibility of enlisting the sympathies and the aid of the United States and France on China's behalf is the principal theme. The American consul, Delano, is mentioned, and suggestions as to the use of American trade as bargaining material are made. A British shipwreck on Taiwan (Formosa) results in depositions by the sailors and

① Earl Swisher, *China's Management of the American Barbarians: A Study of Sino–American Relations, 1841–1861, with Documents*, New York: Octagon Books, 1972, pp. 55–61.

provides the occasion for an early Chinese attempt to distinguish among the various types of "barbarians."

The position of the United States in this period is indicated by the appearance of American naval units at Whampoa. This elicited proposals for the building of an effective Chinese navy and experiments by hong merchants in the construction of Western-type ships and in the manufacture of under-water mines and torpedoes. Americans were involved in these activities as potential allies of China, as friendly neutrals with no love for the British, or as skilled technicians capable of assisting China.

The Western materials parallel to the Chinese documents of this period are summarized by Tyler Dennett, Americans in Eastern Asia, in his chapter entitled "Americans and the Anglo-Chinese War," pages 91 to 113. Some of the pertinent American documents for the same period are the "Memorial of R. B. Forbes and Others," U. S. Cong. 26:1, H. Doc. 40; "Memorial of Edmund Fanning," U. S. Cong. 26:1, H. Doc. 57; "Canton Consular Letters," U. S. Cong. 26:1, H. Doc. 119; "Petition of Boston and Salem Merchants," U. S. Cong. 26:1, H. Doc. 170; "Report of the Secretary of the Treasury on China Trade," U. S. Cong. 26:1, H. Doc. 248; "Canton Consular Letters," U.S. Cong. 26:2, H. Doc. 71; and The Chinese Repository, Canton, for the years 1832–1842, volumes 1–11.

Translations of Documents

1.February 6, 1841. MEMORIAL: Proposal to Use the American Against the British.

I-li-pu further memorializes. Moreover, the attitude of those barbarians now at Canton is extremely refractory. Your slave has received and read a communication from that province and was immeasurably depressed. The said barbarians, after capturing the forts, again sent barbarian letters, stating their demands seriatim. Although Your slave does not know how many items were listed altogether or what the things they asked for were concerned with, he still fears that those barbarians are using force in pressing their demands and that in managing them, fingers are pricked at every turn.

In devising means of restraining the enemy, we should not be afraid to inquire widely. Your slave has received a communication of Juan Yüan, recently occupying the post of Grand Secretary, saying:

"According to rumor, since Ch'i–shan reached Canton, the barbarians have not yet become tractable and I worry about it day and night. I have long since been aware that of the countries trading at Canton, besides England, the United States is the largest and most powerful. In this country, the ground is level and rice plentiful. The English barbarians look to her for supplies and do not dare antagonize her. But the American barbarians at Canton have always been peaceable, not obstinate like the English barbarians. If we treat the American barbarians courteously and abolish their customs duties, and also take the trade of the English barbarians and give it to the American barbarians, then the American barbarians are sure to be grateful for this Heavenly Favor and will energetically oppose the English barbarians. Moreover, the ships and cannon of the English barbarians have mostly been acquired by hire or seizure from other foreign states. If the American barbarians are made use of by us, then other countries will learn of it, and it will not be difficult to break them down. When the American barbarians have received (Imperial) Favor, the English barbarians will certainly not take it lying down. Probably one or two ports will be bombarded by them, but when their strength is expended and we have strengthened fortifications and purged the countryside, then we will meet them and it will not be hard to repel them. Still, this is a plan devised during sickness and I do not yet know whether or not it is practicable. Therefore, I have not ventured to put it into a memorial.

IV–Your slave observes that the present situation at Canton is very critical. If we clash with them, it is extremely difficult to predict whether or not we can win. If we conciliate them along the line requested in this letter, it is feared that their demands will be troublesome and many and, under the circumstances, hard to satisfy. But if we utilize the strength of the American barbarians to curb the English barbarians, it would seem that the effort would be halved and the result doubled.

Although, in view of the greatness of the Heavenly Court, to borrow the help of outside barbarians may not seem to be proper handling, still in the books of strategy there is the theory of "attack by conciliation" and the technique of "using barbarians to curb barbarians." From Han and T'ang times onward it is recorded in history, not once but many times, that such has been done without loss of dignity. Moreover, considering the alternatives of conciliating the English barbarians or utilizing the American barbarians, at least the latter is better than the former. It would seem that the device of Juan Yüan is not entirely without perspicacity. The only question is whether or not the American barbarians can curb the English barbarians; whether or not they are willing to be used by us. That, besides these, there are no other obstacles, Your slave as yet is not fully convinced. Even so, Juan Yüan has been away from Canton for many years and it is feared that there may be differences between then and now. It is only right to append this secret communication and beseech Your Majesty's judgment. If it meets Imperial approval, it is respectfully requested to charge the acting governor general of Liang-kuang [i.e., Kwangtung-Kwangsi], Ch'i-shan, thoroughly to investigate the situation and execute in detail. (IWSM. TK 21; 21b, 1-22b, 8)

2. February 10, 1841. MEMORIAL: Report of Decline of Canton Customs Revenue and Loss of Trade by England and Other Countries.

Governor of Kwangtung, concurrently in charge of Canton customs, I-liang, memorializes. It is found that the Canton Maritime Customs revenue, annual collection and surplus, totals over 899, 000 taels, of which the barbarian customs form a large part. The number of barbarian ships arriving each [sic, copyist's error; should read "the present"] year has not been twenty per cent of that of former years. Not only have the ships of the English barbarians and the Indians stopped trading, but also the ships of other countries have been obstructed by the English barbarians and are unable to enter port. So after the sixth month (July 18–August 17), just when collections of revenues should be the greatest, on the contrary there was a shortage. Not only was there a great disparity with previous administrations, but compared to the amounts collected during the past two years of Yü–k'un's regime, it was again reduced by more than half. (IWSM. TK 21; 38a, 4–10)

3. February 10, 1841. EDICT: Proposal to Capitalize on Resentment of Other Countries against England for Loss of Trade.

Edict to the Grand Councillors. I–liang has memorialized on (his) taking over the management of the Canton Maritime Customs and the shortage in collections, in which he states that in the Canton Maritime Customs revenue, the barbarian customs form a major part; also that the number of foreign ships arriving in the present year is not twenty per cent of that of previous years, because the ships of other countries, being obstructed by the English barbarians, were not able to enter port. So, after the sixth month (July 18–August 17), just when collections of revenues should be the greatest, on the contrary, there was a shortage, etc.

Kwangtung precedent allows the various barbarians to trade. The respectful and obedient states naturally should trade as usual. The English barbarians are overbearing and tyrannical and have interfered with the livelihood of other countries. Are those states willing resignedly to lose their profits? (We) hereby charge I–shan, Lung–wen, and Ch'i Kung, on their respective arrivals at Canton, to investigate carefully the attitudes of the various countries, whether or not they are resentful of the English barbarians' interference with their livelihood or have any disappointment with the Heavenly Court for not yet being able to draw them in and pacify them, leaving them to be neglected and lose their trade, and to memorialize according to the facts. (IWSM. TK 21; 38b, 1–8)

4. March 6, 1841. MEMORIAL: Encouragement of Americans to Trade in Order to Alienate Them from the British.

Memorial of the already degraded Grand Secretary Ch'i–shan. ... Furthermore, at the present time, the American merchant ships coming to Canton are prevented by the English barbarians from entering port, falsely telling them the local officials would take their ships for war purposes. Your slave has already order the hong merchants to inform them that this circumstance does not exist. Moreover, he has issued a statement that the reason they cannot carry on trade lies entirely with the English barbarians but that if they can devise means for entrance (to the port), the Heavenly Court authorizes trade with them as usual; in this way we can quiet their minds and cause them to feel resentful toward the English barbarians and grateful to the Heavenly Court. Thus, while they would not be used by us, there would still be no danger of their siding with evil and abetting treason. ... (IWSM. TK 23; 33a, 8–33b, 3)

5. March 21, 1841. MEMORIAL: Proposal to Encourage Americans to Oppose the English Rebels.

[Imperial Commissioner, Governor of Kiangsu] Y ü –ch'ien further memorializes. Moreover, these marine volunteers are all brigands. In Kwangtung they are called "ragamuffins." To use them against the barbarians would be like using poison to counteract poison. In case they are wounded or killed there will be no regrets; thus there will be no injury to the Heavenly prestige and, at the same time, a local evil can be removed. Furthermore, Your slave has ascertained that the various foreign countries, because the English rebels have stirred up trouble and trade has become slack, are all thoroughly angry and resentful. The strength of such countries as Europe, America, and France is separately equal to that of the (English) rebels. It is not worth while for the Heavenly Court to issue an Edict ordering them to render help, but in the proclamation offering rewards, there is no harm in making clear that no matter whether they be soldiers or civilians, marine volunteers or Chinese traitors, or barbarians of the various countries, all are authorized to kill the rebels and claim the rewards, and also to issue a manifesto informing the various countries:

The Great Emperor as Sovereign over all under Heaven, looks upon Chinese and outsiders with the same benevolence. Those who obey, he soothes; those who rebel, he chastizes. England is rebellious and has resisted authority, and already troops have been sent to punish her. You various other countries are not involved, and are all allowed to trade as usual. If the English rebels brazenly dare to use force to stop you and interfere with your livelihood, you various countries are authorized to fire upon them on the open seas, or separately to use warships to attack their country, or anything else you like.

Thus the minds of the various countries can be pacified, and also the gall of the rebel barbarians be overcome. In addition, (we can) secretly summon the capable and dependable among the hong merchants and order them to act as though this were their own idea, to make use of the policy of disagreement and alienation to meet emergencies as they arise, and to play them off and encourage them until they destroy one another. Our army can merely be quiet and await the opportunity to move, until the said (English) barbarians are left isolated and embarrassed. Then the government troops and marine volunteers can take advantage of their weakened condition and attack them. Such an insignificant rebel can easily be eradicated with one stroke of the drum. (IWSM. TK 24; 36a, 9–37a, 6)

6. March 21, 1841. EDICT: Americans to be Offered Rewards for Killing English Rebels.

Edict to the Grand Councillors. Yü-ch'ien has memorialized asking to offer rewards and recruit marine volunteers in order to dissipate the Chinese traitors and also to allow barbarians of the various countries as a whole to kill rebels and claim rewards. The rebel barbarians at Canton show a great deal of lawlessness. Now the various forces have been mobilized and I-shan and others ordered to attack them quickly. It is hoped that after those generals arrive, they can in one beat of the drum effect their capture and exterminate the evil lot. The government troops sent from various places are experienced only in land warfare; when it comes to going to sea and making captures or attacks, perhaps they are not as able as the marine volunteers. Now Yü-ch'ien's memorial suggests the posting of offers for rewards and the issue of proclamations for recruits to make up the deficiencies in military strength.

(We) charge I-shan and the others immediately to devise means of recruiting and to exert themselves to make them all useful to us in order to dissipate the traitorous bands and extinguish the flames of revolt. His separate memorial proposes, in the proclamations offering rewards, to announce that barbarians of the various countries are all authorized to kill rebels and claim rewards. Whether or not it is practicable, (We) also charge I-shan and the others to take counsel and manage accordingly. The two memorials of Yü-ch'ien are both ordered, copied and sent to them for persual. (IWSM. TK 24; 37a, 7-37b, 4)

II. Common Terms, Words and Phrases for the Text

the First Opium War 第一次鸦片战争

edict 敕令，法令

memorial 年代记，请愿书，纪念碑等

endorsement 支持，代言，票据签字等

notations 标记法，注释，评注

coastal officials 沿海官员

Canton 广州

Yangtze Valley 长江流域

the Treaty of Nanking《南京条约》

the Grand Councilllor 宰相，重臣

the Grand Secretariat 大学士

the American Consul 美国领事

Formosa 台湾

Whampoa 黄埔

under-water mine 水雷

seriatim 依次地

refractory 难治的，不听话的，难熔的

Juan Yüan 阮元

Ch'i-shan 琦善

conciliation 调解，安抚

Maritime Custom 海关

Kwangtung 广东省

brigand 强盗，土匪

ragamuffin 衣衫褴褛的人

sovereign 有主权的，有至高无上权力的，君主等

eradicate 根除，消灭

III. Exercises and Thinking

1. Read this historical material, and figure out what was Qing Dynasty's strategy confronting with Westerners' invasion?

2. Translate main provisions of the Treaty of Nanking.

3. Study on what did American get through treaties with Qing Dynasty before the Second Opium War?

IV. Further Readings and Internet Links

1. Further Readings

（清）文庆等纂辑:《筹办夷务始末》(影印本)，上海古籍出版社 2008 年版。

武堉干:《鸦片战争史》，蒋尊簋校，商务印书馆 1929 年版。

陶文钊:《中美关系史》，重庆出版社 1993 年版。

[美]王栋:《中国的不平等条约：国耻与民族历史叙述》，王栋、龚志伟译，复旦大学出版社 2011 年版。

2. Internet Links

清代外交档案文献汇编全文数据库：https://guji.unihan.com.cn/

鸦片战争博物馆：https://www.ypzz.cn/f/index

中国人民大学清史研究所：http://iqh.ruc.edu.cn/qdzwgxyj/index.htm

Translation of the Peking Gazette Online: https://primarysources.brillonline.com

China and the Modern World: https://www.gale.com/primary-sources

Part V

Modern and Contemporary History of the World

世界现当代史

世界现当代史是资本主义衰落、社会主义兴起和发展的历史。世界现当代史研究以20世纪以来的世界历史作为研究对象，考察1900年至今的人类社会历程。

世界现当代史大致可以分为两个发展阶段。第一个阶段是从20世纪初至1945年第二次世界大战结束。这个阶段最明显的历史主题是战争、危机与革命。20世纪两次世界大战所波及的国家与地区、战争的规模、战争的时间以及战争的损失超过以往时代任何一场战争。斯宾格勒的《西方的没落》预言西方文化走向衰败，代表战争时代西方社会整体的悲观与消沉。一战结束后，欧洲主要资本主义国家兴起了无产阶级革命斗争，其中以俄国为典型，列宁的《告工人、士兵和农民书》宣告了俄国十月社会主义革命的胜利，俄国建立了世界上第一个无产阶级专政的国家，从而打开了资本主义世界的缺口，开启了人类历史发展新纪元。而资本主义世界在这一时间段爆发了严重的经济危机，以1929年美国经济危机为开端，危机迅速波及世界主要资本主义国家。美国制定并实施以凯恩斯经济学为指导思想的罗斯福新政，开创了资本主义国家对经济生活干预的模式，较为顺利地摆脱了经济危机，成为资本主义世界典型样板。然而，德国、意大利、日本通过扩大军事工业加紧对外扩张，以摆脱危机，在政治上建立了法西斯独裁统治，从而形成第二次世界大战欧亚地区两个战争策源地，给人类世界带来严重的灾难。

第二阶段以第二次世界大战结束为起点，从1945年至冷战结束。这一时期，人类经历了战后重建、冷战时期和90年代以来世界呈现多极化的新时期，和平与发展成为世界历史发展的历史潮流，国际合作与和平共处成为时代共识。《联合国宪章》的签署标志着联合国的建立，联合国是国际政治合作与世界人民和平诉求的产物。布雷顿森林体系的建立是各国在世界经济和国际贸易方面所达成的共识。联合国和布雷顿森林体系为战后秩序的恢复和世界经济发展作出重要贡献。为了解决战后的社会危机，二战后资本主义国家开始进行社会改革，调整经济社会发展政策，其中以英国贝弗里奇爵士开创的社会保险制度为典型，该制度缓和了资本主义社会的固有矛盾。战后亚非拉殖民地的人民为了争取民族独立，掀起了民族民主解放运动，殖民地纷纷取得独立。19世纪下半叶形成的世界殖民主义体系彻底崩溃。和平共处五项原则成为各国处理与其他国家关系的基本原则。1961年，不结盟运动首脑会议召开，《不结盟国家和政府首脑宣言》的签署表明第三世界作为一支独立的政治力量从此登上国际政治舞台。

为了反映世界现当代史的总体样貌和不同阶段的历史发展情况，针对世界现当代史这一主题，本编选取了列宁的《告工人、士兵和农民书》、斯宾格勒的《西方的没落》、美国经济大萧条时期的典型原始文献、威廉·贝弗里奇的《贝弗里奇报告》、《布雷顿森林体系》、《联合国宪章》、《不结盟国家和政府首脑宣言》和《顺应时代前进潮流，促进世界和平发展》等。这些文献种类丰富，涉及政治、经济、思想、社会等多个领域的话题，以及资本主义强国和新兴的第三世界国家等区域，力图以点带面，使学生从多方位把握时代主题，理解现当代世界的发展历史与趋势。

Unit 31

To Workers, Peasants, And Soldiers!

列宁《告工人、士兵和农民书》

《告工人、士兵和农民书》是伟大的无产阶级革命家、马克思主义理论家、苏联共产党和苏维埃社会主义国家的主要创建人列宁所著，是俄国十月革命时期一篇重要的纲领性文献。

列宁，原名弗拉米基尔·伊里奇·乌里扬诺夫，无产阶级革命家、政治家、理论家、思想家，1870年4月22日出生于俄国的辛比尔斯克城。1887年，列宁进入喀山大学学习。此后，列宁接触到了马克思的《资本论》，并将德文版的《共产党宣言》翻译成俄文。1892年，列宁的第一本著作《农民生活中新的经济变动》出版。同年，列宁进入彼得堡一家律师事务所从事见习律师的工作，并参加了当地马克思主义者组织的工人小组活动。1895年秋，列宁在彼得堡领导成立了“工人阶级解放斗争协会”。1898年3月初，俄国的一批社会主义者召开第一次党的代表大会，当时还在流亡的列宁宣告了俄国社会民主工党的建立。

1900年，列宁创办《火星报》杂志。1901年到1902年，他完成《怎么办？》一书。在1903年7月俄国社会民主工党召开的第二次代表大会上，通过了党纲和党章。在这次大会上，产生了以列宁为首的布尔什维克和以马尔托夫为首的孟什维克。1905年俄国第一次资产阶级民主革命爆发，在列宁领导下召开了党的第三次代表大会，制定了布尔什维克在这次革命中的策略。在紧张繁忙的革命事业之余，列宁坚持党的理论研究工作，1909年完成了《唯物主义和经验批判主义》一书，该书成为马克思列宁主义的经典文献。

1914年一战爆发后，列宁提出了“变帝国主义战争为国内战争”的革命口号。1917年11月7日（俄历10月25日），俄国爆发革命。当晚，第二次全俄苏维埃代表大会召开，宣布临时政府被推翻，中央和地方全部政权转归苏维埃。阿·瓦·卢那茶尔斯基宣读了列宁起草的《告工人、士兵和农民书》。这篇历史性文献宣告了临时政府已经被推翻，政权已转移到苏维埃手里。这一宣言交付投票表决，代表大会一致通过。第二天，列宁在大会上作了报告，大会通过了《和平法令》和《土地法令》，组成了以列宁为主席的第一届苏维埃政府——人民委员会，世界上第一个社会主义国家宣告诞生。

作为十月革命的重要历史文献，《告工人、士兵和农民书》宣告了全部政权已经归苏维埃，无产阶级革命政府建立。因此，阅读该篇文献，对于了解十月革命史和苏联历史具有重要意义。本文献的俄文版本经过1920年召开的苏维埃社会主义共和国联盟第二次全国会议和俄国共产党（布尔什维克）第九次全国代表大会审议通过，其英文版本以该编辑的俄语版本为基础，由尤里·斯多布尼科夫（Yuri Sdobnikov）和乔治·汉娜（George Hanna）翻译，并由汉娜整理编辑，这也是本书选用的版本。

I. TO WORKERS, PEASANTS, AND SOLDIERS ![①]

Comrades! The Party of Socialist-Revolutionaries, to which Kerensky belongs, appeals to you in its paper *Dyelo Naroda* (of September 30) "*to be patient*" .

The paper asks us "to be patient" and urges that power be left in the hands of Kerensky's government, that power should not pass to the Soviets of Workers' and Soldiers' Deputies. Let Kerensky rely on the landowners, capitalists and kulaks, let the Soviets that have carried through the revolution and vanquished the Kornilovite generals "be patient", we are told. Let them have patience until the Constituent Assembly, which will soon be convened.

---

① George Hanna edited, *Lenin Collected Works*, vol.26, Moscow: Progress Publishers, 1964, pp.137–139.

Comrades! Look around you, see what is happening in the countryside, see what is happening in the army, and you will realise that the peasants and the soldiers cannot tolerate it any longer. *An uprising of the peasants* from whom the land has hitherto been withheld by fraud is sweeping like a broad river over the whole of Russia. The peasants cannot tolerate it any longer. Kerensky sends *troops* to suppress the peasants and to defend the landowners. Kerensky has again come to an agreement with the Kornilovite generals and officers who stand for the landowners.

Neither the workers in the cities nor the soldiers at the front can tolerate this military suppression of the just struggle of the peasants for the land.

As to what is going on in the army at the front, Dubasov, a non–Party officer, has declared before all of Russia: "The soldiers will not fight any longer." The soldiers are tired out, the soldiers are barefooted, the soldiers are starving, the soldiers do not want to fight for the interests of the capitalists, they do not want to "*be patient*" when they are treated only to beautiful words about peace, while for months there has been a delay (as Kerensky is delaying it) in the *peace proposal*, the proposal for a just peace without annexations, to be offered to all the belligerent peoples.

Comrades! Know that Kerensky is again negotiating with the Kornilovite generals and officers to *lead troops against the Soviets* of Workers' and Soldiers' Deputies, to *prevent* the Soviets *from obtaining power*! Kerensky "*will under no circumstances submit*" to the Soviets, *Dyelo Naroda* openly admits.

Go, then, to the barracks, go to the Cossack units, go to the working people and explain the *truth* to them.

If power is in the hands of the Soviets, then not later than October 25 (if the Congress of Soviets opens on October 20) *a just peace will be offered* to all the belligerent peoples. There will *be a workers' and peasants' government* in Russia; it will immediately, without losing a single day, *offer a just peace to all the belligerent peoples*. Then the people will learn who wants the unjust war. Then in the Constituent

Assembly the people will decide.

If power is in the hands of the Soviets, the *landowners'* estates will *immediately* be declared the *inalienable property of the whole people*.

This is what Kerensky and his government fight against, relying on the village exploiters, capitalists and landowners!

This is for whom and for whose interests you are asked to "be patient".

Are you willing to "be patient" in order that Kerensky may use armed force to suppress the peasants who have risen for land?

Are you willing to "be patient" in order that the war may be dragged out longer, in order that the *offer of peace* and the annulling of the former tsar's secret treaties with the Russian and Anglo-French capitalists may be postponed?

Comrades, remember that Kerensky deceived the people once when he promised to convene the Constituent Assembly! On July 8 he solemnly promised to convene it not later than September 17, and he has *deceived the people*. Comrades! Whoever believes in the Kerensky government is a traitor to his brothers, the peasants and soldiers!

No, *not for one more day* are the people willing to suffer postponement. *Not for a single day longer* can we suffer the peasants to be suppressed by armed force, thousands upon thousands to perish in the war, when a *just peace* can and must be *offered* at once.

Down with the government of Kerensky, who is conniving with the Kornilovite landowning generals to suppress the peasants, to fire on the peasants, to drag out the war!

All power to the Soviets of Workers' and Soldiers' Deputies!

Written October 1–2 (14–15), 1917

First published in Pravda No. 93,

April 23, 1924

II. Common Terms, Words and Phrases for the Text

Soviets 苏维埃

comrade 同志

Kerensky 克伦斯基

kulak（沙俄时代的）富农

the Constituent Assembly 立宪会议

fraud 欺骗

Kornilovite 科尔尼洛夫

just struggle 正义斗争

Dubasov 杜巴索夫

the Cossack units 哥萨克部队

the belligerent peoples 交战国

traitor 叛徒

armed force 武力

perish 死亡

down 打倒；击败

drag out 拖延

the Soviets of Workers' and Soldiers' Deputies 工兵代表苏维埃

III. Exercises and Thinking

1. Please discuss the historical background of *To Workers, Peasants, and Soldiers!*.

2. Please comment on the historical implications of *To Workers, Peasants, and Soldiers!*.

3. Who is Kerensky? Please evaluate him objectively and fairly.

IV. Further Readings and Internet Links

1. Further Readings

中共中央马克思恩格斯列宁斯大林编译局编译:《列宁全集》，第 33 卷，人民出版社 1992 年版。

Jeffrey Brooks and Georgey Chernyavskiy, *Lenin and the Making of the Soviet State: A Brief History with Documents*, New York, N.Y.: Palgrave Macmillan, 2007.

Peter Kenez, *A History of the Soviet Union from the Beginning to the End*, Cambridge: Cambridge University Press, 2006.

2. Internet Links

中文马克思主义文库：https://www.marxists.org/chinese/index.html

列宁作品网络资源：https://www.marxists.org/archive/lenin/works/index.htm

Unit 32

The Decline of the West

斯宾格勒《西方的没落》

《西方的没落》是奥斯瓦尔德·斯宾格勒（Oswald Spengler, 1880—1936）的代表性著作，是历史学经典名著，在世界思想史上占有重要地位。斯宾格勒是德国著名哲学家、文学家和历史学家，历史文化形态学的开创者。他于 1880 年出生在德国哈茨山巴的布兰肯堡一个邮政官员的家庭。1890 年，斯宾格勒举家迁到德国中东部的哈雷市，先后就读于慕尼黑大学、柏林大学和哈雷大学，毕业后成为一名中学教师。他除了研究历史和艺术之外，还对数学和博物学有浓厚的兴趣。1904 年，斯宾格勒在哈雷大学获得博士学位，其论文题目为《赫拉克利特基本形而上学思想研究》（*The Fundamental Metaphysical Thought of the Heraclitean Philosophy*）。次年，他又通过考试获得高中教师资格，成为汉堡一名高级中学教师，讲授的科目有数学、物理学、历史、德国文学等。斯宾格勒的教师生活一直持续到 1911 年他母亲去世，那时他得到了一小笔遗产使他得以退出教学领域，以独立作家的身份生活。第一次世界大战以后，他因健康情况未被征召入伍。战争期间，他隐居在南部的慕尼黑的寓所里，终身未婚。他在这里完成了《论自己》（*On himself*），这部作品的创作耗时 7 年时间。从这部作品中可以看出，他饱受精神上的折磨并长期自我怀疑。他在这里也完成了彪炳史册的巨著《西方的没落》。[①] 斯宾格勒的主要著作还有《普鲁士主义和社会主义》（*Prussianism and Socialism*）、《人和技术》（*Man and technics*）、《决战时

① Mark Sedgwick, *Key Thinkers of the Radical Right: Behind the New Threat to Liberal Democracy*, Oxford: Oxford University Press, 2019, pp. 1–7.

刻：德国与世界历史的演变》（*The Hour of Decision: Germany and World Historical Evolution*）、《德国青年的政治义务》（*Politische Pflichten der deutschen Jugend*）、《德国的重建》（*Neubau des Deutschen Reiches*）等。

《西方的没落》是斯宾格勒最著名的代表作。此书构思于1914年以前，那时世界大战已经迫在眉睫。“没落”一词最早可以追溯到1912年，那年斯宾格勒读到慕尼黑大学古代史教授奥拓·泽科（Otto Seeck）的《古代世界没落的历史》书名的时候，受到了该书的启发。《西方的没落》第一卷出版于1917年，第二卷也在1922年出版，全书共100余万字。在他开始写第一卷时，本打算把重点放在欧洲的德国。然而，1911年阿加迪尔危机（the Agadir Crisis）对他的影响巨大，因此他扩大了研究范围。[①] 他在书中描述了第一次世界大战前的几年的情况。“在那个时候，对我而言，世界大战已经迫在眉睫了，这也是历史危机不可弥补的外在表现，我努力通过考察前几个世纪而不是数年的精神来理解它。”[②] 该书的第一卷完成于1914年，但第一版是在1918年夏天一战结束前由维也纳一家出版公司出版，初版印行了1500本。第一卷出版时大获成功，斯宾格勒成为社会名人。这本书不仅在国内受到追捧，在外国也获得很多赞誉。该书出版后，被翻译成多种语言。斯宾格勒逐渐跻身于20世纪最有影响的历史学家之列。1936年5月，斯宾格勒死于心脏病。

斯宾格勒在《西方的没落》中提出，世界历史上曾经存在过8种高级文化，即埃及文化、印度文化、巴比伦文化、中国文化、古典文化（希腊罗马文化）、伊斯兰文化、墨西哥文化、西方文化。每种文化都要经历前文化时期、文化早期、文化晚期和文化时期，或者叫作诞生期、生长期、成熟期、衰老死亡期这样4个发展阶段，它们相当于自然界里的春夏秋冬4个季节，每个阶段都要经历1000年左右的漫长岁月。斯宾格勒说：“每一种文化都有自己的观念，自己的激情，自己的生命、意志和情感，乃至自己的死亡。……每一种文化都有它的自

---

① Klau P. Fischer, *History and Prophecy: Oswald Spengler and The Decline of the West*, Durham: Morre Publishing Company, 1977, p. 241.

② Oswald Spengler, *The Decline of the West*, London: George Allen & Unwin Ltd., 1926, p. 46.

我表现的新的可能，从发生到成熟，再到衰落，永不复返。”[①]斯宾格勒认为，除了西方文化尚存有活力以外，其他文化都已经走完了各自的生命旅程。

《西方的没落》内容丰富，见解独特。我们要以马克思主义为指导对其进行鉴别和借鉴。我国最早对《西方的没落》一书作全面评论的是叶法无，1930 年，她撰写文章全面介绍了斯宾格勒的文化史观。新中国成立后，我国著名历史学家齐世荣等翻译出版了该书的第二卷。齐先生执笔中译本导言，对该书的历史背景与思想内容进行分析，并对其进行了批判与总结。2006 年，《西方的没落》的全译本由上海三联书店出版发行。本篇选自 1926 年由查理・弗兰西斯・爱金孙（Charles Francis Atkinson）翻译的英文版。

I. Excerpt from *The Decline of the West*[②]

CHAPTER I：INTRODUCTION

VI

What, then, *is* world-history? Certainly, an ordered presentation of the past, an inner postulate, the expression of a capacity for feeling form. But a feeling for form, however definite, is not the same as form itself. No doubt we feel world-history, experience it, and believe that it is to be read just as a map is read. But, even to-day, it is only forms of it that we know and not *the* form of it, which is the mirror-image of *our own* inner life.

Everyone of course, if asked, would say that he saw the inward form of History quite clearly and definitely. The illusion subsists because no one has seriously reflected on it, still less conceived doubts as to his own knowledge, for no one has the slightest notion how wide a field for doubt there is. In fact, the *lay-out* of world-history is an unproved and subjective notion that has been handed down from generation to generation (not

① Oswald Spengler, *The Decline of the West*, London: George Allen & Unwin Ltd., 1926, p.21.

② Oswald Spengler, *The Decline of the West*, London: George Allen & Unwin Ltd., 1926, pp. 15-22.

only of laymen but of professional historians) and stands badly in need of a little of that scepticism which from Galileo onward has regulated and deepened our inborn ideas of nature.

Thanks to the subdivision of history into "Ancient," "Mediaeval" and "Modern" — an incredibly jejune and *meaningless* scheme, which has, however, entirely dominated our historical thinking—we have failed to perceive the true position in the general history of higher mankind, of the little part-world which has developed on West-European soil from the time of the German-Roman Empire, to judge of its relative importance and above all to estimate its direction. The Cultures that are to come will find it difficult to believe that the validity of such a scheme with its simple rectilinear progression and its meaningless proportions, becoming more and more preposterous with each century, incapable of bringing into itself the new fields of history as they successively come into the light of our knowledge, was, in spite of all, never whole-heartedly attacked. The criticisms that it has long been the fashion of historical researchers to level at the scheme mean nothing; they have only obliterated the one existing plan without substituting for it any other. To toy with phrases such as "the Greek Middle Ages" or "Germanic antiquity" does not in the least help us to form a clear and inwardly-convincing picture in which China and Mexico, the empire of Axum and that of the Sassanids have their proper places. And the expedient of shifting the initial point of "modern history" from the Crusades to the Renaissance, or from the Renaissance to the beginning of the 19th Century, only goes to show that the scheme *per se* is regarded as unshakably sound.

It is not only that the scheme circumscribes the area of history. What is worse, it rigs the stage. The ground of West Europe is treated as a steady pole, a unique patch chosen on the surface of the sphere for no better reason, it seems, than because we live on it—and great histories of millennial duration and mighty far-away Cultures are made to revolve around this pole in all modesty. It is a quaintly conceived system of sun and planets! We select a single bit of ground as the natural centre of the historical system, and make it the central sun. From it all the events of history receive their real light, from it their importance is judged in *perspective*. But it is in our own West-European conceit alone that this phantom "world-history," which a breath of scepticism would dissipate, is acted out.

We have to thank that conceit for the immense optical illusion (become natural from long habit) whereby distant histories of thousands of years, such as those of China and Egypt, are made to shrink to the dimensions of mere episodes while in the neighbourhood of our own position the decades since Luther, and particularly since Napoleon, loom large as Brocken-spectres. We know quite well that the slowness with which a high cloud or a railway train in the distance seems to move is only apparent, yet we believe that the *tempo* of all early Indian, Babylonian or Egyptian history was really slower than that of our own recent past. And we think of them as less substantial, more damped-down, more diluted, because we have not learned to make the allowance for (inward and outward) distances.

It is self-evident that for the Cultures of the West the existence of Athens, Florence or Paris is more important than that of Lo-Yang or Pataliputra. But is it permissible to found a scheme of world-history on estimates of such a sort? If so, then the Chinese historian is quite entitled to frame a world-history in which the Crusades, the Renaissance, Caesar and Frederick the Great are passed over in silence as insignificant. How, *from the morphological point of view*, should our 18th Century be more important than any other of the sixty centuries that preceded it? Is it not ridiculous to oppose a "modern" history of a few centuries, and that history to all intents localized in West Europe, to an "ancient" history which covers as many millennia—incidentally dumping into that "ancient history" the whole mass of the pre-Hellenic cultures, unprobed and unordered, as mere appendix-matter? This is no exaggeration. Do we not, for the sake of keeping the hoary scheme, dispose of Egypt and Babylon—each as an individual and self-contained history quite equal in the balance to our so-called "world-history" from Charlemagne to the World–War and well beyond it—as a *prelude* to classical history? Do we not relegate the vast complexes of Indian and Chinese culture to foot–notes, with a gesture of embarrassment? As for the great American cultures, do we not, on the ground that they do not "fit in" (with what?), entirely ignore them?

The most appropriate designation for this current West–European scheme of history, in which the great Cultures are made to follow orbits round *us* as the presumed centre of all world–happenings, is the *Ptolemaic system* of history. The system that is put forward in this work in place of it I regard as the *Copernican discovery* in the historical sphere, in that it admits no sort of privileged position to the Classical or the Western Culture as against the Cultures of India, Babylon, China, Egypt, the Arabs, Mexico—separate worlds of dynamic being which in point of mass count for just as much in the general picture of history as the Classical, while frequently surpassing it in point of spiritual greatness and soaring power.

VII

The scheme "ancient–mediaeval–modern" in its first form was a creation of the Magian world–sense. It first appeared in the Persian and Jewish religions after Cyrus, received an apocalyptic sense in the teaching of the Book of Daniel on the four world–eras, and was developed into a world–history in the post–Christian religions of the East, notably the Gnostic systems.

This important conception, within the very narrow limits which fixed its intellectual basis, was unimpeachable. Neither Indian nor even Egyptian history was included in the scope of the proposition. For the Magian thinker the expression "world–history" meant a unique and supremely dramatic act, having as its theatre the lands between Hellas and Persia, in which the strictly dualistic world–sense of the East expressed itself not by means of polar conceptions like the "soul and spirit," "good and evil" of contemporary metaphysics, but by the figure of a catastrophe, an epochal change of phase between world–creation and world–decay.

No elements beyond those which we find stabilized in the Classical literature, on the one hand, and the *Bible* (or other sacred book of the particular system), on the other, came into the picture, which presents (as "The Old" and "The New," respectively) the easily-grasped contrasts of Gentile and Jewish, Christian and Heathen, Classical and Oriental, idol and dogma, nature and spirit *with a time connotation*—that is, as a drama in which the one prevails over the other. The historical change of period wears the characteristic dress of the religious "Redemption." This "world-history" in short was a conception narrow and provincial, but within its limits logical and complete. Necessarily, therefore, it was specific to this region and this humanity, and incapable of any *natural* extension.

But to these two there has been added a third epoch, the epoch that we call "modern," on Western soil, and it is this that for the first time gives the picture of history the look of a progression. The oriental picture was *at rest*. It presented a self-contained antithesis, with equilibrium as its outcome and a unique divine act as its turning-point. But, adopted and assumed by a wholly new type of mankind, it was quickly transformed (without anyone's noticing the oddity of the change) into a conception of a *linear progress*: from Homer or Adam—the modern can substitute for these names the Indo-German, Old Stone Man, or the Pithecanthropus—through Jerusalem, Rome, Florence and Paris according to the taste of the individual historian, thinker or artist, who has unlimited freedom in the interpretation of the three-part scheme.

This third term, "modern times," which in form asserts that it is the last and conclusive term of the series, has in fact, ever since the Crusades, been stretched and stretched again to the elastic limit at which it will bear no more. It was at least implied if not stated in so many words, that here, beyond the ancient and the mediaeval, something definitive was beginning, a Third Kingdom in which, somewhere, there was to be fulfilment and culmination, and which had an objective point.

As to what this objective point is, each thinker, from Schoolman to present-day

Socialist, backs his own peculiar discovery. Such a view into the course of things may be both easy and flattering to the patentee, but in fact he has simply taken the spirit of the West, as reflected in his own brain, for the meaning of the world. So it is that great thinkers, making a metaphysical virtue of intellectual necessity, have not only accepted without serious investigation the scheme of history agreed "by common consent" but have made of it the basis of their philosophies and dragged in God as author of this or that "world-plan." Evidently the mystic number three applied to the world-ages has something highly seductive for the metaphysician's taste. History was described by Herder as the education of the human race, by Kant as an evolution of the idea of freedom, by Hegel as a self-expansion of the world-spirit, by others in other terms, but as regards its ground-plan everyone was quite satisfied when he had thought out some abstract meaning for the conventional threefold order.

On the very threshold of the Western Culture we meet the great Joachim of Floris (c. 1145-1202), the first thinker of the Hegelian stamp who shattered the dualistic world-form of Augustine, and with his essentially Gothic intellect stated the new Christianity of his time in the form of a third term to the religions of the Old and the New Testaments, expressing them respectively as the Age of the Father, the Age of the Son and the Age of the Holy Ghost. His teaching moved the best of the Franciscans and the Dominicans, Dante, Thomas Aquinas, in their inmost souls and awakened a world-outlook which slowly but surely took entire possession of the historical sense of our Culture. Lessing—who often designated his own period, with reference to the Classical as the "after-world" (Nachwelt)—took his idea of the "education of the human race" with its three stages of child, youth and man, from the teaching of the Fourteenth Century mystics. Ibsen treats it with thoroughness in his *Emperor and Galilean* (1873), in which he directly presents the Gnostic world-conception through the figure of the wizard Maximus, and advances not a step beyond it in his famous Stockholm address of 1887. It would appear, then, that the Western consciousness feels itself urged to predicate a sort of finality inherent in its own appearance.

But the creation of the Abbot of Floris was a *mystical* glance into the secrets of the divine world–order. It was bound to lose all meaning as soon as it was used in the way of reasoning and made a hypothesis of *scientific* thinking, as it has been—ever more and more frequently—since the 17th Century.

It is a quite indefensible method of presenting world–history to begin by giving rein to one's own religious, political or social convictions and endowing the sacrosanct three–phase system with tendencies that will bring it exactly to one's own standpoint. This is, in effect, making of some formula—say, the "Age of Reason," Humanity, the greatest happiness of the greatest number, enlightenment, economic progress, national freedom, the conquest of nature, or world–peace—a criterion whereby to judge whole millennia of history. And so we judge that they were ignorant of the "true path," or that they failed to follow it, when the fact is simply that their will and purposes were not the same as ours. Goethe's saying, "What is important in life is life and not a result of life," is the answer to any and every senseless attempt to solve the riddle of historical form by means of a *programme.*

It is the same picture that we find when we turn to the historians of each special art or science (and those of national economics and philosophy as well). We find:

"Painting" from the Egyptians (or the cave–men) to the Impressionists, or

"Music" from Homer to Bayreuth and beyond, or

"Social Organization" from Lake Dwellings to Socialism, as the case may be,

presented as a linear graph which steadily rises in conformity with the values of the (selected) arguments. No one has seriously considered the possibility that arts may have an allotted span of life and may be attached as forms of self–expression to particular regions and particular types of mankind, and that therefore the total history of an art may be merely an additive compilation of separate developments, of special arts, with no bond of union save the name and some details of craft-technique.

We know it to be true of every organism that the rhythm, form and duration of its life, and all the expression-details of that life as well, are determined by the *properties of its species*. No one, looking at the oak, with its millennial life, dare say that it is at this moment, now, about to start on its true and proper course. No one as he sees a caterpillar grow day by day expects that it will go on doing so for two or three years. In these cases we feel, with an unqualified certainty, a *limit*, and this sense of the limit is identical with our sense of the inward form. In the case of higher human history, on the contrary, we take our ideas as to the course of the future from an unbridled optimism that sets at naught all historical, i.e., *organic*, experience, and everyone therefore sets himself to discover in the accidental present terms that he can expand into some striking progression-series, the existence of which rests not on scientific proof but on predilection. He works upon unlimited possibilities—never a natural end—and from the momentary top-course of his bricks plans artlessly the continuation of his structure.

"Mankind," however, has no aim, no idea, no plan, any more than the family of butterflies or orchids. "Mankind" is a zoological expression, or an empty word. But conjure away the phantom, break the magic circle, and at once there emerges an astonishing wealth of *actual* forms—the Living with all its immense fullness, depth and movement—hitherto veiled by a catchword, a dryasdust scheme, and a set of personal "ideals." I see, in place of that empty figment of *one* linear history which can only be kept up by shutting one's eyes to the overwhelming multitude of the facts, the drama of a *number* of mighty Cultures, each springing with primitive strength from the soil of a mother-region to which it remains firmly bound throughout its whole life-cycle; each stamping its material, its mankind, in *its own* image; each having *its own* idea, its *own* passions, *its own* life, will and feeling, *its own* death. Here indeed are colours, lights, movements, that no intellectual eye has yet discovered. Here the Cultures, peoples, languages, truths, gods, landscapes bloom and age as the oaks and the stone-pines, the blossoms, twigs and leaves—but there is no ageing "Mankind." Each Culture has its own new possibilities of self-expression which arise, ripen, decay, and never return. There is not *one* sculpture, *one* painting, *one* mathematics, *one* physics, but many, each in its deepest essence different from the others, each limited in duration and self-contained, just as each species of plant has its peculiar blossom or fruit, its special type of growth and decline. These cultures, sublimated life-essences, grow with the same superb aimlessness as the flowers of the field. They belong, like the plants and the animals, to the living Nature of Goethe, and not to the dead Nature of Newton. I see world-history as a picture of endless formations and transformations, of the marvellous waxing and waning of organic forms. The professional historian, on the contrary, sees it as a sort of tapeworm industriously adding on to itself one epoch after another.

But the series "ancient-mediaeval-modern history" has at last exhausted its usefulness. Angular, narrow, shallow though it was as a scientific foundation, still we possessed no other form that was not wholly unphilosophical in which our data could be arranged, and world-history (as hitherto understood) has to thank it for filtering our classifiable solid residues. But the number of centuries that the scheme can by any stretch be made to cover has long since been exceeded, and with the rapid increase in the volume of our historical material—especially of material that cannot possibly be brought under the scheme—the picture is beginning to dissolve into a chaotic blur. Every historical student who is not quite blind knows and feels this, and it is as a drowning man that he clutches at the only scheme which he knows of. The word "Middle Age," ① invented in 1667 by Professor Horn of Leyden, has to-day to cover a formless and constantly extending mass which can only be defined, negatively, as every thing not classifiable under any pretext in one of the other two (tolerably well-ordered) groups.

① "Middle Age" connotes the history of the space-time region in which Latin was the language of the Church and the learned. The mighty course of Eastern Christianity, which, long before Boniface, spread over Turkestan into China and through Sabaea into Abyssinia, was entirely excluded from this "world-history."

We have an excellent example of this in our feeble treatment and hesitant judgment of modern Persian, Arabian and Russian history. But, above all, it has become impossible to conceal the fact that this so-called history of the world is a limited history, first of the Eastern Mediterranean region and then,—with an abrupt change of scene at the Migrations (an event important only to us and therefore greatly exaggerated by us, an event of purely Western and not even Arabian significance),—of West-Central Europe. When Hegel declared so naively that he meant to ignore those peoples which did not fit into his scheme of history, he was only making an honest avowal of methodic premisses that every historian finds necessary for his purpose and every historical work shows in its lay-out. In fact it has now become an affair of scientific tact to determine which of the historical developments shall be *seriously* taken into account and which not. Ranke is a good example.

II. Common Terms, Words and Phrases for the Text

being 存在

intellect 才智

world-ideas 世界观

polarity 极性

morphologically 形态学

impressionism 印象主义

mechanism 机制

pole 极

the Ptolemaic system of history 历史的托勒密体系

the Gnostic systems 诺斯替体系

time connotation 时间内涵

nachwelt 后期世界

Emperor and Galilean《皇帝和盖利利恩》

Age of Reason 理性时代

the properties of its species 种姓

III. Exercises and Thinking

1. Please comment on Spengler's review on world history.

2. Please briefly summarize on Spengler's theory.

3. Please talk about your understanding of cultural morphology.

IV. Further Readings and Internet Links

1. Further Readings

[德]斯宾格勒:《西方的没落:世界历史的透视》,齐世荣、田农等译,商务印书馆1963年版。

Mark J. Sedgwick, ed., *Key Thinkers of the Radical Right: Behind the New Threat to Liberal Democracy*, Oxford: Oxford University Press, 2019.

Oswald Spengler, *The Decline of the West*, London: George Allen & Unwin Ltd., 1926.

2. Internet Links

奥斯瓦尔德·斯宾格勒协会:https://www.oswaldspenglersociety.com/

Unit 33 Primary Sources of the Great Depression 大萧条相关文献

1929—1933 年，资本主义世界经历了一场严重的经济危机，这场危机首先在美国发生，然后波及德国、英国、法国、奥地利等欧洲主要资本主义国家。这场特大经济危机在美国历史上称为“大萧条”（the Great Depression），这场大萧条的特征是涉及范围特别广、持续时间比较长、破坏性特别大、失业率高。面对危机，美国采取的是较为成功的罗斯福总统改革措施，这一系列改革措施在美国历史上被称为“罗斯福新政”。

富兰克林·德拉诺·罗斯福（Franklin Delano Roosevelt，简称 FDR，1882—1945），美国第 32 任总统，1933—1945 年，连续出任四届美国总统，是迄今唯一连任超过两届的美国总统。罗斯福于 1903 年获得哈佛大学历史学学士学位，并于 1904 年进入哥伦比亚大学法学院学习。1908 年，他进入华尔街著名的律师事务所工作，主要处理有关公司法的事务。1921 年夏天，他患上小儿麻痹症，导致其腰部以下完全永久性瘫痪。1928 年，罗斯福成为纽约州州长。1932 年，罗斯福成为民主党总统候选人，并最终赢得大选。[①] 当 1933 年 3 月罗斯福第一次就任美国总统时，美国正处于大萧条最谷底。罗斯福上台之后，立刻采取了解决经济危机的新政措施。罗斯福新政大体可以分为两个阶段：第一阶段是从 1933 年 3 月罗斯福就职到 1935 年初，这一阶段提出了一系列复兴经济的法案和计划；第二阶段是 1935 年到 1939 年，这一阶段工作重点是对美国的经济机构

---

① Graham, Otis L. and Meghan Robinson Wander, eds., *Franklin D. Roosevelt: His Life and Times*, Boston: G.K.Hall, 1985.

进行全面改革。

罗斯福总统首先对危机影响最深的金融业进行改革。1933 年 3 月 9 日，国会通过了《紧急银行法》（*Emergency Banking Relief Act*），授予总统以管制信贷、通货、黄金、白银和外汇交易的权力，要求政府对全国银行进行整顿；由政府提供 35 亿美元贷款帮助大银行复兴，对缺乏偿付能力的银行进行改组。成立联邦储蓄保险公司（Federal Deposit Insurance Corporation），为所有参与保险的银行提供存款保险，使投保银行免受挤兑之苦。同时公布《存款保险法》，由政府保障存款，恢复储户的信心，防止再发生银行存款挤兑风潮。3 月 12 日晚上，罗斯福发表了第一次“炉边谈话”。1933 年 6 月，国会通过了《银行法》（*Banking Act*），该法又被称为《格拉斯—斯特高尔法》（*Glass-Steagall Act*）。这部法律规定，设立联邦存款保险公司以保证银行存款，建立存款保险制度，使广大储户的存款进一步得到保障。

在救济失业者方面，1935 年 4 月，国会通过了《紧急救济拨款法》，规定拨款 49 亿美元，用于救济、以工代赈和举办有益的公共工程项目，以增加就业机会；并通过了《公共工程和保护自然资源法案》和《田纳西河流管理局法》。为了真正解决就业问题，1933 年 6 月 16 日，国会通过《全国工业复兴法》（*National Industrial Recovery Act*），该法要求保证工人有组织工会和签订集体合同的权利，成立“全国复兴署”，要求每个工业部门制定一个“公平竞争”法规。由国家兴建公共工程以增加就业机会，提高社会购买力。

在第二阶段，罗斯福开始社会改革。针对社会保障，1935 年 6 月，国会通过了《全国劳工关系法》，1935 年 8 月，国会通过了《社会保障法》，联邦政府成立了社会保险署，并规定社会保险包括四个方面：养老金，失业保险，老年保险，对盲人、需抚养的儿童和其他遭遇不幸者给予救济。1938 年 6 月 25 日，通过《公平劳动标准法》，确定最低工资、最高工时以及禁止使用童工的规定。

罗斯福所推行的新政使美国成功走出了经济大危机泥沼，创造了资本主义国家经济干预模式，丰富了凯恩斯经济学理论实践，为资本主义国家克服固有的经济矛盾提供了一种成功案例。这一系列离不开罗斯福的个人努力和贡献。

例如，从1933年3月9日《紧急银行法》到6月16日《全国工业复兴法》通过的100天里，罗斯福发表了10次演说、提交国会10余篇咨文、推动国会通过了10余部法案。这里选取了两篇大萧条时期的文献，分别是“第一次就职演说”和“第一次炉边谈话”，以期使学生加深对罗斯福新政背景和措施的理解。

I. Primary Sources of the Great Depression

First Inaugural Address of Franklin D. Roosevelt①

SATURDAY, MARCH 4, 1933

I am certain that my fellow Americans expect that on my induction into the Presidency I will address them with a candor and a decision which the present situation of our Nation impels. This is preeminently the time to speak the truth, the whole truth, frankly and boldly. Nor need we shrink from honestly facing conditions in our country today. This great Nation will endure as it has endured, will revive and will prosper. So, first of all, let me assert my firm belief that the only thing we have to fear is fear itself; nameless, unreasoning, unjustified terror which paralyzes needed efforts to convert retreat into advance. In every dark hour of our national life a leadership of frankness and vigor has met with that understanding and support of the people themselves which is essential to victory. I am convinced that you will again give that support to leadership in these critical days.

In such a spirit on my part and on yours we face our common difficulties. They concern, thank God, only material things. Values have shrunken to fantastic levels; taxes have risen; our ability to pay has fallen; government of all kinds is faced by serious curtailment of income; the means of exchange are frozen in the currents of trade; the withered leaves of industrial enterprise lie on every side; farmers find no markets for

① Fred L. Israel editor, *The Inaugural Addresses of the Presidents of the United States 1789–2009*, New York: An Imprint of Infobase Publishing, 2010, pp. 281–287.

their produce; the savings of many years in thousands of families are gone.

More important, a host of unemployed citizens face the grim problem of existence, and an equally great number toil with little return. Only a foolish optimist can deny the dark realities of the moment.

Yet our distress comes from no failure of substance. We are stricken by no plague of locusts. Compared with the perils which our forefathers conquered because they believed and were not afraid, we have still much to be thankful for. Nature still offers her bounty and human efforts have multiplied it. Plenty is at our doorstep, but a generous use of it languishes in the very sight of the supply. Primarily this is because the rulers of the exchange of mankind's goods have failed, through their own stubbornness and their own incompetence, have admitted their failure, and abdicated. Practices of the unscrupulous money changers stand indicted in the court of public opinion, rejected by the hearts and minds of men.

True they have tried, but their efforts have been cast in the pattern of an outworn tradition. Faced by failure of credit they have proposed only the lending of more money. Stripped of the lure of profit by which to induce our people to follow their false leadership, they have resorted to exhortations, pleading tearfully for restored confidence. They know only the rules of a generation of self-seekers. They have no vision, and when there is no vision the people perish.

The money changers have fled from their high seats in the temple of our civilization. We may now restore that temple to the ancient truths. The measure of the restoration lies in the extent to which we apply social values more noble than mere monetary profit.

Happiness lies not in the mere possession of money; it lies in the joy of achievement, in the thrill of creative effort. The joy and moral stimulation of work no longer must be forgotten in the mad chase of evanescent profits. These dark days will be worth all they cost us if they teach us that our true destiny is not to be ministered unto but to minister to ourselves and to our fellow men.

Recognition of the falsity of material wealth as the standard of success goes hand in hand with the abandonment of the false belief that public office and high political position are to be valued only by the standards of pride of place and personal profit; and there must be an end to a conduct in banking and in business which too often has given to a sacred trust the likeness of callous and selfish wrongdoing. Small wonder that confidence languishes, for it thrives only on honesty, on honor, on the sacredness of obligations, on faithful protection, on unselfish performance; without them it cannot live.

Restoration calls, however, not for changes in ethics alone. This Nation asks for action, and action now.

Our greatest primary task is to put people to work. This is no unsolvable problem if we face it wisely and courageously. It can be accomplished in part by direct recruiting by the Government itself, treating the task as we would treat the emergency of a war, but at the same time, through this employment, accomplishing greatly needed projects to stimulate and reorganize the use of our natural resources.

Hand in hand with this we must frankly recognize the overbalance of population in our industrial centers and, by engaging on a national scale in a redistribution, endeavor to provide a better use of the land for those best fitted for the land. The task can be helped by definite efforts to raise the values of agricultural products and with this the power to purchase the output of our cities. It can be helped by preventing realistically the tragedy of the growing loss through foreclosure of our small homes and our farms. It can be helped by insistence that the Federal, State, and local governments act forthwith on the demand that their cost be drastically reduced. It can be helped by the unifying of relief activities which today are often scattered, uneconomical, and unequal. It can be helped by national planning for and supervision of all forms of transportation and of communications and other utilities which have a definitely public character. There are many ways in which it can be helped, but it can never be helped merely by talking about it. We must act and act quickly.

Finally, in our progress toward a resumption of work we require two safeguards against a return of the evils of the old order; there must be a strict supervision of all banking and credits and investments; there must be an end to speculation with other people's money, and there must be provision for an adequate but sound currency.

There are the lines of attack. I shall presently urge upon a new Congress in special session detailed measures for their fulfillment, and I shall seek the immediate assistance of the several States.

Through this program of action we address ourselves to putting our own national house in order and making income balance outgo. Our international trade relations, though vastly important, are in point of time and necessity secondary to the establishment of a sound national economy. I favor as a practical policy the putting of first things first. I shall spare no effort to restore world trade by international economic readjustment, but the emergency at home cannot wait on that accomplishment.

The basic thought that guides these specific means of national recovery is not narrowly nationalistic. It is the insistence, as a first consideration, upon the interdependence of the various elements in all parts of the United States—a recognition of the old and permanently important manifestation of the American spirit of the pioneer. It is the way to recovery. It is the immediate way. It is the strongest assurance that the recovery will endure.

In the field of world policy I would dedicate this Nation to the policy of the good neighbor; the neighbor who resolutely respects himself and, because he does so, respects the rights of others; the neighbor who respects his obligations and respects the sanctity of his agreements in and with a world of neighbors.

If I read the temper of our people correctly, we now realize as we have never realized before our interdependence on each other; that we can not merely take but we must give as well; that if we are to go forward, we must move as a trained and loyal army willing to sacrifice for the good of a common discipline, because without such discipline no progress is made, no leadership becomes effective. We are, I know, ready and willing to submit our lives and property to such discipline, because it makes possible a leadership which aims at a larger good. This I propose to offer, pledging that the larger purposes will bind upon us all as a sacred obligation with a unity of duty hitherto evoked only in time of armed strife.

With this pledge taken, I assume unhesitatingly the leadership of this great army of our people dedicated to a disciplined attack upon our common problems.

Action in this image and to this end is feasible under the form of government which we have inherited from our ancestors. Our Constitution is so simple and practical that it is possible always to meet extraordinary needs by changes in emphasis and arrangement without loss of essential form. That is why our constitutional system has proved itself the most superbly enduring political mechanism the modern world has produced. It has met every stress of vast expansion of territory, of foreign wars, of bitter internal strife, of world relations.

It is to be hoped that the normal balance of executive and legislative authority may be wholly adequate to meet the unprecedented task before us. But it may be that an unprecedented demand and need for undelayed action may call for temporary departure from that normal balance of public procedure.

I am prepared under my constitutional duty to recommend the measures that a stricken nation in the midst of a stricken world may require. These measures, or such other measures as the Congress may build out of its experience and wisdom, I shall seek, within my constitutional authority, to bring to speedy adoption.

But in the event that the Congress shall fail to take one of these two courses, and in the event that the national emergency is still critical, I shall not evade the clear course of duty that will then confront me. I shall ask the Congress for the one remaining instrument to meet the crisis; broad Executive power to wage a war against the emergency, as great as the power that would be given to me if we were in fact invaded by a foreign foe.

For the trust reposed in me I will return the courage and the devotion that befit the time. I can do no less.

We face the arduous days that lie before us in the warm courage of the national unity; with the clear consciousness of seeking old and precious moral values; with the clean satisfaction that comes from the stem performance of duty by old and young alike. We aim at the assurance of a rounded and permanent national life.

We do not distrust the future of essential democracy. The people of the United States have not failed. In their need they have registered a mandate that they want direct, vigorous action. They have asked for discipline and direction under leadership. They have made me the present instrument of their wishes. In the spirit of the gift I take it.

In this dedication of a Nation we humbly ask the blessing of God. May He protect each and every one of us. May He guide me in the days to come.

The First "Fireside Chat" ——An Intimate Talk with the People of the United States on Banking. March 12, 1933①

I want to talk for a few minutes with the people of the United States about banking—with the comparatively few who understand the mechanics of banking but more particularly with the overwhelming majority who use banks for the making of deposits and the drawing of checks. I want to tell you what has been done in the last few days, why it was done, and what the next steps are going to be. I recognize that the many proclamations from State Capitols and from Washington, the legislation, the Treasury regulations, etc., couched for the most part in banking and legal terms, should be explained for the benefit of the average citizen. I owe this in particular because of the fortitude and good temper with which everybody has accepted the inconvenience and hardships of the banking holiday. I know that when you understand what we in Washington have been about I shall continue to have your cooperation as fully as I have

---

① Samuel I. Rosenman, by compiled and Collated, *The Public Papers and Addresses of Franklin D. Roosevelt*, vol. 2, New York: Random House, 1933, pp. 61–65.

had your sympathy and help during the past week.

First of all, let me state the simple fact that when you deposit money in a bank the bank does not put the money into a safe deposit vault. It invests your money in many different forms of credit—bonds, commercial paper, mortgages and many other kinds of loans. In other words, the bank puts your money to work to keep the wheels of industry and of agriculture turning around. A comparatively small part of the money you put into the bank is kept in currency—an amount which in normal times is wholly sufficient to cover the cash needs of the average citizen. In other words, the total amount of all the currency in the country is only a small fraction of the total deposits in all of the banks.

What, then, happened during the last few days of February and the first few days of March? Because of undermined confidence on the part of the public, there was a general rush by a large portion of our population to turn bank deposits into currency or gold—a rush so great that the soundest banks could not get enough currency to meet the demand. The reason for this was that on the spur of the moment it was, of course, impossible to sell perfectly sound assets of a bank and convert them into cash except at panic prices far below their real value.

By the afternoon of March 3rd scarcely a bank in the country was open to do business. Proclamations temporarily closing them in whole or in part had been issued by the Governors in almost all the States.

It was then that I issued the proclamation providing for the nationwide bank holiday, and this was the first step in the Government's reconstruction of our financial and economic fabric.

The second step was the legislation promptly and patriotically passed by the Congress confirming my proclamation and broadening my powers so that it became possible in view of the requirement of time to extend the holiday and lift the ban of that holiday gradually. This law also gave authority to develop a program of rehabilitation of our banking facilities. I want to tell our citizens in every part of the Nation that the national Congress—Republicans and Democrats alike—showed by this action a devotion to public welfare and a realization of the emergency and the necessity for speed that it is difficult to match in our history.

The third stage has been the series of regulations permitting the banks to continue their functions to take care of the distribution of food and household necessities and the payment of payrolls.

This bank holiday, while resulting in many cases in great inconvenience, is affording us the opportunity to supply the currency necessary to meet the situation. No sound bank is a dollar worse off than it was when it closed its doors last Monday. Neither is any bank which may turn out not to be in a position for immediate opening. The new law allows the twelve Federal Reserve Banks to issue additional currency on good assets and thus the banks which reopen will be able to meet every legitimate call. The new currency is being sent out by the Bureau of Engraving and Printing in large volume to every part of the country. It is sound currency because it is backed by actual, good assets.

A question you will ask is this: why are all the banks not to be reopened at the same time? The answer is simple. Your Government does not intend that the history of the past few years shall be repeated. We do not want and will not have another epidemic of bank failures.

As a result, we start tomorrow, Monday, with the opening of banks in the twelve Federal Reserve Bank cities—those banks which on first examination by the Treasury have already been found to be all right. This will be followed on Tuesday by the resumption of all their functions by banks already found to be sound in cities where there are recognized clearing houses. That means about 250 cities of the United States.

On Wednesday and succeeding days banks in smaller places all through the country will resume business, subject, of course, to the Government's physical ability to complete its survey. It is necessary that the reopening of banks be extended over a period in order to permit the banks to make applications for necessary loans, to obtain currency needed to meet their requirements and to enable the Government to make common sense checkups.

Let me make it clear to you that if your bank does not open the first day you are by no means justified in believing that it will not open. A bank that opens on one of the subsequent days is in exactly the same status as the bank that opens tomorrow.

I know that many people are worrying about State banks not members of the Federal Reserve System. These banks can and will receive assistance from member banks and from the Reconstruction Finance Corporation. These State banks are following the same course as the National banks except that they get their licenses to resume business from the State authorities, and these authorities have been asked by the Secretary of the Treasury to permit their good banks to open up on the same schedule as the national banks. I am confident that the State Banking Departments will be as careful as the national Government in the policy relating to the opening of banks and will follow the same broad policy.

It is possible that when the banks resume a very few people who have not recovered from their fear may again begin withdrawals. Let me make it clear that the banks will take care of all needs—and it is my belief that hoarding during the past week has become an exceedingly unfashionable pastime. It needs no prophet to tell you that when the people find that they can get their money— that they can get it when they want it for all legitimate purposes—the phantom of fear will soon be laid. People will again be glad to have their money where it will be safely taken care of and where they can use it conveniently at any time. I can assure you that it is safer to keep your money in a reopened bank than under the mattress.

The success of our whole great national program depends, of course, upon the cooperation of the public—on its intelligent support and use of a reliable system.

Remember that the essential accomplishment of the new legislation is that it makes it possible for banks more readily to convert their assets into cash than was the case before. More liberal provision has been made for banks to borrow on these assets at the Reserve Banks and more liberal provision has also been made for issuing currency on the security of these good assets. This currency is not fiat currency. It is issued only on adequate security, and every good bank has an abundance of such security.

One more point before I close. There will be, of course, some banks unable to reopen without being reorganized. The new law allows the Government to assist in making these reorganizations quickly and effectively and even allows the Government to subscribe to at least a part of new capital which may be required.

I hope you can see from this elemental recital of what your Government is doing that there is nothing complex, or radical, in the process.

We had a bad banking situation. Some of our bankers had shown themselves either incompetent or dishonest in their handling of the people's funds. They had used the money entrusted to them in speculations and unwise loans. This was, of course, not true in the vast majority of our banks, but it was true in enough of them to shock the people for a time into a sense of insecurity and to put them into a frame of mind where they did not differentiate, but seemed to assume that the acts of a comparative few had tainted them all. It was the Government's job to straighten out this situation and do it as quickly as possible. And the job is being performed.

I do not promise you that every bank will be reopened or that individual losses will not be suffered, but there will be no losses that possibly could be avoided; and there would have been more and greater losses had we continued to drift. I can even promise you salvation for some at least of the sorely pressed banks. We shall be engaged not merely in reopening sound banks but in the creation of sound banks through reorganization.

It has been wonderful to me to catch the note of confidence from all over the country. I can never be sufficiently grateful to the people for the loyal support they have given me in their acceptance of the judgment that has dictated our course, even though all our processes may not have seemed clear to them.

After all, there is an element in the readjustment of our financial system more important than currency, more important than gold, and that is the confidence of the people. Confidence and courage are the essentials of success in carrying out our plan. You people must have faith; you must not be stampeded by rumors or guesses. Let us unite in banishing fear. We have provided the machinery to restore our financial system; it is up to you to support and make it work.

It is your problem no less than it is mine. Together we cannot fail.

II. Common Terms, Words and Phrases for the Text

curtailment 减少

existence 生存

optimist 乐观主义者

incompetence 无能力

deposit 存款

drawing 取款

state capitols 州议会大厦

legal terms 法律术语

bonds 债券

commercial paper 商业证券

mortgages 抵押

loans 借贷

panic prices 恐慌价格

payroll 工资名单

Federal Reserve Bank 联邦储备银行

the Bureau of Engraving and Printing 铸印局

confidence 信心

III. Exercises and Thinking

1. Please evaluate Roosevelt's New Deal.

2. Please talk about the historical background of Roosevelt's New Deal.

3. What is "Fireside Chat" ?

IV. Further Readings and Internet Links

1. Further Readings

[美]富兰克林·德·罗斯福:《罗斯福选集》,关在汉编译,商务印书馆 2018 年版。

Arthur M.Schlesinger, Jr., *The Coming of the New Deal 1933–1935,* Boston and New York: Houghton Miffin Company, 1958.

Samuel I. Rosenman, Compiled, *The Public Papers and Addresses of Franklin. D. Roosvelt: with a special introduction and explanatory notes by President Roosvelt*, New York: The Random House, 13 vols, 1938–1950.

2. Internet Links

美国国家档案馆:https://www.archives.gov/milestone-documents/list

富兰克林罗斯福总统图书馆和博物馆:https://www.fdrlibrary.org/

Unit 34

Social Insurance and Allied Services

《贝弗里奇报告》

1941年，英国成立社会保险和相关服务部际协调委员会，着手制定战后社会保障计划。英国伦敦经济学院、经济学家、自由党人威廉·亨利·贝弗里奇（William Henry Beveridge, 1879—1963）爵士受英国战后重建委员会主席阿瑟·格林伍德先生委托，出任协调委员会主席，负责对当时的国家社会保险方案及相关服务进行调查与研究，并就战后重建社会保障计划进行构思与设计，提出具体的实施方案和建议。由于贝弗里奇在这个委员会发挥了领导与关键性的作用，因此后来这一委员会又被称为贝弗里奇委员会。

贝弗里奇是英国著名的社会改革家和经济学家。1903年，他在牛津大学取得民法的学位，并开始在汤恩比会馆（Toynbee Hall）里从事对伦敦东区贫困社会状况的研究。这项实践研究为他日后思考英国的社会济贫与社会保障问题打下了基础。1905年，他担任《晨报》（*Morning Post*）特邀撰稿人，针对英国的社会问题展开思考研究，提出自己的主张与建议。第一次世界大战后，贝弗里奇被任命为伦敦经济学院院长。离开伦敦经济学院之后，他一直担任牛津大学一所学院院长。此外，他还分别担任过英国上下两院的议员，并且担任过二战期间英国政府的劳工部次长。[①]

自担任协调委员会主席以来，贝弗里奇从1941年6月开始对英国社会展开了为期18个月的调查，涉及长期失业者问题、医疗服务不完善问题以及儿童

① H. C. G. Matthew and Brian Harrison eds., *Oxford Dictionary of National Biography,* vol. 5, Oxford: Oxford University Press, 2004, pp. 590–595.

和老年人普遍贫困等问题。他走访调查了上百位证人，并咨询了凯恩斯、罗宾斯等经济学家。[①]贝弗里奇委员会在正式报告发表之前，一共召集了44次会议，收集了194份文件。[②]委员会在1942年1月到10月之间举行了数十次听证会，收集了大量资料，并与各方进行了广泛的协商，于10月份拟就最后的报告。这就是著名的《贝弗里奇报告》。为了体现报告的独立性，该报告由贝弗里奇单独署名，是贝弗里奇个人的调查报告，不代表任何政府部门的意见。《贝弗里奇报告》较为全面地总结了英国战前社会中存在的各种问题，分析了当下的社会保障和福利制度的成就和弊端。在此基础上，《贝弗里奇报告》提出了建立战后新型社会保障和福利制度的一整套方案，其中许多是具有划时代意义的改革建议。例如，贝弗里奇提出了“全方位医疗和康复服务”。这一观点为后来著名的英国全民医疗保健服务制度的建立提供了理论基础。

《贝弗里奇报告》发表后遭到了丘吉尔政府的冷遇，但在社会上引起热议。报告在发表后几天时间里，售出超过7万册，最后销售总量为63.5万册，成为当时最畅销的出版物。[③]1943年2月，英国议会就《贝弗里奇报告》进行辩论，各派议员大多对报告表示支持。阿瑟·格林伍德在辩论中宣称：本届议会欢迎贝弗里奇先生关于社会保险以及相关服务的报告，它代表英国对社会保障制度的一种普遍观点，也是英国政府战后重建计划的各种政策所要达到的目标。他专门强调该报告发表后的影响与销量，以此证明民众的支持与要求是正确的。在这种情况下，英国下院最后以“335票赞成、119票反对”通过了《贝弗里奇报告》。

英国政府基本接受了贝弗里奇的建议，于1944年发布了社会保险白皮书，并按照该报告内容制定了相关的法律。1945—1948年，英国相继通过了《家庭

① H. C. G. Matthew and Brian Harrison eds., *Oxford Dictionary of National Biography,* vol. 5, Oxford: Oxford University Press, 2004, p. 593.

② Derek Fraser, *The Evolution of the British Welfare State: A History of Social Policy since the Industrial Revolution*, second Edition, London: Macmillan Press Ltd., 1984, p. 214.

③ H. C. G. Matthew and Brian Harrison eds., *Oxford Dictionary of National Biography,* vol. 5, Oxford: Oxford University Press, 2004, p. 593; John Brown, *The British Welfare State: A Critical History*, Oxford: Basil Blacekwell Ltd., 1995, p. 26.

津贴法》《国民保险法》《国民健康服务法》《儿童法》《国民救助法》等一系列法律。1948 年，英国首相艾德礼宣布英国第一个建成了福利国家，并声明继续坚持遵循《贝弗里奇报告》中的原则建设社会福利国家。贝弗里奇也因此获得了“福利国家之父”的称号。贝弗里奇所开创的社会保险模式在欧洲广泛普及，成为福利国家的一个“样板”。20 世纪 50 年代以后，瑞典、芬兰、挪威、法国、爱尔兰、加拿大、希腊、意大利、西班牙、葡萄牙等国纷纷效仿英国，借鉴贝弗里奇模式，建设福利国家。这里选取的是 1942 年由皇家文书局出版的英文版本。

I. Excerpt from *Social Insurance and Allied Services*①

1.The Inter-departmental Committee on Social Insurance and Allied Services were appointed in June, 1941, by the Minister without Portfolio, then responsible for the consideration of reconstruction problems. The terms of reference required the Committee "to undertake, with special reference to the inter-relation of the schemes, a survey of the existing national schemes of social insurance and allied services, including workmen's compensation and to make recommendations." The first duty of the Committee was to survey, the second to recommend. For the reasons stated below in paragraph 40 the duty of recommendation was confined later to the Chairman of the Committee.

THE COMMITTEE'S SURVEY AND ITS RESULTS

2. The schemes of social insurance and allied services which the inter-departmental Committee have been called on to survey have grown piece-meal. Apart from the Poor Law, which dates from the time of Elizabeth, the schemes surveyed are the product of the last 45 years beginning with the Workmen's Compensation Act, 1897. That Act, applying in the first instance to a limited number of occupations, was made general in

① Sir William Beveridge, *Social Insurance and Allied Services*, London: His Majesty's Stationery Office, 1942, pp. 5-11.

1906. Compulsory health insurance began in 1912. Unemployment insurance began for a few industries in 1912 and was made general in 1920. The first Pensions Act, giving non–contributory pensions subject to a means test at the age of 70, was passed in 1908. In 1925 came the Act which started contributory pensions for old age, for widows and for orphans. Unemployment insurance, after a troubled history, was put on a fresh basis by the Unemployment Act of 1934, which set up at the same time a new national service of Unemployment Assistance. Meantime, the local machinery for relief of destitution, after having been exhaustively examined by the Royal Commission of 1905–1909, has been changed both by the new treatment of unemployment and in many other ways, including a transfer of the responsibilities of the Boards of Guardians to Local Authorities. Separate provision for special types of disability–such as blindness–has been made from time to time. Together with this growth of social insurance and impinging on it at many points have gone developments of medical treatment, particularly in hospitals and other institutions; developments of services devoted to the welfare of children, in school and before it; and a vast growth of voluntary provision for death and other contingencies, made by persons of the insured classes through Industrial Life Offices, Friendly Societies and Trade Unions.

3. In all this change and development, each problem has been dealt with separately, with little or no reference to allied problems. The first task of the Committee has been to attempt for the first time a comprehensive survey of the whole field of social insurance and allied services, to show just what provision is now made and how it is made for many different forms of need. The results of this survey are set out in Appendix B describing social insurance and the allied services as they exist today in Britain. The picture presented is impressive in two ways. First, it shows that provision for most of the many varieties of need through interruption of earnings and other causes that may arise in modern industrial communities has already been made in Britain on a scale not surpassed and hardly rivalled in any other country of the world. In one respect only of the first

importance, namely limitation of medical service, both in the range of treatment which is provided as of right and in respect of the classes of persons for whom it is provided, does Britain's achievement fall seriously short of what has been accomplished elsewhere; it falls short also in its provision for cash benefit for maternity and funerals and through the defects of its system for workmen's compensation. In all other fields British provision for security, in adequacy of amount and in comprehensiveness, will stand comparison with that of any other country; few countries will stand comparison with Britain. Second, social insurance and the allied services, as they exist today, are conducted by a complex of disconnected administrative organs, proceeding on different principles, doing invaluable service but at a cost in money and trouble and anomalous treatment of identical problems for which there is no justification. In a system of social security better on the whole than can be found in almost any other country there are serious deficiencies which call for remedy.

4. Thus limitation of compulsory insurance to persons under contract of service and below a certain remuneration if engaged on non-manual work is a serious gap. Many persons working on their own account are poorer and more in need of State insurance than employees; the remuneration limit for non-manual employees is arbitrary and takes no account of family responsibility. There is, again, no real difference between the income needs of persons who are sick and those who are unemployed, but they get different rates of benefit involving different contribution conditions and with meaningless distinctions between persons of different ages. An adult insured man with a wife and two children receives 38/ – per week should he become unemployed; if after some weeks of unemployment he becomes sick and not available for work, his insurance income falls to 18 / –. On the other hand a youth of 17 obtains 9 / – when he is unemployed, but should he become sick his insurance income rises to 12/ – per week. There are, to take another example, three different means tests for non-contributory pensions, for supplementary pensions and for public assistance, with a fourth test—for unemployment assistance—

differing from that for supplementary pensions in some particulars.

5. Many other such examples could be given; they are the natural result of the way in which social security has grown in Britain. It is not open to question that, by closer co-ordination, the existing social services could be made at once more beneficial and more intelligible to those whom they serve and more economical in their administration.

THREE GUIDING PRINCIPLES OF RECOMMENDATIONS

6. In proceeding from this first comprehensive survey of social insurance to the next task—of making recommendations—three guiding principles may be laid down at the outset.

7. The first principle is that any proposals for the future, while they should use to the full the experience gathered in the past, should not be restricted by consideration of sectional interests established in the obtaining of that experience. Now, when the war is abolishing landmarks of every kind, is the opportunity for using experience in a clear field. A revolutionary moment in the world's history is a time for revolutions, not for patching.

8. The second principle is that organisation of social insurance should be treated as one part only of a comprehensive policy of social progress. Social insurance fully developed may provide income security; it is an attack upon Want. But Want is one only of five giants on the road of reconstruction and in some ways the easiest to attack. The others are Disease, Ignorance, Squalor and Idleness.

9. The third principle is that social security must be achieved by co-operation between the State and the individual. The State should offer security for service and contribution. The State in organising security should not stifle incentive, opportunity, responsibility; in establishing a national minimum, it should leave room and encouragement for voluntary action by each individual to provide more than that minimum for himself and his family.

10. The Plan for Social Security set out in this Report is built upon these principles.

It uses experience but is not tied by experience. It is put forward as a limited contribution to a wider social policy, though as something that could be achieved now without waiting for the whole of that policy. It is, first and foremost, a plan of insurance—of giving in return for contributions benefits up to subsistence level, as of right and without means test, so that individuals may build freely upon it.

THE WAY TO FREEDOM FROM WANT

11. The work of the Inter–departmental Committee began with a review of existing schemes of social insurance and allied services. The Plan for Social Security, with which that work ends, starts from a diagnosis of want—of the circumstances in which, in the years just preceding the present war, families and individuals in Britain might lack the means of healthy subsistence. During those years impartial scientific authorities made social surveys of the conditions of life in a number of principal towns in Britain, including London, Liverpool, Sheffield, Plymouth, Southampton, York and Bristol. They determined the proportions of the people in each town whose means were below the standard assumed to be necessary for subsistence, and they analysed the extent and causes of that deficiency. From each of these social surveys the same broad result emerges. Of all the want shown by the surveys, from three–quarters to five–sixths, according to the precise standard chosen for want, was due to interruption or loss of earning power. Practically the whole of the remaining one–quarter to one–sixth was due to failure to relate income during earning to the size of the family. These surveys were made before the introduction of supplementary pensions had reduced the amount of poverty amongst old persons. But this does not affect the main conclusion to be drawn from these surveys: abolition of want requires a double re–distribution of income, through social insurance and by family needs.

12. Abolition of want requires, first, improvement of State insurance, that is to say provision against interruption and loss of earning power. All the principal causes of interruption or loss of earnings are now the subject of schemes of social insurance. If, in

spite of these schemes, so many persons unemployed or sick or old or widowed are found to be without adequate income for subsistence according to the standards adopted in the social surveys, this means that the benefits amount to less than subsistence by those standards or do not last as long as the need, and that the assistance which supplements insurance is either insufficient in amount or available only on terms which make men unwilling to have recourse to it. None of the insurance benefits provided before the war were in fact designed with reference to the standards of the social surveys. Though unemployment benefit was not altogether out of relation to those standards, sickness and disablement benefit, old age pensions and widows' pensions were far below them, while workmen's compensation was below subsistence level for anyone who had family responsibilities or whose earnings in work were less than twice the amount needed for subsistence. To prevent interruption or destruction of earning power from leading to want, it is necessary to improve the present schemes of social insurance in three directions: by extension of scope to cover persons now excluded, by extension of purposes to cover risks now excluded, and by raising the rates of benefit.

13. Abolition of want requires, second, adjustment of incomes, in periods of earning as well as in interruption of earning, to family needs, that is to say, in one form or another it requires allowances for children. Without such allowances as part of benefit or added to it, to make provision for large families, no social insurance against interruption of earnings can be adequate. But, if children's allowances are given only when earnings are interrupted and are not given during earning also, two evils are unavoidable. First, a substantial measure of acute want will remain among the lower paid workers as the accompaniment of large families. Second, in all such cases, income will be greater during unemployment or other interruptions of work than during work.

14. By a double re-distribution of income through social insurance and children's allowances, want, as defined in the social surveys, could have been abolished in Britain before the present war. As is shown in para. 445, the income available to the

British people was ample for such a purpose. The Plan for Social Security set out in Part V of this Report takes abolition of want after this war as its aim. It includes as its main method compulsory social insurance, with national assistance and voluntary insurance as subsidiary methods. It assumes allowances for dependent children, as part of its background. The plan assumes also establishment of comprehensive health and rehabilitation services and maintenance of employment, that is to say avoidance of mass unemployment, as necessary conditions of success in social insurance. These three measures—of children's allowances, health and rehabilitation services, and maintenance of employment—are described as assumptions A, B and C of the plan; they fall partly within and partly without the plan itself, extending into other fields of social policy. They are discussed, therefore, not in the detailed exposition of the plan in Part V of the Report, but in Part VI, which is concerned with social security in relation to wider issues.

15. The plan is based on a diagnosis of want. It starts from facts, from the condition of the people as revealed by social surveys between the two wars. It takes account of two other facts about the British community, arising out of past movements of the birth rate and the death rate, which should dominate planning for its future; the main effects of these movements in determining the present and future of the British people are shown by Table XI in para. 234. The first of the two facts is the age constitution of the population, making it certain that persons past the age that is now regarded as the end of working life will be a much larger proportion of the whole community than at any time in the past. The second fact is the low reproduction rate of the British community today; unless this rate is raised very materially in the near future, a rapid and continuous decline of the population cannot be prevented. The first fact makes it necessary to seek ways of postponing the age of retirement from work rather than of hastening it. The second fact makes it imperative to give first place in social expenditure to the care of childhood and to the safeguarding of maternity.

16. The provision to be made for old age represents the largest and most rapidly

growing element in any social insurance scheme. The problem of age is discussed accordingly in Part Ⅲ of the Report as one of three special problems; the measures proposed for dealing with this problem are summarised in paras. 254–257. Briefly, the proposal is to introduce for all citizens adequate pensions without means test by stages over a transition period of twenty years, while providing immediate assistance pensions for persons requiring them. In adopting a transition period for pensions as of right, while meeting immediate needs subject to consideration of means, the Plan for Social Security in Britain follows the precedent of New Zealand. The final rate of pensions in New Zealand is higher than that proposed in this Plan, but is reached only after a transition period of twenty-eight years as compared with twenty years suggested here; after twenty years, the New Zealand rate is not very materially different from the basic rate proposed for Britain. The New Zealand pensions are not conditional upon retirement from work; for Britain it is proposed that they should be retirement pensions and that persons who continue at work and postpone retirement should be able to increase their pensions above the basic rate. The New Zealand scheme is less favourable than the plan for Britain in starting at a lower level; it is more favourable in some other respects. Broadly the two schemes for two communities of the British race are plans on the same lines to solve the same problem of passage from pensions based on need to pensions paid as of right to all citizens in virtue of contribution.

SUMMARY OF PLAN FOR SOCIAL SECURITY

17. The main feature of the Plan for Social Security is a scheme of social insurance against interruption and destruction of earning power and for special expenditure arising at birth, marriage or death. The scheme embodies six fundamental principles: flat rate of subsistence benefit; flat rate of contribution; unification of administrative responsibility; adequacy of benefit; comprehensiveness; and classification. These principles are explained in paras. 303–309. Based on them and in combination with national assistance and voluntary insurance as subsidiary methods, the aim of the Plan for Social Security is

to make want under any circumstances unnecessary.

18. A plan which is designed to cover so many varieties of human circumstance must be long and detailed. It must contain proposals of differing orders of certainty and importance. In preparing the Report, the question arose naturally as to how far it was necessary at this stage to enter into details, and whether it might not be preferable to deal with principles only. For two reasons it has appeared desirable, in place of giving an outline only, to set the proposals out in as much detail as the time allowed. The first reason is that the principles underlying any practical reform can be judged only by seeing how they would work in practice. The second reason is that if a Plan for Social Security is to come into operation when the war ends or soon after, there is no time to lose in getting the plan prepared as fully as possible. The many details set forth in Part V are neither exhaustive nor final; they are put forward as a basis of discussion, but their formulation will, it is hoped, shorten subsequent discussion. Even among the major proposals of the Report there are differences of importance and of relevance to the scheme as a whole. There are some proposals which, though important and desirable in themselves, could be omitted without changing anything else in the scheme. Three in particular in the list of major changes in para. 30 have this character and are placed in square brackets to indicate it. This does not mean that everything not bracketed is essential and must be taken or left as a whole. The six principles named above and all that is implied in them are fundamental; the rest of the scheme can be adjusted without changing its character: all rates of benefit and all details are by nature subject to amendment.

19. The main provisions of the plan may be summarised as follows:

(i) The plan covers all citizens without upper income limit, but has regard to their different ways of life; it is a plan all-embracing in scope of persons and of needs, but is classified in application.

(ii) In relation to social security the population falls into four main classes of working age and two others below and above working age respectively, as follows:

I. Employees, that is, persons whose normal occupation is employment under contract of service.

Ⅱ. Others gainfully occupied, including employers, traders and independent workers of all kinds.

Ⅲ. Housewives, that is married women of working age.

Ⅳ. Others of working age not gainfully occupied.

V. Below working age.

Ⅵ. Retired above working age.

(iii) The sixth of these classes will receive retirement pensions and the fifth will be covered by children's allowances, which will be paid from the National Exchequer in respect of all children when the responsible parent is in receipt of insurance benefit or pension, and in respect of all children except one in other cases. The four other classes will be insured for security appropriate to their circumstances. All classes will be covered for comprehensive medical treatment and rehabilitation and for funeral expenses.

(iv) Every person in Class I, II or Ⅳ will pay a single security contribution by a stamp on a single insurance document each week or combination of weeks. In Class I the employer also will contribute, affixing the insurance stamp and deducting the employee's share from wages or salary. The contribution will differ from one class to another, according to the benefits provided, and will be higher for men than for women, so as to secure benefits for Class Ⅲ.

(v) Subject to simple contribution conditions, every person in Class I will receive benefit for unemployment and disability, pension on retirement, medical treatment and funeral expenses. Persons in Class II will receive all these except unemployment benefit and disability benefit during the first 13 weeks of disability. Persons in Class Ⅳ will receive all these except unemployment and disability benefit. As a substitute for unemployment benefit, training benefit will be available to persons in all classes other than Class I, to assist them to find new livelihoods if their present ones fail. Maternity grant, provision for widowhood and separation and qualification for retirement pensions will be secured to all persons in Class Ⅲ by virtue of their husbands' contributions; in addition to maternity grant, housewives who take paid work will receive maternity benefit for thirteen weeks to enable them to give up working before and after childbirth.

(vi) Unemployment benefit, disability benefit, basic retirement pension after a transition period, and training benefit will be at the same rate, irrespective of previous earnings. This rate will provide by itself the income necessary for subsistence in all normal cases. There will be a joint rate for a man and wife who is not gainfully occupied. Where there is no wife or she is gainfully occupied, there will be a lower single rate; where there is no wife but a dependant above the age for children's allowance, there will be a dependant allowance. Maternity benefit for housewives who work also for gain will be at a higher rate than the single rate in unemployment or disability, while their unemployment and disability benefit will be at a lower rate; there are special rates also for widowhood as described below. With these exceptions all rates of benefit will be the same for men and for women. Disability due to industrial accident or disease will be treated like all other disability for the first thirteen weeks; if disability continues thereafter, disability benefit at a flat rate will be replaced by an industrial pension related to the earnings of the individual subject to a minimum and a maximum.

(vii) Unemployment benefit will continue at the same rate without means test so long as unemployment lasts, but will normally be subject to a condition of attendance at a work or training centre after a certain period. Disability benefit will continue at the same rate without means test, so long as disability lasts or till it is replaced by industrial pension, subject to acceptance of suitable medical treatment or vocational training.

(viii) Pensions (other than industrial) will be paid only on retirement from work. They may be claimed at any time after the minimum age of retirement, that is 65 for men and 60 for women. The rate of pension will be increased above the basic rate if retirement is postponed. Contributory pensions as of right will be raised to the full basic rate gradually during a transition period of twenty years, in which adequate pensions according to needs will be paid to all persons requiring them. The position of existing pensioners will be safeguarded.

(ix) While permanent pensions will no longer be granted to widows of working age without dependent children, there will be for all widows a temporary benefit at a higher rate than unemployment or disability benefit, followed by training benefit where necessary. For widows with the care of dependent children there will be guardian benefit, in addition to the children's allowances, adequate for subsistence without other means. The position of existing widows on pension will be safeguarded.

(x) For the limited number of cases of need not covered by social insurance, national assistance subject to a uniform means test will be available.

(xi) Medical treatment covering all requirements will be provided for all citizens by a national health service organised under the health departments and post-medical rehabilitation treatment will be provided for all persons capable of profiting by it.

(xii) A Ministry of Social Security will be established, responsible for social insurance, national assistance and encouragement and supervision of voluntary insurance and will take over, so far as necessary for these purposes, the present work of other Government Departments and of Local Authorities in these fields.

II. Common Terms, Words and Phrases for the Text

social insurance 社会保险

social security 社会保障

children's allowances 子女补贴

budget 预算

compulsory insurance 强制保险

voluntary insurance 自愿保险

national assistance 国家救助

maintenance of employment 维持就业

the Inter-Department Committee 协调委员会

The Poor Law《济贫法》

the Workmen's Compensation Act《工伤赔偿法》

unemployment insurance 失业保险

friendly societies 互助会

Trade Unions 工会

non-manual employee 白领

five giants 五大“巨人”

want 贫困、匮乏

disease 疾病

ignorance 愚昧

idleness 懒散

ministry of social security 社会保障部

medical treatment 医疗服务

the health departments 卫生部

scheme of workmen's compensation 工伤赔偿计划

maternity grant 生育补助金

retirement pensions 退休养老金

insurance document 保险单据

full time education 全日制教育

III. Exercises and Thinking

1. Please summarize briefly the main contents of the Beveridge report.

2. Please summarize and comment on Beveridge's social insurance ideas.

3. Please discuss the implications of the Beveridge report for the development of social security in contemporary China.

IV. Further Readings and Internet Links

1. Further Readings

[英]贝弗里奇:《贝弗里奇报告——社会保险和相关服务》，劳动和社会保障部社会保险研究所组织翻译，中国劳动社会保障出版社2004年版。

Janet Beveridge, *Beveridge and his plan*, London: Hodder and Stoughton, 1954.

Victor George, *Social Security: Beveridge and after*, London: Routledge, 2018.

2. Internet Links

中国人力资源和社会保障部：http://www.mohrss.gov.cn/.

社会工作史：https://www.historyofsocialwork.org/eng/details.php?cps=14.

Unit 35

Bretton Woods Agreement

《布雷顿森林协议》

美国通过罗斯福新政率先走出经济大萧条，实现了经济恢复和发展，二战后成为欧洲乃至世界的债权国，也是世界上最大的资本输出国。英法等老牌资本主义大国经济恢复较慢，并深受两次世界大战的打击，经济地位下降。早在第二次世界大战期间，美国就开始考虑重建战后国际经济新秩序。国际货币体系成为其考虑的重点问题。

1944 年 7 月，来自 44 个国家的 730 名代表齐聚美国新罕布什尔州的布雷顿森林召开会议，这就是著名的布雷顿森林会议。布雷顿森林会议全称为“联合国家货币与金融会议”（United Nations Monetary and Financial Conference），旨在构建战后世界金融秩序。会议通过了以美国提出的“怀特计划”为基础的《联合国家货币金融会议的最后决议书》以及《国际货币基金组织协定》和《国际复兴开发银行协定》两个附件，总称为“布雷顿森林协议”。根据协定，国际货币基金组织和国际复兴开发银行（也称“世界银行”）于 1945 年 12 月 27 日正式成立。世界银行从 1946 年 6 月 25 日开业，国际货币基金组织于 1947 年 3 月 1 日开始业务活动。这两个机构的总部都设在华盛顿。

《布雷顿森林协议》使一个以美元为中心的世界货币体系得以建立，从而确立了美元的霸主地位，这就是著名的布雷顿森林体系。布雷顿森林体系有两大支柱：第一，美元与黄金挂钩，每盎司黄金等于 35 美元；第二，其他会员国货币与美元挂钩，即同美元保持固定汇率关系。这实际上意味着美元就是黄金。布雷顿森林体系实际上是一种国际金汇兑本位制，又称美元—黄金本位制。它使美元在战后国际货币体系中处于中心地位，美元成了黄金的“等价物”，各国货币只有通过美元才能同黄金发生关系。从此，美元就成为国际清算的支付手段和各国的主要储备货币。[①] 以美元为中心的国际货币从 1944 年宣布建立，到 1973 年瓦解，虽然运行时间较短，但对战后世界经济的恢复和发展发挥过重要作用，更是美国建立和维护世界霸权的重要工具，在世界现代史上具有重要地位。这里选取了《布雷顿森林协定：学术评论和重要历史文件》一书收录的《国际货币基金组织协定》和《国际复兴开发银行协定》两份文件原文。

I. *Bretton Woods Agreement*

Articles of Agreement of The International Bank for Reconstruction and Development,[②]

July 22, 1944

The Governments on whose behalf the present Agreement is signed agree as follows:

INTRODUCTORY ARTICLE

The International Bank for Reconstruction and Development is established and shall operate in accordance with the following provisions:

ARTICLE I. PURPOSES

The purposes of the Bank are:

(i) To assist in the reconstruction and development of territories of members by facilitating the investment of capital for productive purposes, including the restoration of economies destroyed or disrupted by war, the reconversion of productive facilities to peacetime needs and the encouragement of the development of productive facilities and resources in less developed countries.

① Giles Scott-Smith and J. Simon Rofe, *Global Perspectives on the Bretton Woods Conference and the Post-War World Order,* Gewerbestrasse: The Palgrave Macmillan, 2017, p. 2.

② Naomi Lamoreaux and Ian Shapiro, *The Bretton Woods Agreements: Together with Scholarly Commentaries and Essential Historical Documents*, London and New Haven: Yale University Press, 2019, pp. 311-341.

(ii) To promote private foreign investment by means of guarantees or participations in loans and other investments made by private investors; and when private capital is not available on reasonable terms, to supplement private investment by providing, on suitable conditions, finance for productive purposes out of its own capital, funds raised by it and its other resources.

(iii) To promote the long-range balanced growth of international trade and the maintenance of equilibrium in balances of payments by encouraging international investment for the development of the productive resources of members, thereby assisting in raising productivity, the standard of living and conditions of labor in their territories.

(iv) To arrange the loans made or guaranteed by it in relation to international loans through other channels so that the more useful and urgent projects, large and small alike, will be dealt with first.

(v) To conduct its operations with due regard to the effect of international investment on business conditions in the territories of members and, in the immediate post-war years, to assist in bringing about a smooth transition from a wartime to a peacetime economy.

The Bank shall be guided in all its decisions by the purposes set forth above.

ARTICLE II. MEMBERSHIP IN AND CAPITAL OF THE BANK

Section 1. Membership

(a) The original members of the Bank shall be those members of the International Monetary Fund which accept membership in the Bank before the date specified in Article XI, Section 2 (e).

(b) Membership shall be open to other members of the Fund, at such times and in accordance with such terms as may be prescribed by the Bank.

Section 2. Authorized Capital

(a) The authorized capital stock of the Bank shall be $10,000,000,000, in terms of United States dollars of the weight and fineness in effect on July 1, 1944. The capital stock shall be divided into 100,000 shares having a par value of $100,000 each, which shall be available for subscription only by members.

(b) The capital stock may be increased when the Bank deems it advisable by a three-fourths majority of the total voting power.

Section 3. Subscription of Shares

(a) Each member shall subscribe shares of the capital stock of the Bank. The minimum number of shares to be subscribed by the original members shall be those set forth in Schedule A. The minimum number of shares to be subscribed by other members shall be determined by the Bank, which shall reserve a sufficient portion of its capital stock for subscription by such members.

(b) The Bank shall prescribe rules laying down the conditions under which members may subscribe shares of the authorized capital stock of the Bank in addition to their minimum subscriptions.

(c) If the authorized capital stock of the Bank is increased, each member shall have a reasonable opportunity to subscribe, under such conditions as the Bank shall decide, a proportion of the increase of stock equivalent to the proportion which its stock theretofore subscribed bears to the total capital stock of the Bank, but no member shall be obligated to subscribe any part of the increased capital.

Section 4. Issue Price of Shares

Shares included in the minimum subscriptions of original members shall be issued at par. Other shares shall be issued at par unless the Bank by a majority of the total voting power decides in special circumstances to issue them on other terms.

Section 5. Division and Calls of Subscribed Capital

The subscription of each member shall be divided into two parts as follows:

(i) twenty percent shall be paid or subject to call under Section 7 (i) of this Article as needed by the Bank for its operations;

(ii) the remaining eighty percent shall be subject to call by the Bank only when required to meet obligations of the Bank created under Article IV, Sections I (a) (ii) and (iii).

Calls on unpaid subscriptions shall be uniform on all shares.

Section 6. Limitation on Liability

Liability on shares shall be limited to the unpaid portion of the issue price of the shares.

Section 7. Method of Payment of Subscriptions for Shares

Payment of subscriptions for shares shall be made in gold or United States dollars and in the currencies of the members as follows:

(i) under Section 5 (i) of this Article, two percent of the price of each share shall be payable in gold or United States dollars, and, when calls are made, the remaining eighteen percent shall be paid in the currency of the member;

(ii) when a call is made under Section 5 (ii) of this Article, payment may be made at the option of the member either in gold, in United States dollars or in the currency required to discharge the obligations of the Bank for the purpose for which the call is made;

(iii) when a member makes payments in any currency under (i) and (ii) above, such payments shall be made in amounts equal in value to the member's liability under the call. This liability shall be a proportionate part of the subscribed capital stock of the Bank as authorized and defined in Section 2 of this Article.

Section 8. Time of Payment of Subscriptions

(a) The two percent payable on each share in gold or United States dollars under Section 7 (i) of this Article, shall be paid within sixty days of the date on which the Bank begins operations, provided that

(i) any original member of the Bank whose metropolitan territory has suffered from enemy occupation or hostilities during the present war shall be granted the right to postpone payment of one-half percent until five years after that date;

(ii) an original member who cannot make such a payment because it has not recovered possession of its gold reserves which are still seized or immobilized as a result of the war may postpone all payment until such date as the Bank shall decide.

(b) The remainder of the price of each share payable under Section 7 (i) of this Article shall be paid as and when called by the Bank, provided that

(i) the Bank shall, within one year of its beginning operations, call not less than eight percent of the price of the share in addition to the payment of two percent referred to in (a) above;

(ii) not more than five percent of the price of the share shall be called in any period of three months.

Section 9. Maintenance of Value of Certain Currency Holdings of the Bank

(a) Whenever (i) the par value of a member's currency is reduced, or (ii) the foreign exchange value of a member's currency has, in the opinion of the Bank, depreciated to a significant extent within that member's territories, the member shall pay to the Bank within a reasonable time an additional amount of its own currency sufficient to maintain the value, as of the time of initial subscription, of the amount of the currency of such member which is held by the Bank and derived from currency originally paid in to the Bank by the member under Article II, Section 7 (i), from currency referred to in Article IV, Section 2 (b), or from any additional currency furnished under the provisions of the present paragraph, and which has not been repurchased by the member for gold or for the currency of any member which is acceptable to the Bank.

(b) Whenever the par value of a member's currency is increased, the Bank shall return to such member within a reasonable time an amount of that member's currency equal to the increase in the value of the amount of such currency described in (a) above.

(c) The provisions of the preceding paragraphs may be waived by the Bank when a uniform proportionate change in the par values of the currencies of all its members is made by the International Monetary Fund.

Section 10. Restriction on Disposal of Shares

Shares shall not be pledged or encumbered in any manner whatever and they shall be transferable only to the Bank.

Articles of Agreement of the International Monetary Fund,①

July 22, 1944

The Governments on whose behalf the present Agreement is signed agree as follows:

TRODUCTIORY ARTICLE

The International Monetary Fund is established and shall operate in accordance with the following provisions.

Article I. Purposes

The purposes of the International Monetary Fund are:

(i) To promote international monetary cooperation through a permanent institution which provides the machinery for consultation and collaboration on international monetary problems.

(ii) To facilitate the expansion and balanced growth of international trade, and to contribute thereby to the promotion and maintenance of high levels of employment and real income and to the development of the productive resources of all members as primary objectives of economic policy.

(iii) To promote exchange stability, to maintain orderly exchange arrangements among members, and to avoid competitive exchange depreciation.

(iv) To assist in the establishment of a multilateral system of payments in respect of current transactions between members and in the elimination of foreign exchange restrictions which hamper the growth of world trade.

(v) To give confidence to members by making the Fund's resources available

---

① Naomi Lamoreaux and Ian Shapiro, *The Bretton Woods Agreements: Together with Scholarly Commentaries and Essential Historical Documents*, London and New Haven: Yale University Press, 2019, pp.275-310.

to them under adequate safeguards, thus providing them with opportunity to correct maladjustments in their balance of payments without resorting to measures destructive of national or international prosperity.

(vi) In accordance with the above, to shorten the duration and lessen the degree of disequilibrium in the international balances of payments of members.

The Fund shall be guided in all its decisions by the purposes set forth in this Article.

ARTICLE II. MEMBERSHIP

Section 1. Original Members

The original members of the Fund shall be those of the countries represented at the United Nations Monetary and Financial Conference whose governments accept membership before the date specified in Article XX, Section 2 (e).

Section 2. Other Members

Membership shall be open to the governments of other countries at such times and in accordance with such terms as may be prescribed by the Fund.

ARTICLE VIII. GENERAL OBLIGATIONS OF MEMBERS

Section 1. Introduction

In addition to the obligations assumed under other articles of this Agreement, each member undertakes the obligations set out in this Article.

Section 2. Avoidance of Restrictions on Current Payments

(a) Subject to the provisions of Article VII, Section 3 (b), and Article XIV, Section 2, no member shall, without the approval of the Fund, impose restrictions on the making of payments and transfers for current international transactions.

(b) Exchange contracts which involve the currency of any member and which are contrary to the exchange control regulations of that member maintained or imposed consistently with this Agreement shall be unenforceable in the territories of any member. In addition, members may, by mutual accord, co-operate in measures for the purpose of making the exchange control regulations of either member more effective, provided that such measures and regulations are consistent with this Agreement.

Section 3. Avoidance of Discriminatory Currency Practices

No member shall engage in, or permit any of its fiscal agencies referred to in Article V, Section 1, to engage in, any discriminatory currency arrangements or multiple currency practices except as authorized under this Agreement or approved by the Fund. If such arrangements and practices are engaged in at the date when this Agreement enters into force the member concerned shall consult with the Fund as to their progressive removal unless they are maintained or imposed under Article XIV, Section 2, in which case the provisions of Section 4 of that Article shall apply.

Section 4. Convertibility of Foreign held Balances

(a) Each member shall buy balances of its currency held by another member if the latter, in requesting the purchase, represents

(i) that the balances to be bought have been recently acquired as a result of current transactions; or

(ii) that their conversion is needed for making payments for current transactions.

The buying member shall have the option to pay either in the currency of the member making the request or in gold.

(b) The obligation in (a) above shall not apply

(i) when the convertibility of the balances has been restricted consistently with Section 2 of this Article, or Article VI, Section 3; or

(ii) when the balances have accumulated as a result of transactions effected before the removal by a member of restrictions maintained or imposed under Article XIV, Section 2; or

(iii) when the balances have been acquired contrary to the exchange regulations of the member which is asked to buy them; or

(iv) when the currency of the member requesting the purchase has been declared scarce under Article VII, Section 3 (a); or

(v) when the member requested to make the purchase is for any reason not entitled to buy currencies of other members from the Fund for its own currency.

Section 5. Furnishing of Information

(a) The Fund may require members to furnish it with such information as it deems necessary for its operations, including, as the minimum necessary for the effective discharge of the Fund's duties, national data on the following matters:

(i) Official holdings at home and abroad, of (1) gold, (2) foreign exchange.

(ii) Holdings at home and abroad by banking and financial agencies, other than official agencies, of (1) gold, (2) foreign exchange.

(iii) Production of gold.

(iv) Gold exports and imports according to countries of destination and origin.

(v) Total exports and imports of merchandise, in terms of local currency values, according to countries of destination and origin.

(vi) International balance of payments, including (1) trade in goods and services, (2) gold transactions, (3) known capital transactions, and (4) other items.

(vii) International investment position, i.e., investments within the territories of the member owned abroad and investments abroad owned by persons in its territories so far as it is possible to furnish this information.

(viii) National income.

(ix) Price indices, i.e., indices of commodity prices in wholesale and retail markets and of export and import prices.

(x) Buying and selling rates for foreign currencies.

(xi) Exchange controls, i.e., a comprehensive statement of exchange controls in effect at the time of assuming membership in the Fund and details of subsequent changes as they occur.

(xii) Where official clearing arrangements exist, details of amounts awaiting clearance in respect of commercial and financial transactions, and of the length of time during which such arrears have been outstanding.

(b) In requesting information the Fund shall take into consideration the varying ability of members to furnish the data requested. Members shall be under no obligation to furnish information in such detail that the affairs of individuals or corporations are disclosed. Members undertake, however, to furnish the desired information in as detailed and accurate a manner as is practicable, and, so far as possible, to avoid mere estimates.

(c) The Fund may arrange to obtain further information by agreement with members. It shall act as a centre for the collection and exchange of information on monetary and financial problems, thus facilitating the preparation of studies designed to assist members in developing policies which further the purposes of the Fund.

Section 6. Consultation between Members Regarding Existing International Agreements

Where under this Agreement a member is authorized in the special or temporary circumstances specified in the Agreement to maintain or establish restrictions on exchange transactions, and there are other engagements between members entered into prior to this Agreement which conflict with the application of such restrictions, the parties to such engagements will consult with one another with a view to making such mutually acceptable adjustments as may be necessary. The provisions of this Article shall be without prejudice to the operation of Article VII, Section 5.

II. Common Terms, Words and Phrases for the Text

Special Drawing Rights (SDR) 特别提款权

Special Disbursement Account (SDA) 特别支付账号

investment account 投资账号

real income 实际收入

quotas 份额

subscriptions 认缴费

securities 证券

general resources accounts 普通资金账户

exchange 汇兑

exchange rates 汇率

international monetary system 国际货币制度

surveillance 监督

par values 平价

stabilization fund 平准基金

waiver 放弃

charges 收费

currency 货币

reserve tranche 储备档

service charge 服务费

remuneration 酬金

criterion 准则

computations 计算

maintenance of value 价值的维持

per capita income 人均收入

capital transfers 资金转移

capital transactions 资本交易

replenishment 补充

administration of restrictions 限制的实施

effect 效果，影响

current payment 经常性支付

exchange contracts 汇兑契约

furnishing of information 提供信息

foreign exchange 外汇

national income 国民收入

exchange controls 外汇管制

official clearing arrangements 官方的清算安排

arrears 逾期欠款

corporation 公司

consultation 协商

reserve assets 储备资产

customs duties 关税

investment 投资

international balance 国际收支，国际结算

disequilibrium 不平衡

III. Exercises and Thinking

1. Please talk about the background of the establishment of the World Bank and the International Monetary Fund.

2. Please talk about the main functions and objectives of the World Bank and the International Monetary Fund.

3. Please discuss about what are the differences between the World Bank and the International Monetary Fund.

IV. Further Readings and Internet Links

1. Further Readings

[加] 埃里克赫莱纳:《布雷顿森林被遗忘的基石：国际发展与战后秩序的构建》，张士伟译，人民出版社 2019 年版。

Naomi Lamoreaux and Ian Shapiro, *The Bretton Woods Agreements: Together with Scholarly Commentaries and Essential Historical Documents*, London and New Haven: Yale

University Press, 2019.

2. Internet Links

Proceedings and Documents of the United Nations Monetary and Financial Conference, Bretton Woods, New Hampshire: https://fraser.stlouisfed.org/title/proceedings-documents-united-nations-monetary-financial-conference-bretton-woods-new-hampshire-july-1-22-1944-430

Unit 36

Charter of the United Nations
《联合国宪章》

联合国成立于 1945 年 10 月 24 日，截至 2024 年 7 月，共有 193 个成员国，是当今世界上最重要的国家间合作组织，在维护世界和平与发展、协调解决国际纠纷、共同应对全人类面临的问题等方面发挥着重要作用。联合国是第二次世界大战的产物，也是 20 世纪国际社会的一件大事。

二战期间，反法西斯国家就已经开始商讨战后国际秩序的重建问题，其中建立联合国就是各国关心的话题。1941 年 6 月，英、美、法联合发表《同盟国宣言》，提出了制止侵略、维护和平以及促成国际合作的原则。1941 年 8 月，英、美发表《大西洋宪章》，标志着国际反法西斯统一战线正式形成。1942 年 1 月 1 日，包括中、美、英、苏在内的 26 国代表在美国华盛顿签订了《联合国家宣言》，又称《二十六国宣言》。该宣言表示支持《大西洋宪章》，第一次使用“联合国”（United Nations）一词，为这个新组织的建立奠定了基础。1944 年 8 月至 12 月，苏、英、美 3 国和中、英、美 3 国代表先后在华盛顿的敦巴顿橡树林举行会议，提出了组织联合国的方案，并拟定出宪章的基本轮廓。1945 年 4 月 25 日，50 国代表在美国旧金山举行联合国国际组织会议，两个月后即 1945 年 6 月 26 日，50 国代表正式签署了《联合国宪章》。中共代表董必武作为中国代表团成员参加了这次会议，并在宪章上签字。《联合国宪章》于同年 10 月 24 日正式生效，联合国正式宣告成立。这是“联合国日”的由来。

《联合国宪章》是联合国的创始文件，不仅是联合国各成员国共同遵守的法律文件，也是公认的国际法文献。除序言和结语外，《联合国宪章》共分为 19

章111条。序言表达了创建联合国是各国政府及其人民的共同理想和目标。第一章规定了联合国组织的四项宗旨与七项原则。第一条规定了联合国的四项宗旨：（1）维护国际和平与安全；（2）发展各国间的友好关系；（3）促进国际间有关经济、社会及文化等方面的合作；（4）协调各国行动。第二条为联合国本身及其成员国规定的应遵循的七项基本原则：（1）联合国组织基于所有会员国主权平等的原则；（2）各会员国应该忠实履行其依据宪章规定所承担的义务；（3）各会员国应该以和平方法解决其国际争端；（4）各会员国在其国际关系中不得以不符合联合国宗旨的任何方式进行武力威胁或者使用武力；（5）各会员国对联合国依照宪章所采取的任何行动应给予一切协助；（6）联合国在维护国际和平与安全的必要范围内，应确保使非会员国遵循上述原则；（7）联合国不得干涉在本质上属于任何国家内管辖的事项，但此项规定不应妨碍联合国对威胁和平、破坏和平的行为及侵略行径采取强制行动。第二章规定了联合国的会员。其中第三条规定：凡曾经参加旧金山联合国国际组织会议或此前曾签字于1942年1月1日《联合国宣言》之国家，签订本《宪章》，且依宪章第一百一十条规定而予以批准者，均为联合国之创始会员国。第四条规定了联合国会员国的资格：凡其他爱好和平之国家，接受宪章所规定之义务，经本组织认为确能并愿意履行该项义务者，即可成为联合国成员国。要成为联合国的会员国还需经过安理会推荐决定。第三章至第十五章规定了联合国六大主要机关的组成、职权范围、活动程序与主要工作内容。根据第七条的规定，联合国的六大主要机构包括：联合国大会、安全理事会、经济与社会理事会、托管理事会、秘书处和国际法院。第十六章是杂项条款，主要规定了条约应该尽速登记，未登记条约的效力，宪章义务的优先地位，联合国及其代表的特权与豁免；第十七章规定了过渡安全办法，主要规定了安理会5个常任理事国的特殊权利以及“敌国条款”；第十八章规定了宪章的修正；第十九章规定了宪章的批准及其签字。《联合国宪章》生效后，随着国际社会的变化又进行了个别条款的修订。

这里选取了《联合国宪章》原文，以及《联合国大会议事规则》和《联合国礼宾手册》的一部分内容，旨在加深理解联合国的国际地位、议事程序和日常安排。《联合国大会议事规则》的英文版本采用的是 2021 年 9 月 10 日审议通过的版本。《联合国礼宾手册》的英文版本采用的是 2023 年 9 月第 78 届联合国大会通过的版本。以上文献均见于联合国网站。

I. *CHARTER OF THE UNITED NATIONS*①

WE THE PEOPLES OF THE UNITED NATIONS DETERMINED

to save succeeding generations from the scourge of war, which twice in our lifetime has brought untold sorrow to mankind, and

to reaffirm faith in fundamental human rights, in the dignity and worth of the human person, in the equal rights of men and women and of nations large and small, and

to establish conditions under which justice and respect for the obligations arising from treaties and other sources of international law can be maintained, and

to promote social progress and better standards of life in larger freedom,

AND FOR THESE ENDS

to practice tolerance and live together in peace with one another as good neighbours, and

to unite our strength to maintain international peace and security, and

to ensure, by the acceptance of principles and the institution of methods, that armed force shall not be used, save in the common interest, and

to employ international machinery for the promotion of the economic and social advancement of all peoples,

HAVE RESOLVED TO COMBINE OUR EFFORTS TO ACCOMPLISH THESE AIMS.

Accordingly, our respective Governments, through representatives assembled in the city of San Francisco, who have exhibited their full powers found to be in good and due

---

① Ian Shapiro and Joseph Lampert, edited, *Charter of the United Nations: Together with Scholarly Commentaries and Essential Historical Documents*, New Haven and London: Yale University Press, 2014, pp.14−45.

form, have agreed to the present Charter of the United Nations and do hereby establish an international organization to be known as the United Nations.

CHAPTER I: PURPOSES AND PRINCIPLES

Article 1

The Purposes of the United Nations are:

1. To maintain international peace and security, and to that end: to take effective collective measures for the prevention and removal of threats to the peace, and for the suppression of acts of aggression or other breaches of the peace, and to bring about by peaceful means, and in conformity with the principles of justice and international law, adjustment or settlement of international disputes or situations which might lead to a breach of the peace;

2. To develop friendly relations among nations based on respect for the principle of equal rights and self-determination of peoples, and to take other appropriate measures to strengthen universal peace;

3. To achieve international co-operation in solving international problems of an economic, social, cultural, or humanitarian character, and in promoting and encouraging respect for human rights and for fundamental freedoms for all without distinction as to race, sex, language, or religion; and

4. To be a centre for harmonizing the actions of nations in the attainment of these common ends.

Article 2

The Organization and its Members, in pursuit of the Purposes stated in Article 1, shall act in accordance with the following Principles.

1. The Organization is based on the principle of the sovereign equality of all its Members.

2. All Members, in order to ensure to all of them the rights and benefits resulting from membership, shall fulfill in good faith the obligations assumed by them in

accordance with the present Charter.

3. All Members shall settle their international disputes by peaceful means in such a manner that international peace and security, and justice, are not endangered.

4. All Members shall refrain in their international relations from the threat or use of force against the territorial integrity or political independence of any state, or in any other manner inconsistent with the Purposes of the United Nations.

5. All Members shall give the United Nations every assistance in any action it takes in accordance with the present Charter, and shall refrain from giving assistance to any state against which the United Nations is taking preventive or enforcement action.

6. The Organization shall ensure that states which are not Members of the United Nations act in accordance with these Principles so far as may be necessary for the maintenance of international peace and security.

7. Nothing contained in the present Charter shall authorize the United Nations to intervene in matters which are essentially within the domestic jurisdiction of any state or shall require the Members to submit such matters to settlement under the present Charter; but this principle shall not prejudice the application of enforcement measures under Chapter Ⅶ.

CHAPTER II: MEMBERSHIP

Article 3

The original Members of the United Nations shall be the states which, having participated in the United Nations Conference on International Organization at San Francisco, or having previously signed the Declaration by United Nations of 1 January 1942, sign the present Charter and ratify it in accordance with Article 110.

Article 4

1. Membership in the United Nations is open to all other peace–loving states which accept the obligations contained in the present Charter and, in the judgment of the Organization, are able and willing to carry out these obligations.

2. The admission of any such state to membership in the United Nations will be effected by a decision of the General Assembly upon the recommendation of the Security Council.

Article 5

A Member of the United Nations against which preventive or enforcement action has been taken by the Security Council may be suspended from the exercise of the rights and privileges of membership by the General Assembly upon the recommendation of the Security Council. The exercise of these rights and privileges may be restored by the Security Council.

Article 6

A Member of the United Nations which has persistently violated the Principles contained in the present Charter may be expelled from the Organization by the General Assembly upon the recommendation of the Security Council.

CHAPTER III: ORGANS

Article 7

1. There are established as principal organs of the United Nations: a General Assembly, a Security Council, an Economic and Social Council, a Trusteeship Council, an International Court of Justice and a Secretariat.

2. Such subsidiary organs as may be found necessary may be established in accordance with the present Charter.

Article 8

The United Nations shall place no restrictions on the eligibility of men and women to participate in any capacity and under conditions of equality in its principal and subsidiary organs.

CHAPTER IV: THE GENERAL ASSEMBLY

Composition

Article 9

1. The General Assembly shall consist of all the Members of the United Nations.

2. Each Member shall have not more than five representatives in the General Assembly.

Functions and Powers

Article 10

The General Assembly may discuss any questions or any matters within the scope of the present Charter or relating to the powers and functions of any organs provided for in the present Charter, and, except as provided in Article 12, may make recommendations to the Members of the United Nations or to the Security Council or to both on any such questions or matters.

Article 11

1. The General Assembly may consider the general principles of co-operation in the maintenance of international peace and security, including the principles governing disarmament and the regulation of armaments, and may make recommendations with regard to such principles to the Members or to the Security Council or to both.

2. The General Assembly may discuss any questions relating to the maintenance of international peace and security brought before it by any Member of the United Nations, or by the Security Council, or by a state which is not a Member of the United Nations in accordance with Article 35, paragraph 2, and, except as provided in Article 12, may make recommendations with regard to any such questions to the state or states concerned or to the Security Council or to both. Any such question on which action is necessary shall be referred to the Security Council by the General Assembly either before or after discussion.

3. The General Assembly may call the attention of the Security Council to situations

which are likely to endanger international peace and security.

4. The powers of the General Assembly set forth in this Article shall not limit the general scope of Article 10.

Article 12

1. While the Security Council is exercising in respect of any dispute or situation the functions assigned to it in the present Charter, the General Assembly shall not make any recommendation with regard to that dispute or situation unless the Security Council so requests.

2. The Secretary-General, with the consent of the Security Council, shall notify the General Assembly at each session of any matters relative to the maintenance of international peace and security which are being dealt with by the Security Council and shall similarly notify the General Assembly, or the Members of the United Nations if the General Assembly is not in session, immediately the Security Council ceases to deal with such matters.

Article 13

1. The General Assembly shall initiate studies and make recommendations for the purpose of: a. promoting international co-operation in the political field and encouraging the progressive development of international law and its codification; b. promoting international co-operation in the economic, social, cultural, educational, and health fields, and assisting in the realization of human rights and fundamental freedoms for all without distinction as to race, sex, language, or religion.

2. The further responsibilities, functions and powers of the General Assembly with respect to matters mentioned in paragraph 1 (b) above are set forth in Chapters IX and X.

Article 14

Subject to the provisions of Article 12, the General Assembly may recommend measures for the peaceful adjustment of any situation, regardless of origin, which it deems likely to impair the general welfare or friendly relations among nations, including situations resulting from a violation of the provisions of the present Charter setting forth the Purposes and Principles of the United Nations.

Article 15

1. The General Assembly shall receive and consider annual and special reports from the Security Council; these reports shall include an account of the measures that the Security Council has decided upon or taken to maintain international peace and security.

2. The General Assembly shall receive and consider reports from the other organs of the United Nations.

Article 16

The General Assembly shall perform such functions with respect to the international trusteeship system as are assigned to it under Chapters XII and XIII, including the approval of the trusteeship agreements for areas not designated as strategic.

Article 17

1. The General Assembly shall consider and approve the budget of the Organization.

2. The expenses of the Organization shall be borne by the Members as apportioned by the General Assembly.

3. The General Assembly shall consider and approve any financial and budgetary arrangements with specialized agencies referred to in Article 57 and shall examine the administrative budgets of such specialized agencies with a view to making recommendations to the agencies concerned.

Voting

Article 18

1. Each member of the General Assembly shall have one vote.

2. Decisions of the General Assembly on important questions shall be made by a two–thirds majority of the members present and voting. These questions shall include: recommendations with respect to the maintenance of international peace and security, the election of the non–permanent members of the Security Council, the election of the

members of the Economic and Social Council, the election of members of the Trusteeship Council in accordance with paragraph 1 (c) of Article 86, the admission of new Members to the United Nations, the suspension of the rights and privileges of membership, the expulsion of Members, questions relating to the operation of the trusteeship system, and budgetary questions.

3. Decisions on other questions, including the determination of additional categories of questions to be decided by a two-thirds majority, shall be made by a majority of the members present and voting.

Article 19

A Member of the United Nations which is in arrears in the payment of its financial contributions to the Organization shall have no vote in the General Assembly if the amount of its arrears equals or exceeds the amount of the contributions due from it for the preceding two full years. The General Assembly may, nevertheless, permit such a Member to vote if it is satisfied that the failure to pay is due to conditions beyond the control of the Member.

RULES OF PROCEDURE OF THE GENERAL ASSEMBLY[①]

RULES OF PROCEDURE

I. SESSIONS: REGULAR SESSIONS

Opening date

Rule 1

(a) The General Assembly shall meet every year in regular session commencing on the Tuesday of the second week in September, counting from the first week that contains at least one working day.

(b) The general debate in the General Assembly shall open on the Tuesday of the fourth week in September, counting from the first week that contains at least one working

① https://www.un.org/en/ga/about/ropga/

day, and shall be held without interruption over a period of nine working days.

Closing date

Rule 2

On the recommendation of the General Committee, the General Assembly shall, at the beginning of each session, fix a closing date for the session.

Place of meeting

Rule 3

The General Assembly shall meet at the Headquarters of the United Nations unless convened elsewhere in pursuance of a decision taken at a previous session or at the request of a majority of the Members of the United Nations.

Rule 4

Any Member of the United Nations may, at least one hundred and twenty days before the date fixed for the opening of a regular session, request that the session be held elsewhere than at the Headquarters of the United Nations. The Secretary–General shall immediately communicate the request, together with his recommendations, to the other Members of the United Nations. If within thirty days of the date of this communication a majority of the Members concur in the request, the session shall be held Accordingly.

Notification of session

Rule 5

The Secretary–General shall notify the Members of the United Nations, at least sixty days in advance, of the opening of a regular session.

Temporary adjournment of session

Rule 6

The General Assembly may decide at any session to adjourn temporarily and resume its meetings at a later date.

SPECIAL SESSIONS

Summoning by the General Assembly

Rule 7[①]

The General Assembly may fix a date for a special session.

Summoning at the request of the Security Council or Members

Rule 8

(a) Special sessions of the General Assembly shall be convened within fifteen days of the receipt by the Secretary–General of a request for such a session from the Security Council or from a majority of the Members of the United Nations or of the concurrence of a majority of Members as provided in rule 9.

(b) Emergency special sessions pursuant to General Assembly resolution 377 A (V) shall be convened within twenty–four hours of the receipt by the Secretary–General of a request for such a session from the Security Council, on the vote of any nine members thereof, or of a request from a majority of the Members of the United Nations expressed by vote in the Interim Committee or otherwise, or of the concurrence of a majority of Members as provided in rule 9.

Request by Members

Rule 9

(a) Any Member of the United Nations may request the Secretary–General to convene a special session of the General Assembly. The Secretary–General shall immediately inform the other Members of the request and inquire whether they concur in it. If within thirty days of the date of the communication of the Secretary–General a majority of the Members concur in the request, a special session of the General Assembly shall be convened in accordance with rule 8.

(b) This rule shall apply also to a request by any Member of the United Nations

---

① Rule based directly on a provision of the Charter (Article 20).

for an emergency special session pursuant to resolution 377 A (V). In such a case, the Secretary–General shall communicate with the other Members by the most expeditious means of communication available.

Notification of session

Rule 10

The Secretary–General shall notify the Members of the United Nations, at least fourteen days in advance, of the opening of a special session convened at the request of the Security Council, and at least ten days in advance in the case of a session convened at the request of a majority of the Members or upon the concurrence of a majority in the request of any Member. In the case of an emergency special session convened pursuant to rule 8 (b), the Secretary–General shall notify Members at least twelve hours before the opening of the session.

ANNEX X

Oath of office

"I solemnly declare that I shall truthfully perform my duties and exercise the functions entrusted to me as President of the General Assembly of the United Nations in all loyalty, discretion and conscience, and that I shall discharge these functions and regulate my conduct with the interest of the United Nations only in view and in accordance with the Charter of the United Nations and the code of ethics for the President of the General Assembly, without seeking or accepting any instruction in regard to the performance of my duties from any Government or other source external to the Organization."

ANNEX XI

Code of ethics for the President of the General Assembly

1. The President of the General Assembly in performing his or her duties and responsibilities as an elected official, fully in line with the Charter of the United Nations and the rules of procedure of the General Assembly, shall at all times from the date of

election observe the highest standards of ethical conduct.

2. The President shall perform his or her duties and responsibilities in an impartial and equitable manner and in full honesty and good faith.

3. The President shall avoid any action that might result in or create the appearance of:

(a) The use of the office of the Presidency or resources attached thereto for private gain;

(b) Giving unwarranted preferential treatment to any State, organization or person;

(c) Impeding the work of the Organization, or taking a preferential, biased or prejudged approach;

(d) Affecting adversely the confidence of Member States in the integrity of the work of the Organization.

4. The President shall engage with Member States in a consultative and cooperative manner, while at the same time refraining from receiving or accepting instructions from any individual or governmental or non–governmental organization or group whatsoever.

5. The President shall avoid any situation involving a conflict between his or her own personal or private interest and the interests of the Presidency or the United Nations.

6. The President shall ensure the greatest possible transparency in the utilization of property, premises, services and resources made available for the discharge of the functions of the office and ensure that they are used only for the official business of the Presidency and not for other purposes.

7. The President shall ensure the greatest possible transparency in any external activities, and any commercial dealings, to protect against conflict of interest. Holding of any commercial office during his or her term in office is not compatible with the post of the President.

8. In the event that the President considers that a conflict of interest may arise, he or she shall recuse himself or herself from handling the matter and, in accordance with the rules of procedure of the General Assembly, appoint an Acting President in relation

to that matter or meeting.

9. In the fulfilment of his or her mandate, the President is accountable to the General Assembly.

10. Any reference to the President in the present code shall also include members of his or her office while in the exercise of their functions as members of the Office of the President of the General Assembly.

11. Nothing in this code shall preclude the President or members of his or her Office from being seconded from their Government or from retaining the privileges, immunities and diplomatic status granted by a Member State.

Delegates Handbook Seventy-eighth session of the General Assembly of the United Nations①

III. Conference services

Programme of meetings

The programme of meetings is prepared by the Meetings Management Section. The daily programme of meetings is published online in the *Journal of the United Nations*.

All authorized clients, including permanent missions and United Nations entities, that wish to book conference rooms and meeting services should submit a request through the gMeets one-stop shop portal (conferences.unite.un.org/gMeets). The portal is a self-service, single-entry point to submit requests for conference rooms and meeting services at Headquarters. All mandatory fields, including the screening questions, must be completed. Requests are reviewed and confirmed by the Meetings Management Section. Requestors can track the status of their requests in the "All My Requests" section of the portal. For additional information, please contact the Meetings Management Section (gmeets@un.org). For technical support related to the gMeets one-stop shop portal and user accounts, please contact the Helpdesk (gmeets-helpdesk@un.org).

① https://www.un.org/dgacm/en/content/protocol/delegates-handbook.

Statements in plenary meetings and in meetings of the Main Committees

Delegations are requested to submit their statements (in both PDF and Microsoft Word formats, whenever possible) by email to the eStatements section of the *Journal* (estatements@un.org) well in advance of the meeting but no later than two hours before delivery and not in hard-copy format. The name of the meeting and the speaker, as well as the agenda item, should be indicated in the subject line of the email message and in the heading of the statement. The statements will not be released until their delivery.

Only statements presented during the course of the meeting will be posted in the eStatements section of the *Journal*.

Questions related to eStatements should be addressed to the Chief of the Meetings Support Section (chiefmss-dgacm@un.org).

Interpretation

In meetings where interpretation is provided, statements made in any of the six official languages of the United Nations are interpreted into the other official languages. Speakers are requested to deliver their statements at a speed that is interpretable. Although delegations are increasingly being given a time frame in which to deliver their statements, they are kindly requested to do so at a normal speed, if possible, to enable the interpreters to give an accurate and complete rendition of their statements. When statements are delivered at a fast pace to comply with the time limit, the quality of interpretation may suffer. It is suggested that statements be delivered at a speed not exceeding the equivalent of 100 to 120 words per minute in English.

Any speaker may also make a statement in a language other than the official languages. In such cases, in accordance with rule 53 of the rules of procedure of the General Assembly, the delegation in question must provide an interpreter from the non-official language into an official language. Exceptional arrangements for bidirectional interpretation facilities for Heads of States or Government may be requested. However, there will be only limited facilities to accommodate such non-official language interpreters on site. Delegations seeking to provide their own interpreters for non-official languages are requested to inform the Meetings Management Section well in advance by email (gmeets@un.org) and to copy the Interpretation Service (is-unhq@un.org) and the Broadcast and Conference Support Section (request-for-services@un.org). The Meetings Management Section will provide further instructions.

II. Common Terms, Words and Phrases for the Text

international court 国际法院

the Security Council 安全理事会

the Economic and Social Council 经济及事务委员会

review 审查

human rights 人权

human person 人格

worth 价值

international law 国际法

treaty 条约

international peace 国际和平

security 安全

common interest 公共利益

international machinery 国际机构

international relations 国际关系

self-determination 自决

sovereignty 主权

sovereignty equality 主权平等

good faith 善意

justice 正义

independence 独立

trusteeship system 托管制度

trusteeship council 托管委员会

representative 代表

secretary-general 秘书长

subsidiary organs 辅助机构

conciliation 和解

equal rights 平等的权利

specialized agencies 专门机关

territory 领土

miscellaneous provisions 杂项条款

immunity 豁免

amendment 修正，修订

constitutional processes 宪法程序

protocol 协议，外交礼节

administering authority 管理当局

ratification 批准

interpretation 口译

translation 笔译

III. Exercises and Thinking

1. Please talk about the historical background and significance of the establishment of the United Nations.

2. Please talk about the main organizational structures of the United Nations and their basic functions.

3. Please discuss with students about the role of the United Nations in today's world.

IV. Further Readings and Internet Links

1. Further Readings

郑瑞珺、席桂桂:《联合国研究》,时事出版社 2021 年版。

Ian Shapiro and Joseph Lampert, edited, *Charter of the United Nations: Together with Scholarly Commentaries and Essential Historical Documents*, New Haven and London: Yale University Press, 2014.

2. Internet Links

联合国：https://www.un.org/en

Unit 37

Declaration of the Heads of State or Government of Non-Aligned Countries

《不结盟国家和政府首脑宣言》

第二次世界大战结束后，长期受到帝国主义国家侵略压迫的殖民地和半殖民地纷纷独立。当时国际上形成了以美苏为首的两大政治军事阵营。这两大阵营竭力把新独立的主权国家纳入到各自的集团。许多新兴独立国家为了维护国家的主权独立，不依附集团、不参与美苏双方的争霸斗争，宣布奉行独立自主的“不结盟政策”。

不结盟运动始于二战之后，在南斯拉夫总统铁托、印度总理尼赫鲁、埃及总统纳赛尔、柬埔寨亲王西哈努克、印尼总统苏加诺等共同倡导下，不结盟运动得以开展。1961 年 2 月至 4 月，铁托展开一次为期两个月的非洲和亚洲的旅行，向各个独立国家游说，建议举行不结盟国家首脑会议。1961 年 6 月 5 日至 13 日，不结盟国家会议筹备会议在埃及的开罗召开。发起国是南斯拉夫、阿拉伯联合共和国、印度、印度尼西亚和阿富汗 5 国，共有 21 个国家派外长或大使参加。筹备会议决定 1961 年 9 月 1 日在南斯拉夫的贝尔格莱德召开不结盟国家和政府首脑会议。其后又召开了不结盟国家大使级会议、不结盟国家预备会议。[①] 第一次不结盟国家和政府首脑会议于 1961 年 9 月 1 日至 6 日在贝尔格莱德举行，这次会议宣告不结盟运动正式成立。会议通过了不结盟国家和政府首脑会议宣言、关于战争的危险和呼吁和平的声明等文件。

1961 年于贝尔格莱德第一次不结盟国家和政府首脑会议确定的不结盟运动

---

① 中国国际问题研究所编辑部编：《不结盟运动主要文件集》，中国对外翻译出版公司 1987 年版，第 3 页。

的最初原则包括：在和平共处的基础上对不同政治和社会制度的国家奉行独立政策，支持民族解放运动，反对集团和建立军事基地，要求解决经济问题和消除经济不平等现象，所有国家都有参与解决影响所有国家地位和生活的国际问题的平等权利等。这些原则和目标代表了不结盟国家和广大发展中国家的根本利益和要求。不结盟运动不设总部，无常设机构（1973 年成立了协调局），无成文章程；各种会议均采取协商一致原则；遇有不同意见，各成员国可以书面形式向主席国正式提出保留，以示不受有关决议或文件的约束。不结盟运动一般每 3 年召开一次会议。至今不结盟运动共举行了 19 次峰会。第 19 次峰会于 2024 年 1 月 19 日至 20 日在乌干达举行。乌干达为 2024—2027 年的主席国。目前，不结盟运动共有 120 个成员，18 个观察员国家。中国于 1992 年成为不结盟运动的观察员国家。

这里选取了第一次不结盟国家首脑会议通过的《不结盟国家和政府首脑宣言》，以期读者更深入地理解不结盟运动的初衷。

I. *DECLARATION OF THE HEADS OF STATE OR GOVERNMENT OF NON-ALIGNED COUNTRIES*①

The conference of heads of state or government of the following non-aligned countries:

1. Afghanistan　　2. Algerua
3. Burma　　4. Cambodia
5. Ceylon　　6. Congo
7. Cuba　　8. Cyprus
9. Ethiopia　　10. Ghana
11. Guinea　　12. India
13. Indonesia　　14. Iraq

① Henry M. Christman ed, *Neither East Nor West: The Basic Documents of Non-Alignment*, New York: Sheed & Ward, 1973, pp. 53–65.

15. Lebanon
16. Mali
17. Morocco
18. Nepal
19. Saudi Arabia
20. Somalia
21. Sudan
22. Tunisia
23. United Arab Republic
24. Yemen
25. Yugoslavia

and of the following countries represented by observers:

1. Bolivia 2. Brazil 3. Ecuador

was held in Belgrade from September 1 to 6, 1961, for the purpose of exchanging views on international problems with a view to contributing more effectively to world peace and security and peaceful cooperation among peoples.

The heads of state or government of the aforementioned countries have met at a moment when international events have taken a turn for the worst and when world peace is seriously threatened. Deeply concerned for the future of peace, voicing the aspirations of the vast majority of people of the world, aware that, in our time, no people and no government can or should abandon its responsibilities in regard to the safeguarding of world peace, the participating countries—having examined in detail, in an atmosphere of equality, sincerity and mutual confidence, the current state of international relations and trends prevailing in the present-day world—make the following declaration:

The heads of state or government of non-aligned countries noting that there are crises that lead towards a world conflict in the transition from an old order based on domination to a new order based on cooperation between nations, founded on freedom, equality and social justice for the promotion of prosperity; considering that the dynamic processes and forms of social change often result in or represent a conflict between the old established and the new emerging nationalist forces; considering that a lasting peace can be achieved only if this confrontation leads to a world where the domination of colonialism-imperialism and neo-colonialism in all their manifestations is radically eliminated;

and recognizing the fact that acute emergencies threatening world peace now exist in this period of conflict in Africa, Asia, Europe and Latin America and big power rivalry likely to result in world conflagration cannot be excluded;

that to eradicate basically the source of conflict is to eradicate colonialism in all its manifestations and to accept and practice a policy of peaceful co–existence in the world;

that guided by these principles the period of transition and conflict can lay a firm foundation of cooperation and brotherhood between nations, state the following:

I

War has never threatened mankind with graver consequences than today. On the other hand, never before has mankind had at its disposal stronger forces for eliminating war as an instrument of policy in international relations.

Imperialism is weakening. Colonial empires and other forms of foreign oppression of peoples in Asia, Africa and Latin America are gradually disappearing from the stage of history. Great successes have been achieved in the struggle of many peoples for national independence and equality. In the same way, the peoples of Latin America are continuing to make an increasingly effective contribution to the improvement of international relations. Great social changes in the world are further promoting such a development. All this not only accelerates the end of the epoch of foreign oppression of peoples, but also makes peaceful cooperation among peoples, based on the principles of independence and equal rights, an essential condition for their freedom and progress.

Tremendous progress has been achieved in the development of science, techniques and in the means of economic development.

Prompted by such developments in the world, the vast majority of people are becoming increasingly conscious of the fact that war between peoples constitutes not only an anachronism but also a crime against humanity. This awareness of peoples is becoming a great moral force, capable of exercising a vital influence on the development of international relations.

Relying on this and on the will of their peoples, the governments of countries participating in the conference resolutely reject the view that war, including the cold war, is inevitable, as this view reflects a sense both of helplessness and hopelessness and is contrary to the progress of the world. They affirm their unwavering faith that the international community is able to organize its life without resorting to means which actually belong to a past epoch of human history.

However, the existing military blocs, which are growing into more and more powerful military, economic and political groupings, which, by the logic and nature of their mutual relations, necessarily provoke periodic aggravations of international relations, the cold war and the constant and acute danger of its being transformed into actual war, have become a part of the situation prevailing in international relations.

For all these reasons, the heads of state or government of non–aligned countries wish, in this way, to draw the attention of the world community to the existing situation and to the necessity that all peoples should exert efforts to find a sure road towards the stabilization of peace.

II

The present–day world is characterized by the existence of different social systems. The participating countries do not consider that these differences constitute an insurmountable obstacle for the stabilization of peace, provided attempts at domination and interference in the internal development of other peoples and nations are ruled out.

All peoples and nations have to solve the problems of their own political, economic, social and cultural systems in accordance with their own conditions, needs and potentialities.

Furthermore, any attempt at imposing upon peoples one social or political system or another by force and from outside is a direct threat to world peace.

The participating countries consider that under such conditions the principles of peaceful co–existence are the only alternative to the cold war and to a possible general nuclear catastrophe. Therefore, these principles—which include the right of peoples to self–determination, to independence and to the free determination of the forms and methods of economic, social and cultural development—must be the only basis of all international relations.

Active international cooperation in the fields of material and cultural exchanges among peoples is an essential means for the strengthening of confidence in the possibility of peaceful co–existence among states with different social systems.

The participants in the conference emphasize, in this connection, that the policy of co–existence amounts to an active effort towards the elimination of historical injustices and the liquidation of national oppression, guaranteeing, at the same time, to every people their independent development.

Aware that ideological differences are necessarily a part of the growth of the human society, the participating countries consider that peoples and governments shall refrain from any use of ideologies for the purpose of waging cold war, exercising pressure, or imposing their will.

III

The heads of state or government of non–aligned countries participating in the conference are not making concrete proposals for the solution of all international disputes, and particularly disputes between the two blocs. They wish, above all, to draw attention to those acute problems of our time which must be solved rapidly, so that they should not lead to irreparable consequences.

In this respect, they particularly emphasize the need for a great sense of responsibility and realism when undertaking the solution of various problems resulting from differences in social systems.

The non–aligned countries represented at this conference do not wish to form a new bloc and cannot be a bloc. They sincerely desire to cooperate with any government which seeks to contribute to the strengthening of confidence and peace in the world.

The non–aligned countries wish to proceed in this manner all the more so as they are aware that peace and stability in the world depend, to a considerable extent, on the mutual relations of the great powers.

Aware of this, the participants in the conference consider it a matter of principle that the great powers take more determined action for the solving of various problems by means of negotiations, displaying at the same time the necessary constructive approach and readiness for reaching solutions which will be mutually acceptable and useful for world peace.

The participants in the conference consider that, under present conditions, the existence and the activities of non-aligned countries in the interests of peace are one of the more important factors for safeguarding world peace.

The participants in the conference consider it essential that the non–aligned countries should participate in solving outstanding international issues concerning peace and security in the world as none of them can remain unaffected by or indifferent to these issues.

They consider that the further extensions of the non–committed area of the world constitutes the only possible and indispensable alternative to the policy of total division of the world into blocs, and intensification of cold war policies. The non–aligned countries provide encouragement and support to all peoples fighting for their independence and equality.

The participants in the conference are convinced that the emergence of newly liberated countries will further assist in narrowing of the area of bloc antagonisms and thus encourage all tendencies aimed at strengthening peace and promoting peaceful cooperation among independent and equal nations.

1. The participants in the conference solemnly reaffirm their support for the "Declaration of the Granting of Independence to Colonial Countries and Peoples,"

adopted at the fifteenth session of the General Assembly of the United Nations and recommend the immediate unconditional, total and final abolition of colonialism and resolve to make a concerted effort to put an end to all types of new colonialism and imperialist domination in all its forms and manifestations.

2. The participants in the conference demand that an immediate stop be put to armed action and repressive measures of any kind directed against dependent peoples to enable them to exercise peacefully and freely their right to complete independence and that the integrity of their national territory should be respected. Any aid given by any country to a colonial power in such suppression is contrary to the Charter of the United Nations.

The participating countries, respecting scrupulously the territorial integrity of all states, oppose by all means any aims of annexation by other nations.

3. The participating countries consider the struggle of the people of Algeria for freedom, self-determination and independence, and for the integrity of its national territory including the Sahara, to be just and necessary and are, therefore, determined to extend to the people of Algeria all possible support and aid. The heads of state or government are particularly gratified that Algeria is represented at this conference by its rightful representative, the Prime Minister of the Provisional Government of Algeria.

4. The participating countries draw attention with great concern to the developments in Angola and to the intolerable measures of repression taken by the Portuguese colonial authorities against the people of Angola and demand that an immediate end should be put to any further shedding of blood of the Angolan people, and the people of Angola should be assisted by all peace-loving countries, particularly member states of the United Nations, to establish their free and independent state without delay.

5. The participants in the conference demand the immediate termination of all colonial occupation and the restoration of the territorial integrity to the rightful people in countries in which it has been violated in Asia, Africa and Latin America as well as the

withdrawal of foreign forces from their national soil.

6. The participating countries demand the immediate evacuation of French armed forces from the whole of the Tunisian territory in accordance with the legitimate right of Tunisia to the exercise of its full national sovereignty.

7. The participating countries demand that the tragic events in the Congo must not be repeated and they feel that it is the duty of the world community to continue to do everything in its power in order to erase the consequences and to prevent any further foreign intervention in this young African state, and to enable the Congo to embark freely upon the road of its independent development based on respect for its sovereignty, unity and its territorial integrity.

8. The participants in the conference resolutely condemn the policy of apartheid practiced by the Union of South Africa and demand the immediate abandonment of this policy. They further state that the policy of racial discrimination anywhere in the world constitutes a grave violation of the Charter of the United Nations and the Universal Declaration of Human Rights.

9. The participating countries declare solemnly the absolute respect of the rights of ethnic or religious minorities to be protected in particular against crimes of genocide or any other violation of their fundamental human rights.

10. The participants in the conference condemn the imperialist policies pursued in the Middle East, and declare their support for the full restoration of all the rights of the Arab people of Palestine in conformity with the Charter and resolutions of the United Nations.

11. The participating countries consider the establishment and maintenance of foreign military bases in the territories of other countries, particularly against their express will, a gross violation of the sovereignty of such states. They declare their full support to countries who are endeavoring to secure the vacation of these bases. They call upon those countries maintaining foreign bases to consider seriously their abolition as a

contribution to world peace.

12. They also acknowledge that the North American military base at Guantanamo, Cuba, to the permanence of which the government and people of Cuba have expressed their opposition, affects the sovereignty and territorial integrity of that country.

13. The participants in the conference reaffirm their conviction that:

(a) All nations have the rights of unity, self-determination and independence by virtue of which rights they can determine their political status and freely pursue their economic, social and cultural development without intimidation or hindrance.

(b) All peoples may, for their own ends, freely dispose of their natural wealth and resources without prejudice to any obligations arising out of international economic co-operation, based upon the principle of mutual benefit, and international law. In no case may a people be deprived of its own means of subsistence.

The participating countries believe that the right of Cuba as that of any other nation to freely choose their political and social systems in accordance with their own conditions, needs and possibilities should be respected.

14. The participating countries express their determination that no intimidation, interference or intervention should be brought to bear in the exercise of the right of self-determination of peoples, including their right to pursue constructive and independent policies for the attainment and preservation of their sovereignty.

15. The participants in the conference consider that disarmament is an imperative need and the most urgent task of mankind. A radical solution of this problem, which has become an urgent necessity in the present state of armaments, in the unanimous view of participating countries, can be achieved only by means of a general, complete and strictly and internationally controlled disarmament.

16. The heads of state or government point out that general and complete disarmament should include the elimination of armed forces, armaments, foreign bases, manufacture of arms as well as elimination of institutions and installations for

military training, except for purposes of internal security; and the total prohibition of the production, possession and utilization of nuclear and thermo-nuclear arms, bacteriological and chemical weapons as well as the elimination of equipment and installations for the delivery and placement and operational use of weapons of mass destruction on national territories.

17. The participating countries call upon states in general, and states exploring outer space at present in particular, to undertake to use outer space exclusively for peaceful purposes. They express the hope that the international community will, through collective action, establish an international agency with a view to promote and coordinate the human actions in the field of international cooperation in the peaceful uses of outer space.

18. The participants in the conference urge the great powers to sign without further delay a treaty for general and complete disarmament in order to save mankind from the scourge of war and to release energy and resources now being spent on armaments to be used for the peaceful economic and social development of all mankind. The participating countries also consider that:

(a) The non-aligned nations should be represented at all further world conferences on disarmament;

(b) All discussions on disarmament should be held under the auspices of the United Nations;

(c) General and complete disarmament should be guaranteed by an effective system of inspection and control, the teams of which should include members of non-aligned nations.

19. The participants in the conference consider it essential that an agreement on the prohibition of all nuclear and thermo-nuclear tests should be urgently concluded. With this aim in view, it is necessary that negotiations be immediately resumed, separately or as part of negotiations on general disarmament. Meanwhile, the moratorium on the testing

of all nuclear weapons should be resumed and observed by all countries.

20. The participants in the conference recommend that the General Assembly of the United Nations should, at its forthcoming session, adopt a decision on the convening either of a special session of the General Assembly of the United Nations devoted to discussion of disarmament or on the convening of a world disarmament conference under the auspices of the United Nations with a view to setting in motion the process of general disarmament.

21. The participants in the conference consider that efforts should be made to remove economic imbalance inherited from colonialism and imperialism. They consider it necessary to close, through accelerated economic, industrial and agricultural development, the ever–widening gap in the standards of living between the few economically advanced countries and the many economically less–developed countries. The participants in the conference recommend the immediate establishment and operation of a United Nations capital development fund. They further agree to demand just terms of trade for the economically less–developed countries and, in particular, constructive efforts to eliminate the excessive fluctuations in primary commodity trade and the restrictive measures and practices which adversely affect the trade and revenues of the newly developing countries. In general, to demand that the fruits of the scientific and technological revolution be applied in all fields of economic development to hasten the achievement of international social justice.

22. The participating countries invite all the countries in the course of development to cooperate effectively in the economic and commercial fields so as to face the policies of pressure in the economic sphere, as well as the harmful results which may be created by the economic blocs of the industrial countries. They invite all the countries concerned to consider to convene as soon as possible an international conference to discuss their common problems and to reach an agreement on the ways and means of repelling all damage which may hinder their development; and to discuss and agree upon the most

effective measures to ensure the realization of their economic and social development.

23. The countries participating in the conference declare that the recipient countries must be free to determine the use of the economic and technical assistance which they receive, and to draw up their own plans and assign priorities in accordance with their needs.

24. The participating countries consider it essential that the General Assembly of the United Nations should, through the revision of the Charter, find a solution to the question of expanding the membership of the Security Council and of the Economic and Social Council in order to bring the composition and work of these two most important organs of the General Assembly into harmony with the needs of the organization and with the expanded membership of the United Nations.

25. The unity of the world organization and the assuring of the efficiency of its work make it absolutely necessary to evolve a more appropriate structure for the Secretariat of the United Nations, bearing in mind equitable regional distribution.

26. Those of the countries participating in the conference who recognize the Government of the People's Republic of China recommend that the General Assembly in its forthcoming session should accept the representatives of the Government of the People's Republic of China as the only legitimate representatives of that country in the United Nations.

27. The countries participating in the conference consider that the German problem is not merely a regional problem but liable to exercise a decisive influence on the course of future developments in international relations.

II. Common Terms, Words and Phrases for the Text

non-aligned countries 不结盟国家

observer 观察员

colonialism 殖民主义

neo-colonialism 新殖民主义

independence 独立

moral force 道义力量

anachronism 时代错误

Cold war 冷战

military blocs 军事集团

social systems 社会制度

national oppression 民族压迫

ideological differences 意识形态差异

manifestation 表现

territorial integrity 领土完整

the Provisional Government 临时政府

Angola 安哥拉

apartheid（南非政府过去推行的）种族隔离制度

genocide 种族灭绝

ethnic 种族

sovereignty 主权

unity 统一

the principle of mutual benefit 互利原则

subsistence 生存

disarmament 裁军，裁减军备

general disarmament 全面裁军

foreign bases 外国基地

thermo-nuclear arms 热核武器

weapons of mass destruction 大规模杀伤性武器

collective action 集体行动

moratorium 暂停，中止

United Nations capital development fund 联合国资本发展基金

the scientific and technological revolution 科学与技术革命

international social justice 国际社会正义

the recipient countries 受援国

the Secretariat of the United Nations 联合国秘书处

III. Exercises and Thinking

1. Please talk about the background, symbol and influence of the rise of the Non-Aligned Movement.

2. Please talk about the content and characteristics of the Non-Aligned Movement.

3. Please read the relevant literature and talk about China's role in the Non-Aligned Movement.

IV. Further Readings and Internet Links

1. Further Readings

中国国际问题研究所编辑部编:《不结盟运动主要文件集》, 中国对外翻译出版公司 1987 年版。

Guy Arnold, *Historical Dictionary of the Non-aligned Movements and Third World*, London: Scarecrow Press, 2006.

2. Internet Links

Non-Aligned Movement (NAM): https://nam.go.ug/

Unit 38

Follow the Trend of the Times and Promote Global Peace and Development

《顺应时代前进潮流，促进世界和平发展》

《顺应时代前进潮流，促进世界和平发展》是 2013 年 3 月 23 日习近平主席在俄罗斯莫斯科国际关系学院的演讲。这次访问俄罗斯，是习近平同志担任中国国家主席后第一次出访。习近平主席在这次出访中提出了人类命运共同体理念，具有重大的历史意义。

习近平主席在演讲中指出了当今时代背景和国际局势，深入阐释了中国对世界形势的看法和对国际关系的立场与主张。他指出：这个世界，人类越来越成为你中有我、我中有你的命运共同体，和平、发展、合作、共赢成为时代潮流。要跟上时代前进步伐，就不能身体已进入 21 世纪，而脑袋还停留在过去，停留在殖民扩张的旧时代里，停留在冷战思维、零和博弈的老框架内。面对国际形势的深刻变化和世界各国同舟共济的客观要求，各国应该共同推动建立以合作共赢为核心的新型国际关系，各国人民应该一起来维护世界和平、促进共同发展。

在演讲中，习近平主席向世界提出重大倡议，呼吁国际社会树立人类命运共同体意识，在国际社会产生广泛积极的影响。人类命运共同体逐渐成为全世界各国人民的普遍共识。2017 年 1 月 18 日，习近平主席在联合国日内瓦总部发表题为《共同构建人类命运共同体》的主旨演讲。2017 年 10 月 18 日，习近平总书记在党的十九大报告中提出，坚持和平发展道路，推动构建人类命运共同体，同时倡导构建人类命运共同体，促进全球治理体系变革。2018 年 3 月 11

日，第十三届全国人民代表大会第一次会议通过的宪法修正案，将宪法序言第十二自然段中“发展同各国的外交关系和经济、文化的交流”修改为“发展同各国的外交关系和经济、文化交流，推动构建人类命运共同体”。本文选自习近平主席出访俄罗斯时发表的演讲，意在使读者学习人类命运共同体的思想内涵。本篇外文选自北京外文出版社出版的版本。

I. *Follow the Trend of the Times and Promote Global Peace and Development*[①]

Distinguished Mr Anatoly Vasilyevich Torkunov, Rector of the Moscow State Institute of International Relations,

The Honorable Olga Golodets, Deputy Prime Minister of the Russian Federation,

Dear faculty members and students,

I am very pleased to come to the beautiful Moscow State Institute of International Relations today and meet so many faculty members and students here.

The Moscow State Institute of International Relations is a prestigious school of world renown, boasting an outstanding faculty and distinguished alumni. I wish to express my warm congratulations on the remarkable successes you have achieved in various fields.

Russia is a friendly neighbor to China. My current visit to Russia is the first leg of my first overseas trip since becoming China's president. It is also my second visit to your beautiful and richly endowed country in three years. Yesterday, I had fruitful talks with President Putin, and together we attended the launch of the Tourism Year of China in Russia.

The month of March marks the return of spring, a season of sowing and great

① Xi Jinping, *The Governance of China*, Beijing: Foreign Languages Press, 2014, pp. 297–304.

renewal. As a popular Chinese saying goes, "he who hopes for a good year starts planning in spring." China and Russia, having taken advantage of this season to plough and hoe not only for our bilateral relations but also for peace and development in the world, will surely reap a bumper harvest to the benefit of our two peoples and those of other countries.

Dear faculty members and students,

The Institute of International Relations, as an institution of higher learning specialized in the study of international issues, pays close attention to the international landscape and can appreciate especially keenly the enormous changes the world has gone through over the past decades. Indeed, we live in a time of kaleidoscopic changes that make the world constantly different.

It is a world where peace, development, cooperation and mutual benefit have become the trend of the times. The old colonial system has long since disintegrated, and confrontations between blocs as during the Cold War have long gone. No country or group of countries can dominate world affairs single-handedly.

It is a world where emerging markets and developing countries in large numbers have embarked on the track of fast development. Billions of people are moving towards modernization at an accelerating pace. Multiple growth engines have emerged in regions across the world. And the international balance of power continues to evolve in a direction favorable for peace and development.

It is a world where countries are linked with and dependent on one another at a level never seen before. Mankind, by living in the same global village in the same era where history and reality meet, has increasingly emerged as a community of shared future in which everyone has in himself a little bit of others.

And it is a world where mankind is beset with numerous difficulties and challenges. They range from the continued underlying impact of the international financial crisis, an apparent upsurge of all kinds of protectionism, incessant regional flashpoints, rising hegemonism, power politics and neo-interventionism, to a web of conventional and non–conventional security threats, such as the arms race, terrorism and cyber security. Upholding world peace and promoting common development remain a long and uphill battle.

We hope that the world will become a better place. We have every reason to believe that it will. At the same time, we are soberly aware that while the future is bright, the path leading to it can be tortuous. Chernyshevsky once wrote, "The path of history is not paved like Nevsky Prospekt; it runs across fields, either dusty or muddy, and cuts across swamps or forest thickets." Yet as shown by humanity's progress, history always moves forward according to its own laws despite twists and turns, and no force can hold back its rolling wheels.

The tide of the world is surging forward. Those who submit to it will prosper and those who resist it will perish. Keeping up with the times, one cannot live in the 21st century while thinking in the old fashion, lingering in the age of colonial expansion or with the zero–sum mentality of the Cold War.

In the face of the profoundly changed international landscape and the objective need for the world to rally together like passengers in the same boat, all countries should join hands in building a new model of international relations featuring cooperation and mutual benefit, and all peoples should work together to safeguard world peace and promote common development.

We stand for the sharing of dignity by all countries and peoples in the world. All countries, irrespective of size, strength and wealth, are equal. The right of the people to independently choose their development paths should be respected, interference in the internal affairs of other countries opposed, and international fairness and justice maintained. Only the wearer of the shoes knows if they fit or not. Only the people can best tell if the development path they have chosen for their country suits or not.

We stand for the sharing of the fruits of development by all countries and peoples. Every country, while pursuing its own development, should actively facilitate the common development of all countries. There cannot be sustainable development in the world when some countries are getting richer and richer while others languish in prolonged poverty and backwardness. Only when all countries achieve common development can there be better worldwide development. Such practices as beggar–my–neighbor, shifting crises onto others and feathering one's nest at the expense of others are both immoral and unsustainable.

We stand for the sharing of security by all countries and peoples. Countries should make concerted efforts to properly address the issues and challenges they face. As challenges often take on global dimensions, there is all the more need for countries to take them on cooperatively, turning pressure into motivation and crises into opportunities. Confronted with complex threats to international security, fighting alone or fighting with a blind faith in the use of force will not get one anywhere. The only solution lies in cooperative, collective and common security.

As the trends of world multipolarity and economic globalization grow and those of upholding cultural diversity and applying information technology in social life continue to make progress, mankind has never been better blessed with opportunities for taking strides towards peace and development. And mutually beneficial cooperation provides the only practical way to achieve such a goal.

The destiny of the world must be left in the hands of the peoples of all countries. Matters that fall within the sovereign rights of a country should be managed only by the government and people of that country. And affairs of the world should be addressed by the governments and peoples of all countries through consultation. Herein lies the democratic principle for the handling of international affairs which should be universally observed.

II. Common Terms, Words and Phrases for the Text

the old colonial system 旧的殖民体系

global village 地球村

protectionism 保护主义

hegemonism 霸权主义

power politics 强权政治

neo-interventionism 新干涉主义

Chernyshevsky 车尔尼雪夫斯基

world multipolarity 世界多极化

economic globalization 经济全球化

III. Exercises and Thinking

1. Please talk about how you understand “a Community with a Shared Future for Mankind”.

IV. Further Readings and Internet Links

1. Further Readings

Xi Jinping, *The Governance of China*, Beijing:Foreign Languages Press, 2014.

习近平:《论坚持推动构建人类命运共同体》,中央文献出版社 2018 年版。

习近平:《习近平著作选读》,人民出版社 2023 年版。

2. Internet Links

中国共产党新闻网:http://theory.people.com.cn

Postscript
后　记

这部著作最为突出的一个特点是，为贯彻落实“两个结合”，编者专门收录了马克思主义经典文献和中华优秀传统文化经典文献的英文版。有关版本均是经过精心考证和选择的，均以我国外文出版社出版的马克思主义经典文献为主，同时参考欧美学者整理出版的马克思主义经典文献版本。据编者了解，在世界史文献解读相关著作中收录英文版马克思主义经典文献和中华优秀传统文化经典文献，这一做法在国内似乎还是首次。本书可作为普通高等学校世界史专业教材。

在国内，似乎还没有中国学者用英语讲授马克思主义原理，而外国学者中用英语讲授马克思主义原理的似乎也只有中国人民大学哲学院的薄国强（Roland Boer）教授。他是一位来自澳大利亚的学者。2024 年 6 月 12 日至 14 日，我有幸参加了中国历史研究院历史理论研究所主办的“中华民族现代文明与世界文明交流互鉴”国际学术研讨会。会上我遇见了 10 余位参会的外国学者，其中就有薄国强教授。他作了题为“马克思主义中国化：外国学者的视角”的主旨演讲，并在演讲中提到，他是首位在中国用英语讲授马克思主义原理的外国学者。在与薄国强教授的交谈中，我了解到，他似乎并不讲授马克思主义经典文献。因此，无论是用英语讲授马克思主义原理，还是用英语讲授马克思主义经典文献，中国学者似乎还未曾系统开展过。至于用英语讲授中华优秀传统文化经典文献，国内外学者都比较重视，但从“两个结合”的高度来理解和讲授则是全新的挑战。

因此，无论是从课程思政建设角度还是从国际学术交流视角来看，本书作为大学的历史专业教材，收录马克思主义经典文献和中华优秀传统文化经典文献是很有必要的。教材是学习贯彻落实马克思主义唯物史观的重要阵地，是通过“两个结合”实现历史学人才培养高质量发展的重要途径。我们中国学者不仅不应丢掉这个阵地，而且还应主动把握住这个阵地的领导权、管理权、话语权。

本书编写的具体分工如下：

序言和后记、第一编，由天津师范大学历史文化学院暨欧洲文明研究院张乃和老师编写。第二编由天津师范大学历史文化学院袁指挥老师编写。第三编由天津师范大学历史文化学院陈建军老师编写。第四编第二十二至二十六单元由天津师范大学历史文化学院周芬老师编写。第四编第二十七、二十八单元以及第五编由河北大学历史学院袁跃华老师编写。天津师范大学文学院资料室吴冬杰老师校对了序言、后记和第一编的初稿。天津师范大学欧洲文明研究院博士研究生姚海宁校对了全文的初稿。全书由张乃和与袁跃华统稿。

在编写过程中，我们有幸得到了中国社会科学院中国历史研究院《历史研究》杂志社焦兵研究员、清华大学张绪山教授、河北师范大学倪世光教授、首都师范大学姚百慧教授、吉林大学于洪教授和李国红研究员提供的帮助。他们有的在百忙中无偿地提供了多种文献资料，有的从一开始就参与讨论确定编写思路和大纲目录，有的从世界历史文献学角度提出了很好的意见和建议，为本书增色添彩。在此，本书编写组对他们的无私帮助表示衷心感谢！

我们还要感谢东方出版社领导和编辑的辛勤付出。他们认真负责、任劳任怨、精益求精的工作态度以及良好的工作作风和工作能力，给我们留下了极为深刻的印象。他们为本书的出版付出了大量心血和汗水，在此对他们表示衷心感谢！

张乃和
2024 年 6 月于天津